Studies in Church History

37

THE USE AND ABUSE OF TIME IN CHRISTIAN HISTORY

THE USE AND ABUSE OF TIME IN CHRISTIAN HISTORY

PAPERS READ AT
THE 1999 SUMMER MEETING AND
THE 2000 WINTER MEETING OF
THE ECCLESIASTICAL HISTORY SOCIETY

EDITED BY

R. N. SWANSON

PUBLISHED FOR
THE ECCLESIASTICAL HISTORY SOCIETY
BY
THE BOYDELL PRESS
2002

First published 2002

A publication of the Ecclesiastical History Society
in association with The Boydell Press
an imprint of Boydell & Brewer Ltd
PO Box 9, Woodbridge, Suffolk IP12 3DF, UK
and of Boydell & Brewer Inc.
PO Box 41026, Rochester, NY 14604-4126, USA

ISBN 0 9529733 7 5

ISSN 0424-2084

A catalogue record for this book is available
from the British Library

Library of Congress Cataloging-in-Publication Data
applied for

Details of previous volumes are available from Boydell & Brewer Ltd

This book is printed on acid-free paper

Typeset by Joshua Associates Ltd, Oxford
Printed in Great Britain by
St Edmundsbury Press Ltd, Bury St Edmunds, Suffolk

CONTENTS

CONTENTS

PREFACE

A theme focusing on attitudes to time was highly appropriate for a volume of *Studies in Church History* whose production schedule would straddle the transition between the second and third millennia of the Christian calendar. The volume's title modifies that adopted by Dr Stuart Mews as the theme for the Ecclesiastical History Society conferences held at Fitzwilliam College, Cambridge, in July 1999, and at the Institute of Historical Research in London in January 2000; its contents reflect the wide range of approaches adopted by the speakers. The seven main papers delivered at the conferences appear here, with a selection of the communications offered at the Cambridge meeting. As ever, the process of selecting the papers to be included has been difficult; I am grateful to all who commented on texts and thereby assisted me considerably in that process. I am also grateful to the authors for their tolerance of editorial comments requesting revisions of the original papers as the conference theme was honed to that of the volume.

The Society thanks Fitzwilliam College for accommodating the summer conference, and is particularly indebted to Dr David Thompson for acting as prime liaison with the College. Thanks are also due to the Institute of Historical Research in London and its staff for accommodating the January meeting and ensuring that the day ran smoothly.

* * *

It is with regret that we record the death of Douglas Murray, one of the contributors to this volume, which occurred during the final stages of the editing process.

Robert Swanson

CONTRIBUTORS

STUART MEWS (*President*)
Reader in Religious Studies, University of Gloucestershire

FRANCES ANDREWS
Lecturer in Mediaeval History, University of St Andrews

JANE BAUN
Assistant Professor of History and Hellenic Studies, New York University

SUSAN BOYNTON
Assistant Professor of Historical Musicology, Columbia University

STUART K. BURNS
Ordinand, St John's College, Nottingham

HILARY M. CAREY
Associate Professor in History, University of Newcastle, New South Wales, Australia

BARRY COLLETT
Senior Lecturer in History, University of Melbourne

KRISTA COWMAN
Senior Lecturer in History, Leeds Metropolitan University

ALLAN K. DAVIDSON
Lecturer in Church History, St John's College, Auckland, and Honorary Lecturer in Theology, University of Auckland, New Zealand

JANE GARNETT
Fellow and Tutor in Modern History, Wadham College, Oxford

CAROL HARRISON
Lecturer in Theology, University of Durham

K. S. JEFFREY
Minister, Parish Church of Coupar Old and St Michael of Tarvit

ANNE LAURENCE
Senior Lecturer in History, Open University

TIM MACQUIBAN
Director, Wesley and Methodist Studies Centre, Westminster Institute of Education, Oxford Brookes University

JUDITH MIDDLETON-STEWART
Tutor for the Board of Continuing Education, University of East Anglia

ANGELA MONTFORD
Research Student, University of St Andrews

MICHAEL A. MULLETT
Professor of Cultural and Religious History, University of Lancaster

†DOUGLAS M. MURRAY
Late Principal of Trinity College; Lecturer in Ecclesiastical History, University of Glasgow

JANET L. NELSON
Professor of Medieval History, King's College, University of London

JOHN F. POLLARD
Professor of History, Anglia Polytechnic University

JILL SÖDERSTRÖM
Research Student, Murdoch University, Western Australia

JOKE SPAANS
Lecturer in the History of Christianity, University of Amsterdam

JOHN WALSH
Emeritus Fellow, Jesus College, Oxford

MARTIN WELLINGS
Secretary, British Section, World Methodist Historical Society

LINDA WILSON
Tutor, Open Theological College, Cheltenham

DIANA WOOD
Senior Research Fellow in History, University of East Anglia,

Assistant Tutor in Local History, Department for Continuing Education, University of Oxford

DAVID L. WYKES
Director, Dr Williams's Trust and Library, London

ABBREVIATIONS

Abbreviated titles are adopted within each paper after the first full citation. In addition, the following abbreviations are used throughout the volume.

BL	London, British Library
BN	Paris, Bibliothèque Nationale
CChr	*Corpus Christianorum* (Turnhout, 1953–)
CChr.CM	*Corpus Christianorum, continuatio medievalis* (1966–)
ChH	*Church History* (New York/Chicago, 1932–)
CIC	*Corpus iuris canonici*, ed. E. Richter and E. Friedberg, 2 vols (Leipzig, 1879–81)
DNB	*Dictionary of National Biography* (London, 1885–)
EETS	*Early English Text Society* (London, 1864–)
e.s.	extra series
HistJ	*Historical Journal* (Cambridge, 1958–)
JEH	*Journal of Ecclesiastical History* (Cambridge, 1950–)
MGH	*Monumenta Germaniae historica inde ab a. 500 usque ad a. 1500*, ed. G.H. Pertz et al. (Hanover, Berlin, etc., 1826–)
n.d.	no date
n.s.	new series
ODCC	*Oxford Dictionary of the Christian Church*, ed. F. L. Cross (Oxford, 1957), 2nd edn with E. A. Livingstone (1974), 3rd edn (1997)
o.s.	old series
P&P	*Past and Present: A Journal of Scientific History* (London/Oxford, 1952–)
PG	*Patrologia Graeca*, ed. J. P. Migne, 161 vols (Paris, 1857–66)
PL	*Patrologia Latina*, ed. J. P. Migne, 217 vols + 4 index vols (Paris, 1841–61)
RS	*Rerum Brittanicarum medii aevi scriptores*, 99 vols (London, 1858–1911) = *Rolls Series*
SC	Sources chrétiennes (Paris, 1942–)
SCH	*Studies in Church History* (London/Oxford/Woodbridge, 1964–)

ScHR	*Scottish Historical Review* (Edinburgh/Glasgow, 1904–)
SCH.S	*Studies in Church History: Subsidia* (Oxford/Woodbridge, 1978–)
Speculum	*Speculum: A Journal of Medieval Studies* (Cambridge, MA, 1925–)
tr.	translated (by)

* * *

Canon law citations are laid out according to the 'modern form' (see James A. Brundage, *Medieval Canon Law* [London and New York, 1995], app. 1), with quotations from *CIC*.

INTRODUCTION

SINCE 1958, Professor C. Northcote Parkinson's famous 'law' has unforgettably linked time and work: 'work expands to fill the time available for its completion'; a dictum which all involved in the production of this volume might ruefully ponder! The additional notion that 'time is money' has also become inextricably associated with Parkinson's Law, but has a longer pedigree. The linkage was not lost on the eighteenth-century evangelical hymn-writer, William Cowper, when he penned a secular rhyme to *John Gilpin*, a citizen 'of credit and renown'. Although he had already mounted his horse to set off on holiday, Gilpin delayed his departure to deal with three customers who turned up just at that moment –

> for loss of time,
> Although it grieved him sore,
> Yet loss of pence, full well he knew,
> Would trouble him much more.[1]

The use and abuse of time, as demonstrated by attitudes to work and leisure, both spiritual and secular, seemed an appropriate theme for the conference of the Ecclesiastical History Society in the year which, at least in the popular view, was the last of the twentieth century; and whose proceedings, for those of mathematical precision, would provide the first volume of *Studies in Church History* to appear in the twenty-first. Millennium doomsters were already proclaiming the 'End of Work' as the outcome of technological development and globalization, with all its consequent problems for leisure and individual identity. To be millennial about work is one thing; to be historical another. 'Work' itself is a complex concept; attitudes to and understandings of it have changed over time – as they have to its antithesis, no work, whether treated as rest and play, or leisure and idleness or sloth. The full *Oxford English Dictionary* lists thirty-four definitions for the noun 'work', and thirty-nine for the verb. As the

1 *The Poems of William Cowper*, ed. J. D. Baird and C. Ryskamp, 3 vols (Oxford, 1980–95), 2, p. 297.

editor of the *Oxford Book of Work* (1999), Sir Keith Thomas includes also entries on rest, leisure, and idleness, because their meaning derives from their 'implicit opposition to the activity of work'.[2] When the economist J. K. Galbraith received an honorary degree from the London School of Economics in 1999, as part of the tribute to his ninetieth birthday, he said:

> The word 'work' is our most misleading social term. It designates the occupation of those who would be very unhappy without it. And we use the same word for hard, repetitive, even physically painful toil. No word in the English language stretches over such different conditions. There is the further perverse fact that those who most enjoy what is called work are those who are best paid. And they are also allowed the most leisure.

He went on to stress the evolution in attitudes to work in the twentieth century, when 'many have graduated from the miseries to the enjoyments of work'.[3] Yet the miseries are still there, not least in the contemporary bane of work-induced stress.

The theorists and practitioners of the Christian religion have made both responses and contributions to the changing views on work and leisure, and the attendant debates on the use and abuse of time. Throughout Christian history, the Genesis accounts of creation and life in the Garden of Eden have been important sources for those living in the fallen world. In the beginning, according to Genesis, God separated the light (day) from the darkness (night), and created the earth in six days, after which he rested. He created humans, and gave them work to do: 'the Lord God took the man and put him into the garden of Eden to dress it and to keept it' (Genesis 2.15). After the Fall, the work remained, but with a new imperative: it became hard labour.

Whether those living in societies influenced by Christian teaching have followed the divine command to divide their time appropriately between work and rest is one of the recurrent questions in religious history. Whether they have been good gardeners, hoers, pruners, waterers, pickers; whether they have used or abused the time allotted to them; is a major theme running through this volume. From the beginning, work has been seen as a divine command legitimizing what is also an economic necessity. For most people, and for most of the

[2] Keith Thomas, ed., *The Oxford Book of Work* (Oxford, 1999), pp. xvi–xvii.

[3] *Guardian*, 29 June 1999, p. 13.

time, work has been monotonous and exhausting, recompensed by rest, leisure, and play, by holiday. For some, work has been a form of religious asceticism. For both theorists and practitioners, work's subsidiary purpose has also been to fill time, to provide a bulwark against the dangers of idleness and sloth – that deadly sin which wastes time. Idleness has been seen as equally dangerous: the devil has long been known to find work, often devilish work, for idle hands. That need to be on guard, and to affirm the links between time, work, and godliness, is memorably expressed in the verse of Isaac Watts, writing 'Against Idleness and Mischief':

How doth the little busy Bee
   Improve each shining Hour,
And gather Honey all the day
   From every opening Flower!

. . . . .

In Works of Labour or of Skill
   I would be busy too:
For *Satan* finds some Mischief still
   For idle hands to do.[4]

Yet, if the necessity of work is accepted as part of the human condition, how is work actually to be defined? St Benedict valued both manual labour and sacred reading: the notion that prayer is a form of work had its consolations; those engaged in it doubtless considered it preferable to tilling fields or mining coal. Work can be satisfying, and a job well done can bring satisfaction. If it also brings spiritual rewards, so much the better. Yet even prayer-as-work could have its drawbacks: rushing through daily Mattins without a congregation might be considered nothing more than a humdrum chore. To maintain the right balance in attitudes to the demands of work, the obligations which go with labour, and the calls of leisure and alternative uses of time, has also been an issue at different periods of Christian history, for societies as a whole, and for groups and individuals within them.

The essays in this volume reflect the wide range of perspectives on work and leisure, on the use and abuse of time, which have been evident in Christian history over the past two millennia. A refreshing feature of several of the contributions is their concern to move beyond

[4] Thomas, *Oxford Book of Work*, p. 104.

the usual boundaries of what is usually thought of as '*ecclesiastical* history', and to look across the barriers of national histories. Others also suggest the need to look beyond – and indeed reject – stereotypes, notably about Quakers, Methodists, and Roman Catholics, with particular reference to the Weberian cliché of 'the Protestant ethic and the spirit of capitalism'. Elsewhere, two bishops of Winchester living centuries apart are seen to have similar attitudes to work and the use of time. Attitudes to religious work in the cities of thirteenth-century Italy; medieval concern about the misuse and exploitation of time through usury; more modern clerical views on the withdrawal of labour; the use of the strike weapon in the armoury of the Labour movement; and women's work; are among the other issues which receive attention.

Taken together, the contents of this volume make a real contribution to an understanding of attitudes to the use and abuse of time in Christian history; especially with regard to work and leisure. They clearly demonstrate that the authors have not been idle, and like Watts's busy bee they know how to 'improve each shining hour'. Some of them may also at times enjoy idleness, or even get up to mischief; but that is another matter entirely.

Stuart Mews

PSEUDO-MACARIUS AND THE MESSALIANS: THE USE OF TIME FOR THE COMMON GOOD

by STUART K. BURNS

IN the year AD 431 the Council of Ephesus anathematized the 'Messalians' (Syriac) or 'Euchites' (Greek) – both terms meaning 'those who pray'[1] – referring to them as 'impious' and 'contaminating'.[2] A defining characteristic of this group was their emphasis on constant prayer. The Messalian phenomenon, which originated in Syria and Mesopotamia, spread to Armenia and Asia Minor during the late fourth century, causing concern amongst the ecclesiastical hierarchy of many areas. In condemning the movement in AD 431 the Council of Ephesus confirmed the judgement of the synods of Antioch (*c.* 380) and Side (*c.* 390) that the Messalians, who were also known as 'enthusiasts', were a dangerous and divisive group who rejected work and discipline for the sake of prayer and individual advancement. The Messalians could be considered negligent and wasteful in their use of time.

Pseudo-Macarius was active *c.* AD 385–430, and the writings that bear his name were once thought to have been the work of the Egyptian desert father Macarius (d. 390). However, identification with Macarius of Egypt is unlikely, and it is now assumed that Ps-Macarius lived in and around Syria and Cappadocia, teaching and preaching in small 'brotherhoods' or communities of ascetics. The similarities between the teachings of the Messalian movement and the writings attributed to Ps-Macarius have been known since 1920, but of late consideration has been given to other formative influences on the author and his communities. This paper will briefly consider the Messalian movement and the place of Ps-Macarius within it. The Macarian focus of the 'common good' will be examined, to evaluate the distinct Macarian approach to prayer, community, and the use of time.

The Messalian movement is difficult to isolate with any precision, and such are its reported characteristics that it is easy to taint with a

[1] *ODCC*, 3rd edn, p. 1075 (art. 'Messalians').

[2] H. R. Perceval, ed., *The Seven Ecumenical Councils of the Undivided Church*, A Select Library of Nicene and Post-Nicene Fathers of the Christian Church, 2nd ser., 14 (Oxford and New York, 1900), p. 240.

tinge of heresy otherwise orthodox beliefs that touch upon the areas of belief of the group. The Messalian characteristics include a rejection of work, a rejection of discipline, the need for constant prayer to drive out sin and demons from the soul, men and women sleeping in the same house (in warm weather in the streets), and the rejection of marriage.[3] Part of the evidence against the Messalians was a book presented to the synod of Antioch and subsequently to the Council of Ephesus. This became known as the *Asceticon*, and has come to be understood as associated with the work of Ps-Macarius. The *Asceticon*, although not extant, is assumed to have contained material taken from the Macarian corpus. This corpus is primarily made up of homilies supplemented by records of questions and answers. It is a heavily edited collection, with its present form the result of collation by fourteenth-century Hesychast communities. The conclusion was often drawn that the author of the Macarian corpus was a major figure in the Messalian movement, a proposal which is now open to question.[4] The accusation of Messalianism within the Macarian corpus led some to reject the authority of Ps-Macarius, and to question the place of the author within the tradition of the Church.[5] Today the orthodoxy of the Macarian corpus is generally accepted, and the consensus is that the corpus has a Syrian or Mesopotamian origin, rather than an Egyptian origin as previously thought. However, the identity of Ps-Macarius is still a matter of discussion. It has also been generally accepted by scholars that there is a connection between Ps-Macarius and the Messalians, although the precise nature of this connection is uncertain, and is a matter of continuing research.[6]

One connection between Ps-Macarius and the Messalians has been their common approach to prayer. The lists of Messalian practices stress their teaching that prayer is the only way to drive out the demon

[3] For a full discussion of the lists see C. Stewart, *Working the Earth of the Heart* (Oxford, 1991), pp. 52–69.

[4] The connections were first brought to light in 1920: L. Villecourt, 'La Date et l'origine des "Homélies spirituelles" attribuées à Macaire', *Comptes rendues des sessions de l'Académie des Inscriptions et Belles-Lettres* (Paris, 1920), pp. 250–8. See J. Gribomont, 'Le Dossier des origines du messalianisme', in J. Fontaine and C. Kannengiesser, eds, *Epektasis: Mélanges patristiques offerts au Cardinal Jean Daniélou* (Beauchesne, 1972), pp. 611–25. Recent suggestions that the connections between Ps-Macarius and the Messalians have been exaggerated include Stewart, *Working the Earth*, pp. 52–9; K. Fitschen, *Messalianismus und Antimessalianismus. Ein Beispiel ostkirchlicher Ketzergeschichte*, Forschungen zu Kirchen- und Dogmengeschichte, 71 (Göttingen, 1998), p. 218; S. Burns, 'Charisma and spirituality in the early Church: a study of Messalianism and Pseudo-Macarius' (University of Leeds, Ph.D. thesis, 1999), pp. 244–7.

[5] See Gribomont, 'Dossier'.

from the soul, and to achieve purity; the Macarian homilies similarly stress the importance of prayer for progress in the spiritual life. However, between the two there are crucial differences both in the approach to prayer, and in the use of time within the community. This paper will briefly examine some of those differences in prayer before considering the use of time and community benefit in the Macarian corpus.[7]

* * *

The Messalian approach to prayer can be seen from lists of condemned Messalian practices[8] which were collated through the fourth to sixth centuries. Initial evidence against the Messalians came in the form of the lists of heresies compiled by Ephrem (pre-373) and Epiphanius (*c.* 374 and 377). Theodoret (*c.* 440) includes evidence concerning specific Messalian teachings, providing a list of their leaders before

[6] See Fitschen, *Messalianismus und Antimessalianismus*, p. 218; Burns, 'Charisma and spirituality', pp. 244–7.

[7] The Macarian corpus exists in three published collections: **Collection I** - H. Berthold, ed., *Makarios/Symeon: Reden und Briefe. Die Sammlung I des Vaticanus Graecus 694 (B)*, 2 vols, Die griechischen christlichen Schriftsteller der ersten drei Jahrhunderte [hereafter GCS] (Berlin, 1973).

Collection II – H. Dörries, E. Klostermann, and M. Kroeger, eds, *Die 50 Geistlichen Homilien des Makarios*, Patristische Texte und Studien, 4 (Berlin, 1964); G. L. Marriott, *Macarii Anecdota (Seven Unpublished Homilies of Ps-Macarius)*, Harvard Theological Studies, 5 (Cambridge, MA, 1918).

Collection III – E. Klostermann and H. Berthold, eds, *Neue Homilien des Makarius/Symeon*, Texte und Untersuchungen zur Geschichte des altchristlichen Literatur, 72 (Berlin, 1961); V. Desprez, ed., *Pseudo-Macaire, Œuvres spirituelles, I: Homélies propres à la Collection III*, SC, 275 (Paris, 1980). See also 'The Great Letter', in R. Staats, *Makarios-Symeon: Epistola Magna. Eine Messalianische Mönchsregel und ihre Umschrift in Gregors von Nyssa 'De instituto Christiano'*, Abhandlungen der Akademie der Wissenschaften in Göttingen, philologische-historische Klasse, 3/134 (Göttingen, 1984).

Hereafter the collections are cited by collection number, homily number, and paragraph.

[8] The lists of condemnations of the movement include those by Ephrem the Syrian in *Contra haereses* (ed. E. Beck, 2 vols, Corpus Scriptorum Christianorum Orientalium, 169–70 [Louvain, 1957]), Madrashe 22, stanza 4 (1, p. 79); Epiphanius, in *Ancoratus*, ch. 13 and *Panarion*, ch. 80, in *Epiphanius (Anacoratus und Panarion)*, 3 vols, ed. K. Holl (Leipzig, 1915–33), 1, pp. 21–2, 3, pp. 484–96; Theodoret, in his *Haereticorum fabularum compendium*, IV.11 (*PG* 83, cols 429–32), and *Historia ecclesiastica*, IV.11 (*Theodoret: Kirchengeschichte*, ed. L. Parmentier, GCS, 44 [Berlin, 1954], pp. 229–31); Severus of Antioch, *Contra additiones Juliani*, 34.17–21 (in *Sévère d'Antioche: La Polémique antijulianiste. Contra additiones Juliani*, ed. R. Hespel, Corpus Scriptorum Christianorum Orientalium, 295 [Louvain, 1927], p. 34); Philoxenus, *Letter to Patrikos* (in *La Lettre à Patricius de Philoxène de Mabboug*, ed. R. Lavenant, Patrologia Orientalis, 30/v (Paris, 1963), pp. 850–5); Timothy of Constantinople, *De iis qui ad ecclesiam ab haereticis accedunt* (*PG* 86, cols 12–74), and *De receptione haereticorum* (*PG* 86, cols 45–52); John of Damascus, *De haeresibus* (in *Die Schriften des Johannes von Damaskos*, ed. P. B. Kotter, 4, Patristische Texte und Studien, 22 [Berlin, 1981], pp. 42–6).

chronicling the steps taken against them by Letoïs, Bishop of Melitene, and the trial of Adelphus, a known Messalian leader. There is also a brief list associated with Severus of Antioch in the sixth century. The later records of Timothy of Constantinople (*c.* 600) and John of Damascus (749) also provide details of the perceived heretical nature and practices of the Messalian adherents. A synopsis of these lists has been compiled by Columba Stewart,[9] who suggests that there were ten basic Messalian doctrines and practices which were commonly seen to be heretical or objectionable by hierarchs in Asia Minor. However, Stewart is careful to avoid using the lists as a means of assessing the orthodoxy of the Messalian movement. Furthermore it must be remembered that the individual lists are descriptions of the perceived objectionable elements of the movement rather than exact theological statements written by its members. In this regard they may have more to tell us of the theological agenda and fears of the accusing church than they do of the theological position of the Messalians, isolating as they do the perceived negative aspects of the group. Those isolated teachings specifically relating to prayer and the use of time within the lists are the presence of an indwelling demon in each human soul; the inefficacy of baptism for the expulsion of the demon; the sole efficacy of prayer for the expulsion of the demon; stress on the coming of the Holy Spirit or the heavenly bridegroom; avoidance of work and the desire for sleep; excessive sleep and claims that dreams are prophetic.[10]

From an examination of the lists of perceived Messalian doctrines and practices it can be seen that prayer is, for them, a purifying activity; indeed it is the only means of ridding the soul of the indwelling demon.[11] As such, prayer takes priority in their use of time, taking precedence over all other activities. This imbalance may have been a cause of the disquiet felt by the established ecclesiastical hierarchy in the areas where Messalianism flourished. This assertion is given credibility by a recorded conversation between Flavian, Bishop of Antioch, and Adelphus, a known Messalian leader, at the Synod of Antioch in *c.* 380. Flavian elicits, somewhat dubiously, from Adelphus the admission that

[9] Stewart, *Working the Earth*, pp. 55–6, App. 1–2.

[10] Ibid., pp. 55–6; Gribomont, 'Dossier'.

[11] See also the reports of the conversation between Adelphus and Flavius at the Synod of Antioch: ibid., pp. 615–16.

> Holy baptism is of no use to those to whom we administer it, only persevering prayer can succeed in chasing the devil which lives in us, for each one at birth, receives through Adam, along with his nature, the servitude to demons. Once these demons are chased out by prayer then at last the Holy Spirit can arise, who manifests his presence in a way that can be felt and seen, liberating the body from the movement of the passions and freeing completely the soul, which is no longer inclined towards evil.[12]

Prayer is seen as an activity in which divine communications and experiences are received in a way, as Adelphus states, that can be both felt and seen; it is also a means to purify the soul. Thus, within Messalianism, time should be so arranged that prayer is the principal activity. This insistence on 'constant prayer' is elsewhere described in the lists of Messalian heresy as an excuse for the avoidance of work, on the assumption that the work of the hands is not considered fit for Christians.[13] Timothy of Constantinople records that

> They [the Messalians] say that after what is called by them *apatheia* they give themselves over to much sleep, and the dreams which occur by the inspiration of the evil demon energizing them they herald as prophecies; and they teach that these things are to be believed as inspired by the Holy Spirit.[14]

Furthermore, Theodoret records that the Messalians pretend to be devoted to prayer, but exercise sleep when they say they are actually praying.[15] The emphasis on prayer which is found in both the Macarian writings and the known Messalian practices continued within emergent monasticism long after the Messalian movement was anathematized by the Council of Ephesus in 431. The idea of constant prayer was to become a major emphasis within eastern monastic Christianity.[16] Indeed, the charge of Messalianism almost became a generic accusation levelled against any 'experiential',

[12] Theodoret (ed. Parmentier), *Kirchengeschichte*, IV.11 (pp. 230–1).

[13] Timothy of Constantinople, *De iis qui ad ecclesiam*, XIII (*PG* 86, cols 45–52); see Stewart, *Working the Earth*, p. 263.

[14] Timothy of Constantinople, *De iis qui ad ecclesiam*, XIV (*PG* 86, cols 45–52); see Stewart, *Working the Earth*, p. 267.

[15] Theodoret, *Haereticarum fabularum compendium*, IV.11 (*PG* 83, cols 429–32); see Stewart, *Working the Earth*, p. 266.

[16] For a summary of the influence of the Messalian Homilies see G. Maloney, *Pseudo-Macarius: the Fifty Spiritual Homilies and the Great Letter*, Classics of Western Spirituality (New York and Mahwah, NJ, 1992), pp. 20–7.

'charismatic', or 'prayerful' group or practice.[17] The Messalians stood accused of individualism to the detriment of community, of following the way of excessive prayer to the detriment of a community lifestyle, as well as having a theological stance that rejected the efficacy of baptism and taught that there was an indwelling demon in the soul of each believer.

Persevering prayer then, was an issue to the Church in the fourth century, and it was linked to the question of authority and experience. For the Messalians prayer was not only the way to attain purity of soul by the expulsion of the inner demon; it was also a way of acquiring authoritative status within a group of believers. The lack of detailed evidence on Messalian teaching (the only evidence we have being the lists of perceived heretical practices) precludes definite conclusions. There is, however, evidence that some Messalian groups rejected the authority of the Church due to a lack of celibacy amongst its hierarchy.[18] It remains clear that the Messalian approach to prayer was one of 'perseverance' to attain purity, perseverance to receive visions and dreams, and (to quote Adelphus) perseverance to receive an experience of the Holy Spirit that was both 'felt and seen'. This experience brought kudos, and hence authority.

* * *

When the allegedly Messalian approach to prayer and work is considered in comparison with the approach and teaching of Ps-Macarius, certain differences and discrepancies appear between the two, which cast doubt on the designation of Ps-Macarius as a Messalian. Such doubts are not new. Recent scholarship has shown how new approaches to the Macarian Corpus reveal new insights into the persona and position of Ps-Macarius, as well as confirming the doubts concerning the Messalian element within his work.

An example of this is seen in the approach to prayer of Ps-Macarius, as compared to that of the Messalians outlined above, although at times his language is ambiguous. For example, Ps-Macarius describes prayer as 'the head of every good endeavour and the guiding force of right action',[19] and he too emphasises the need for perseverance in

[17] See L. Bouyer, 'The spirituality of the New Testament and the Fathers', in idem, *History of Christian Spirituality*, vol. 1: *The Spirituality of the New Testament and the Fathers* (London, 1963), p. 371.

[18] Burns, 'Charisma and spirituality', pp. 240–7.

[19] I.4.1–5; II.40.2.

prayer. Similar sentiments are included among the condemned Messalian views, and in the words of Adelphus recorded above. However, Ps-Macarius goes out of his way to affirm the communal element of prayer. He states that prayer is built on a foundation of 'vigilance of thought, in tranquillity and peace', and crucially insists that prayer should not be a source of offence to others.

> The true foundation of prayer is this, to concentrate attention, and to pray in great quietness and peace, so as to give no offence to those outside. Such a man . . . will edify other people more. For God is not the God of confusion but of peace. Those who pray noisily . . . cannot pray everywhere. . . . But those who pray quietly edify everybody everywhere. A man's whole labour should be employed upon his thoughts.[20]

This desire to pray in peace and harmony with others is a crucial difference from the Messalian practice of prayer which, according to the extant accounts, caused disharmony and offence. For Ps-Macarius prayer is conducted in response to an act of the will, and is an opportunity to examine oneself for purity of thought: 'Go to prayer, and observe your heart and mind, and determine to send up your prayer to God pure, and look well there, whether there be nothing to hinder it, whether the mind is fully occupied with the Lord.'[21] Prayer does involves the reception of vision, and wisdom, and divine mysteries, and there is an undoubted experiential element that is required within effective prayer. These experiences are the reward of having nothing to do with the world, and are to be taught and passed on to others rather than kept hidden in oneself.

> Oftentimes . . . the unlearned man goes to prayer, and bends the knee, and his own mind enters into rest, and deep as he may dig and get below, the wall of evil that withstands him breaks down, and he enters into vision and wisdom, where potentates and wise men and orators cannot penetrate to understand and know the delicacy of his mind, since he is engrossed in divine mysteries.[22]

Simply put, the deeper a person's prayer life, the more the person praying is drawn towards God,[23] and the greater the experience of

20 II.6.3.

21 I.32.1–8; II.15.13.

22 I.48.3; II.15.15.

23 I.4.1–5; II.40.3.

God. However, Ps-Macarius also cautions that prayer is a means of falling from grace, for the visions and power received can lead to pride in the person who prays.[24] Thus prayer alone is not sufficient, humility is required. Coupled with prayer a person must seek after humility, charity, and meekness,[25] all elements not usually associated with the Messalian practices.

Ps-Macarius teaches that prayer is not to be conducted within a vacuum, and there is a need to pray whilst waiting on God; not according to custom and habit, but with the mind concentrated on God.[26] Ps-Macarius speaks of the teaching that the person will receive from the Spirit, and the corresponding gift of worship, and in so doing enlarges upon the reception of visions and dreams that occur while the soul is caught up in the presence of the Divine, and is in a state of spiritual intoxication. For Ps-Macarius the Spirit must be present in pure prayer, and act as a teacher in prayer,[27] teaching the soul not to stray in distraction but to be attentive and actively discern the thoughts of the mind.[28] For the soul waiting upon Christ will receive true prayer; 'And thus will He lighten it, teaching it the true asking, giving it the pure spiritual prayer, which is worthy of God, and the worship which is in spirit and truth.'[29] Prayer, then, is a means of making the soul a throne of glory for the Lord. Ps-Macarius states: 'So let us also fit our souls out with versatility and skill, to obtain the great true gain, even God, who teaches us truly to pray. In this way the Lord rests upon the soul's good intention, making it a throne of glory, and sitting and resting upon it.'[30] The result of prayer is that the 'person who daily forces himself to persevere in prayer is inflamed with divine passion and fiery desire rising from a spiritual love toward God, and he receives the grace of the sanctifying perfection of the Spirit'.[31]

Prayer in Ps-Macarius is more than contemplation. It is an active process, an activity of the heart as much as of the body. Here we see the beginnings of prayer as an activity of life, of attitude, of constant progress, rather than prayer as limited in time, primarily a means of

[24] II.17.14.
[25] I.56.1–2; II.19.2,4.
[26] E.g. II.33.
[27] I.56.1–2; II.19.9.
[28] II.31.2,6.
[29] II.33.2.
[30] II.33.1,2,3.
[31] I.4.1–5; II.40.2.

reception of experience. Ps-Macarius emphasises the progression within the life of the believer. To advance in prayer it is necessary to subdue the thoughts by an act of the will, and this is portrayed as a 'battle' in the soul and mind.

A further example of the discrepancy between Messalianism and Ps-Macarius is seen in the relationship between prayer and work. The Messalian approach to work was, from the available accounts, lax, with prayer being the foremost activity and work being regarded as unnecessary. The Macarian rules for communal living recognize that communal life, prayer for the community, is necessary for progression in the life of the believer. This communal life includes work, and prayer is not to be engaged in to the detriment of the community. Ps-Macarius writes that

> The one who works should say of him who is praying: 'I also possess the treasure which my brother possesses since it is common.' And let him who prays say of him who reads: 'What he gains from reading redounds also to my advantage.' . . . But let each one do whatever he is doing for the glory of God. He who reads should regard the one praying with love and joy with the thought, 'For me he is praying'; and let him who prays think of him who is at work, 'What he is doing, is done for the common good.'[32]

This affirmation of community responsibility and 'collective faith' is typical of Ps-Macarius, and finds no echo in the known Messalian practices. Ps-Macarius draws from the body analogy of I Corinthians 12.12, of the idea of the 'common good'. For him, prayer is not only an individual activity, it is a corporate endeavour, whose practise benefits all. The aim of the Macarian community is to live on earth as angels, in one accord, in unanimity, in peace, with mutual love and sincerity.[33] This community attitude validates a diverse use of time, with some free to devote themselves to prayer for 'six hours' whilst others 'kindly serve' and others 'do their own work'.[34] Thus in the Macarian corpus there is a community structure that allows freedom of activity, and whose adoption brings release. In contrast the Messalian phenomenon is difficult to isolate and define, precisely

[32] II.3.2.
[33] II.3.1.
[34] II.3.1.

because of the ephemeral nature of the movement which had no known structure. Hence the lack of precision on the use of time in the lists of Messalian practices.

The common good, the life of angels on earth, the mutual progression of all towards the Godhead is a binding force within the Macarian community. The attitude to the common good allows the purifying activity of the Holy Spirit within the heart of the individual whilst that individual is seeking the 'common good' for all.[35] Therefore, work and leisure are seen as 'spiritual' activities. That is, there is no demarcation between what is spiritual and what is not. The attitude of the heart is what is crucial for effective prayer. The use of time is such that all activities, however mundane, can be conducive to the believer's progress on the journey towards the Divine.

* * *

The realm of experience offers a further characteristic of the Macarian community. Experience is a qualification for leadership within the community. Those who teach are to have experienced what they are teaching about. Thus, those who have experienced divine communion (like Ps-Macarius) are therefore qualified to teach, having experienced this divine communication not just for personal gain, but for didactic purposes. The accusation against the Messalians of selfishness, laziness, and prevarication,[36] cannot be levelled against Ps-Macarius, as teaching and passing on divine communications plays such an important part within his community. Indeed, in his teaching Ps-Macarius is at pains to stress that any ecstatic experience is not permanent, since if it were the recipient of the divine communication would be unable to pass on the experience to others. The goal of the Macarian community is thus communal progress, the progression of all members of the community to the level of experience of the Spirit which the teacher has received. The individual can only progress within the body of the community. Once again this understanding of community life and aims contradicts what is known about the Messalian movement, while still sharing some

[35] II.3.2.

[36] See Stewart, *Working the Earth*, App. 2, p. 262. Timothy of Constantinople, *De iis qui ad ecclesiam*, *PG* 86, cols 45–52: 'They say that the work of the hands is to be shunned as loathsome'; John of Damascus, *De haeresibus*, 80 (ed. Kotter, pp. 42–6): 'Yet they shun the work of the hands as not fit for Christians'; Theodoret (ed. Parmentier), *Kirchengeschichte*, IV.11, pp. 229–31: 'Those who are fully taken into the complete sickness shun manual labour as if it were vice.'

of the expressions and desire for spiritual experience seen in that movement.

Implicit in the explanation of the role of the teacher within the community is a criticism that some teachers (outside the community) were teaching without having experienced what they were teaching about. In an ecclesiastical setting those teaching outside the community were most likely to be bishops and the local church leadership, which allows the inference of an understated criticism of the leadership of some of the churches in the area of Macarian activity. Rather than this being seen as an anti-ecclesiastical or anti-establishment characteristic, it reflects a concern of Ps-Macarius for the genuineness and purity of teaching within the Church, as an enduring aspect of the tension between 'monastic' and 'urban' forms of Church experience and organization. Ps-Macarius is obviously a person of responsibility within the Macarian communities, who could also be seen as authoritative by those outside the community structure. This suggests that it is not inconceivable that Ps-Macarius was a bishop.

* * *

It is the essence of Ps-Macarius' thought that there is no dichotomy between theology and spirituality. For him there is only the life of being a follower of Christ, under the control of the Holy Spirit, imbued by his power, and gazing directly at God the Father. Ps-Macarius does not shy away from the difficulty of living a life in total devotion to God, nor does he ignore those who leave the ascetic way for other pastures. His understanding of the presence of the Spirit in the heart of a believer, and of the co-operation and discipline required to experience fully the Christian life, leads to his theological stance. In many ways his practice and experience formulate his theological understanding and teaching, generating a theology based on and grounded in the reality of his faith.

The relationship of Ps-Macarius to Messalianism becomes clearer when the fluid nature of the Messalian phenomenon is taken into account. Rather than being a figurehead of the movement, or one attempting to reform it from within, Ps-Macarius must be seen as one engaged in the broader debate on the role of experience and prayer within the Church. Ps-Macarius shows some 'enthusiastic' traits which were common to Messalians and attractive to Syrians in general. However, it should be noted that by the nature of his corpus and the volume of his work we are able to isolate a significant degree of

Macarian theology, whereas in comparison the extant lists of Messalian traits allow only a limited deduction of Messalian theology. Ps-Macarius cannot simply be read as Messalian, particularly when the Messalian phenomenon is recognized as being highly ephemeral in nature.

This consideration of the use of time within the Macarian community reveals a focus on prayer, and the preparation for prayer, but not to the detriment of the community and, in particular, not to the detriment of the wider ecclesiastical community outside the Macarian brotherhoods. The use of time is for the common good. Prayer, working, and reading, whether conducted individually or corporately, all benefit the community, and as such all contribute to 'prayer'. Prayer is more than the reception of visions and experience, more than a purifying activity (as it was for the Messalians). It is a unifying entity within the community, a means by which community values are strengthened, and by which the community is enabled to live 'as angels' whilst still on earth. Ps-Macarius' use of time marks him out as different from the Messalians, and his focus on the corporate 'common good' is a further characteristic by which his distinct theology may be identified.

St John's College, Nottingham

AUGUSTINE AND THE ART OF GARDENING

by CAROL HARRISON

ANY description of man's ideal state tells us a lot about the culture, society, and character of its author. Early Christian writers, as one might expect, tended to turn to Scripture, to the authoritative account in the book of Genesis of God's creation of man and woman and of their life in the garden of Eden, in order to define their conception of the ideal life. There they discovered what to us, and perhaps to them, seems a rather strange, alien portrait of the life of two celibate naturists, at ease in a luxuriant garden which provided for all their needs. By some obscure and generally unspecified means, the Church fathers thought Adam and Eve were to be the founder members and originators of a society which, on condition it obeyed one simple rule, would become an immortal society.

It was clear to the fathers of the Church that the application of this ideal state to their own experience of the world demanded a huge, and daring, imaginative leap of interpretation. This was once again informed for them primarily by Genesis and its account of the Fall. Having disobeyed the one rule which constrained their otherwise undemanding life, the first couple found themselves forced to assume clothes and exiled into a hostile world characterized by toil and suffering. This was something the fathers could more readily identify with: alienation and dissociation, not only from their Creator, but from themselves and from each other because of their disordered, darkened, and fractured wills. This was a life characterized by necessity – the need to work, to labour, to suffer, to fight in order to survive.

The contrast between paradisal rest and leisure and the necessity of everyday work is at its starkest here. It raises a host of questions. This paper examines how St Augustine, the fourth/fifth-century African Bishop of Hippo, reflected upon and responded to them. In doing so we may appreciate, despite the predominantly secular nature of modern culture, and the rather different approach to Scripture and authority which Augustine shared with his culture, just how influential his thought has been in shaping Western attitudes to work, rest, and leisure.

When Augustine turns to reflect on the Genesis account in the longest of his five attempts at interpreting this text, the *Literal Commentary on Genesis* (Genesis was something of an obsession for him), it is the apparent inconsistencies in what he regards as the authoritative text of Scripture which occasion his reflection on the nature of work, rest, and leisure. The idea of God's rest on the seventh day, having completed the work of creation, is one that puzzles and, in its obvious meaning, offends him. The author cannot possibly mean that God needed to put his feet up because he was tired. Augustine opts for a more philosophical, theological line of interpretation: God, Augustine suggests, is 'at rest' in himself because he is self-sufficient and stands in need of nothing outside himself; he is 'always in a state of tranquillity', always 'happy in himself'. God in turn gives man rest in himself because only in him, the Creator, can we be said not to lack anything, and to attain happiness.[1] Rest is to be understood, in Augustinian terms, not as a box of chocolates in a comfy armchair, but as a humble acknowledgement of our created dependence on God as our ultimate good, in whom alone we can find wholeness and happiness. As Augustine puts it, 'We must rest in an immutable God, that is, in him who made us. This will be our most exalted state of rest, a truly holy state, free from all pride.'[2] I will come back to this.

Augustine is also puzzled as to why Genesis speaks of Adam being placed in paradise to 'cultivate and protect it' (Genesis 2.15), when it is clear that there are 'nourishing crops' and 'fruit bearing trees' aplenty to provide for all his needs, and the toil of cultivating the earth is later described as one of the punishments of the Fall in Genesis. Augustine's response is to assume that Adam was one of that noble breed, a 'gentleman gardener', who freely pursued the art of horticulture because of the simple pleasure and delight it afforded him. Moreover, there were no weeds, no inclement weather, no slugs or snails to contend with in paradise, rather everything was propitious for an abundant harvest. We discover the frustrated gardener in Augustine as he warms to his theme and asks,

> What more impressive and wonderful spectacle than this? Where is human reason better able to speak, as it were, to nature than

[1] *De Genesi ad litteram*, IV.xiii.24–xvii.29. All references to Augustine's works are to the Benedictine edition, which is reprinted in *PL* 32–47. The best English translation of the *De Genesi ad litteram* is by J. H. Taylor: Augustine, *The Literal Meaning of Genesis*, 2 vols, Ancient Christian Writers, 41–2 (New York, 1982).

[2] *De Genesi ad litteram*, IV.xvii.29.

> when man sows the seed, plants a tree, transplants a bush, grafts a mallet shoot, and thus asks, as it were, each root and seed what it can or cannot do, why it can or cannot do it.[3]

It is an art far removed from the wearisome toil mankind now experiences in working the soil in order to eat. Rather, as he puts it, 'The exercise of this art . . . was filled with delights, suggesting noble and salutary thoughts to the mind of a wise man.'[4]

Here then is a portrait of man at his most noble, freely practising an art which affords him pleasure and delight, exercises the body, engages with nature and lifts the mind to spiritual thoughts. It is the ideal portrait of man at work, a work undertaken not through obligation or necessity but freely, satisfyingly, and with spiritual profit.

We need to pause and reflect on terminology. I have used the language of 'work' in relation to Adam's gentlemanly occupation of gardening intentionally. The word 'leisure' might suggest itself as more appropriate in this context but I would like to resist it for a number of reasons. Whereas 'leisure' probably suggests to us something free from the necessity of everyday work, free from the obligations which must necessarily be met in order to provide food, clothing, and shelter, something of an indulgence for free time, like playing golf, watching TV, or collecting hat pins, I would like to follow Augustine's suggestion that it is, in fact, the highest form of 'work', of human occupation, which engages the highest part of ourselves in the most fruitful way.

On the one hand, then, there is 'work' which must be done to provide the basic necessities of human existence, and, as we shall see, to order, govern, and protect human society – let us call this 'enforced work'. On the other there is 'work' which is motivated by love, undertaken by choice, for the pleasure and delight it affords – we might call this 'free work'. Just because an occupation is not a matter of basic necessity does not mean that it is of a lower value than, or should not be taken as seriously as, work viewed as labour; but it is precisely this which our use of the language of 'leisure' would suggest. In fact, much of what we regard as leisure turns out to be pure idleness (but that is another question).[5]

Augustine suggests that real work, true work, ideal work, is that in

[3] Ibid., VIII.viii.15.

[4] Ibid., VIII.x.22.

[5] See Josef Pieper, *Leisure the Basis of Culture* (London, 1952), pp. 30–48.

which man freely engages because he loves it, for the delight and, as he puts it, the 'spiritual pleasure' it affords,[6] and which leads him to engagement with the nature of reality. This is 'free work' and is the ideal, natural state of humankind. Work undertaken purely out of necessity, 'enforced work', is alien to human existence and a mark of its fallenness.

I have used the language of free work and enforced work. The ancients would use the language of *otium* and *negotium*; of leisure and the absence of leisure. Leisure, or *otium*, in fact covers a broad spectrum of meaning, from idleness, rest, and spare time, to the idea of freedom or retirement from business to pursue other activities, especially cultural ones. The idea of philosophical *otium*, of withdrawing from the world in order to pursue a life devoted to wisdom, or of a cultured sabbatical in the middle of one's career, in order to pursue the philosophical life, was a common one, and one that fits in well with Augustine's description of free work.

Augustine's actual example, however – of gardening, rather than the more well-known and widely accepted one of life devoted to wisdom – might well suggest an implicit criticism of the classical ideal, or at least a desire to broaden it out to include in man's pre-fallen condition other aspects of life worthy to be counted as free, leisure work. This is indeed suggested when, having discussed the question of Adam's cultivating of the soil in *The Literal Commentary on Genesis*, he proceeds, in the next chapter, to describe the two aspects of God's providential action in the world.[7] What he calls 'natural providence' refers to God's natural and inward ordering of nature, in, for example, the movement and growth of the body, plants, the elements, and in the life and sensation of the soul; 'voluntary providence', on the other hand, refers to the external work of men or angels, acting on the things God has given in order, as Augustine puts it, 'to acquire knowledge and live in harmony'. By the work of voluntary providence, he observes, 'creatures are instructed and learn, fields are cultivated, societies are governed, the arts are practised'. Since the context makes clear that Augustine is referring to man's life before the Fall, one must, I think, therefore presume that education, the government of human society, the practice of the arts (whatever they were – we will return to this later), were pursued in the same way as Adam's gardening, as

[6] *De Genesi ad litteram*, VIII.xi.18.

[7] Ibid., VIII.ix.17–18. See the whole of book VIII for an extended discussion.

Augustine puts it, not 'in servile labour but with a spiritual pleasure befitting his dignity'.[8] He certainly mentions Adam's intention to educate Eve,[9] his loving rule over her as head of the first couple,[10] the society which, potentially, they were meant to establish, and also, as we have seen, his occupation as a gardener. The arts are not, however, given any further attention before the Fall – perhaps because Adam and Eve's time in paradise was so short that they did not have the opportunity to practise them. What is interesting, however, is the range and variety of the first humans' 'work': freely willed, pleasurable and fulfilling work, unconstrained by any necessity, before the Fall. These occupations give us some insight into the sort of pursuits, the sort of 'work', which is natural and desirable for man.

But as always with Augustine, we must now turn to consider what is in fact the case, what man's position actually is, not in the few idyllic moments before the Fall, but in the world as he now finds it, a world he described as one of 'utter misery', a 'kind of hell on earth', where man lives a life of such 'wretched necessity' that it might best be described as a 'living death'.[11]

For, according to Augustine, after the Fall the world has become an alien and hostile place for mankind. Following Genesis he will note that man must now work the soil with the sweat of his brow – gardening is no longer a delightful and elevating activity but a penal labour fraught with difficulties, a battle against the hostile elements, against thorns and thistles. Gardening, along with education, government, and the arts, is no longer freely chosen, but an unavoidable labour and necessity.

More generally, by disobeying God, Augustine asserts, man has lost the 'rest' and peace he found in acknowledging his subjection to, and dependence upon him. Man is now subject to disorder, disruption, division, and darkness, not only in his experience of the world in which he lives, but within himself. The natural order of human society, of man's subjection to God, of the body to the soul, has been upturned. Within, man finds himself alienated and dissociated from himself; his will so flawed and vitiated that it can no longer control his body and its desires. Externally, human society is characterized by division, war, the urge to subject, conquer, and dominate. Justice, which Augustine

[8] Ibid., VIII.ix.18.

[9] Ibid., XI.xlii.59.

[10] Ibid., XI.xxxvii.50.

[11] *Ciuitas Dei*, XIX.x, XXII.xxii, XIX.vi.

describes as rendering to each his due, and which in a Christian context meant love of God and of one's neighbour, has also been destroyed. What remains is simply a 'shadow peace', a travesty of true justice, no longer based on the will of God, but on a 'compromise', as Augustine puts it, 'between human wills'.[12] This is manifested in the 'temporal laws' of human society and the way it now organizes and governs itself so that it might protect itself from the violent and destructive forces unleashed by the Fall, so that it might function as harmoniously as possible in a fallen world and not destroy itself.[13] It is his conviction that 'rest', or true peace and justice, in rightly ordered love of God and man, is now unattainable in this life, which determines what Augustine has to say about every aspect of the life and work of the Christian in the world.

It is therefore appropriate to examine the various aspects of Christian life in the world, and the sort of work Augustine understood them to entail. The most obvious starting point is perhaps the family, that group which Augustine and the ancients regarded as the basic constituent of human society.[14]

Augustine is convinced that both before and after the Fall, and in the life to come, human life is meant to be a social life. Before the Fall he perceives a natural pattern of rule and obedience governing the relationship of Adam and Eve which he believes is continued in the Roman family. The *paterfamilias*, like Adam, rules his wife, and husband and wife rule their children. But whereas before the Fall Eve turned towards Adam in love,[15] family relations are now characterized by fear and subjection. The most obvious sign of how the original hierarchy of human relations has been subverted by fallen man was, for Augustine, the institution of slavery. Slavery did not exist in paradise; but the present subjection of slaves to their masters, in captive and enforced service rather than freely willed, loving obedience, is for him a sign and punishment of the Fall. Slavery, for Augustine, is the paradigm of 'enforced work', and is actually the state of all mankind after the Fall. It is perhaps this insight that underlies his toleration of it.

Although he evidently abhorred the institution itself, and did what

12 *Ciuitas Dei*, XIX.xvii.

13 The contents of this paragraph are discussed by Augustine, ibid., XIX.

14 Harmony or *concordia* in the family constituted the basis for harmony and unity in the city and in the state – *De bono coniugali*, iv.3, iv.4, vii.6.

15 *De Genesi ad litteram*, XI.xxxvii.50.

he could, as bishop, to ameliorate it,[16] he did not seek to abolish slavery. His conviction that all men are now slaves, that slavery is 'ordained by the law which enjoins the preservation of nature and forbids its disturbance'[17] – in other words it is part of man's just punishment for sin against the original order – means that instead of objecting to it on humanitarian grounds, as we would no doubt do, he rather feels compelled to suggest ways in which slaves and masters should behave, how they should make the best of things, within the unavoidable constraints of their fallen world. Slaves, he recommends, should try to create their own limited freedom by freely obeying their masters with a good will and 'fidelity of affection'.[18] They should take comfort that they are probably better off in slavery than in many other supposedly 'free' occupations, and that slavery to a master is infinitely preferable to slavery to lust.[19] The master, on his side, should treat his slave with benevolence and compassion, try to ensure that he is encouraged to become, or to continue as, a Christian, and be included, on a par with the rest of the household and 'with equal affection', in matters of worship.[20] He should, as it were, become the slave of those whom he appears to command.[21]

And what of women within the family? They were not, of course, expected to work in the formal sense of following a career or profession. They were not educated or trained for it; rather the expectation was, at least among the elite for whom we have evidence, that they would make a good marriage and oversee the household administration, childcare, and servants. They might also spin and weave.

The woman's sphere was very much the private one of the household; the man's, the public one of the city. The fathers tended to see this state of affairs as divinely ordained. Ambrose traces it to Eve's original creation when he writes on Genesis 2.21–2: 'God built the rib he took from Adam into a woman.'

[16] E.g. in *Epistula*, XXIV* (J. Divjak, *Œuvres de saint Augustin, 46B: Lettres 1*–29**, Bibliothèque Augustinienne [(Paris), 1987], pp. 382–7), he insists that free-born men should not be sold into slavery. He used the church chest, on occasion, to liberate slaves in bad households.

[17] *Ciuitas Dei*, XIX.15.

[18] Ibid.

[19] *Sermones*, CLIX.5; *Ciuitas Dei*, XIX.15.

[20] *Civitas Dei*, XIX.16. On ensuring that slaves are converted and baptized see *Epistula*, XCVIII.6.

[21] *Ciuitas Dei*, XIX.14.

> 'He built' [the reading of the Septuagint and the Vulgate] is well put in that verse where he was speaking of woman's creation, because the domestic edifice of man and woman seems to be rich in a certain kind of perfection. The man who is without a wife is accordingly considered to be without a home. Just as a man is thought to be more skilful at public duties, so a woman is thought more skilful in domestic services.[22]

It was also quite clear to the fathers that the main purpose of Eve's creation was to bear children. If God had wanted to create a companion for Adam he would, Augustine rather unfortunately but self-evidently observes, have created another man. Nevertheless, in paradise, Eve turned to Adam in love, which knows no domination; after the Fall she is subjected to him as a servant to her lord.[23] Although Augustine, rather surprisingly, is emphatic that, morally and intellectually[24] – even physically[25] – women are equal to men, and that inferiority is not their natural state, it is now, he believes, part of their lot as helper and childbearer. Of course, this was reinforced in Augustine's mind by Scripture and the traditional customs and practices of his society. A woman's lot was generally regarded as a highly unenviable one, and many of the fathers go out of their way to give long rhetorical descriptions of the trials of marriage – especially in treatises on virginity! Women, too, then, are effectively slaves: their 'work' is not freely chosen because of the pleasure and rewards it affords, but is rather enforced by social expectation and the punishment of fallen necessity.

When we turn to examine the nature of work in the wider society which took the family as its base we are immediately confronted with a stark divide between rich and poor: the elite (for whom documentary evidence exists) and the vast majority – probably about 80–90 per cent – who were either slaves and tenants, or engaged in trade, such as craftsmen, merchants, or shopkeepers.

The occupations pursued by the 'silent majority' were recognized and accepted as useful and good by Augustine so long as they were conducted with integrity and honesty. He tends to favour manual work

[22] *On Paradise*, XI.50 (*PL* 14, col. 299), quoted by E. A. Clark, *Women in the Early Church* (Collegeville, MN, 1983), p. 33. Cf. Tertullian, *An Exhortation to Charity*, xii (*PL* 2, col. 927).

[23] *De Genesi ad litteram*, XI.xxxvii.50.

[24] *Contra Faustum*, XXIV.2; *De Genesi ad litteram*, III.xxii.34; *De trinitate*, XII.iii.10.

[25] *Ciuitas Dei*, XXII.17–18.

for precisely this reason: it was much less likely to present a man with the dilemmas and temptations which those engaged in trade and business frequently had to face,[26] and kept his mind free from worldly preoccupations in order to dwell on more spiritual matters.[27] In fact, as one might expect given Augustine's theology of grace and human freedom, he sometimes reflects that when the workman loves what he is doing rather than finding it a necessary and burdensome chore, he can find joy and delight in his job; it becomes, as it were, 'free work'. He writes,

> The labours of those who love are never tiresome, but they are even a source of pleasure as in the case of hunters, fowlers, fishermen, vine-dressers, merchants and those who amuse themselves at some game. It all depends on what one loves, for there is either no weariness in work that is loved, or the weariness itself is loved.[28]

This is a reminder that, for Augustine, it is in love, above all, that God's redemptive grace makes itself felt and makes possible the free action of man's fallen will, even in contexts which might otherwise be regarded as necessitated by the Fall.

The elite minority was set apart and moulded by an exclusive system of education which, although it did not really prepare them, at least put them in the position of being able to pursue occupations fitting for their class. These were almost wholly related to the government and administration of the empire, in other words to the imperial service (a place in the senate, a governorship, military command), or to overseeing a large estate with its slaves and tenants. Augustine himself, the son of a town councillor with very modest means, is a good example of how it was possible to work one's way into the aristocracy, not through birth but by the right education. Having attended the village school at Thagaste, and then, thanks to a benefactor, the schools of rhetoric at Madura and Carthage, he was able to teach rhetoric at Carthage and Rome, and finally obtain the

[26] See R. Arbresmann, 'The attitude of Saint Augustine toward labor', in D. Neiman and W. Schatkin, eds, *The Heritage of the Early Church. Essays in Honor of Georges Florovsky* (Rome, 1973), p. 254 nn.31–2.

[27] *De opere monachorum*, XIV, XVI; see Arbresmann, 'Attitude', pp. 252–3. In XIV Augustine cites the example of the Patriarchs who were shepherds, the Greek philosophers who were shoemakers, and Joseph, who was a carpenter.

[28] *De bono viduitatis*, XXI.26, quoted by Arbresmann, 'Attitude', p. 251.

municipal rhetorship of Milan, the imperial capital. Here he had every hope of, perhaps, becoming a provincial governor and obtaining senatorial rank. Instead, as we know, he converted to Christianity.

Perhaps the most pressing question for Augustine and his Christian contemporaries when considering the Christian's place in the world – his role in society; the sort of occupation he might pursue; his attitude to everyday customs, traditions, and practices; the way in which he might entertain himself – was the question of the relation between Christianity and paganism. As we know, for the first three centuries of its existence the Church had grown in the shadow of a largely hostile and persecuting pagan society. It had been forced to understand and define itself in contradistinction to pagan religion, society, and practices. With the conversion of Constantine the situation began – slowly, erratically, and falteringly – to be reversed, until paganism was proscribed, and pagans were persecuted by a Christian Emperor.

Augustine lived during this period of transition, an ambiguous period of conflicting loyalties and uncertainties; of definition, distinction, and division between what should be identified and condemned as pagan or accepted as Christian; between what was simply part of 'secular' life and what was 'sacred' to either paganism or Christianity.[29] The pagan past was still very much part of the present; the Church itself was made up of men and women who came from, and were moulded by, it. It is obvious from Augustine's sermons that conversion did not – could not – bring about a final and decisive break with that past, but rather that it lingered on in popular superstitious practices and customs and especially in enthusiasm for pagan festivals and the games.

Some of Augustine's predecessors, such as Tertullian (at least in his more severe moods), had advocated a total separation from, and rejection of, all things pagan.[30] Augustine, however, was clear that the legacy of paganism, like the inheritance of original sin, could not simply be obliterated. There was to be no dramatic Christianization of

[29] Peter Brown, *Authority and the Sacred* (Cambridge, 1995).

[30] See e.g., *De praescriptione haereticorum*, VII, in *Tertullien: Traité de la prescription contre les hérétiques*, ed. R. F. Refoulé and P. de Labriolle, SC, 46 (Paris, 1957), pp. 96–9 ('nothing could be more foreign to the Christian than the State'), and *De idololatria*, ed. J. H. Waszink and J. C. M. van Winden, Supplements to Vigiliae Christianae, 1 (Leiden, New York, Copenhagen, and Cologne, 1987). But see *Apologeticum*, XXXII, XLII (*PL* 1, cols 447, 490–1) for an attitude which, in fact, comes very close to Augustine's compromise with the world.

the empire as Eusebian theology had optimistically proclaimed. Rather, the pagan context of Christianity, like original sin, was a feature which confirmed the ambiguity, the uncertainty, and the essential compromise of Christian life in the world.

Compromise, then, is the key to understanding Augustine's attitude to the way in which a Christian should occupy himself in the world. It was pointless, he believed, to think that a Christian empire, or any other sort of ideal society, could be attained in this life. The Christian is, rather, a captive, a foreigner in a strange land; Augustine's favourite image is that of a pilgrim, a resident alien, a *peregrinus* - someone who is passing through this world and who makes use of its laws, customs, and institutions on the way to his true homeland, the heavenly City of God.[31] His attitude should be a detached one: he uses what is necessary but takes nothing as an end or ultimate in itself. In other words, he does not 'rest' in anything of this world, but is continually seeking 'rest', as we defined it earlier, only in God.[32]

How, we might ask, does this work out on a practical, everyday level? In common with a long line of Christian apologists before him, Augustine is emphatic that Christians should, as Paul had enjoined, obey the powers that be; they should 'render to Caesar', whether those powers represent Christianity or not. Like the Israelites using the peace of Babylon,[33] they should use and support the laws, institutions, customs, and traditions of the society in which they find themselves, so long as they do not conflict with their devotion to God.[34] This is because, in Augustine's view, human law, government, and politics serve above all to order, control, and set limits on the anarchy, disruption, and division which otherwise vitiates human society as a result of the Fall. These institutions are indeed human, temporal, and all too fallible and flawed – they are based on coercion, violence, lust for domination, and subjection. They work, not according to God's eternal law, but on a relative and shifting 'compromise between human wills about the things relevant to this life'.[35] Unlike the family they are not part of man's natural or intended state; man is naturally social but

[31] *Ciuitas Dei*, XIX is the key text here. See esp. XIX.17.

[32] Ibid., XIX.19. Augustine describes these ideas theoretically in *De doctrina Christiana*, I, in terms of *uti* and *frui*; use and enjoyment. They recur frequently throughout his works (especially in sermons).

[33] *Ciuitas Dei*, XIX.26.

[34] Ibid., XIX.17.

[35] Ibid.

not naturally political.[36] Nevertheless, all men, including Christians, have an obligation to uphold them if the vicious and destructive forces unleashed by the Fall are not completely to undermine and destroy human society.

Roman government, then, Augustine regards as part of God's voluntary providence following the Fall. It is a divinely given means whereby people might act to protect themselves, as it were, against themselves. The Christian is therefore obliged not only to obey and support it, but actively to participate in it by holding, or at least not shirking, civil, secular posts, such as those of governor, magistrate, councillor, or judge. The latter is the subject of one of the most disturbing passages of book 19 of the *City of God*, for although fallen man is blind to the truth, both in himself and in the mind of another, and is consequently forced to reason in a context which makes clear insight and balanced judgement impossible, the judge, for the sake of whatever remnants of peace and justice might be salvaged, is still obliged to hear and try cases. His duty is invidious: such is the darkness which attends man's fall that the innocent are tortured and put to death whilst the guilty are set free.[37] Many Christians are in a similar position; for wherever public office is exercised, it is more a matter of stemming the tide of man's sin with the sandbags of authority than of creating the perfect state. Nevertheless, they are thereby serving and loving their neighbour, and, as Augustine encourages two public servants, Caecilian and Macedonius, what they do is pleasing to God.[38]

The emperor himself, for Augustine, was simply another, more prominent, example of a public officer acting in the interests of temporal peace and security. He is, of course, distinguished by the extent of his powers and responsibilities, and if he is a Christian, by the ends to which he directs his actions and the manner – especially the degree of humility – in which he performs them.[39] It has sometimes been remarked that Augustine's later support of coercion is incompatible with his 'secularization' of the state and his emphasis on the

[36] Outside the family, Augustine argues, man was originally created to exercise rule only over irrational creatures, the animals, not over men: 'hence the first just men were set up as shepherds of flocks, rather than as kings of men': ibid., XIX.15.

[37] Ibid., XIX.6.

[38] *Epistulae*, CLI.14, CLII.2, CLIII.19, CLV.vii.17, cited by R. A. Markus, *Saeculum: History and Society in the Theology of Saint Augustine* (Cambridge, 1970), p. 100.

[39] See *Ciuitas Dei*, V.24–6 for Augustine's description of the Christian emperors.

Christian's obligation to simply accept and co-operate with the powers that be, without seeking to change or reform them, except in cases where he is hindered from worshipping. His strong advocacy of coercion, albeit in a predominantly pastoral context of concern and love for the reformation of the sinner, certainly breaks with the idea of a secular state and of passive acceptance of the world by the Christian, in favour of vigorous action to transform a particular state of affairs in the Church. Robert Markus finds the key to this apparent incongruity in Augustine's emphasis on the fact that when a Christian official acts in matters related to the well-being of the Church he acts not as a representative of the state, but as a Christian individual.[40] Nowhere is this more apparent than in the actions of a Christian emperor, initiating and authorizing the coercion of schismatics and heretics: he is acting, not as emperor, but as a Christian with special powers and responsibilities for, and on behalf of, the Church:

> A man serves God in one way in that he is man, in another way in that he is also king. In that he is man, he serves him by living faithfully; but in that he is also king, he serves him by enforcing with suitable rigour such laws as ordain what is righteous, and punish what is the reverse.[41]

Similarly, pleading with a proconsul for leniency with regard to the imposition of the law against a schismatic faction, Augustine comments, 'For when you act, the Church acts, for whose sake and as whose son you act.'[42]

Augustine also endorsed Christian military service and engagement in war on the same grounds as other civil occupations: quite simply, they prevented human society from lapsing into utter anarchy and ruin. Of course, there were wars which were unjust – those motivated by a desire for territorial expansion,[43] greed, revenge, a lust for power, glory, or domination[44] – and these he utterly abhorred. But wars fought *against* these motivations,[45] in order to prevent the annihilation of the state, and to secure peace and safety for human society, with the

[40] Markus, *Saeculum*, ch.6.

[41] *Epistulae*, CLXXXV.19. Cf. *Contra litteras Petiliani*, II.xcii.210, II.xcvii.224; *In Johannis euangelium tractatus*, XI.14; *Epistulae*, LXXXXV.19.

[42] Ibid., CXXXIV.3, cited by Markus, *Saeculum*, p. 148.

[43] *Ciuitas Dei*, IV.6.

[44] Ibid., III.14.

[45] *Contra Faustum*, XXII.74.

interests of the common good at heart, were to be approved and supported. Augustine writes to the military commander of North Africa, Boniface: 'Peace should be your aim; war should be a matter of necessity so that God might free you from necessity and preserve you in peace.'[46] If soldiers are forced to kill in the course of duty they are not to be held guilty, he urges, if they act under the orders of a recognized authority,[47] even if the war or the commander is unjust. He did not believe it was legitimate, however, for individuals or groups simply to take power into their own hands; this was no better than anarchy, whatever their motives.[48]

Although clergy were barred from military service,[49] Augustine was keen to encourage others to remain at their posts. He travelled many miles, for example, to talk with Count Boniface, in order to dissuade him from abandoning his military command in order to become a monk.[50]

At a theological level, Augustine evidently regarded war as part of God's providence in a fallen world. Like the rest of the machinery of state it served to control and order fallen man. Even when the evil were victorious he saw God's providence at work, humbling the pride of the defeated.[51] And like the duty of coercion, he believed that war does not exclude, but should be motivated by, benevolence and love, by a concern for other human beings, that they might live in peace and security: 'if the commonwealth observe the precepts of the Christian religion, even its wars themselves will not be carried on without the benevolent design that, after the resisting nations have been conquered, provision may be more easily made for enjoying in peace the mutual bond of piety and justice.'[52]

This is not to say that Augustine advocated war, but rather that he recognized and lamented its necessity and encouraged any means which might avoid it whilst achieving the same ends. As he writes to

[46] *Epistulae*, CLXXXIX.6. Cf. *Ciuitas Dei*, III.10, XIX.7, XXII.6; *Contra Faustum*, XXII.74; *Quaestionum in Heptateuchum*, VI.10.

[47] *De libero arbitrio*, I.v.11; *Contra Faustum*, XXII.70, 75; *Ciuitas Dei*, I.21, 26.

[48] E.g. *Sermones*, CCCII; *Epistulae*, XLIV; *Ciuitas Dei*, I.17, cited by J. Rist, *Augustine* (Cambridge, 1994), p. 232.

[49] See Ambrose, *De officiis*, I.xxxv.175 (*PL* 16, cols 74–5); *Epistulae*, XX.22 (*PL* 16, cols 1000–1).

[50] *Epistulae*, CCXX.3, LXXXIX.4–7, where he points out the similarities between the two vocations.

[51] *Ciuitas Dei*, XIX.15.

[52] *Epistulae*, CXXXVIII.14. Cf. ibid., CLXXIII.2.

the imperial ambassador Darius, who had been sent to negotiate a settlement with Boniface, 'Preventing war through persuasion, and seeking or attaining peace through peaceful means rather than through war, are more glorious things than slaying men by the sword.'[53]

As for specifically Christian occupations and work, the Church had long possessed its own hierarchy of officials, ranging from doorkeepers to bishops. The way in which bishops were literally press-ganged into office – in one case bound and gagged[54] – might come as something of a shock to us today. Augustine wept when the congregation of Hippo laid hands on him to forcibly ordain him priest – not, as some thought, because he had aspired to be a bishop, but because he did not want to relinquish his present way of life.[55]

The bishop had risen enormously in influence and status following the conversion of Constantine, and had been granted particular privileges, such as exemption from military service and taxes. Bishops like Augustine now found themselves not only responsible for the customary duties of preaching, teaching, celebrating the liturgy, baptizing, administering charity, and doing pastoral work; they were now also responsible for the administration of the donations, gifts, and bequests which the Church could legally receive. Above all, a bishop became a source of free, relatively impartial, legal arbitration for any two parties, rich or poor, pagan or Christian, who chose to consult him and agreed to abide by his judgement. Augustine frequently complains that a good deal of each day was spent in this way, listening to minor cases – tedious, petty, family disputes and wrangling over inheritances, property, debt, or children.[56]

The bishop also acted very much as the public face of the Church, as a sort of mediator who represented the concerns of his congregation to high-ranking Roman officials. Again, Augustine complains of how much time he wastes hanging around in an ante-chamber, waiting to see an official, only to have his request turned down.[57]

Augustine's experiences reveal a great deal about the ambiguous relation between the Church and secular government in the fourth and

[53] Ibid., CCXXIX.2.

[54] See the account of B. Ramsay, *Ambrose* (London, 1997), pp. 19–20.

[55] *Vita*, 4. He had established a lay community, called the *servi dei*, in his home town of Thagaste.

[56] *De opere monachorum*, XXXVII; *Epistulae*, CXXIX.3; *Enarrationes in Psalmos*, XCVIII.xxiv.3; *Sermones*, CCCXL.1, CCCII.17.

[57] E.g. ibid., CCCII.17.

fifth century. On the one hand, bishops had legal powers and a public voice and influence; on the other their petitions and representations could be overturned by the merest whim of a Roman official.[58] This was, again, not a situation he wished to change: he was acutely conscious of his obligation to act as a legal arbitrator, given that it afforded him the opportunity to apply Christian principles to the cases in hand. He was also respectful of, and deferential to, Roman authority, and willing to acknowledge the Church's subjection to it in order to enjoy its protection.

Nevertheless, Augustine's longing for a quieter life, for time to read, think, meditate, and pray, is often poignantly evident in his writings.[59] The 'enforced work' necessitated by the Fall seemed to impose an incessant, sometimes nearly intolerable, burden on him in his role as bishop.

Augustine longed for leisure, for *otium* in the classical sense, for the opportunity to study, to read, to pursue the truth. In a secular context this would primarily involve study of the liberal arts: literally, those disciplines which were pursued by free men – and therefore, of course, by a small, privileged, elite, leisured minority. These were the disciplines which formed the core of late antique education and moulded the governing classes – the disciplines of grammar, mathematics, music, geometry, astronomy, dialectic, and, pre-eminently, rhetoric.

In his early years as a Christian Augustine was enthusiastic about the role of the liberal arts in enabling the student to attain to truth; they exercised and trained his mind, gradually allowing him to ascend from concrete to abstract truths, from corporeal to incorporeal, from the temporal to the eternal, and ultimately, perhaps, to an understanding of the divine. Later, as a pastor responsible for a congregation which included representatives of every level of society, their rather exclusive, recherché nature seems to have been forcibly brought home to him. They were of limited relevance and use in relation to the farmer from Carthage, the shopkeeper from Hippo, or the peasant from a nearby

[58] For C. Lepelley (*Les Cités de l'Afrique romaine au Bas-Empire*, 2 vols [Paris, 1979], 1: 398) this is evidence of the Church's marginal role in civil life and of the limited nature of the Christianization of the city structures in North Africa.

[59] E.g. *De opere monachorum*, XXXVII: 'I would much prefer to do some manual work every day at certain hours as is the custom in well-regulated monasteries and to have the remaining hours free for reading, prayer, or for the study of the Scriptures than to have to bear the most confusing perplexities of other men's disputes involving worldly concerns which I have to decide or settle in my capacity of judge or arbitrator, respectively.'

estate. Indeed, they began to appear to Augustine to be all too representative of a proud, philosophical culture which thought it could attain the truth without the need for faith or acceptance of the discipline of the Christian life. His criticism of them is, in fact, a criticism and disavowal of his own past.

However, the fact that, as we noted earlier, Augustine includes education and the practice of the arts as activities characteristic of voluntary providence *before* the Fall, indicates that he did not reject them completely. As his hugely influential work, *De doctrina Christiana*, makes clear, he was acutely aware of the need to articulate, define, and practise a Christian culture, in contradistinction to secular, pagan culture; a Christian culture centred on the authority and interpretation, not of the Greek and Latin classics, but of the divinely inspired Scriptures. In doing so, he works on the principle, common to Christian apologists, that since Christianity possesses the true religion and true philosophy it is therefore at liberty, like the Israelites plundering the Egyptians, to take back the various elements of pagan culture which are, in fact, its rightful possession.[60] He is therefore prepared to take over and use whatever aspects of pagan culture he regards as compatible with, valuable to, and useful for, the definition of Christian culture, its faith, doctrine, and (especially) its exegesis of its Scriptures and preaching on them. Having been formed, intellectually, culturally, and socially, by late antique culture, Augustine is more than aware that the liberal arts, and other carefully selected elements of secular culture and its institutions (suitably freed of their pagan dress), might indeed prove useful in shaping and informing Christian society and in enabling it to cohere by making possible communication and self-understanding in the interpretation of, and (especially) in preaching on, its Scriptures.[61] Rhetoric, the art of public speaking, the goal of the liberal arts and the acme of the late antique culture, is, he is forced to acknowledge in book four of *De doctrina Christiana*, indispensable in a Christian context. Scripture must be made attractive, delightful, and pleasing. How else could he move, persuade, and teach his congregation and inspire them to take to heart and act upon the truths of Scripture? How else (though this is an unstated subtext) could he defend the somewhat strange, crude, badly

[60] *De doctrina Christiana*, II.xl.60.

[61] See esp. ibid., II.xix.29–xlii.63, and L. M. J. Verheijen, 'Le *De Doctrina Christiana* de saint Augustin: Un manuel d'herméneutique et d'expression chrétienne avec, en II.xix.29–lxii.63, une "charte fondamentale pour une culture chrétienne"', *Augustiniana*, 24 (1974), pp. 10–20.

written text of Scripture against its pagan critics if it could not be shown to demonstrate the rules of classical 'eloquence'?

So, the traditional elements of late antique culture, those disciplines which were the product of privilege and leisure, have an indispensable place in Christian life since they facilitated the study and articulation of the literature of Christian culture, the Scriptures.[62]

In common with the other activities which Augustine assigned to Adam before the Fall, education and the practice of the arts (what we have here described as culture), like gardening and the government of human society, are irreversibly affected by the Fall. It is, in fact, unclear just what exactly Augustine has in mind when he mentions 'the arts' before the Fall. Since Adam had an intuitive grasp of truth and had no need for either written or spoken language, the arts, the disciplines, we must presume, would have been practised, not out of necessity, as an attempt to attain some insight into the truth, but purely as a matter of intellectual pleasure and exercise.

After the Fall, however, language, the cement of society and culture, in Augustine's experience generally assumes the nature of a veil which obscures the truth and makes lies, deceit, and misunderstanding all too possible.[63] The use of language becomes a difficult and frustrating battle with material alien and hostile to the task of communicating one's inward thoughts. It is an 'enforced labour'[64] which always risks a 'shipwreck of misrepresentation'. Nevertheless, we cannot begin to understand without it – and in this context Scripture is crucial.

Other activities, which we might well incline to assign to what I have described as 'free work' (or leisure), and which we would naturally include as intrinsic elements of culture, Augustine rejects outright. These include the work of the artist, the sculptor, the musician, the dancer, and the actor. For Augustine, these were crafts (*artes/techne*). Because they are primarily involved in the deceitful, misleading, mendacious activity of imitating, copying, or distorting the real world, they serve only to distract and tempt man away from the true and into the realm of profitless curiosity and attachment to the temporal.[65]

[62] See *Ciuitas Dei*, XXII for evidence of Augustine's appreciation of the achievements of human culture.

[63] *De Genesi aduersus Manichaeos*, II.iv.5–v.6. C. Harrison, *Revelation and Beauty in the Thought of Saint Augustine* (Oxford, 1992), pp. 59–63.

[64] See e.g. Augustine's reflections in *De catechizandis rudibus*.

[65] See Harrison, *Revelation and Beauty*, ch.1, in reference to the early works where these ideas are primarily discussed.

This no doubt strikes us as rather puritanical – but we must remember that for Augustine and his contemporaries many of these activities were also inseparably linked with the pagan games, shows, and spectacles which were such a prominent feature of civic life in the ancient world. Actors, musicians, dancers, and athletes were ranked together with prostitutes, astrologers, and diviners by Christian thinkers and rejected outright as representatives of the immorality, idolatry, depravity, and inhumanity characteristic of such entertainments. In his sermons Augustine often had occasion to extol the drama, excitement, and spectacle of the Christian liturgy in contrast to the pagan games, performances, and banquets which were enticing his congregation away from attendance at church.[66]

Christian culture, then, had no place for anything that did not lend itself either to Christian learning, interpretation of Scripture, and teaching, or to the encouragement of a life of single-minded, single-hearted devotion to God and love of neighbour. These were the unique elements which enabled it to build up its own customs, traditions, conventions, authorities, and texts – the essential elements without which any society or culture cannot cohere. They were not to be undermined.

Having considered Augustine's ideas on work, rest, and leisure we are now in a position to appreciate the basic polarities and tensions of his thought. In the beginning, and presumably after death, in eternity, man was, and will be, able freely to choose his occupation and to pursue it simply because of the pleasure, delight, and fulfilment he derives from it. There was and will be no sense of necessity, toil, or difficult labour in the face of hostile and alien elements. Rather, everything was and will be natural to him; it will be ordered, harmonious, fitting, and propitious to the work in hand. This was and will be possible primarily because Adam was, and human individuals in the resurrection will be, at rest in God – they will rest from the works of the world and turn wholly to God to find the source of their being, and their ultimate happiness, in their Creator. Nothing will distract them from him but they will enjoy an eternal Sabbath.[67]

In this life, however, caught in time, our hearts are restless – they

[66] E.g. *Enarrationes in Psalmos*, XXXII; *Sermones*, II.25, LXXX.23. See R. A. Markus, *The End of Ancient Christianity* (Cambridge, 1990), p. 118, for further references and discussion.
[67] See *De Genesi ad litteram*, IV.ix.16–xvii.29.

seek rest but will never attain it until the life to come, in God: 'our hearts are restless until they rest in You'.[68] Here man is a foreigner, an alien, a pilgrim in the world, caught up in the inescapable tensions, darkness, difficulties, and hard labour which are the result of, and punishment for, the Fall. There is no true rest, no freely chosen leisure, but a continual battle both internally against the fallen will, and externally against the distractions and temptations of this world.

Augustine obviously felt that the best way to endure this life and to prepare oneself for the next was to embrace the monastic life. This was not because he saw it as an escape from the world or an opportunity to retreat into peace and tranquillity. He was all too well aware that the repercussions of the Fall were felt just as forcibly within the confines of the monastery as outside it; monks were just as prone to pride, greed, lack of charity, and temptation as people in the world.[69] What the monastic life did allow however, was the opportunity to practise charity by living in community.[70] In *De opere monachorum* (*The Work of Monks*), written to counter a group of monks at Carthage who claimed that because they consecrated themselves to prayer, meditation, and reading, they should not have to do physical work,[71] he makes it clear that all monks are obliged to work,[72] according to their capabilities and background, as a matter of service and love towards the community, and in order to further the common good.[73] Since their work was motivated by love it would be experienced less as a burdensome necessity and more in the manner of Adam's freely motivated, delightful, pleasurable, and fulfilling work in Paradise.[74] Monks were also expected to practise celibacy. The most important aspect of this,

[68] *Confessiones*, I.i.1.

[69] See *De uirginitate*, which is more occupied with the problem of pride and the virtue of humility than with the nature of virginity as such. Cf. *Enarrationes in Psalmos*, XCIX.10.

[70] See Augustine's *Regula*.

[71] For a discussion of the possible Messalian origins of this group see Arbresmann, 'Attitude', pp. 246–7.

[72] *De opere monachorum*, XXII, XXXIII. Only those with duties in the church (e.g. preaching, catechizing, celebrating: ibid., IV, IX, XIX, XXIV), and the sick and infirm (ibid., XXII, XXV, XXXV) are exempt. Those from the upper classes, unaccustomed to manual work, who have already benefited the monastery by handing over all their possessions, should be shown due consideration and given work, such as administration, which they can manage (ibid., XXXIII). References are taken from Arbresmann, 'Attitude'.

[73] *De opere monachorum*, XIX, XXXIII, and *Regula*, V.2. See G. Madec, *Petites études Augustiniennes* (Paris, 1994), p. 13: 'Le communisme spirituel'.

[74] The liberating aspect of love is the key to Augustine's theology of grace and human freedom following the fall. See C. Harrison, 'Delectatio Victrix: grace and freedom in Saint Augustine', *Studia patristica*, 27 (1993), pp. 298–302.

for Augustine, was not bodily celibacy, but the single-minded, single-hearted devotion to God it allowed in those who had, by this divinely given means, separated themselves from the concerns of this world.[75] In a sense, it too allowed the monks to regain, albeit partially, some of the rest which Adam had lost at the Fall.

It was clear to Augustine that only in subjecting themselves to God, and in acknowledging their complete dependence on him, can men and women enjoy 'rest' and therefore the freedom to engage in true work, the freely chosen, pleasurable activity of Adam the gardener.

University of Durham

[75] E.g. *De uirginitate*, II.2, XI.11. Augustine distinguishes between *virginitas carnis, virginitas in carne, virginitas corporis*; and *virginitas cordis, virginitas in corde, virginitas mentis*.

THE CHURCH AND A REVALUATION OF WORK IN THE NINTH CENTURY?

by JANET L. NELSON

MY title poses what may seem an unpromising question. Even to consider the possibility of such fundamental change in ecclesiastical perceptions in the very midst of the Dark Ages may seem anachronistic. After all, were not Christian attitudes to work already well and truly fixed? There is, for instance, the story of Adam and Eve from Genesis 3.16–19, as displayed in words and pictures in the mid-ninth-century Moutier-Grandval Bible:

> Unto the woman [the Lord] said, I will greatly multiply thy sorrow and thy conception; in sorrow thou shalt bring forth children. . . . And to Adam he said, Because thou hast hearkened unto the voice of thy wife . . . cursed is the ground for thy sake; in sorrow shalt thou eat of it all the days of thy life. . . . In the sweat of thy face thou shalt eat bread, till thou return unto the ground; for out of it wast thou taken.
>
> Mulieri . . . dixit [Dominus]: Multiplicabo aerumnas tuas, et conceptus tuos (thy sorrows and thy conceptions); in dolore paries filios. . . . Adae vero dixit [Dominus]: . . . maledicta terra in opere tuo; in laboribus comedes ex ea cunctis diebus vitae tuae. . . . In sudore vultus tui vesceris pane, donec reverteris in terram de qua sumptus es.

Here work is presented as the punishment for fallen man, the gendered male equivalent for the female agony of childbirth. In the Moutier-Grandval Bible illumination, Adam must delve, while Eve's nursing of her baby symbolizes all the physical labour of birth and child-care.[1]

To biblical templates add monastic ones. In chapter 48 of the Rule of St Benedict, work is presented as the monk's every-day obligation:

[1] The 'strip-cartoon' fol. 5v of the Moutier-Grandval Bible, BL, MS Add. 10546, is reproduced in D. Bullough, *The Age of Charlemagne* (London, 1965), facing p. 162. To his curse in Gen. 3.16–19, the Lord added, in Gen. 4.12, additional pain as punishment for the sin of Cain: 'when thou tillest the ground, it shall not henceforth yield unto thee her strength.' Cain was, it has been justly said, the first peasant.

> Of the Daily Manual Labour. Idleness is the enemy of the soul. The brethren, therefore, must be occupied at stated hours with manual labour . . . for then they are truly monks when they live by the labour of their hands, like our fathers and the apostles. Yet let all things be done in moderation on account of the faint-hearted.[2]

Thus monasticism reinforced the idea of work as punitive and penitential. But that was not quite all – for the association with the fathers, that is, the avatars of monasticism, and with the apostolic life, endowed manual labour with a positive value. Further, in chapter 57, 'The Craftsmen of the Monastery', the Rule considers a rather different kind of work, here called *artes*, crafts, to be pursued in the monastery, yet only so long as it was done with humility and with the abbot's permission: any craftsman who becomes 'puffed up on account of his skill in his craft [*scientia artis suae*], supposing that he is conferring some benefit on the monastery', is to be banned from practising his skill until suitably humbled.[3] If Benedict's monastery was, as Peter Brown wrote recently, 'an up-country cottage',[4] the work done therein might be considered by way of cottage industry. But it was not therefore small beer to those who performed it. For though it must be admitted that a strong impression conveyed by earlier medieval texts written by monks and clerics who were also nobles is of the transposition of classical aristocratic attitudes, that is, of contempt for rustic labour, into Christian asceticism,[5] yet in the Rule of Benedict a value, however qualified, however associated with the humiliation of the body, is put on manual labour in field or garden or workshop alike.

Not forgetting the Rule, which remained fundamental to Carolingian monasticism, I want briefly to consider another ninth-century set of images: the earliest extant medieval depiction of the labours of

[2] *Regula Benedicti*, c.48, ed. and (French) tr. by A. de Vogüe and J. Neufville, *La Règle de Saint Benoît*, 7 vols, SC, 181–6 (Paris, 1971–2), 2: 598–601: 'De opere manuum cotidiano. Otiositas inimica est animae . . . et ideo certis temporibus occupari debent fratres in labore manuum . . . tunc veri monachi sunt si labore manuum suarum vivunt sicut et patres nostri et apostoli. Omnia tamen mensurate fiant propter pusillanimes.' English tr., J. McCann, *The Rule of St Benedict* (London, 1976), p. 53.

[3] *Regula Benedicti*, c.57: 'De artificibus monasterii'. De Vogüe and Neufville, *La Règle*, 2: 624–5; McCann, *Rule*, p. 62.

[4] P. Brown, *The Rise of Western Christendom* (Oxford 1996), p. 138.

[5] J. Le Goff, 'Les Paysans et le monde rural dans la littérature du haut Moyen Age', in *Agricoltura e mondo rurale in occidente nell'alto medioevo*, Settimane di studio del Centro italiano di studi sull'alto medioevo, 13 (Spoleto, 1966), pp. 723–41, reprinted in idem, *Pour un autre moyen âge: temps, travail et culture en Occident* (Paris, 1977), pp. 131–44, tr. A. Goldhammer, *Time, Work and Culture in the Middle Ages* (Chicago and London, 1980), pp. 87–97, 306–8.

the months, in a collection of computistical and astronomical material (with a set of Easter Tables running through to 1063) in a manuscript, now in Vienna, Codex 387, made in 809/10.[6] Much imitated in medieval art, and much reproduced in modern art histories, these pictures are at once charming and thought-provoking. How should we read them? Put them together with Charlemagne's well-known renaming of the months 'according to his own language',[7] and you have the attractive answer offered by a lively modern tradition of scholarly exegesis: these pictures are signs of 'how large the new agricultural cycle loomed in [Charlemagne's] thinking';[8] or, even more literal-mindedly, snapshots of

> hardworking peasants . . . and their implements, hence of the local everyday . . . [which] gives the impression that peasant labour . . . was thoroughly revalued; now the representations of work in book-miniatures attest a positive shift of attitudes: it is striking that, in a way quite different from Antiquity, peasants were now thought worthy of being represented.[9]

The recent work of Carl I. Hammer has deflated this balloon. The Vienna Codex 387 can now be seen to have reproduced, precisely, a classical model. It was made for a patron, Charlemagne's ally and client Archbishop Arn of Salzburg. The point of these images was to affirm Charlemagne's recently-assumed imperial task of 'ordering human

[6] Vienna, Österreichische Nationalbibliothek, Codex 387, fol. 90v. See now the penetrating, and well illustrated, study of C. I. Hammer, *Charlemagne's Months and their Bavarian Labours. The Politics of the Saxons in the Carolingian Empire*, British Archaeological Reports, International Series 676 (Oxford, 1997), to which I am much indebted. For an accessible reproduction of this set of images, see Bullough, *Age of Charlemagne*, facing p. 145, and for the artistic genre see J. C. Webster, *The Labors of the Months in Antique and Medieval Art to the End of the Twelfth Century*, Princeton Monographs in Art and Archaeology, 21 (Princeton, NJ, 1938).

[7] Einhard, *Vita Karoli*, 6th edn, ed. O. Holder-Egger, MGH Scriptores rerum germanicarum in usum scholarum (Hanover and Leipzig, 1911), c.29 (p. 33).

[8] L. White, *Medieval Technology and Social Change* (Oxford, 1962), p. 78; cf. Bullough, *Age of Charlemagne*, p. 192. See also R. Morrissey, *L'Empereur à la barbe fleurie* (Paris, 1997), p. 50, noting Charlemagne's 'concern to master time'.

[9] A. Borst, *Buch der Naturgeschichte. Plinius und seine Leser im Zeitalter des Pergaments*, Abhandlungen der Heidelberger Akademie der Wissenschaften, philosophisch-historische Klasse, 1994/ii (Heidelberg, 1994), p. 173: 'schwer arbeitende . . . Bauern samt ihrem Werkzeug, mithin den örtlichen Alltag. . . . [E]s hat den Anschein, als sei die bäuerliche Arbeit . . . durchaus geachtet gewesen; schon die Arbeitsdarstellungen auf Buchminiaturen zeugen . . . von einer positives Einstellung: es ist bemerkenswert . . . daß man den Bauern – anders als in der Antike – überhaupt für darstellungswürdig crachtete.'

affairs in the context of nature and the cosmos'.[10] Imperial time and sacred time coincided. This is ideology, Hammer concludes, its reference not to work as such, but to a revived Roman Empire.

In a quest for a ninth-century revaluation of work, then, art turns out to be a red herring. Nevertheless, struck by the sheer ideological effrontery of Charlemagne's renaming of the months, and the medieval Church's ultimate success (given, admittedly, a very long run) in achieving a wholesale reconfiguration of cyclical time – something that French revolutionaries and twentieth-century totalitarian regimes attempted and signally failed to achieve – I am not yet ready to abandon the question in my title.

Consider three other distinctively Carolingian products. First, there is the early ninth-century *Capitulare de villis*, in which the ruler regulates the management of 'our estates which we have organized to serve our needs' ('villae nostrae quae ad opus nostrum serviendi institutas habemus').[11] It would be hard to imagine a text that expressed more powerfully the value of the work performed on royal estates: this, more than plunder and tribute, was the foundation of Carolingian power. Then, there are records of monastic estate ownership. A dozen or so polyptychs (surveys) have survived from the ninth century, more or less intact.[12] I say 'more or less' because it occurred to me that it might be worth checking the prefaces of these texts, to see if they contained some positive statement about the fruits of peasant labour, but I fear that this turned out to be a blind alley. Either the polyptych survives only in a much later copy (Prüm) or incorporated into a monastic history (St-Bertin), or the opening bit is missing (St Germain). Perhaps, simply, this was not the genre for ideological reflection. Still, it is hard to imagine that the monk-managers of great estates were anything but keenly aware of the importance of the combined labour of their peasant tenants. After all, monastic agents patiently detailed thousands of peasant households and individuals, together with, in virtually every case, the labour-

[10] Hammer, *Charlemagne's Months*, p. 51.

[11] J. Martindale, 'The Kingdom of Aquitaine and the "dissolution" of the Carolingian fisc', *Francia*, 11 (1984), pp. 134, 148, 154, 160–2, with a helpful discussion of the historiography at n. 152 (reprinted in eadem, *Status, Authority and Regional Power* [Aldershot, 1997], ch. II); E. Magnou-Nortier, 'Capitulaire *De villis et curtis imperialibus,* vers 810–813. Texte, traduction et commentaire', *Revue Historique*, 607 (1998), pp. 643–89.

[12] Y. Morimoto, 'État et perspectives de recherches sur les polyptyques carolingiens', *Annales de l'est*, 40 (1988), pp. 99–149; J.-P. Devroey, *Études sur le grand domaine carolingien* (London, 1993).

service they owed. In charters too, recording donations to these monasteries and written by members of the monastic community, we can find traces of careful attention paid to the presence of *laboratores*, operators of the heavy plough, on land consisting of *novalia*, or *labores* – fields newly-cleared from the waste, or sometimes, simply, income from agricultural produce. Credit for spotting these peasant improvers, and 'agricultural progress', goes to a philologist, J. F. Niermeyer, and a historian, Jacques Le Goff.[13]

Which brings me to another type of monastic record and my third kind of evidence: the biblical commentary. It was in this genre, in the ninth century, that the Three Orders made their first appearance in medieval Europe.[14] Haymo and Heiric of Auxerre 'baptized' the senators, knights (*equites*), and plebs of pagan Rome, and of Isidore, to make of them 'those who fight, those who pray, and those who work the land' (*bellatores/militantes*, *oratores*, and *agricolae/agricultores*). Picking up the theme in his *Commentary on Romans*, and discussing social debts, Haymo wrote of what was owed by *agricolae* as well as *milites*.[15] Commenting on II Timothy 2.6, 'The husbandman that laboureth must be first partaker of the fruits' ('Laborantem agricolam oportet primum fructus percipere'), Haymo elaborated, first, 'in the literal sense: it is worthy that the peasant and the vinegrower must first taste the fruit of their labours' ('dignum est ut agricola et vinitor primum fructus sui laboris degustent' – note the addition of the *vinitor* and the evocative verb *degustare*), but 'in a higher sense, the field is this world of the Church' ('ager est hic mundus vel ecclesia'), in which the peasants and winegrowers must support the preachers, by handing

[13] J. F. Niermeyer, 'En marge du nouveau Ducange', *Le Moyen Age*, 63 (1957), pp. 329–60; J. Le Goff, 'Note sur la société tripartite, idéologie monarchique et renouveau économique dans la chrétienté du IXe au XIIIe siècle', in T. Manteuffel and A. Gieysztor, eds, *L'Europe aux IXe–XIe siècles: Aux origines des états nationaux* (Warsaw, 1968), pp. 63–71 (reprinted in Le Goff, *Pour un autre moyen âge*, pp. 80–90; idem, *Time, Work and Culture*, pp. 53–7, 296–300).

[14] What follows owes much to the pioneering work of D. Iogna-Prat, 'Le "baptême" du schéma des trois ordres fonctionnels', *Annales*, 41 (1986), pp. 101–26, and E. Ortigues, 'L'Élaboration de la théorie des trois-ordres chez Haymon d'Auxerre', *Francia*, 14 (1988), pp. 27–43, both of whom acknowledge the pioneering work of J. Le Goff (see preceding note) and G. Duby, *Les Trois ordres ou l'imaginarie du féodalisme* (Paris, 1978), tr. A. Goldhammer, *The Three Orders. Feudal Society Imagined* (Chicago, 1980). See further O. G. Oexle, '*Tria genera hominum*. Zur Geschichte eines Deutungsschemas der sozialen Wirklichkeit in Antike und Mittelalter', in L. Fenske et al., eds, *Institutionen, Kultur und Gesellschafter im Mittelalter. Festschrift für Josef Fleckenstein zum 65. Geburtstag* (Sigmaringen, 1984), pp. 483–500.

[15] *Commentarium in Romanos*, *PL* 116, col. 482.

over some of their surplus ('quae supersunt') to support them, 'that is, food, footwear, and clothing' ('id est victum, et calciamentum et vestimentum'). Haymo adds a little apology for Timothy who, unlike St Paul, did not live 'by the labour of his hands', for he was old and ill.[16] In his *Miracles of St Germanus*, written for the monastic community, but also presented to King Charles the Bald, and so for consumption by the royal entourage too, in the early 870s, Heiric of Auxerre, Haymo's former student, wrote that the 'third order' (that is, the ecclesiastical one), had been picked by God as his 'private domain' (*privata sors*):[17] 'those who fight and those who labour undergo for your sake harsh conditions, whether of military service or of manual toil, . . . while you continue to serve them so that you can be of use to them by zealous performance of prayers and masses' ('pro vobis [i.e. the monks] duras conditiones subeunt vel militiae vel laboris, . . . itidem vos illis obnoxii persistis ut eos orationum et officii instantia prosequamini').[18]

This was indeed, as Edmond Ortigues observes, to moralize the third function, that is, peasant labour.[19] Commenting on I Corinthians 12.8, 'For to one is given by the Spirit the word of wisdom; to another the word of knowledge' ('Alii quidem per Spiritum datur sermo sapientiae'), Haymo distinguished between wisdom (*sapientia*) and practical knowledge (*scientia*): the former concerned with discrimination between good and evil, the latter with 'organizing and managing human affairs', as in 'cultivating farms and fields, building a house intelligently, organizing a household in a suitable way [fundos sive agros excolere, domum prudenter aedificare, familiam competenter ordinare]. . . . And they shall have their reward.'[20] In Haymo's commentary on Revelation 12.1, the woman clothed with the sun represents the 'more perfect in the Church [*perfectiores in Ecclesia*] who, leaving everything, have followed Christ', while the moon represents the 'common folk who toil for the benefit of others, by planting, building, working the land. . . . [Y]et they shall not lack their reward, although they are not made equal to those others in every respect, provided that they carry out their job faithfully' ('simplices qui

16 *Expositio in Pauli epistolas*, *PL* 117, col. 802.

17 For the material meaning of *sors* as 'share of an inheritance', 'estate', 'tenure', in the Latin of this period, see J. F. Niermeyer, *Mediae latinitatis lexicon minus* (Leiden, 1997), p. 981.

18 *Miracula sancti Germani*, *PL* 124, col. 1269.

19 Ortigues, 'L'Élaboration', pp. 36–7.

20 *Expositio in Pauli epistolas*, *PL* 117, col. 577.

laborant ad aliorum usus in plantando, aedificando, et agricolando . . . non tamen illi mercede carebunt, licet illis non per omnia coaequentur, si fideliter ministerium impleverint').[21]

Is this just learned monastic word-spinning from antique and biblical threads? Of course it *is* that, but monks, even monks, do not word-spin in ivory towers. Is it also a reflection, as Le Goff has suggested, of an ecclesiastical re-evaluation of peasant labour?[22] The monk of Auxerre expatiated on the surpluses from farms and fields, and was anxious to justify monastic demands for sustenance therefrom, because these were the material conditions of his own Auxerrois, and the material preconditions of that monastic culture that was one of the most striking features of what we call the Carolingian Renaissance. The monk of Auxerre added the wine-grower to his biblical model because he knew well the taste – and the value – of the local wine. The monk's assessment is amply confirmed by the polyptychs, which show the transport of wine as a vital feature of monastic estate management, and by annalistic and capitulary evidence, showing wine as the key commodity bought and sold in the Paris basin during the ninth century.[23] It was in this context of increased production and consumption of wine and other products, of a lively economy of exchanges and hefty monastic cash incomes, that a re-evaluation of peasant labour was evoked.

If Le Goff is right, why have so few, if any, historians followed up his insight? I fear it is a bad case of intradisciplinarity rather than interdisciplinarity, of the right hand knowing not. Look through the index of Peter Brown's *The Rise of Western Christendom*, or Pierre Riché's *Instruction et vie religieuse dans le haut moyen âge*, or *The New Cambridge Medieval History*, volume 2, and there is no entry for 'work'. Le Goff's collected papers were entitled *Time, Work and Culture*; but look in the splendid collection of essays recently edited by Miri Rubin in honour of Le Goff and you will not find anything much about work,

[21] *Expositio in Apocalypsin*, *PL* 117, col. 1081; cf. Iogna-Prat, 'Le "baptême"', p. 115.

[22] Le Goff, 'Note'.

[23] R. Doehaerd, 'Au Temps de Charlemagne et des Normands. Ce qu'on vendait et comment on le vendait dans le bassin parisien', *Annales*, 3 (1947), pp. 268–80; J.-P. Devroey, 'Un Monastère dans l'économie d'échanges: les services de transport à l'abbaye de Saint-Germain-des-Prés au IXe siècle', *Annales*, 39 (1984), pp. 570–89. For the implications of c.31 of the Edict of Pîtres (*MGH*: *Capitularia regum francorum*, 2, ed. A. Boretius and V. Krause [Hanover, 1897], no. 273, p. 324) ordering that peasant migrants be allowed to keep the earnings made from working in the vineyards, see J. L. Nelson, *Charles the Bald* (London, 1992), p. 38.

nor who dunnit.[24] You will find Jean Dunbabin gently mocking Le Goff's idealization of thirteenth-century Intellectuals, men in his own image, she reckons: 'as one reads, the whiff rises up the nostrils of mingled Gauloises and roasting chestnut braziers on the boulevard St Germain in the late 1950s.'[25] Jean Dunbabin's own calculation of the costs of university education in the thirteenth century shows clearly that the income generated by peasant work was simply not up to sending the peasant's son to study in Paris.[26] Marxist/marxisant intellectuals, would-be organic intellectuals, still have not quite cracked the problem of how to justify their existence. Most *annalistes* these days seem to have given up even trying to crack it.

But the problem is not just *their* problem: it is ours too, for it lies deep within the modern discipline of History itself. Over there are the economic historians busy decoding the polyptychs; over here in another part of the wood are ecclesiastical historians busy unpacking the Three Orders from hitherto cunningly locked exegetical trunks. Is it not time the two groups met somewhere? Maybe there were some in the ninth century who contrived to close a comparable gap. Perhaps Charles the Bald, his *familiares*, and his counsellors (who included monks), were on the way to doing so as they pondered the miracles of St Germanus. But I have in mind particularly King Alfred of Wessex and his circle of helpers, who included scholarly churchmen and also *fasselli*, which is how Alfred's biographer (he was a Welshman) wrote, and presumably said, 'vassals'. Alfred had his own version of the three orders: *gebedmen*, and *fyrdmen*, and *weorcmen*: praying men, fighting men, and working men.[27] I do not think the third group here are primarily *laboratores*, workers on the land, but those whom Alfred's biographer calls *aurifices*, *artifices*, and *operatores* - goldsmiths, craftsmen, and builders: practitioners, in other words, of the *artes* needed by the fabricator of a court society. I have not spotted in Alfred's writings any

[24] M. Rubin, ed., *The Work of Jacques Le Goff and the Challenges of Medieval History* (Woodbridge, 1997).

[25] J. Dunbabin, 'Jacques Le Goff and the intellectuals', ibid., pp. 157–67, at p. 158.

[26] Ibid., p. 162.

[27] J. L. Nelson, 'The political ideas of Alfred of Wessex', in A. Duggan, ed., *Kings and Kingship in Medieval Europe* (London, 1993), pp. 125–58, esp. 141–6, reprinted in Nelson, *Rulers and Ruling Families in Early Medieval Europe* (Aldershot, 1999), ch. IV; see also G. Constable, *Three Studies in Medieval Religious and Social Thought* (Cambridge, 1995), esp. Pt III, 'The Three Orders', and pp. 277–82, but cf. also Pt I, 'The interpretation of Mary and Martha'. See further a pathbreaking paper of C. J. Holdsworth, 'The blessings of work: the Cistercian view', *SCH*, 10 (1973), pp. 59–76.

reference to peasant improvers, yet I find in his vision of three 'fellowships' (*geferscipas*) who together 'keep the land fully manned', each deploying his *cræft*, an attractive practical imagination in its own terms, raising at the very least a nostalgic whiff of Gauloises and chestnuts. . . . Manual work in the sense of craft-work was certainly re-evaluated by Alfred and his courtly contemporaries.

Maybe, then, those presentist interpretations of the ninth-century labours of the months I began with were not so anachronistic after all. Maybe the taste for those particular images arose not only from courtiers' classicizing imperialism, but also from their interest in their own contemporary world of work. It comes down, as usual, to how we practise our historian's craft. It is fitting to end with a quote from a master-craftsman:

> As for *homo religiosus, homo oeconomicus, homo politicus* and all that rigmarole of Latinised men . . . there is a grave danger of mistaking them for something other than they really are: phantoms which are convenient providing they don't become nuisances. The man of flesh and bone, reuniting them all simultaneously, is the only real being.[28]

King's College, University of London

[28] M. Bloch, *The Historian's Craft* (Manchester, 1954), p. 151.

TABOO OR GIFT? THE LORD'S DAY IN BYZANTIUM

by JANE BAUN

CHURCH history has tended to trace the development of doctrine, either orthodox or heretical, canonical or *anti*-canonical. This paper, however, examines '*para*-canonical' ideas, those which develop alongside the canonical – not quite heretical, but not fully orthodox either. Canonical norms, while constant in principle, have always been subject in practice to multiple understandings. Most of these shifting understandings, among groups or individuals, are fleeting and can never be recovered; this is why the history of the reception of canonical norms is so elusive. But for the social historian of religion, reception is often more interesting than the norms themselves.

What actually 'trickles down' from what the bishops teach? This paper will maintain that some record of how things 'trickled down' is preserved in para-canonical religious texts, commonly known as 'apocryphal' literature. It considers various ways in which the canonical norms of the Greek Orthodox Church concerning the Lord's Day were understood in a specific time and place: medieval Byzantium, between the ninth and the twelfth centuries. This was a crucial formative period for Orthodox Church culture, both Greek and Slav, during which ritual and moral attitudes that still obtain today were being worked out.

The essential teaching for the Orthodox Churches on most normative questions was set by the canons of the early church councils and bishops. The parameters of the debate over the proper reverence due the Lord's Day were all set by the early fifth century. Another great wave of religious literature in the Greek Church came between the ninth and the twelfth centuries, as various Middle Byzantine authors – both with and without official sanction – interpreted the earlier conciliar and episcopal norms for their own times. The effort resulted in a proliferation of two very different types of text, which this study will juxtapose: canonical judgements and commentaries, and para-canonical visions and revelations.

The canonical texts originate in the sphere of high-ranking ecclesiastical and imperial officials, such as the canonists John Zonaras

(†1159) and Theodore Balsamon (†1195). The anonymous para-canonical texts – visionary otherworld journeys, fantastic saints' lives, messages that fall from the sky – represent a world far from the ordered certainties of scholarship and law. It quickly becomes apparent that the two types of text record widely varying attitudes towards the use of time on the Lord's Day.

Two poles towards which most texts gravitate may be identified: towards understanding Sunday as a 'taboo' day, or as a 'gift' day.[1] Is the Lord's Day a joyful day of worship and rest, given by a benevolent deity for the refreshment of his people – a gift? Or is it a fearful day, on which one must engage in ritual propitiation of an angry, jealous deity who will exact supernatural revenge if snubbed – a taboo? Does one observe the Lord's Day as a free response, motivated by gratitude – or under compulsion, motivated by fear? Does one make satisfaction for having violated the Lord's Day voluntarily and privately, in sacramental confession – or involuntarily and publicly, by enduring terrible calamity sent from God? Ultimately, as Christ himself phrased it in Mark 2.27, was the Sabbath made for man or man for the Sabbath?

This analytical construct of 'taboo' and 'gift' should be understood less as an absolute dichotomy and more as marking two ends of a continuum, with most texts falling somewhere in between. The 'taboo–gift' model is meant to allow an analytical placement of human attitudes and behaviour that accommodates their rich variousness.

Overall, the surprise is that the general pattern in the texts is not one of canonical authorities imposing rigid negative demands, while the unofficial texts propose a more flexible, positive approach. Rather, the imperial and ecclesiastical authors seem to promote positive understandings of norms (Sunday as gift), while the medieval apocrypha suggest that, in parish and village, the same norms are being received negatively (Sunday as taboo). What the bishops and canonists teach is trickling down in perverse and strange ways.

The conciliar canons of the fourth to seventh centuries, together with their medieval commentators, unanimously proclaim Sunday as a day of Resurrection joy. Repeatedly, they teach that one must neither

[1] The antithesis of 'taboo' and 'gift' is particular to this paper, and the terms are used non-technically. Among the many anthropological discussions of 'taboo', the most pertinent here is Hutton Webster, *Rest Days: the Christian Sunday, the Jewish Sabbath, and their Historical and Anthropological Prototypes* (New York, 1916, repr. Detroit, 1992), which, despite its evolutionism, remains the comprehensive ethnographic survey of 'taboo days'.

fast nor kneel on Sundays, the penitential nature of both acts being out of keeping with the spirit of the day.[2] It is a day to spend in the temples, united in praise and worship, abstaining from all earthly things – chief among them work and sex, but also the theatre, games, and horse races.[3] The motivation given by the canons and their commentators is gratitude towards a benevolent God, and joyful celebration of Christ's Resurrection. The modality is gift: the Sabbath was made for man.

This was the understanding also of the Emperor Leo VI (r. 886–912) when he issued a 'new law' about the Lord's Day, Novel no. 54, in the late ninth century.[4] Previous emperors had allowed farmers to work on Sundays, but Leo the Wise now decreed that all should abstain from work on Sundays.[5] Why? God the benevolent creator, through his benevolent agent, the Emperor, has bestowed the blessing of rest, for his people's benefit and preservation. Like most Byzantine emperors, Leo styled himself a lawgiver in the biblical mode as well as the Roman; the highly rhetorical exposition of his Sunday law is deliberately scriptural in tone. Leo was not, however, a strict sabbatarian. And strikingly, no mention at all is made of penalties for violation, though these figure prominently in his Old Testament models.[6] The closest Leo comes to a warning is a genial play on words, admonishing farmers who labour on the Lord's Day with the excuse of saving their fruits that such logic is faulty, since abundance of fruits is furnished not by human labour, but by the mercy of the giver of all fruits.[7] With 'fruit', 'benefit', and 'salvation' its most frequently-repeated terms, the law's discourse is all of benevolence, grace, respite from labour, and free gift.

What to do with one's day off from work? Well into the medieval period in Byzantine and formerly Byzantine urban areas the public baths remained a favourite place to unwind. Among the sixty-four canonical questions that Mark, the Orthodox Patriarch of Alexandria,

[2] Relevant canons, together with twelfth-century commentary by Balsamon, Zonaras, and Alexios Aristenos: Apostolic Canons 64/66, Nicaea 20, Trullo 55, 90, Gangra 18 (*PG* 137, cols 169–72, 308–9, 708–9, 821–5, 1265–6); also, Peter of Alexandria, canon 15; Nicholas III Grammatikos, question 2 (*PG* 138, cols 516, 940).

[3] Carthage 70 (*PG* 138, cols 247–50), Trullo 66 (*PG* 137, cols 744–5).

[4] P. Noailles and A. Dain, eds, *Les Novelles de Léon VI le Sage* (Paris, 1944), pp. 205–9.

[5] C. S. Mosna, *Storia della Domenica dalle origini fino agli inizi del V secolo* (Rome, 1969), pp. 216–27, gives a detailed summary and analysis of prior legislation.

[6] E.g., 'Whoever works on that day shall be put to death' (Exod. 35.2); also Exod. 20.8–11, 23.12; Deut. 5.12–15.

[7] Noailles and Dain, *Novelles*, p. 207, ll.14–17.

put to Theodore Balsamon in 1195 was this: 'Is it licit to go to the baths on the Lord's day, and to wash in the thermal baths, or not?'[8] There will be no pardon, replies Balsamon, for the believer 'who keeps apart from the prayer, and stands aloof from the many-hymned praises and teachings of the Lord's day, and occupies himself with waiting patiently for hot water'. The primary concern of Balsamon's commentary, though, is not condemnation of the believer who bathes, nor does he allude to potential moral dangers lurking in the steam. Instead, quoting the Emperor Leo's Sunday law at length, Balsamon's main consideration as the commentary develops is for the welfare of the bath attendants. Balsamon does not say one should not bathe at all, only that one should not miss church to bathe, and that bath attendants should not have to work on Sundays. The accent is not on deprivation of pleasure, but on the pleasure of rest extended to all: again, the Sabbath was made for man.

Following Jesus' saying, both Balsamon and Zonaras assert that human welfare should take precedence over ritual considerations. Zonaras, commenting on Canon 88 of the Council in Trullo, provides the fullest discussion.[9] Echoing Exodus 23.12 and Deuteronomy 6.12–15, he explains the sabbatical rest from labour in strictly utilitarian terms, as a gift from God to refresh both man and beast – so that they might work more vigorously afterwards. Such a rationalist approach is far from the realm of taboo.

In Jewish culture, the Sabbath rest has traditionally been seen as an especially blessed time to engage in the renewal of families. But as the Christian Sabbath rest developed, it borrowed more from the Jewish priestly tradition that sex is ritually defiling (Leviticus 15). The early episcopal canons and the medieval canonists teach that in preparation for the Sunday liturgy, and on Sunday itself, spouses should abstain from sexual relations. The exact requirements of Sunday abstinence never seem to have been formalized in a conciliar canon. Perhaps because of this ambiguity, questions on the topic often appear in the Eastern Orthodox canonical question-and-answer collections, preserving intriguing hints of how the question may have been discussed among bishops, parish clergy, and believers.

First, the foundational response, by Timothy of Alexandria in the fourth century. Question: 'if a woman comes together with her

[8] Question 51: *PG* 138, cols 997–1000.

[9] *PG* 137, cols 813–16.

husband during the night, or a man with his wife, and intercourse happens, should they receive [Communion] or not?'[10] No, replies the bishop, but his answer, far from condemning conjugal relations, takes care to affirm them as a priority for married couples:

> They should not [receive], for the Apostle proclaims, 'Do not refuse one another except perhaps by agreement for a season, that you may devote yourselves to prayer; but then come back together again, lest Satan tempt you through lack of control' (I Corinthians 7.5).

Asked on which days married couples ought to abstain, Timothy repeats the Pauline injunction about spouses not denying each other, then adds, 'Of necessity, one ought to abstain on the Sabbath and the Lord's day, because on these days the spiritual sacrifice is offered to the Lord.'[11] The wording of this second question is particularly interesting, since among the several possibilities available in Greek for 'intercourse', it uses the word *koinonia*, 'communion', the word also commonly used to denote eucharistic Communion. Literally, the question reads, 'For those yoked together in the communion of marriage, what days of the week ought to be set aside to abstain from communion with each other, and on which days is it authorized to have it?'

The two fourth-century *responsa* state unambiguously that sacramental Communion and sexual 'communion' do not mix. But neither does the bishop dictate how married couples should spend their weekends: both types of communion, in their separate spheres, seem to be affirmed. One ought to abstain on days when the Divine Liturgy is celebrated, but if sex 'happens', the worst penalty for the married couple is that they cannot receive Communion. Nothing further is said; and the repetition of the Pauline quotation together with the choice of words seems to affirm sexual relations within Christian marriage as a communion unto itself.

Seven centuries later, Theodore Balsamon was also asked twice about the same issues, by Mark of Alexandria.[12] May spouses have sex and still receive Communion? No. Like Timothy, whom he quotes, Balsamon begins by citing I Corinthians, but a sterner and more

10 Question 5: *PG* 138, col. 893.

11 Question 13: *PG* 138, col. 900.

12 *PG* 138, cols 899–964.

explicitly eucharistic verse: 'Let each person examine himself, and thus eat of the bread and drink of the cup' (11.28). In comparison with Timothy, Balsamon raises the stakes. His long reply, quoting Exodus at length, introduces Old Testament concepts of ritual purity and defilement.[13] Moreover, the communicant should not engage in sexual relations or wild parties *after* the receiving of Communion either – Balsamon refers particularly to wedding parties after church that get out of hand. Violators, he rules, should be subjected to a 'more austere' penalty. Note that while Balsamon clearly requires would-be communicants to stay pure, nothing is said expressly about worshippers who do not communicate. Sunday *per se* would not seem to be off-limits for spousal 'communion'.

Or would it? Mark's second question complicates things: 'on the eve of the divinely-sanctioned first day, if spouses meld together carnally, are they to be penalized as transgressors or not?'[14] The query itself is not limited to would-be communicants only, indicating that at least some in twelfth-century Alexandria considered sexual abstinence on Saturday nights (and thus by extension on Sundays as well) incumbent upon *all* believers, no matter what their Sunday plans.

Balsamon's response seems to admit a number of interpretations. He begins by citing Timothy's earlier reply: on Saturdays and Sundays, spouses ought to abstain from 'fleshly communion' because the sacrifice is offered on those days. For how, he asks rhetorically, can one who is not continent expect to pray properly, in harmony with God? The severe wording of Mark's question clearly expects a punishment beyond simple exclusion from Communion; but Balsamon himself seems to treat the question less strictly, ruling that violators should be corrected with a 'moderate' penalty. Balsamon's replies clearly uphold an ideal of abstinence from all fleshly indulgence in preparation for worship on Saturdays, Sundays, and feast days – and that ideal's application to all believers, not just would-be communicants, may be implicit, but why is there no explicit statement? Especially when one considers that such *responsa* were often used by confessors looking for concrete guidelines, his treatment seems puzzlingly vague. Was the point too obvious to be stated, or might Balsamon be leaving some space for discretion (*oikonomia*)? That even so seemingly obvious an issue as sexual abstinence before receiving

13 Question 10: *PG* 138, cols 961–4.
14 Question 49: *PG* 138, col. 997.

Communion kept having to be clarified, from the fourth century to the twelfth, could suggest that there was some room in Orthodox practice for differing interpretations on such matters.

The talk of penalties implies a penitential context. In what spirit did Balsamon wish the penitent to understand pre-Communion abstinence? His explanations are all cast positively: one abstains to show proper reverence for the Holy Mysteries and for the sacred character of the Lord's Day. Out in the parishes, however, the reception of these norms seems to have been overwhelmingly negative. Moving from the canonical world to the para-canonical, abstention from sex on Sundays is represented not as a positive choice for personal holiness, but as a fearsome taboo, to be violated only at great peril to the soul.

The point is made memorably in an anecdote from the *Life* of Andrew the Fool, an extremely colourful (and probably fictitious) saint's life of the tenth century.[15] One Sunday morning in Constantinople, Andrew saw a high official on his way to the palace, presumably to attend Liturgy. Andrew, who could tell that the courtier and his wife had copulated that morning, shouted out, 'Look at the fool who defiled the holy Sunday and is going to defile the palace as well!' How did he know? Andrew had seen 'a queen wearing an imperial crown set with pearls and jewels', who rebuked the courtier, saying,[16]

> How did you dare to defile my palace, you wretch? Is it not enough for you, insatiable man, to bark for lust during the whole week? Do you have to act recklessly on the holy day? By Christ my bridegroom, if you do it a second time, you will not do it a third!

The introduction of a female personification for Sunday projects the author's point about defilement on to a much more intense conceptual plane. An abstract prohibition becomes disturbingly personal. Sexual abstinence on the Lord's Day is represented not as a bloodless canonical ideal, the violation of which elicits Balsamon's 'moderate penalty' from the confessor, but graphically as a disgraced woman, whose violation provokes terrible supernatural punishment: 'By Christ my bridegroom, if you do it a second time, you will not do it a third!' Sunday has become a fully-fledged taboo.

Another tenth-century apocryphon, the *Apocalypse of Anastasia*,

15 *The Life of St. Andrew the Fool*, ed. and tr. Lennart Rydén (Uppsala, 1995), ll. 2869–92.
16 Ibid., p. 199.

presents Sunday as a 'taboo woman' with even greater vehemence: she is shown dishonoured and disgraced before the very throne of God.[17] In the course of their tour of the otherworld, Anastasia and her guide, the Archangel Michael, stumble into the middle of a tense courtroom drama, in which all mankind is on trial. Four women stand before the throne. The accusers are St Wednesday, St Friday, and St Sunday (*Hagia Tetradē, Hagia Paraskevē, Hagia Kyriakē*), while Mary, the Theotokos, pleads for the defence. The charges? Indulging in meat, cheese, and copulation on Wednesdays and Fridays, and working on Sundays. As recorded in three of the four Greek manuscripts, St Sunday complains:[18]

> Master, cast the faithless and merciless ones into the sea, for I am not able to endure their shameful deeds. Behold – from the ninth hour of the Sabbath[19] until the second drawing towards dawn, they work the works of their hands, not honouring the day of your Resurrection. They light their ovens and go off into their streets and work other works of [their] hands. So cast them into the sea, since their vices mount up to me, and my countenance is thoroughly disgraced, and I stand before you thoroughly disgraced.

In answer, a Voice thunders from the throne: 'Cursed is that house which from the ninth hour of the Sabbath until the second dawning of the sun engages in work, for the eternal fire awaits it, and I will not bless it upon the earth.'

Wednesday and Friday present their complaint, and all await God's reply. But the Lord turns his face from the sons of men. The Mother of God marshals the heavenly hosts, and leads them in a mass *proskynēsis* before the throne. All fall on their faces and plead for mercy: 'Master, have mercy on the sinners, and do not destroy the works of your

[17] *Apocalypsis Anastasiae*, ed. Rudolf Homberg (Leipzig, 1903) [hereafter *Anastasia*], ch. 2 (pp. 12–16).

[18] Ibid., pp. 12–13, bottom text. The apocalypse is known in four Greek manuscripts: BN, MS Graecus 1631; Milan, Ambrosianus, MS A 56 Sup.; Oxford, Bodleian, MS Selden Supra 9; Palermo, Panormitanus, MS III.B.25. The Paris, Milan, and Oxford MSS form the 'long' recension of the text; the Palermo version the 'short' recension. See further Jane Baun, 'The *Apocalypse of Anastasia* in its middle Byzantine context' (Princeton University, Ph.D. thesis, 1997), ch. 2.

[19] I.e., Saturday. Both Greek and Russian have kept 'Sabbath' as the standard name for Saturday – in Greek, *sabbaton*; in Russian, *subbota*. Accordingly, Byzantine authors rarely use the word 'Sabbath' to refer to Sunday.

hands.' But the Voice is now silent. Will God, disgusted at mankind's violation of the appointed fast and feast days, wipe mankind off the face of the earth? Reader and audience are left in suspense, while Anastasia and the angel continue their tour.

Observance of Wednesday, Friday, and Sunday is not the only ritual responsibility that the *Apocalypse of Anastasia* endeavours to reinforce, but it is given by far the most prominence. And this violation is the only sin in the text to achieve truly universal significance. All the other sins noted bring punishment for the individual, but the ritual violation of Sunday, Wednesday, and Friday has the potential to wreak disaster upon the entire human race. This is classic taboo.

As in Andrew the Fool's courtier anecdote, the personification of Sunday as a majestic woman invests the message with greater moral impact, allowing the author to draw on the strong convictions regarding the purity and defilement of women so deeply rooted in traditional societies. The passage opens with 'St Sunday, her countenance luminous like the sun', but the image is swiftly violated, as Sunday describes how mankind's sins foul her radiance.[20]

With regard to the earlier discussion of sexual relations on Sunday, it is noteworthy that while the fast days of Wednesday and Friday complain of being defiled by copulation, Sunday, in the three manuscripts of the long recension of *Anastasia*, does not. The moral and ritual norms that at least three copyist-compilers chose to reinforce for Sunday do not seem to include sexual abstinence. Elsewhere in the long recension of the apocalypse, among the approximately seventy-two different types of sin mentioned, Anastasia sees in a river of fire sinners who went to church and received Communion in a state of anger, or with liquor on their breath,[21] but nothing is said about sex on Sundays for laypeople. One manuscript of the four, however, does mention sex on Sundays. The heart of St Sunday's complaint in the Palermo version reads: 'Behold – they work the works of their hands, not honouring your holy Resurrection. They light their ovens and copulate with their wives, and swear oaths falsely and make wicked counsels.'[22] In all four manuscripts, *priests* who slept with their wives on Sundays or other feasts are seen being punished,[23] but the manuscripts

[20] *Anastasia*, p. 12 (Palermo and Milan MSS only).

[21] Ibid., p. 17. The four manuscripts often show variant readings. Here, the Milan MS has 'liquor', while Palermo reads 'anger'.

[22] Ibid., p. 12, top text.

[23] Ibid., p. 20.

do not present a united front as regards laypeople. This preservation of different opinions could signal the presence of a larger social debate over the issue – which would enhance the plausibility of the more nuanced reading proposed above of Balsamon's *responsa* to Mark on the topic.

Also notable in the late tenth-century apocalypse is an unrelenting sabbatarianism. From the ninth hour on Saturday until dawn on Monday, the text insists, one should not work, go out into the streets, or light fires.[24] Sabbatarian tendencies were not unknown in Byzantium; for example, almost two centuries earlier the Patriarch Nikephoros I (806–11) had ruled that 'one ought not to walk abroad, without necessity or compulsion, on the Lord's Day'.[25] The mainstream of Byzantine thought on Sunday activity, though, as represented by the twelfth-century canonists, was more flexible. Canon 29 of the local council at Laodicea decreed that Christians should not 'judaize' and rest on Saturday, but should work on Saturdays and, as far as possible, take Sunday as their rest day.[26] The commentaries of both Balsamon and Zonaras are quick to pick up on the equivocal phrase, 'as far as possible', and to counsel *oikonomia* for those in difficult situations. The ideal is for Christians to abstain from working, and to go to church; but, says Balsamon, if through some difficulty or necessity someone is forced to work, he should not be punished.

St Sunday, as portrayed by *Anastasia*'s compiler, does not agree: one should not even light fires on Sunday – and violation courts disaster. Whence the text's literalist views? In addition to the book of Exodus, the compiler of the earliest version of the apocalypse most certainly knew a Greek version of that notorious sabbatarian tract, the *Letter of Our Lord that Fell from the Sky*. Several Greek versions of the *Skyletter* have numerous points of convergence with Anastasia's apocalypse, and it is clear that the text served *Anastasia*'s original compiler as a source.

The *Letter of Our Lord that Fell from the Sky*, also known as the 'Letter about Sunday', was a wildly popular 'chain letter', with versions circulating from the fifth century to the nineteenth, in languages

[24] *Anastasia*, p. 12; compare Exod. 35.3. Trullo 90 (see n.2) also makes the Christian Sabbath last 'for a whole day and a whole night'.

[25] Canons, 2nd ser., no. 2 (*PG* 100, col. 852). See Mosna, *Storia*, pp. 353–62, for sabbatarian debates in the early Church.

[26] *PG* 137, cols 1376–7 (Balsamon citation at 1377-B).

ranging from Arabic to Icelandic.[27] The text was truly a chain letter: most versions end with copious blessings for those who make multiple copies and send them out to every village and town – and even more copious curses for those who scoff and refuse. Some versions even promise forgiveness of all sins to those who make and distribute copies. Is this indeed why so many manuscripts survive, in so many different languages?

While each manuscript's version adapts the basic message to its own circumstances, the fundamental material of the letter remained remarkably constant across languages and centuries. In origin, the *Skyletter* owes much in tone and content to biblical models, such as Leviticus 26. The message of the letter is plain: honour Sunday in the Old Testament way, or you and your entire community and all your animals and crops will suffer. The tone is violent and intemperate, the goal, to inspire terror and compliance. No threat significant to an agricultural community is left unspoken. Most importantly, the *Skyletter* is sure that this is mankind's Last Chance; unlike the scene in Anastasia's apocalypse, there is no ambiguity. Among countless heated passages in the various Greek versions, is the following threat:[28]

> Cursed is the person who does not honour the holy Sunday from the ninth hour of the Sabbath until the second dawning . . . if you will not do these things, I will not send another letter, but I will open the heavens and rain fire, hail, boiling water, such as man has not known, and I will make fearsome earthquakes and rain blood and drops in April, and wipe out all the seed, vines and plants, and obliterate your sheep and flocks, for the sake of the holy Sunday.

Specific curses are pronounced on those who work or copulate on Sundays (no room for *oikonomia* here), and, in one version, on whose who 'taste the Holy Sunday quickly' (spend ten minutes in church and call it a day?).[29]

Blessings are also pronounced on those who take their families to

[27] M. Bittner, ed., 'Der vom Himmel gefallene Brief Christi in seinem morgenländischen Versionen und Rezensionen', *Denkschriften der Kaiserlichen Akademie der Wissenschaften in Wien, Philosophisch-Historische Klasse*, 51/i (Vienna, 1905). Possible fifth-century origins: M. van Esbroeck, 'La Lettre sur le dimanche, descendue du ciel', in his *Aux origines de la Dormition de la Vierge* (Aldershot, 1995), no. XIII; nineteenth-century circulation: H. Delehaye, 'Note sur la légende de la Lettre du Christ tombée du ciel', *Bulletins de l'Académie Royale de Belgique, Classe des lettres* (1899), pp. 171–213.

[28] Bittner, 'Der Brief Christi', p. 19, §17.

[29] Ibid., p. 32, §53.

church, offer candles and oil, participate in the Liturgy, and, duly prepared, receive Communion.[30] But the real interest is in accentuating the negative, in spelling out the supernatural vengeance that will come upon those who ignore Sunday. It is a day to inspire fear and trembling, not gratitude. These texts are far from the benevolent canonical Sabbath rest, refreshment, and beatitude with which this paper began.

How to account for such a striking divergence? An immediate question is: who was actually composing, copying, sponsoring, and disseminating apocryphal texts such as the *Skyletter* and Anastasia's apocalypse? Answers can be teased out only laboriously from each different version of each text, and conclusions remain tentative at best. Some scholars have seen the hand of frustrated pastors, trying to scare their flocks sinless. It is all very well, a parish priest might reason, for bishops and emperors sitting in their palaces to radiate benevolence and talk positively about ritual and moral norms – but on the front line of parish work, different realities obtain, and fear is a more effective motivator than gratitude. Elements of such thinking may be represented in individual texts, but frustrated pastors and centre–periphery tension do not exhaust the possible range of circumstances surrounding the texts' composition and circulation.

Why was the *Skyletter* copied so many times, in so many places and eras? What motivated *Anastasia*'s compiler to create her vision, and translators in Bulgaria and Serbia to develop Slavonic versions of it? Clearly something in the essential message of these texts struck a chord. And the message is this: violating ritual responsibilities brings disaster, not just upon the individual, but upon the entire community. The canonists talk mostly about individuals and their moral and ritual health, about the state of the individual's soul. The apocryphal texts, in contrast, are concerned primarily with the state of the community's soul, and the role of individual moral and ritual choice in its well-being. Sunday, the apocrypha insist, is not just about you and God. It is rather about you and your neighbour, your village, the world. Sunday is part of the moral order of the universe itself, violated only at great peril. This was indeed a message worth copying.

New York University

[30] Bittner, 'Der Brief Christi', pp. 32–3.

WORK AND PLAY IN SACRED MUSIC AND ITS SOCIAL CONTEXT, *c.* 1050–1250

by SUSAN BOYNTON

IN the central and high Middle Ages, liturgical singing was a form of work, even if it is absent from the typology of 'work' as understood by modern historians.[1] The notion of the 'three orders', dividing society into those who work, those who pray, and those who fight,[2] does not acknowledge the laborious character of the medieval monastic *horarium*. On occasion, however, singers could also experience the liturgy in a lighter vein. Clerical celebrations during the Octave of Christmas transformed musical work into its mirror image, resulting in musical play that was structured in the image of work, as illustrated by cathedral ordinals and liturgical dramas. Indeed, the opposition between the strictly maintained daily liturgical structure and the release from routine was the central ludic element of the annual festivities – the crossing of the boundary between the use and the abuse of liturgical time. To demonstrate the significance of that boundary, this paper will analyse texts that show the perception of singing as work, and then turn to sources demonstrating the process by which liturgical material was subverted into play.

Psalmody as 'sacred work' is the central metaphor of the Western monastic tradition, as indicated by the expression *opus Dei* in the early Latin rules. The Rule of Benedict suggests a correlation between liturgical 'work' and manual labour through the use of the terms *opus Dei* and *opus manuum*.[3] Liturgical singing was an all-consuming use of time, causing the daily schedule of a monastic community to be based almost entirely on the exigencies of the office. As Joseph Dyer has pointed out, the Rule's injunction to 'let nothing come before the *opus Dei*' furnished justification for the vast amount of time devoted to the

[1] See, for instance, Jacques Heers, *Le travail au moyen âge*, Que sais-je?, 1186 (Paris, 1982) which refers to the liturgy only in the context of confraternities (pp. 98–104).

[2] Georges Duby, *The Three Orders: Feudal Society Imagined*, tr. Arthur Goldhammer (Chicago and London, 1980), influentially distinguished between the activities of monks and anything that could be considered labour; see esp. pp. 178–9, on Cluny.

[3] As in the juxaposition of the terms in the titles of ch. 47 ('de significanda hora operis Dei') and ch. 48 ('de opera manuum cotidiana'); see *RB 1980: The Rule of St. Benedict in Latin and English*, ed. Timothy Fry (Collegeville, MN, 1981), p. 248.

liturgy.[4] Expansions of the monastic office, additional intercessory masses, and other services introduced during the Carolingian period were further intensified during the tenth and eleventh centuries.[5] Some historians have interpreted these accretions as a substitute for the manual labour that had lost most of its importance in Latin monasticism by the Carolingian period.[6] At the abbey of Cluny in the late eleventh century, the daily *horarium* reached an extraordinary degree of compression commented on by contemporary observers such as Peter Damian.[7] In addition to the choir liturgy, complex liturgical observances accompanied ordinary activities throughout the day, including manual labour. The psalmody and prayers preceding, accompanying, and following work are so numerous in the *Liber tramitis*, an eleventh-century Cluniac customary, that they left only a small amount of time for the work in question.[8]

Besides the prevalence of the expression *opus Dei*, medieval writers rarely characterize singing explicitly as work. Some texts do suggest an equivalence between singing and manual labour, however. Two customaries of Augustinian canons describe singing as a replacement for work by those who are not physically able. The *Liber ordinis* written in the early twelfth century for abbeys affiliated with the Augustinians at St Victor in Paris prescribes that those remaining behind when the canons go out to work 'can sing masses if they are priests, and the others can help them, and those who have nothing to do should sit in peace in the cloister and they should sing their hours and psalms, like those who are working'.[9] Another Augustinian customary from the

[4] Joseph Dyer, 'Monastic psalmody of the Middle Ages', *Revue Bénédictine*, 99 (1989), p. 41.

[5] On the additions to the Benedictine office, in general, see *The Monastic Breviary of Hyde Abbey*, ed. J. B. L. Tolhurst, 6 vols, Henry Bradshaw Society, 69–71, 76, 78, 80 (London, 1932–42), 6: 46–137; Kassius Hallinger, 'Überlieferung und Steigerung im Mönchtum des 8. bis 12. Jahrhunderts', in *Eulogia: miscellanea liturgica in onore di P. Burckhard Neunheuser O.S.B.*, Studia Anselmiana, 68 (Rome, 1979), pp. 125–87.

[6] Tolhurst, *Monastic Breviary*, pp. 46–7. Barbara Rosenwein, 'Feudal war and monastic peace: Cluniac liturgy as ritual aggression', *Viator*, 2 (1971), p. 139, cites Cuthbert Butler's thesis to this effect in his *Benedictine Monachism* (Cambridge, 1924), p. 296.

[7] For descriptions of developments in Cluniac liturgy during the central Middle Ages, see Kassius Hallinger, 'Das Phänomen der liturgischen Steigerungen Klunys (10/11. Jh.)', in Isaac Vázquez, ed., *Studia historico-ecclesiastica. Festgabe für Prof. Luchesius G. Spätling O.F.M.* (Rome, 1977), pp. 183–236; Rosenwein, 'Feudal war', esp. pp. 129–40. On Peter Damian's reaction see most recently Irven Resnick, 'Peter Damian on Cluny, liturgy, and penance', *Studia liturgica*, 18 (1988), pp. 170–87.

[8] *Liber tramitis aeui Odilonis abbatis*, ed. Peter Dinter, Corpus consuetudinum monasticarum, 10 (Siegburg, 1980), chs 140, 148 (pp. 200–1, 213–14).

[9] *Liber ordinis S. Victoris Parisiensis*, ed. Luc Jocqué and Ludo Milis, *CChr.CM*, 61

1120s takes the equivalence of work and psalmody further, stating that those who are too old to work at all should occupy themselves with psalmody while the others work, so that 'in the diverse performance of work, the unity of brotherly love rules'.[10]

In the Rule of Benedict, punishment takes the form of prohibition from full participation in the liturgy. A monk who has committed a minor offence cannot lead a psalm or refrain (chapter 24); if he is guilty of a serious fault, he is excluded from the liturgy altogether, for he is forbidden to enter the oratory (chapter 25). Once he is readmitted to the choir, he cannot lead a psalm while doing penance for his crime (chapter 44). Some texts from the high Middle Ages, however, prescribe singing itself as a form of punishment. In the customary from Bury St Edmunds written around 1234, the prescriptions for both a serious offence ('gravis culpa') and for minor penitence include singing among the acts of atonement. After being accused in chapter of a serious offence, if he is not immediately pardoned, the offender must cover his face with his cowl up to his mouth, leave the chapter house, and proceed to a stall in between the pulpit and the entrance to the church, where he must remain during each hour of the office, including Matins, singing the psalter and lamenting his deeds.[11] A monk guilty of disobedience, hardness of heart, or carelessness had to perform a penance involving tasks usually assigned to junior members of the community, such as reading the first lesson at Matins, carrying a lamp for the other monks, gathering the crumbs in the refectory, carrying the candelabrum for Mass, and singing the choral sections of the gradual, Alleluia, or tract on a feast of twelve lessons.[12]

Some liturgical commentators of the twelfth century interpret the Divine Office as a form of manual labour. The *Summa de ecclesiasticis officiis* of John Beleth, for instance, casts the six psalms of monastic

(Turnhout, 1984), p. 144: 'Qui autem de labore remanent, si sacerdotes fuerint, possunt missas cantare, et alii eos iuuare, et qui nichil facere habent, in claustro quieti sedere debent, et horas suas et psalmos, sicut hii, qui in labore sunt, cantent.'

10 *Consuetudines canonicorum regularium Springirsbacenses-Rodenses*, ed. Stephan Weinfurter, *CChr.CM*, 48 (Turnhout, 1978), XXI, civ (p. 62): 'Qua finita incipiunt operari, qui norunt et possunt, cęteri uero consuetudine delicatiores uel ualitudine debiliores aut ętate imbecilliores in claustro operentur, quod pater monasterii statuerit. Qui uero processu ętatis nihil omnino operari ualuerint, dum cęteri operantur, psalmodię uacabunt, ut in diuersa actione laboris unitas fraterni regnet amoris.'

11 *The Customary of the Benedictine Abbey of Bury St Edmunds in Suffolk (from Harleian Ms. 1005 in the British Museum)*, ed. Antonia Gransden, Henry Bradshaw Society, 99 (Chichester, 1973), p. 82.

12 Ibid., p. 88.

Lauds as the works of mercy performed by the labourers in the vineyard of the Lord, referring to Matthew 20.[13] This passage in Beleth's *Summa* probably reveals the influence of Honorius Augustodunensis, who in the *Gemma animae* works every element of the night office into an allegory of the labourers in the vineyard.[14] As an unusually thorough interpretation of singing as work, this text is worth quoting at length:

> The night office is an imitation of those working in the vineyard. When we sing in church at night in the service of God, we come together as if to work in the vineyard. . . . When we begin the praise of God with *Domine, labia mea aperies* we commence, as it were, the work of the vineyard. And as soon as we invoke divine aid with *Deus, in adjutorium meum intende*, so that we may accomplish the work begun, with the *Venite*, we stimulate each other, like those working to serve God. Then we sing a hymn to God, since we have overcome nocturnal delusions, and in this we imitate those who sing while they work. Then, while we sing psalms in alternation, we press on as if eagerly in work; while we read the lessons, we prepare ourselves as if for work; while we sing the responsories, we give thanks as when after work is finished. For reading is refreshment of the mind; therefore while we read lessons, we refresh our tired minds, the labourers in the vineyard, so to speak, in divine work; while we sing the responsories, we express praise as if after refreshment. Whence, when we sing psalms again, we rise to work as if refreshed.[15]

[13] John de Beleth, *Summa de ecclesiasticis officiis*, ed. Herbert Douteil, 2 vols, *CChr.CM*, 41A (Turnhout, 1976), c. 30b: 1, p. 58.

[14] On the *Gemma animae*, see most recently Valerie J. Flint, *Honorius Augustodunensis of Regensburg*, Authors of the Middle Ages, 6 (Aldershot, 1995), pp. 138–9.

[15] Honorius Augustodunensis, *Gemma animae*, II, 18: *PL* 172, col. 621: 'Nocturnale officium quoque est imitatio in vinea laborantium. Cum in Ecclesia ad servitium Dei noctu canimus, quasi in vinea ad operandum convenimus. . . . Cum laudem Dei per *Domine, labia mea aperies* incipimus, quasi opus vineae inchoamus. Moxque divinum auxilium per *Deus, in adjutorium meum intende* invocamus, quatenus incoeptum opus perficiamus, per *Venite* ver alterutrum ad servitium Dei, quasi operantes instigamus. Deinde hymnum Deo canimus, quod nocturnas illusiones superavimus, et illos per hoc imitamur, qui cantant, dum operantur. Deinde dum alternatim psallimus, quasi certatim operi insistimus, dum lectiones legimus, quasi nos ad opus instruimus, dum responsoria canimus, quasi post peractum opus gratias agimus. Est enim lectio mentis refectio; dum ergo lectiones legimus, quasi animas in divino opere lassas velut vineae operarios reficimus; dum responsoria canimus, quasi post refectionem laudes solvimus. Unde cum iterum psallimus, quasi refecti ad laborandum surgimus.'

Honorius interprets each of the participants in the service as corresponding to a member of the group involved in the work of the vineyard. The priest is the proprietor of the estate (*paterfamilias*), while the cantor who sings the Invitatory (Psalm 94, 'Come, let us rejoice in the Lord') represents the overseer (*procurator*) who summons the workers to cultivate the vineyard. Honorius then assigns new meanings to the chants of the office. The hymn represents the song that workers begin after work is finished; the psalms teach the works of the saints. Honorius follows this allegory with an interpretation of each psalm of the office both typologically and tropologically. The first example is Abel, as the first labourer in the vineyard, and the subject of the first psalm, 'who taught us to meditate day and night on the law of the Lord, as it were, to work in the vineyard'.[16] In the section devoted specifically to the monastic office, Honorius comments, like Beleth, that 'therefore through the six psalms, those labouring in the vineyard of the Lord are manifested' and further that 'the alacrity of the labourers is denoted by the responsories'.[17]

Monastic sources emphasise the difficulty of getting up for the night office and then staying awake, an effort that seems particularly important in the life of a monk because of the length of monastic Matins. We should not underestimate the challenge of this task: Isidore of Seville's *Rule* begins the duties of the monk with 'let him flee the torpor and laziness of sleep, and exert himself in vigils and prayers without interruption.'[18] The temptations of sleep and the difficulty of rising in the middle of the night permeate the liturgical texts of the night office themselves, and references to these concerns appear in commentary on the hymns for Matins. A gloss on 'Primo dierum omnium' in an eleventh-century manuscript refers to the spiritual need of the singer to force himself out of bed: 'He who hastens to celebrate the divine office or a service must cast off all somnolence and laziness; otherwise he cannot find the Lord whom he seeks.'[19] In the

[16] Ibid., II, 19: *PL* 172, col. 622.

[17] *PL* 172, col. 624: 'Per sex ergo psalmos in vinea Domini laborantes declarantur ... per Responsoria alacritas laborantium denotatur.'

[18] Isidore of Seville, *Regula monachorum*, III, *De monachis*, in *Reglas monásticas de la España visigoda (San Leandro, San Isidoro, San Fructuoso); Los Tres libros de las "Sentencias"*, ed. Julio Campos Ruiz and Ismael Roca Meliá, Santos Padres Españoles, 2 (Madrid, 1971), p. 93: 'Torporem somni adque pigritiam fugiat, uigiliisque et orationibus sine intermissione intendat.'

[19] BN, MS lat. 11550, fol. 243r: 'Qui ad celebrandum diuinum offitium uel obsequium festinat, necesse est ut a se omnem somnolentiam et torporem repellat. Aliter dominum

same manuscript, a gloss on the phrase 'drive out somnolence' ('expelle somnolentiam') in the hymn 'Consors paterni luminis' seems to point out the danger of falling asleep during the service: 'he who is sleepy and lazy is overwhelmed by that very somnolence, so his prayer cannot reach God.'[20] The preoccupation with sleep in the Matins hymns arises from the function of the texts as poetic glosses on the hours of the Divine Office. Drawing upon the patristic commonplace of the 'sleep of sin' ('somnus peccati'),[21] the glosses reify this figurative, spiritual sleep as the nightly rest of monks. Since the hymns were used in monastic education as well as in the liturgy, the hymn glosses concerned with mastering sleep in order to attend the Divine Office would seem to have a didactic purpose.[22]

The difficulties of overcoming somnolence also appear in narrative texts, which seem to offer the personal perspective of singers more than liturgical commentary, albeit with intentions no less didactic. Radulfus Glaber's *Histories* provide a particularly intriguing example. Book Five begins with a curious anecdote about a devil who convinced a monk to stay in bed and miss Matins by telling him that the monks' excessive labours were superfluous.[23] Turning to his own personal experience, Glaber describes a demon he saw in three different places; the last occasion was a night during which he stayed in bed in the dormitory, along with a few other monks, after the bell rang for Matins. As most of the brothers rushed off to the church, the demon entered the dormitory breathless, announcing, 'It is I, it is I, who stay with those who remain behind.' Three days later, one of the brothers who had stayed in bed that night left the monastery at the instigation of the demon, and lived 'tumultuously' for six days with laypeople, then returned, chastized, on the

quem querit, inuenire non poterit.' The gloss comments on vv. 5–6, 'pulsis procul torporibus surgamus omnes ocius'. For a text of the hymn, see *Early Latin Hymns*, ed. A. S. Walpole (Cambridge, 1922), pp. 262–3.

[20] BN, MS lat. 11550, fol. 248r: 'qui somnolentus et piger est, ipsa somnolentia obruit eum ne oratio eius possit peruenire ad Deum.' For the hymn text, see Walpole, *Early Latin Hymns*, p. 268.

[21] See, for instance, Cassian, *Collatio*, ed. M. Petschenig, Corpus scriptorum ecclesiasticorum latinorum, 13 (Vienna, 1886), xxii.5, p. 620.

[22] For an analysis of the hymn glosses in my critical edition currently in preparation, see Susan Boynton, 'Latin glosses on the office hymns in eleventh-century continental hymnaries', *The Journal of Medieval Latin*, 11 (2001).

[23] Radulfus Glaber, *Historiae*, ed. John France (Oxford, 1989), V.1, p. 216. This narrative is based on a text written for Abbot Odo of Saint-Germain; see R. A. Shoaf, 'Raoul Glaber et la *Visio Anselli Scholastici*', *Cahiers de civilisation médiévale*, 23 (1980), pp. 215–19.

seventh.[24] In this story, singing the night office seems to be as much a matter of physical or psychological well-being as a spiritual obligation; while Glaber acknowledges the difficulty of adhering to the *horarium*, the story reflects the perceived dangers that could be avoided by carrying out liturgical work as required.

The Cistercian prior Caesarius of Heisterbach, writing in the early thirteenth century, also portrays the Divine Office as work. In his *Dialogus miraculorum* we read of a monk who, while sweating to overcome an illness, was convinced by the devil to miss Matins. As in Glaber's *Histories*, the devil gives himself away by speaking to the monk (in this case, from under his bed), verbalizing the monk's self-indulgence: 'don't get up, don't interrupt your sweating, it's not advisable.'[25] These anecdotes fit into a broader context of punishments prescribed in monastic rules and customaries for monks missing the night office or arriving late, and the role of officials such as the *circator*, who kept monks awake during Matins.[26]

Caesarius of Heisterbach also evokes persistent problems of somnolence even on the part of those who do make it to Matins. We read of the *conversus* who sees the eyes of another *conversus* closed by a tomcat as he fell asleep in the choir; yet another sleepy *conversus*, observing a serpent creeping in broad daylight over the back of one of the brothers who often falls asleep in his stall, remarks that such somnolence comes from the devil.[27] A novice is distracted from his psalmody by a demon who has transformed himself into a calf's tail.[28] Older, more experienced monks fared no better: one older monk known for his somnolence found filthy straw thrown into his eyes by the devil when he fell asleep during Matins.[29] Another monk sat in the choir unconsciously harbouring a demon; he was more than a little lazy, willingly sleeping in choir, but unwillingly singing, happier to drink

[24] Glaber, *Historiae*, V.5, pp. 220–2.

[25] Caesarius of Heisterbach, *Dialogus miraculorum*, ed. Joseph Strange, 2 vols (Cologne, 1851), IV.28 – 1: 197–8.

[26] For a convenient overview of the office of the *circator* beginning with the Rule of Benedict, see Hugh Feiss, '*Circatores*: from Benedict of Nursia to Humbert of Romans', *American Benedictine Review*, 40 (1989), pp. 346–79, and most recently S. G. Bruce, '"Lurking with spiritual intent": a note on the origin and functions of the monastic roundsman (*circator*)', *Revue Bénédictine*, 109 (1999), pp. 75–89. Bruce notes that '*circatores* were ever on the watch for somnolent monks' (p. 85). Ch. 43 of the Rule prescribes the punishment for monks who were late to services.

[27] Caesarius of Heisterbach, *Dialogus miraculorum*, IV.31 – 1: 202–3.

[28] Ibid., V.5 – 1: 282.

[29] Ibid., IV, 33, 34 – 1: 203–4.

than to sing ('hilarior ad potandum, quam ad cantandum'). Even the shorter vigils seemed extremely long to him.[30] A similar monk, who habitually fell asleep in the choir, and whom Caesarius described as 'often silent and singing too little' ('multum tacens et parum psallens'), was frequently seen surrounded by audibly grunting pigs. Following this last story, a monk in dialogue with a novice comments that 'there are certain people who as soon as they have begun to sing, pray, or read, immediately begin to be drowsy. . . . When they hear secular words, they stay quite awake; when the word of God is proposed to them, they soon fall asleep.'[31] In Caesarius' text, it seems that extraordinary solutions were needed. One resourceful abbot resorted to startling drowsy monks with Arthurian tales, only to reprove them for falling asleep during his sermon. The case of one particularly unlucky monk must have made an impressive *exemplum*: one night when he dozed during the psalmody, the crucifix itself came down from the altar, woke him up, and hit him in the jaw with such force that he died three days later.[32] These anecdotes, along with prescriptive texts, suggest that singing the night office was experienced more often as drudgery than as a spiritual act.

Indeed, some of Caesarius' stories about the night office emphasise the danger of singing without the requisite humility. One concerns the time that a devil interfered with the co-operation between the two choirs of monks in the chanting of the Invitatory psalm. After the weekly cantor intoned the psalm on a rather low pitch, a youth in the other choir, possessed by a devil, raised the pitch a fifth above the intonation, violating the injunction found in monastic customaries against raising the pitch of a chant once the cantor has decided upon it.[33] The conflict between the two choirs continued, as the demon who had started the trouble moved from one side to the other.[34] Musical pride presents a temptation to the devil: in another anecdote of

[30] Caesarius of Heisterbach, *Dialogus miraculorum*, V.5 – 1: 283.

[31] Ibid., IV.35 – 1: 204.

[32] Ibid., IV.36, 38 – 1: 205–6.

[33] For instance, Margot Fassler, 'The office of the cantor in early Western monastic rules and customaries: a preliminary investigation', *Early Music History*, 5 (1985), p. 49, cites a passage from the late-eleventh-century Cluniac customary of Bernard stating that 'no one should ever presume to begin any chant higher, or to raise it, once it is begun, or vary it in any way, unless the armarius begins first' ('nullus enim praesumere umquam debet quemlibet cantum altius incipere, aut inceptum elevare, seu quovis modo variare, nisi Armarius prius incipiat').

[34] Caesarius of Heisterbach, *Dialogus miraculorum*, V.5 – 1: 283–4.

Caesarius, two singers congratulate themselves on their excellent performance, and then discover that a demon has collected their prideful voices in a sack. As he points out, they have sung not just well, but a 'sack full'.[35] These anecdotes serve to remind the reader that singing should be work rather than play.

Another moralizing story appears in the early twelfth-century Farfa Register compiled by Gregory of Catino, in a passage interpreting musical play as abuse of liturgical tradition. The 1120s were a crucial moment in the history of the imperial abbey of Farfa. Abbot Guido, who held his office against the veto of Henry V, profoundly violated the abbey's imperial patronage by turning to Pope Calixtus II to moderate his dispute with the community. The monks had elected Guido but then, in May 1121, they sought to replace him with the imperial candidate, Berard Ascarellus. Guido occupied the abbey by force and sent the protesting monks into exile. The monks who left at this time later returned only under duress, after three events that compelled them to accept Guido as abbot against their will. Calixtus arrived at Farfa in the summer of 1121 with an army to confirm Guido, then in 1122 signed the Concordat of Worms, essentially giving the Pope control over the abbey. Finally, Calixtus excommunicated Berard Ascarellus during the Lateran Council of 1123.[36]

According to Gregory of Catino, on the return of the monks to Farfa, Abbot Guido took his revenge by deforming the solemnity of the liturgy, making them wear tattered everyday clothing in the choir instead of their former rich vestments. Gregory deplored the fact that the younger brothers no longer sang the traditional chant repertoire with spiritual sincerity or solemnity:

> they were eager to sing in the manner of actors, and they busied themselves with introducing many ditties and foreign songs; they did not care to cultivate the custom of this place but instead [sang] frivolities and flighty things from elsewhere, which they had heard or seen in the foreign places where they had stayed.[37]

[35] Ibid., IV.9 – 1: 181. I am grateful to Margot Fassler for referring me to this text.

[36] For the most recent discussion of these events, see Mary Stroll, *The Medieval Abbey of Farfa* (Leiden, 1998), pp. 235–47.

[37] *Il Regesto di Farfa compilato da Gregorio di Catino*, ed. Ignazio Giorgi and Ugo Balzani, 5 vols (Rome, 1883–1914), 5: 322: 'Adolescentes vel minores fratres cantuum neumas et organa solita respuebant, et non spirituali honestate aut gravitate, sed istrionum more canere studebant, et multas nenias extraneasque cantilenas introducere satagebant, nec huius loci consuetudinem sed diversarum partium levitates et extollentias, quas in exteris locis quibus degebant audierant vel viderant, exercere curabant.'

For Gregory, the degeneration of liturgical music, expressed in the choice of more playful repertoire, corresponds to the spiritual and political decay of the abbey.

This is one of the rare medieval texts that refer directly to musical style, and particularly to musical play. Although we cannot be entirely sure what Gregory meant by 'foreign' music, it is possible to deduce what would have seemed foreign (and perhaps, by extension, frivolous) in central Italy in the early twelfth century. A *Benedicamus Domino* song that was added to a Farfa manuscript during the period described by Gregory provides a good example of such a new and foreign style. In *Splendor patris*, lines of newly composed rhymed verse complement the text of the pre-existing office versicle (indicated below in bold):

Splendor patris et sol iustitiæ
fit particeps nostre materiæ;
intrat uentrem[38] sed sine semine
egreditur ex matre uirgine.
Ergo **benedicamus Domino**.
Hic egressus et haec ingressio
deitatis fiunt probatio;
probat namque matris integritas
quod filius eius est deitas.
Ergo **Deo** dicamus **gratias**.
Benedicamus Domino.
Orthodoxorum coetus
cherichorum iubilorum.
Deo dicamus **gratias**.[39]

In style, *Splendor patris* most resembles the modern *Benedicamus Domino* songs and *versus* found in northern French manuscripts of the early twelfth century, and in fact a closely related text is found, albeit with a somewhat different melody, in a manuscript copied in Norman Sicily during the second third of the twelfth century.[40] Since most of the repertory in this manuscript comes from northern France,[41] it seems

[38] The manuscript reading is *uentre*, which I emend to *uentrem* at the kind suggestion of Charles Witke.

[39] Rome, Biblioteca Nazionale, MS Farfa 4, fol. 77r.

[40] Madrid, Biblioteca Nacional, MS 289, fol. 134r.

[41] Wulf Arlt, *Ein Festoffizium des Mittelalters aus Beauvais in seiner liturgischen und musikalischen Bedeutung*, 2 vols (Cologne, 1970), 2 (= Darstellungsband), p. 176.

possible (if unprovable) that *Splendor patris* is one of the 'imported' compositions deplored by Gregory of Catino. To conservative monks in early twelfth-century central Italy, *Splendor patris* would certainly have sounded foreign because it differs markedly from the traditional Gregorian chant of the abbey's liturgical repertoire, and would contrast even with some of the new liturgical compositions introduced at the abbey in the later eleventh century.[42] The transparent structure is based on textual rhyme and melodic repetition.[43] Musical phrases with an antecedent-consequent structure give symmetry to lines 1–4 and 6–9; repetition in lines 5 and 10–14 reinforces the listener's sense of tonal goals. In lines 1–10, a decorative cadence emphasises the end of each text line. The melody moves quickly up and down through the range of an octave, a characteristic associated with newer compositions. The predominantly syllabic first part (set to the first ten lines of text) resembles many twelfth-century *Benedicamus Domino* songs associated with the Christmas season, such as *Super omnes alias*, which is transmitted by manuscripts from Norman Sicily and preserved in the Circumcision offices from Beauvais and Sens.[44] The melismatic setting of lines 10–14 recalls some twelfth-century *versus*, as does the language of the text in general.[45] *Splendor patris* seems intuitively appropriate for performance by young voices, and indeed many monastic customaries indicate that boys performed the *Benedicamus Domino*.[46]

With its focus on the Incarnation suggesting performance in the Christmas season, *Splendor patris* exemplifies the new compositions created in the twelfth and thirteenth centuries for the clerical festivities of the Christmas Octave. In contrast to the liturgical

[42] For examples of these new compositions, see Susan Boynton, 'Liturgy and history at the abbey of Farfa in the late eleventh century: Hymns of Peter Damian and other additions to BAV Chigi C.VI.177', *Sacris Erudiri*, 39 (2000), pp. 317–44.

[43] See the transcription in the Appendix. I am grateful to Peter Bergquist for preparing a camera-ready version of my handwritten transcription.

[44] Edited in Arlt, *Festoffizium*, 1 (= Editionsband), pp. 147–8. For other editions, see p. 257.

[45] For a recent discussion of this repertory, with further bibliography, see James Grier, 'A new voice in the monastery: tropes and *versus* from eleventh- and twelfth-century Aquitaine', *Speculum*, 69 (1994), pp. 1023–69.

[46] E.g. *Consuetudines Fructuarienses – Sanblasianae*, ed. L. G. Spätling and Peter Dinter, 2 vols, Corpus consuetudinum monasticarum, 12 (Siegburg, 1987), 2: 215–16; Ulrich of Zell, *Antiquiores consuetudines Cluniacensis monasterii*, 11: *PL* 149, col. 654D. The Cluniac *Liber tramitis* and the Cluniac customary from Vallombrosa, among other sources, are cited by Anne Walters Robertson, '*Benedicamus Domino*: the unwritten tradition', *Journal of the American Musicological Society*, 41 (1988), pp. 5–9.

structuring of time in the monastic tradition, this 'abuse' of liturgical time was an important tradition in the high Middle Ages. The clerical festivities that took place in the week after Christmas in many northern cathedrals by the twelfth century consisted of several celebrations associated with different ecclesiastical orders: deacons on St Stephen's Day, 26 December; priests on the feast of St John, the 27th; acolytes on the feast of the Innocents, the 28th; and the subdeacons on the feast of the Circumcision on 1 January (or sometimes on Epiphany).[47] While all these feasts were celebrated with their own elaborate proper liturgies, two in particular are notorious for a degree of celebration that went far beyond sheer solemnity: Innocents' Day and 1 January.[48] These two days, not coincidentally the festivities of younger clergy in minor orders, were the occasion for mischievous fun and riotous merrymaking that literally turned the clerical hierarchy upside down. On Innocents' Day, primarily in northern European cathedrals, a Boy Bishop officiated in place of the real bishop; he was chosen from among the acolytes on the feast of St Nicholas or the vigil of Innocents' Day. The reversal of the ecclesiastical hierarchy represented by the Boy Bishop was apparently less outrageous than the Feast of Fools, a day of all-out clowning and misbehaviour associated primarily with the feast of the subdeacons. According to John Beleth, the subdeacons' uncertain place in the ecclesiastical hierarchy was manifested in their celebration of their feast with a 'confused office'. *Tripudia*, Beleth's intriguing term for the feasts after Christmas, carries a connotation of dancing and music.[49] The secular connotations of the word *tripudia* were part of a generalized perception of the clerical festivities in the twelfth century. Gerhoh of Reichersberg, for example, deplored the fact that the regular canons of the cathedral of Augsburg, when he taught there in the early twelfth century, ate in their refectory and slept in their dormitory only on feasts when there

[47] While the festivities are best documented in cathedrals, some version of them took place in monasteries as well. Two texts by Ekkehard IV refer to celebrations after Christmas at St Gall; Ekkehard IV, *Casus Sancti Galli*, ed. Hans F. Haefele, Ausgewahlte Quellen zur deutschen Geschichte des Mittelalters, 10 (Darmstadt, 1980), 14 (p. 40); 'Notkero magistro pro pace et solito scolarium otio in die post Epiphaniam', in *Der Liber Benedictionum Ekkeharts IV*, ed. Johannes Egli, Mitteilungen zur vaterländischen Geschichte, 31 (St Gall, 1909), pp. 383–7. I am grateful to Peter Stotz for these references.

[48] On the Feast of Fools through the thirteenth century, see E. K. Chambers, *The Mediaeval Stage*, 2 vols (Oxford, 1903), 2, pp. 274–91, 321–5, 336–41; on the Boy Bishop, see 2: 349–71; S. Shahar, 'The boy bishop's feast: a case-study in Church attitudes towards children in the High and Late Middle Ages', *SCH*, 31 (1994), pp. 243–60.

[49] Beleth, *Summa*, ch. 72b, p. 134.

was dramatic entertainment.[50] Beleth criticized the custom of the 'libertas Decembris' observed in some churches, 'where in the cloisters bishops or archbishops play with their clergy, descending even to a game of ball'. He attributed the origin of this custom to the ancient pagan tradition of giving banquets to shepherds and servants after the harvest, and concludes that this practice was not praiseworthy, although maintained by some great churches.[51] While Beleth does not link the 'libertas Decembris' explicitly to either the Christmas octave or the feast of St Nicholas, its atmosphere of boundary-crossing seems connected to these clerical festivities, both of which took place in December.

The traditions associated with the Boy Bishop and the Feast of Fools are known from a wide variety of sources, including liturgical commentators, complaints and legislation by church reformers, ordinals for the day's liturgy, and music dramas. Many of these texts show that music was central to the ludic activities of the clerical festivities. However, liturgical commentators generally do not mention music. A notable exception is a legend about the proper office of St Nicholas, which exists in several versions transmitted during the thirteenth century. In the *Rationale* of Guillaume Durand, the legend occupies the entirety of the chapter in Book 7 concerning the feast of St Nicholas:

> In a certain church called Crux, subject to the monastery of Saint Mary of Charity, the proper office of Blessed Nicholas was not yet performed. The brothers of this place asked their prior to let them sing it, but he refused this absolutely, saying that it would be unsuitable to change the former custom for novelties. When they insisted, he responded indignantly: 'Leave me, since new songs, indeed certain jocular ones, will not be sung in my church.' When the feast of the saint arrived, the brothers with a certain sadness of the soul sang the vigils of Matins. And when they had all gone back to bed, behold blessed Nicholas appeared visibly terrible to the prior, whom he pulled out of bed by his hair, and dashed him to the floor of the dormitory, and beginning the antiphon 'O pastor eterne', pouring very heavy blows on the back of the prior

[50] *PL* 194, cols 890–1; same text in K. Young, *The Drama of the Medieval Church*, 2 vols (Oxford, 1933), 2: 411. See also Susan Boynton, 'Performative exegesis in the Fleury *Interfectio puerorum*', *Viator*, 29 (1998), pp. 42–3.

[51] Beleth, *Summa*, ch. 120, p. 223.

> with the rods he held in his hand, with each cadence of the melody, he led him, singing that entire antiphon mournfully in order to the end. All the brothers having been awakened by his cries, he was carried to his bed half alive, and when he came to himself he said: 'Go, and henceforth sing the new office of St Nicholas.'[52]

This story illustrates the importance of musical play to liturgical singers, and the social conflicts that the need for play could cause between ecclesiastical authorities and those subject to them. While the monks' request to sing an office of St Nicholas seems unobjectionable enough, the prior knew that a new proper office of St Nicholas could include 'new songs, indeed certain jocular ones' ('nova cantica immo joculatoria quaedam'). The word *joculatoria* has multiple connotations: in addition to meaning jesting or jocular, it could also constitute an allusion to the music associated with minstrels or jongleurs (*ioculatores*). A similarly ambiguous use of *joculatoria* appears in William of Malmesbury's *De gestis pontificum Anglorum.* William describes Thomas, Archbishop of York from 1070 to 1100, as a composer who could transform jocular or jongleur song into sacred music: 'if anyone in his hearing sang anything vocal in a jocular manner, he instantly fashioned it into divine praise.'[53] In the legend of the proper office of St Nicholas, the prior's conservatism could be interpreted as resistance not only to new styles of music common in cathedrals, but also to the riotous merrymaking of their clergy during the Christmas

[52] Guillaume Durand, *Rationale diuinorum officiorum, VII–VIII*, ed. Anselme Davril and Timothy Thibodeau, *CChr.CM,* 140B (Turnhout, 2000), p. 105 (VII.xxxix): '*De beato nicolao.* Legitur quod cum in quadam ecclesia que dicitur Crux, subiecta monasterio sancte Marie de Caritate, nondum ystoria beati Nicolai cantaretur. Fratres eiusdem loci priorem suum ut eam sibi cantare liceret instanter rogauerunt; ille uero hoc precise negauit dicens incongruum fore pristinum morem nouitatibus immutare. Illis uero instantibus, indignatus respondit: Recedite a me quia noua cantica immo ioculatoria quedam in mea ecclesia non cantabuntur. Adueniente autem eiusdem sancti festiuitate, fratres cum quadam animi tristitia matutinarum uigilias peregerunt. Cumque omnes se in lectis recepissent, ecce beatus Nicolaus priori uisibiliter terribilis apparuit, quem a lecto extrahens per capillos dormitorii pauimento illisit, et incipiens antiphonam "O pastor eterne", per singulas uocum differentias uirgis quas in manu tenebat grauissimos ictus super dorsum illius ingeminans, per ordinem, morose cantando antiphonam ipsam ad finem usque perduxit. Omnibus ergo illius clamoribus excitatis, semiuiuus ad lectum deportatur qui tandem ad se rediens dixit: Ite et ystoriam nouam sancti Nicolai amodo decantate.'

[53] William of Malmesbury, *De gestis pontificum Anglorum libri quinque*, ed. N. E. S. A. Hamilton, *RS*, 52 (London and Cambridge, 1870), p. 258: 'Nec cantu nec voce minor, multa ecclesiastica composuit carmina. Si quis in auditu ejus arte joculatoria aliquid vocale sonaret, statim illud in divinas laudes effigiabre.'

octave. Perhaps, therefore, one dimension of the story's meaning is a conflict in musical values between traditional Benedictine monasticism and the secular clergy. In fact, in a lengthier version of the story the prior denounces the chants of the proper office as 'new songs of secular clerics' ('nova *saecularium* cantica *clericorum*').[54] We have some examples of 'new songs' that could illuminate the prior's reaction to them as 'jocular': for instance, a two-part piece of twelfth-century English polyphony in honour of St Nicholas, published by Christopher Page, contains interpolated vernacular French phrases of secular song to humorous effect, evoking the light-hearted spirit of the festivities for St Nicholas:

> Let us rejoice and be glad / let us venerate Nicholas
> Let us sing his praises / and those of sweet Alice;
> Let us preach through singing / and do listen to me![55]

Already by the twelfth century, clerical festivities were associated with a distinctive body of music, both monophonic and polyphonic; the musical genres include tropes (a genre of liturgical poetry consisting of musical and/or poetic additions to pre-existing chants) and versus and conductus (newly composed Latin songs, not necessarily liturgical or even sacred), with other types of rhythmical poetry, as well as music dramas that were a mixture of poetry and prose. As at other important times of the church year, liturgical music on this day derives much of its richness from the heightened solemnity of the occasion. As the thirteenth-century ordinal from the cathedral of Bayeux states, the deacons, priests, and acolytes must all celebrate their feasts as solemnly as possible – with as much splendour as they could muster.[56]

One of the feasts of the Christmas Octave, Innocents' Day was associated in the Middle Ages with both mourning and rejoicing. Commentators on the liturgy, beginning with Amalarius of Metz, remarked that the Gloria and Alleluia were omitted from the Mass to

[54] This expanded version of the legend found in Durand's *Rationale* is translated in Charles W. Jones, *The Saint Nicolas Liturgy and its Literary Relationships (Ninth to Twelfth Century)* (Berkeley and Los Angeles, CA, 1963), pp. 47–9.

[55] Christopher Page, *The Owl and the Nightingale: Musical Life and Ideas in France, 1100–1300* (London, 1989), pp. 4–6: 'Exultemus et letemur / Nicolaum veneremur / Eius laudes decantemus / Et suef Aleis; Decantando predicemus / Et si m'entendeiz!'

[56] *Ordinaire et coutumier de l'église cathédrale de Bayeux*, ed. Ulysse Chevalier (Paris, 1902), p. 64: 'omnes enim isti quam sollennius possunt festa sua celebrant.'

express the sorrow of the bereaved mothers. Sermons and liturgical poetry for the feast, however, juxtapose the lament of Rachel and the other mothers after the slaughter of the Innocents with the positive meaning of the martyrdom in salvation history. Tropes for the feast refer to celebrations by the choirboys and acolytes, and establish an equivalence between the boy singers and the Innocents themselves. In liturgical dramas on the massacre of the Innocents, this equivalence is taken further by means of visual and textual references.[57] On Innocents' Day, then, both the sacrifice of biblical children for Christ and the festivity of contemporary children were commemorated simultaneously within the framework of the liturgy. The ceremony of the Boy Bishop affirmed the joyful aspect of the feast; the choirboys celebrated their own festivity but were identified with the Holy Innocents through the proper chants and readings of the day.

Thirteenth-century ordinals from the cathedrals of Bayeux and Padua provide some of the most detailed extant prescriptions for the Boy Bishop's feast. The thirteenth-century ordinal from Bayeux provides general instructions for the three feasts immediately after Christmas. These are the only duplex feasts, in addition to the feast of the Rod (probably New Year's Day), on which the canons of the cathedral are not required to perform all the chants and readings, singing the chants of the Mass from the high stalls. All the members of clerical orders in charge of the feasts of St Stephen, the Innocents, and St John – respectively the deacons, the choirboys ('pueri'), and the priests – should celebrate their feasts as solemnly as they can, and can sing in the high stalls usually reserved for the canons. The gradual and Alleluia at Mass are sung in polyphony. While liturgical assignments were normally determined by the cantor, on each of the three feasts of the Christmas Octave the order celebrating that day chooses the readers and singers to be written on the tablet that contains the order of the services. They are free to choose the hymn, versicle, and *Benedicamus Domino* at Compline.[58]

Each of the three feasts began after Vespers of the previous day with a procession to an appropriate church or altar. On the vigil of Innocents' Day, the boys process to the altar of St Nicholas. They

[57] For an expanded version of this argument, see Boynton, 'Performative exegesis', pp. 41–5.

[58] Chevalier, *Ordinaire*, pp. 3, 64, 67.

have their own cantor and chaplain; their Boy Bishop, to whom they show all the reverence due to the real bishop, bears all the insignia of the real bishop except the ring, and carries out all the offices of a priest except for the Mass. Only boys may participate, and all the boys are included, even those who are not choir clerks; they occupy the high stalls throughout the entire next day, while the Boy Bishop sits in the stall of the dean of the cathedral. Like the deacons, the boys sing a Compline of their own devising.[59]

During the procession to the altar of St Nicholas, on the way to bed, and back to the church for Matins, the boys sing the prose *Sedentem in superne*. They repeat it after the last responsory of Matins, with the choir singing melismas after the boys sing every verse.[60] The text of this prose concludes with an image frequently associated with the Holy Innocents: a 'most innocent flock, who are without any blemish, singing with a high voice: "Glory be to you, Christ"'.[61] The Bayeux ordinal makes it clear that the feast of the Innocents is a day of highly controlled liturgical play; the ceremonial adheres to the orderly structure of a regular duplex feast, despite some individual licences and choices. Since most of the chants are those usually sung on Innocents' Day, the boys were apparently not at liberty to make extensive substitutions, distinguishing the festivity of the Boy Bishop from that of the Feast of Fools on the Circumcision. The tablet with the order of services is written in the customary fashion and read aloud in the choir at the required hour. Several elements of the service must replicate those usually performed by the bishop, and the boys' cantor must carry out his office exactly as the real cantor would.[62] Most of the play involved in this ceremony is tied to the visual imagery of the substitute bishop with his clergy. The Boy Bishop sings chants associated with the real bishop, and he and his clergy sing from the higher stalls reserved to the cathedral canons. The ordinal contains no musical humour of the kind found in the Beauvais Circumcision Office, except for the playful prolongation of one verse of the Magnificat: *Deposuit potentes*, 'He hath put down the mighty from their seat: and hath exalted the humble and meek.' The boys move to

[59] Ibid., pp. 69–70.

[60] Ibid., p. 69.

[61] *Analecta Hymnica*, 10: 56 and 47: 298: 'innocentissimo grege, qui sine ulla sunt labe, dicentes excelsa voce: Laus tibi sit Domine'. On this prose, which is also found in Matins of the Beauvais Circumcision office, see Arlt, *Festoffizium*, 1: 223, 2: 99–100.

[62] Chevalier, *Ordinaire*, p. 71.

the middle of the church to repeat this verse several times after the Boy Bishop. It was at this moment that a Boy Bishop for the following year could be designated, apparently indicated by receiving the episcopal staff from the previous one. After many repetitions of *Deposuit potentes* they return to the choir to finish Vespers, and the new Boy Bishop, if one has been named, presides over Compline.[63] The text of *Deposuit potentes* is thus appropriate on several levels. It signifies simultaneously the reversal at the centre of the feast, with the glorious martyrdom of the infant martyrs, the role reversal in the celebration by the choirboys and Boy Bishop, the subsequent return to order, and the handing over of the episcopal office to another boy.

The feast of the Innocents in the thirteenth-century ordinal from Padua differs in many ways from the Bayeux *ordo*. The Padua text includes complete prescriptions for the feast as celebrated both with and without a Boy Bishop, called here an 'episcopellus'.[64] As in the Bayeux ordinal, most of the chants are those customarily sung on Innocents' Day. In the evening, the Episcopellus with his canons go to the home of the real bishop, and sing the antiphon *Sinite paruulos* at the entrance. This antiphon has a double meaning in the same manner as the repetition of the verse *Deposuit potentes* at Bayeux: as a chant for Innocents' Day, also employed in plays for the feast, it refers to the Innocents' ascent to God; during the processional entry of the Episcopellus into the bishop's residence, it alludes humorously to the bishop's reception of the youngest members of his clergy. As in the Bayeux text, the Episcopellus is required to employ the same ceremonial gestures as the bishop and to follow the order of the feast.[65] However, some alterations signal the special festivity of the day when a Boy Bishop is celebrating: after the ninth lesson of Matins, the Episcopellus and his 'clergy' sing the ninth responsory, then all of Lauds, behind the high altar; when there is no Boy Bishop, these offices are sung in the choir. At the Mass of the Episcopellus, the chants are the usual ones for the feast, but a dramatic element adds a playful touch: during the epistle, someone meant to represent Herod throws a wooden spear at the people in attendance, and armed soldiers move through the church seeking the Christ child and Mary; the Holy

[63] Chevalier, *Ordinaire*, p. 72.

[64] The text is published in *Uffici drammatici padovani*, ed. Giuseppe Vecchi (Florence, 1954), pp. 174–8, and in Young, *Drama*, 1: 106–9.

[65] Vecchi, *Uffici drammatici*, pp. 174–5.

Family, with Mary and Jesus mounted on an ass, walk through the church as well.[66]

Alongside the humorous tenor of Mass on Innocents' Day, the martyrdom of the Innocents is commemorated in the customary omission of the Gloria and the Alleluia. A further commemoration takes place after the main Mass, when a second, abbreviated Mass begins in commemoration of dead children, 'pro pueris', recited without music ('plana voce') with some of the same liturgical items as the high Mass. This Mass ends after the gospel, when women offer money and candles on behalf of dead children.[67] This combination of rejoicing and mourning is typical of the feast of the Innocents in the high Middle Ages. The Matins service on Epiphany in the Padua ordinal is even more lively than the Boy Bishop's Mass: Herod furiously throws a spear at the choir, and reads the ninth lesson just as furiously, while his attendants run around the choir beating the bishop and canons with inflated bladders, as well as all others in the church. This ceremony, like that of the Boy Bishop, achieves its humorous effect by combining outrageous behaviour with an incongruously ordinary performance of the chants proper to the feast.[68]

The thirteenth-century Circumcision Office from the cathedral of Beauvais exhibits a similar combination of clowning and liturgical decorum. This office was composed for the subdeacons' festivity on the Circumcision, 1 January, often the occasion for the Feast of Fools. Margot Fassler has argued convincingly that the Beauvais office, and the Play of Daniel in the same manuscript, represent reformed versions of the feast.[69] Much of our information about the way the Feast of Fools was celebrated before it was reformed is gleaned from ecclesiastical legislation. The richest text on this subject from a musical point of view is the decree of 1198 by the Bishop of Paris, Odo of Sully.[70] The decree established a new *ordo* for the Circumcision in place of the Feast of Fools at Paris. It is significant that most of the provisions concern music; although ecclesiastical authorities generally deplored the diverse misbehaviour promoted by the Feast of Fools,

[66] Ibid., p. 176.

[67] Ibid., pp. 176–7.

[68] Ibid., p. 179.

[69] Margot Fassler, 'The Feast of Fools and *Danielis Ludus*: popular tradition in a medieval cathedral play', in Thomas Forrest Kelly, ed., *Plainsong in the Age of Polyphony*, Cambridge Studies in Performance Practice, 2 (Cambridge, 1992), pp. 85–6.

[70] For the text of the decree, see *PL* 212, cols 71–2.

Odo of Sully was especially concerned with the musical conduct of the services. The bells should sound in an orderly way; there could be no rhythmic poetry or impersonations; the lord of the feast could no longer be conducted between his house and the church in a procession with chant; all the canonical hours, and the Mass, should be celebrated in a solemn, orderly fashion. Odo's prescriptions for the music of the feast seem to acknowledge the elements that were usually ludic, and take charge of organizing them in a dignified but festive manner. He allowed for polyphonic performances of the responsories and the *Benedicamus Domino* of Vespers, of the third and sixth responsories of Matins, and of the gradual and Alleluia of the Mass. The cantor was in charge of the responsories of Matins, probably indicating that the subdeacons had previously been free to choose them, just as at Beauvais, the deacons, acolytes, and priests were free to perform Compline as they wished on their own feasts. The epistle at Mass could be farsed, meaning that its verses could be interspersed with interpolated material. Finally, the clergy and canons had to remain in their stalls throughout the feast, and the verse *Deposuit* of the Magnificat could be sung no more than five times. This last prescription is clearly a reference to ceremonies in which it was repeated innumerable times, as explicitly indicated in the ordinal from Beauvais for the Boy Bishop.[71]

The decree shows how central music was to the Feast of Fools. How would this music have sounded? The office of the Circumcision from Beauvais, preserved in an early thirteenth-century manuscript,[72] provides examples of all the genres amd styles associated with festive music of the Christmas octave: conductus, *Benedicamus Domino* songs, polyphony, triadic melodies, a farced epistle, Credo, and Pater Noster, and texts with phrases in the vernacular.

With the freedom inherent in a genre of newly-composed music set to rhythmical verse in a modern style, the conductus was particularly appropriate to the ludic function of the Feast of Fools. The Circumcision office from the cathedral of Sens, which is closely related to the office from Beauvais, includes several humorous examples. The 'conductus ad ludos' exhibits extensive and presumably comic repetitions. The 'conductus ad bacularium', indicating processional motion towards the subdeacon holding the cantor's rod, contains written-out

[71] Chevalier, *Ordinaire*, p. 72.

[72] BL, MS Egerton 2615, compiled between 1227 and 1234; see Arlt, *Festoffizium*, 2: 29.

laughter and reference to the 'poculum uitale'. The structures of the 'conductus ad poculum' and 'conductus ad subdiaconum' are full of playful repetition.[73]

The best known piece associated with a Circumcision office, the conductus *Orientis partibus* (also known as 'the prose of the ass') was used at Beauvais, Sens, and Bourges, appearing in the Beauvais Circumcision office both at First Vespers, and in polyphony at Mass.[74] At the beginning of First Vespers, *Orientis partibus* was sung while the ass is led into the church ('quando asinus adducitur'). With its simple musical structure, based on four short phrases of rhymed text, and its boisterous vernacular refrain ('hez, hez, sire asne, hez') it must have immediately established the jocular character of the feast, along with the entrance of the ass. *Orientis partibus* was used on other occasions as well and apparently continued in use long after the Middle Ages: according to a canon of Beauvais writing at the end of the seventeenth century, on the first day after the Octave of the three kings, a young girl rode an ass in procession from the cathedral to the church of St Stephen. *Orientis partibus* served as the sequence at Mass. The Introit, Kyrie, Gloria, Credo, and other chants ended in hee-haws, and the priest said 'hee-haw' three times to the people instead of 'Ite missa est'. In response, the people hee-hawed three times instead of singing *Deo gratias*.[75] In the Circumcision office, after the entrance of the ass, the first Vespers service continues with an abundance of lively rhythmic poetry. The usual antiphons and psalms are enhanced by the rubric that they begin 'cum falseto' (meaning with polyphony, or perhaps in falsetto).[76] Most of the pieces in the office that are not based on chant, but rather newly composed in the twelfth or thirteenth century, exhibit the same predominant musical style as *Orientis partibus*: syllabic settings, short rhyming lines, and symmetrical phrase structure. The London manuscript of the Circumcision Office also contains the Beauvais Play of Daniel. Margot Fassler's analysis of the play as a reformed Circumcision office has revealed musical references to *Orientis partibus* at key moments in the play; she argues that allusions

[73] The Sens office has been published as *Office de Pierre de Corbeil (Office de la Circoncision) improprement appelé 'Office des Fous'*, ed. Henri Villetard, Bibliothèque musicologique, 4 (Paris, 1907). The conductus described here are on pp. 101 and 121–2.

[74] Edited in Arlt, *Festoffizium*, 1: 3, 104.

[75] Henry Copley Greene, 'The song of the ass *Orientibus partibus*, with special reference to Egerton MS. 2615', *Speculum*, 6 (1931), pp. 534–49, esp. p. 534.

[76] Arlt, *Festoffizium*, 1: 113.

to the Circumcision office reinforce the identification of the Babylonians in the play with the subdeacons of Beauvais Cathedral.[77]

The controlled subversion of the liturgy in the Beauvais Circumcision office and the *Ludus Danielis* transformed the Feast of Fools into a new type of liturgical art: *ordines* created by reformers. If we view the clerical festivities as the transformation of work into play, we can better understand that some of the efforts of Church authorities did not abolish the celebrations altogether, but instead modified them by endowing them with an orderly structure. Thus were the notorious abuses of the Feast of Fools and the Octave of Christmas made spiritually useful.

Columbia University

77 Fassler, 'Feast of Fools', pp. 89–92.

APPENDIX

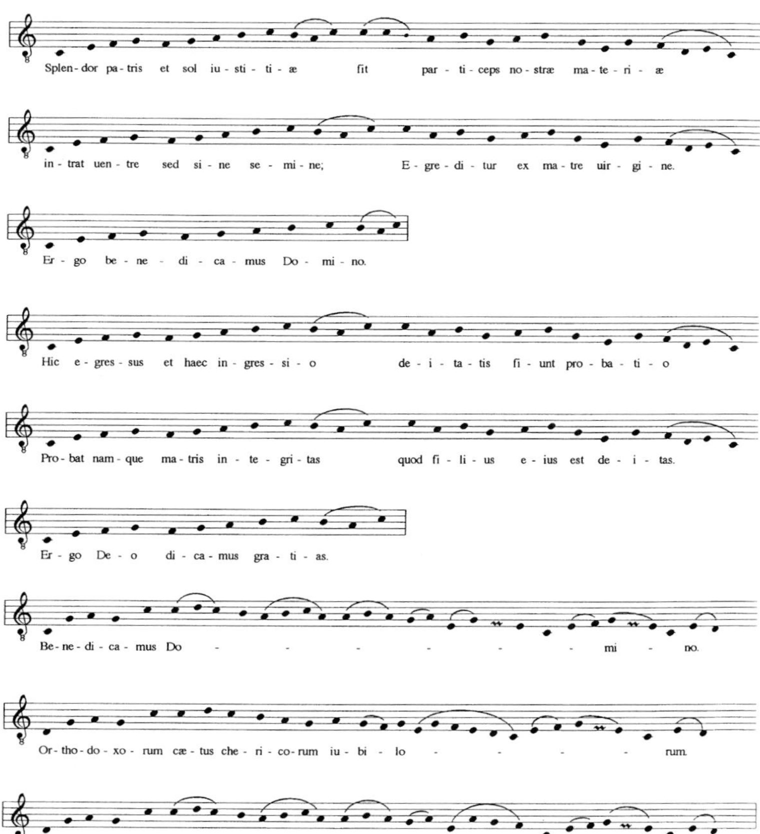
Splen- dor pa- tris et sol iu - sti - ti - æ fit par - ti - ceps no - stræ ma - te - ri - æ
in - trat uen - tre sed si - ne se - mi - ne; E - gre - di - tur ex ma - tre uir - gi - ne.
Er - go be - ne - di - ca - mus Do - mi - no.
Hic e - gres - sus et haec in - gres - si - o de - i - ta - tis fi - unt pro - ba - ti - o
Pro - bat nam - que ma - tris in - te - gri - tas quod fi - li - us e - ius est de - i - tas.
Er - go De - o di - ca - mus gra - ti - as.
Be - ne - di - ca - mus Do - - - - - - mi - no.
Or - tho - do - xo - rum cæ - tus che - ri - co - rum iu - bi - lo - - - - rum.
De - o di - ca - mus gra - - - - - - ti - as.

BY THE LABOUR OF THEIR HANDS? RELIGIOUS WORK AND CITY LIFE IN THIRTEENTH-CENTURY ITALY

by FRANCES ANDREWS

IN his *Historia occidentalis*, written in the 1220s after wide travels and varied experience, the Augustinian canon, bishop, and finally cardinal, Jacques de Vitry, described the recent and contemporary history of the West and in particular the many orders of both regular and secular persons in the Church, some of whom he had encountered in his journeying. He covered monks, canons, and secular religious, and it is an extensive list, including the Cistercians (male and female), the Carthusians, the Grandmontines, various hospital Orders, and new Orders such as the Valiscaulians, Trinitarians, Friars minor, Friars preacher, and the Humiliati of northern Italy. His text outlines the activities of the religious in these communities, giving us some sense of how such religious used their time. Manual labour was a long-established part of the regular life, and he naturally and frequently refers to it, the 'labour of their hands' of my title. Thus, according to Vitry, after daily chapter the Cistercians spent the rest of the day in manual labour, reading, and prayer; while the Valiscaulians had gardens, herbs, and orchards within their enclosure to which they went at set times 'so that they might eat by the labour of their hands', a direct allusion to Psalm 127.2: 'Thou shalt eat the labour of thine hands: happy shalt thou be and it shall be well with thee.'[1] Premonstratensian canons likewise went out at fixed times 'ad labores manuum', and he describes the Humiliati as keeping sluggishness at bay by assiduous reading, prayer, and manual labour, by which they lived for the most part ('ex magna parte'). By contrast, the canons of Bologna (as he calls the early Friars preacher or Dominicans) spent their days listening to Scripture, preaching, and working to save the souls of sinners from the jaws of the Leviathan (Job 40.20) through learning, so that they might 'shine like perpetual stars in eternity'.[2]

[1] On the Valiscaulians, or Order of Val-des-Choux, see *Dizionario degli istituti di perfezione*, 9 (Rome, 1997), s.v.

[2] *The 'Historia Occidentalis' of Jacques de Vitry: a Critical Edition*, ed. J. F. Hinnebusch (Freibourg, 1972), pp. 112, 120, 133, 144–5.

There is no reference to manual work in his accounts of either the Friars preacher or the Friars minor, the two great new Orders of the thirteenth century.

Vitry's *Historia* has an idealistic quality, but it is an informed view and serves as a snapshot of the different solutions chosen by regular communities in response to the biblical and patristic requirement for manual labour, as well as the pragmatic need to support and feed a community. The role of manual labour in the regular religious life enjoyed a long and occasionally controversial history but the essential elements may be summarized by reference to three of the key texts, the authorities around which the regular religious life constructed the role of physical labour.[3] The fundamental document is of course the Bible, but this is not an unequivocal authority on the value of work since, to take only two of the texts most frequently cited in the Middle Ages, labour is described as a punishment after the Fall in Genesis 3.16–19 while, as we have seen, in Psalm 127.2 living by the labour of one's hands is implicitly a source of happiness and well-being. Paul perhaps had these two texts in mind when he wrote to the Thessalonians, 'for if any would not work, neither should he eat.'[4]

These passages and others inform the writings of two of the most influential legislators for the regular life, saints Benedict and Francis, here chosen as a shorthand guide to a long and complex history. Chapter 48 of the Benedictine rule famously ordains that the monks shall do manual labour: 'Idleness is the enemy of the soul, and therefore the brethren should occupy some time with manual labour, other hours with divine reading.' Later in the same chapter this requirement for manual labour is further explained: 'for then they are true monks if they live by the labour of their hands, just like

[3] For further detail see, for example, J. Dubois, 'Le Travail des moines au moyen âge', in J. Hamesse and C. Muraille-Samaran, eds, *Le Travail au moyen âge. Une approche interdisciplinaire* (Louvain-la-neuve, 1990), pp. 61–100; G. Ovitt, 'Manual labor in early monastic rules', *Viator*, 17 (1986), pp. 1–18; idem, 'The cultural context of western technology: early Christian attitudes toward manual labour', in A. J. Frantzen and D. Moffat, eds, *The Work of Work: Servitude, Slavery, and Labour in Medieval England* (Glasgow, 1994), pp. 71–94 (originally in *Technology and Culture*, 27 [1986], pp. 471–500); idem, *The Restoration of Perfection: Labor and Technology in Medieval Culture* (New Brunswick, NJ, 1987).

[4] II Thess. 3.6–10. For more detailed discussion see P. De Leo, 'L'Esegesi medievale dell'immagine biblica del lavoro (Gen. III, 17–19; Lc. X. 7, 2 Thess. III, 10)', in *Lavorare nel medio evo: rappresentazioni ed esempi dell'Italia dei secc. x–xvi, 12–15 ottobre 1980*, Convegni del centro di studi sulla spiritualità medievale, Università degli studi di Perugia, 21 (Todi, 1983), pp. 219–55.

both the Fathers and the Apostles.'[5] Manual labour is thus a spiritual aid, a way to use time which, when combined with divine reading, will allow the monk to avoid danger to the soul. It is also a means to imitate patristic and apostolic models and an essential part of true monasticism.

Elsewhere, of course, the Benedictine rule acknowledges both that work may not always be attractive and that heavy manual labour may not be all that routine. The monks are explicitly warned not to be sad if necessity or poverty forces them to busy themselves in gathering produce.[6] The implication is evident: the realities of physical labour were usually to be left to others, a practice which was later to be institutionalized, for example by Cistercian or Carthusian use of *conversi*. On the other hand, to return one last time to Benedict, if a monk were already an artisan before entering the community, he may continue his craft with all humility (if the abbot allows).[7]

Our second authority is Francis, the model of evangelical perfection for the thirteenth century. Vitry does not describe the Friars minor undertaking manual labour and indeed Francis dedicated his life to preaching, working with his hands only intermittently, though enthusiastically, such as in the rebuilding of San Damiano and other churches in Assisi.[8] Franciscan legislation concerning work endorses and elaborates that of Benedict though it does not impose manual work indiscriminately. The *Regula non bullata* of 1221 required that 'the brethren who know how to work shall work and exercise a craft [*ars*] if they already know one as long as it is no obstacle to their spiritual progress and can be practised with honesty.'[9] The papally approved *Regula bullata* issued in 1223 established that

> those brothers to whom the Lord has given the grace to work, shall work faithfully and devotedly, in such manner that idleness, the soul's enemy, is kept at bay, that they extinguish not the spirit of holy prayer and devotion, to which other, temporal cares should be subjected. They shall accept as reward of their work, for

[5] *Benedicti Regula*, ed. R. Hanslik, Corpus scriptorum ecclesiasticorum latinorum, 75 (Vienna, 1960), ch. 48, pp. 114, 116.

[6] Ibid., p. 116.

[7] Ibid., ch. 57, p. 132.

[8] See Thomas of Celano, 'Vita Prima Sancti Francisci, Legendae S. Francisci', ed. Quaracchi Fathers, *Analecta Francescana*, 10 (1941), pp. 1–126.

[9] 'Regula non bullata', *Fontes Franciscani*, ed. E. Menestò and S. Brufani (Assisi, 1995), c.vii, pp. 191–2.

> themselves and their brothers, the body's needs, but never coins or money, and accept them humbly as befits God's servants and the followers of holiest poverty.[10]

Finally, in his *Testament*, Francis reminded his brethren that he himself had worked with his hands and had wished to work and that he wanted the friars to work at honest tasks. Those who did not know how to were to learn, not out of greed for the recompense, but so as to give an example and, once more, to keep idleness at bay. Only when they do not receive recompense for their work are they to turn to God's table, seeking alms from door to door.[11]

These texts do not give a full account of Franciscan approaches to work, but already we see that among the Friars minor, as with the Benedictines, those with a craft are to continue to exercise it. While work is advocated as a means to avoid danger to the soul and to feed the body, it is to be subordinate to holy prayer and devotion, undertaken in such a way as to avoid scandal, and it is not to be rewarded with money. It is also intended to provide an example to others. There is however one glaring (and long-acknowledged) difference between the Benedictines and the Franciscans: whereas Benedict accepted that the monks would have property to support them, Francis expects his brothers to live by the labour of their hands, or, if this fails, by begging from door to door.

Before turning to the question of what work religious actually did (the 'religious work' of my title) it is worth considering the meaning and value of *labor* undertaken in the secular world. The tripartite model of society devised by churchmen in the eleventh century of *oratores*, *bellatores*, and *laboratores* (those who pray, those who fight, and those who work) placed *laboratores* firmly at the bottom of the hierarchy, reflecting the humble and penitential status of *labor*. Jacques Le Goff and others have argued that pressure from an expanding artisan world and an increasingly mobile population created new pressures which led to a gradual acquisition of greater spiritual dignity for certain kinds of work.[12] This can be illustrated by reference to the enormously influential work of Peter the Chanter, a Paris theologian at the end of the twelfth century, and

[10] 'Regula bullata', *Fontes Franciscani*, c.v, pp. 175–6.

[11] 'Testamentum', *Fontes Franciscani*, p. 229.

[12] See for example J. Le Goff, 'Discours de clôture', in Hamesse and Muraille-Samaran, *Le Travail au moyen âge*, pp. 413–24.

his circle of students who were particularly concerned with practical morality. John Baldwin has written an authoritative study of their works which illustrates the type of arguments which might allow *labor* greater dignity. Bearing in mind the passage in Luke 10.7, 'The labourer is worthy of his hire', the Chanter argued, for example, that if a lawyer lacked regular income he could accept fees from his clients as remuneration in proportion to the labour expended in study and defence of the case. Likewise, canonists argued that an artisan who bought materials and improved their quality through additional expenses and labour could sell this merchandise at a higher price and this might be permitted even to clergy whose ecclesiastical income was insufficient.[13] By contrast, the usurer who lent money at interest was immoral because he profited without labour, making a livelihood even while sleeping.

This stark portrayal of the related issues of time and work cannot do justice to the complexity of the debate surrounding the value of work in the late twelfth and thirteenth centuries, and an equally fair translation of 'labor' in the examples given might be 'effort'. It is the effort expended in study and defence of the case which earns the lawyer his fee. It should also be noted that although the passage from Luke can be rendered in English as labourer ('the labourer is worthy of his hire'), in the Latin familiar to the Chanter and his circle, the word used is *operarius*: 'dignus sit operarius mercede sua', though the Chanter immediately links this to Genesis 3, that man should live by his own labour and sweat: 'ex labore et sudore suo'.

With these precautions in mind, let us return to the question of manual labour and the religious life. What did regular religious do in practice? Vitry gives us some idea: gardening or orchard work perhaps occasionally interspersed with going 'out' to the fields. This is close to the picture envisaged in the Rule of Benedict which mentions three main places where monks might work: the garden, the mill, and workshops. Later texts suggest a similar pattern. The twelfth-century *Ecclesiastica officia* of the Cistercians, for example, describes the distribution of tools and the departure of the monks to work, but it also reveals that monks apparently did not enthuse about manual labour: they had to be warned that they might not read during times of work (*tempore laboris*) and even that they were not to take a book with

[13] J. Baldwin, *Masters, Princes and Merchants. The Social Views of Peter the Chanter and his Circle*, 2 vols (Princeton, NJ, 1970), 1: 125, 263.

them.[14] The basic argument is I hope clear: manual labour was for monks a secondary affair, secondary to the work of their servants and labourers on their land, and secondary to their life of prayer, study, and devotion, the *vita contemplativa.* Indeed, as has frequently been demonstrated, for many monks work had been largely substituted by more intellectual tasks such as the copying of texts. In practice, the fact that monasteries were great landowners also meant that many, at least of the obedientiaries, spent their time managing their estates and defending their rights. One question nonetheless remains: does this picture change in any way with the new Orders of the thirteenth century? What did *labor* or *labor manuum* mean for the religious of thirteenth-century Italy; and if we can find the evidence, did this have any impact on those amongst whom they lived and worked? Can we detect any secular understanding of or interest in 'religious work'?

The evidence is not easy to find and further research in the archives will be necessary to provide a comprehensive picture. Moreover, although records kept by regular communities are notoriously strong survivors, it is difficult to find in them accounts of religious at work. This might be surprising if it were not that such records were preserved to document the things that those who kept them wished to remember or prove: land ownership, dispute settlements, the names of the dead and members of confraternal associations and patrons (there are many other types of information, but the point is clear, such sources tend not to record the routine activities of communities). Rules and other normative texts, as we have seen, do set down habitual activities which might include manual work, but such texts present their own pitfalls for the historian: what is the relationship between text and community, between norm and observance? (We all know individuals who see rules as there to be broken.)

Other types of record provide sporadic references to religious work. Last wills and testaments give occasional hints: in Padua in 1292 a testator's tomb was to be made by a Franciscan, Brother Clarello, who was perhaps a stone-cutter; and the same year saw the completion of a mosaic which portrayed some extraordinarily prominent mendicant artisan workers. In the (now much restored) apse mosaic of St John Lateran in Rome, Brother James of Camerino is shown with a mosaicist's hammer breaking tessera and the master of works is also

[14] *Les 'Ecclesiastica officia' cisterciens du xiie siècle*, ed. and tr. D. Choisselet and P. Vernet (Reiningue, 1989), p. 220.

represented as a Franciscan, whether or not this is Jacopo Torriti himself, as argued most recently by Valentino Pace.[15] Two Franciscans are thereby portrayed as artisans (as well as two craftsmen as artists), suggesting that it was acceptable to portray religious as humble manual workers in a place as conspicuous as the apse of the bishop of Rome's cathedral.

If we turn to the Humiliati of northern Italy, it is not difficult to broaden the range of evidence to show that some regular religious in the towns were involved in artisan work. The Humiliati encompassed three separate orders: the first Tertiaries as the third order, lay people living a life of devotion while remaining in the world; a second order of enclosed regulars living in houses which might accommodate both men and women in separate communities; and a 'first order' of men and women sharing the rule of the second order, but also observing the *ordo canonicus*.[16] The rule of the first and second orders allows for the brethren to work throughout the day, interrupting this rhythm only for the Office, chapter, meals, and an evening drink. Even at night work is permitted as an alternative to sleep or prayer.[17] Precisely what work they were doing is not always clear: evidence from Genoa and sporadic references to wool and to cloth from other cities implies that wool-working was their primary activity and certainly this was a tradition in the histories of the Order by the fifteenth century.[18] This has been widely accepted by modern historians,[19] but it should be remembered that the regular Humiliati were also traditional property owners, acquiring substantial lands, mills, and other property early in their history. Nonetheless, the emphasis on artisan work may perhaps be seen as a reflection of the artisan-based, mercantile economy in which they found themselves. Working as artisans echoes the

[15] V. Pace, 'Per Iacopo Torriti, frate architetto e "pictor"', *Mitteilungen des Kunsthistorischen Instituts in Florenz*, 40 (1996), pp. 212–21.

[16] For a general introduction see F. Andrews, *The Early Humiliati* (Cambridge, 1999).

[17] Ibid., pp. 115–16.

[18] See the Chronicle of John of Brera compiled in 1419, ed. G. Tiraboschi, *Vetera Humiliatorum monumenta*, 3 vols (Milan, 1766–8), 3: 229–86.

[19] See L. Zanoni, *Gli Umiliati nei loro rapporti con l'eresia, l'industria della lana ed i comuni nei secoli xii e xiii sulla scorta di documenti inediti* (Milan, 1911, reprinted Rome, 1971); R. Manselli, 'Gli umiliati, lavoratori di lana', in M. Spallanzani, ed., *Atti della seconda settimana di studio (10–16 aprile 1970): produzione, commercio e consumo dei panni di lana (nei secoli XII–XVIII)*, Pubblicazioni del istituto internazionale di storia economica F. Datini, Prato: ser. 2, Atti delle settimane di studi e altri convegni, 2 (Florence, 1976), pp. 231–6; L. Paolini, 'Le Umiliate al lavoro. Appunti fra storiografia e storia', *Bullettino dell'Istituto storico italiano per il medio evo e archivio muratoriano*, 97 (1991), pp. 229–65.

pragmatic idea of both Benedictine and Franciscan legislators that those who had a craft should continue to exercise it on entering the regular life, as long as it would not cause scandal. This desire to exploit the skills of new recruits may also have lain behind other activities in which the Humiliati and other religious became involved.

An unexpectedly interesting category of sources for the activities of religious in the cities is to be found in the surviving statutes of city corporations. These are not easy sources to use.[20] The relationship between legislation and community is not always obvious or immediate. Each city government and the corporate bodies within them produced their own statutes, so that the group of people to whom such legislation applied is not always clear. Moreover, as Manlio Bellomo notes, 'recasting and updating the statutes was carried on at such a dizzying pace that proverbs sprang up: "Legge di Verona non dura da terza a nona".'[21] The great advantage of statutes, however, is that they are not primarily the product of ecclesiastical writers (though on issues such as heresy, churchmen might influence their content very substantially, as they did following the Great Devotion of 1233).[22] They may therefore help with trying to establish whether we can detect any secular understanding or interest in 'religious work'. On one hand statutes reveal the rhetoric of competing propaganda, with rubrics designed to restrict the autonomy of churchmen and religious communities both theoretically and in practice, for example by imposing taxation on all property. On the other, they show religious communities as the focus for alms-giving, and for the public ritual life of the city, as Vauchez and, more recently, Diana Webb have amply demonstrated.[23] From the statute-makers' point of view, religious communities were also part of the economic life of the city, users of water, contributors to city expenses such as wall-building, and also in need of workers. (A neat, if late, illustration of this last point is provided by the statutes of Arezzo for 1327, in which the podestà and his magistrates were required to ensure that all those taking the religious habit had first paid off all debts, notwithstanding any

[20] But for an introduction see M. Bellomo, *The Common Legal Past of Europe, 1000–1800*, tr. L. G. Cochrane (Washington, DC, 1995) and D. Webb, *Patrons and Defenders. The Saints in the Italian City-states* (London and New York, 1996), pp. 95–127.

[21] Bellomo, *Common Legal Past*, p. 85.

[22] On clerical rewriting of statutes see A. Thompson, *Revival Preachers and Politics in Thirteenth-Century Italy. The Great Devotion of 1233* (Oxford, 1992), pp. 179–204.

[23] A. Vauchez, *La Sainteté en occident aux derniers siècles du moyen âge d'après les procès de canonisation et les documents hagiographiques* (Rome, 1981); Webb, *Patrons and Defenders*.

privilege to the contrary. If any should try to resist, no person from the city or contado of Arezzo might work their land or possessions on pain of a ten lire fine.)[24] For the question of work by religious themselves, however, statutes are particularly interesting when they turn to the question of public officialdom. The statutes of the city of Novara of 1277 ordain that the office of *canevarius* is to be held either by two Friars minor *boni et legales* ('good and lawful') or by two of the best ('ex melioribus') of the brethren of either Sta Marta, SS. Simone e Giuda, S. Elena or Sta Croce (at least three of which were Humiliati communities) with the proviso that those chosen are always to be from a house or from the same house ('et sint semper de una domo'), which I take to mean that they must be regulars.[25] The rubric describes their task as keeping and administering the key documents and accounts of the commune and making a copy to be shown to the podestà or other officials when needed (and without charge). They are also to receive and pay all monies owed to or by the commune and to write it all down in order. For this they are to be paid twenty-five lire per year, 'pro eorum salario et labore' – which can reasonably be translated as 'as their salary and for their labour'. This is not an isolated instance: twenty-one years earlier, in 1256, the statutes of the city of Alessandria ordained that the *clavarius* (literally the key holder or treasurer) of the commune of Alessandria should be 'a *Humiliatus* of the Order of the Humiliati'. This *clavarius* was to be chosen by the provost of the Humiliati and to remain in office for the same length of time as the other officials of Alessandria, always changing when the other officials changed. As in Novara, he must always be chosen from among those brethren who live in a house ('qui morantur in domibus') and who know how to write, and must write all his accounts himself or have a notary according to the wish of the general council. The same requirement is again made that all monies of the commune from whatever source must pass through his hands, and that the *clavarius* must keep a book of the receipts and a book of expenses, correctly recording the details of each. The rubric closes with the instruction that the said *clavarius* is to be 'subject to the *arbitrium* of the podestà, like the other officials of the commune, at the bell-tower or communal palace, to carry out this office; and there at the said bell-tower, he shall

24 *Statuto di Arezzo (1327)*, ed. G.M. Camerani, Fonti di storia Aretina, 1 (Florence, 1946), p. 160.

25 *Statuta communitatis Novariae anno mcclxxvii lata*, ed. A. Ceruti (Novara, 1879), p. 15.

have a chest in which to keep the books . . . and he shall have 23 *denarii* per day for his salary.'[26] In Cremona, still earlier surviving account records enable us to illustrate the kind of work involved in such book-keeping in more detail: on Wednesday, 11 October 1234, two *massarii* of the commune paid out money to various officials, including Guglielmo de Barbata, *humiliatus*, the *massarius* (supervisor) of the mills.[27] By 1239, according to a fragment of the statutes of the city and militia of Cremona copied in the fifteenth century, the role of such regular religious had expanded in new directions: a *massarius* was to follow the army or cavalcade of the commune and this was to be a *Humiliatus*, accompanied by a notary, *bono et leali*, chosen by the Orders of the Franciscans, Dominicans, and Humiliati, and the two men were to have a horse each and sixteen *denarii* per day.[28]

The special position of the Humiliati here, and their relationship with the Friars minor and preacher, requires some comment; but first it may be helpful to look at the will of Homobono Morixius, drawn up in 1259, with a codicil of 1261, which will help to illustrate the point. Homobono had been an itinerant teacher of law in Mantua, Vercelli, Padua, Turin, and Reggio Emilia, and left his books to the Friars preacher of his home town of Cremona to be sold to purchase a Bible in his memory. He also left a substantial estate, with houses, arable land, meadows, trees, and various equipment, to the house of San Cataldo of the Humiliati in Cremona. From the revenues on the estate the Humiliati are to give alms of bread and wine each Sunday to the Friars preacher, Friars minor, and Sisters minor (Franciscan women), slightly less to the Eremitani (the Austin hermit friars), and other amounts to various hospitals and groups of religious women. The Friars preacher and the guardian of the Friars minor are to provide advice about what to do should there be more to distribute amongst the poor, and the Friars preacher are given particular instructions to ensure that all this is carried out, and should they in turn neglect their duty the Eremitani are to replace them. Various masses are to be said for the soul of Homobono and his mother and father, and whenever the Humiliati, their minister, or the Friars preacher give alms from his revenues they are to say to the recipient, 'these alms are given for the soul of Homobono de Morixius from his property', and the recipient is

[26] Statutes of Alessandria, cited by Zanoni, *Gli Umiliati*, pp. 221–2, n.1.

[27] *Codex diplomaticus Cremonae 715–1334*, ed. L. Astegiano, 2 vols (Turin, 1896), 1: 266.

[28] Ibid., 1: 272.

to say the Our Father for his soul. In the codicil, dated 31 August 1261, Homobono adds a yearly gift of wheat and wine for the Humiliati 'pro labore et remuneratione sua' – for their work and remuneration.[29]

There are two points which need to be highlighted here. The first is the relationship between the Humiliati and the other Orders mentioned: the Humiliati are entrusted with the administration of property, but their activities are to be monitored by the Dominicans or the Eremitani. The Cremona statute concerning the activities of *massarii* had reflected a similar pattern: a *Humiliatus* was to travel with the army, but the individual was to be chosen by a combination of the Humiliati and the Friars minor and preacher. Secondly, the distribution of alms and the administration that this will necessitate can be described as *labor* – just as the office of *canevarius* in Novara involved *labor*. The idea that such administrative tasks are *labor* and should be paid is fairly clear. Before leaving Cremona, we should note that by 1271 the *massarii* (the treasurers) of the commune itself were brothers Monachus and Nicholas 'of the Order of the Humiliati of San Guglielmo of Cremona', and that members of the Order recur as *massarii* with varying responsibilities in 1281, 1283, 1284, 1286, 1287 and 1290. In the 1320s we still find a brother Job, of the Order of the Humiliati, described as *massarius* of the commune and gabelles.[30] A similar pattern of office-holding over a period of years by Humiliati can equally be demonstrated in Parma, while in Verona in the 1320s one of the two *massarii* or treasurers of the commune (who must both be Humiliati) was required to stay at work continuously day and night so as to do the business fully.[31]

The involvement of religious of whatever Order in the activities of secular government and administration did not go unresisted by ecclesiastical authority. Already in 1232, Goffredus, cardinal priest of San Marco and apostolic legate in northern Italy, had instructed the podestà and commune of Pavia not to force the Humiliati to hold office, and similar restrictions were issued by Innocent IV in 1247 for the whole Order in Lombardia.[32] By 1251 Innocent was writing to the Archbishop of Milan instructing him to prevent the podestà and

29 Ibid., 1: 305–10.

30 Ibid., 2: 193, 198–200, 209.

31 *Liber iurium communis Parme*, ed. G. La Ferla Morsia (Parma, 1993), nos 11, 18–20, 28–30, 33–6, 41, 102–4; *Statuti di Verona del 1327*, ed. S.A. Bianchi and R. Granuzzo (Rome, 1992), p. 169.

32 Andrews, *Early Humiliati*, app. 1, nos. *40, 66.

commune of Milan from forcing the Humiliati of the first and second orders to carry out public or communal offices and other duties detrimental to church liberty.[33] In 1252 the same prohibition was issued in a letter to the Bishop of Novara sent in response to a petition from the Humiliati of the second order in Milan; and again in December 1253, in response to a petition from the Master, provosts, prelates, and brothers of the first and second orders of the Humiliati in Milan, the Pope authorized the Master of the Order to ensure that the Humiliati were no longer required to undertake the affairs of the commune ('comuni negotia'), or to collect tolls.[34] It is worth noting that these restrictions focus increasingly on the first and second orders. Although perhaps undesirable, such office-holding was not considered so inappropriate for members of the third order who had not withdrawn from the world, and indeed, the same point was in practice acknowledged in the constitutions of the Order of Penance. The statutes of the *popolo* of Bologna issued in the 1280s and 1290s required members of the Order of Penance to take responsibility for overseeing the building of bridges and other works undertaken at the expense of the commune and even, in one case, to supervise the straightening and widening of a street, which required the demolition of buildings and compensation of owners.[35] Yet the ordinances of the general chapter of the Order of Penance held in Bologna in 1289 are distinctly half-hearted in their resistance:

> no brother of penance can or should receive or work [*operari*] in any public office in any city or place. If however they should be elected to an office . . . they may take it with a dispensation from their minister and according to the wish of the majority of the brethren of the city or place in which they have been elected.[36]

In the same city (as in many others) the Eremitani and the Friars minor were required to act as scrutineers at elections and to undertake various tasks for the public good and 'out of love and understanding of the popolo of Bologna' ('amore et intuitu popoli Bononie').

[33] Andrews, *Early Humiliati*, app. 1, no 95.

[34] Ibid., nos 98, 102.

[35] *Statuti di Bologna dell'anno 1288*, ed. G. Fasoli and P. Sella, 2 vols, *Studi e Testi*, 73, 85 (Vatican City, 1937–9), e.g. 1: 48, 2: 158, 161.

[36] 'Ordinazioni del capitolo generale di Bologna, 14 Nov. 1289', from 'Il manuale dei penitenti de Brescia', ed. G. G. Meersseman, *Ordo fraternitatis. Confraternite e pietà dei laici nel medioevo*, 3 vols, Italia Sacra, 24–6 (Rome 1977), 1: 446–8.

So what is to be made of this? The evidence presented here is preliminary and fragmentary and much more work needs to be done on both the language of work and the sources available. The categories are sometimes confused, occasionally the sources are paradoxical, and much of the evidence concerns tertiaries not regulars.[37] This line of enquiry may nonetheless bring further information about the way the activities of religious interacted with the cities in which they found themselves, and in the process may show how work by religious might be part of the expansion of activities which could be termed *labor*. One thing, however, is already clear: to the statute writers of Novara and elsewhere, calling on the skills and probity of the religious in their towns was an appropriate use, not an abuse, of their time and *labor*.

University of St Andrews

[37] But for other evidence concerning regulars see R. C. Trexler, 'Honor among thieves. The trust function of the urban clergy in the Florentine republic', in S. Bertelli and G. Ramakus, eds, *Essays presented to Myron P. Gilmore*, 2 vols, Villa I Tatti, 2 (Florence, 1978), 1: 317–34.

FIT TO PREACH AND PRAY: CONSIDERATIONS OF OCCUPATIONAL HEALTH IN THE MENDICANT ORDERS

by ANGELA MONTFORD

FOLLOWING their foundation in the thirteenth century, the mendicant Orders came to occupy an increasingly important role in the religious life of the medieval city. The mendicant spiritual mission and way of life was arduous, and the prayer and preaching which filled (or ought to have filled) a friar's working and waking hours demanded both strength and stamina. As a result of these demands, the leaders of the Orders had to ensure that those men whom they admitted as their brothers were physically capable of undertaking their intended duties. This paper accordingly considers the idea of the 'use and abuse of time' by approaching some of the questions concerning health and fitness as requirements for the friars of the Franciscan and Dominican Orders.

The issue was raised concisely in a Franciscan statute from the French province in 1337: 'Novices must publicly acknowledge and witness that they are not concealing any latent illness they have, otherwise the Order shall not have any obligation to them.'[1] Any such illness would make them not only unsuited to the life of a friar but would also involve the Order in physical care and expense for advice and medical treatment if required. Sickness, or any bodily weakness which in other circumstances might be considered a blessing and spiritual benefit, here becomes something to be avoided, a practical inconvenience which, by affecting a friar's ability to pursue his vocation, wasted money and resources that could be better used in other ways. One of these resources was time, the hours, days, and years of a friar's life which were intended to be usefully devoted to the performance of God's work.

In his text of advice to the friars of the Order of Preachers, Humbert of Romans (Master-general of the Order 1257–63) indicated the benefits of health for those following the Dominican way of life:

[1] Michael Bihl, 'Statuta provincialia provinciae Aquitainiae et Franciae', *Archivum Franciscanum Historicum* [hereafter *AFH*], 7 (1914), p. 485.

> It is . . . useful to the preacher to be strong in body so that he can stay up late at night studying, speak loudly when he is preaching, endure the labours of travelling and the poverty of not having the things he needs and many other hardships.[2]

Elsewhere he wrote:

> the Preacher needs a strong constitution like a woman in childbirth because both suffer from great bodily hardships, numerous privations and much anxiety.[3]

The ascetic and mendicant lifestyle undertaken by the friars had put particular demands on the individual's stamina and strength, especially in the early years of the Orders' existence when food might be meagre and housing rudimentary. The Franciscan convent member sent to a provincial chapter in the thirteenth century had to be able to walk six leagues in a day, somewhere in the region of eighteen miles.[4] Friars might spend months or years in inhospitable climates, becoming weak from hunger, ill from dysentery, depressed, lonely, or crippled with frost bite.[5] Rising from one's bed to sing the night office was physically exhausting and could damage the health, as noted by both Humbert and the Franciscan chronicler Salimbene de Adam of Parma (1221–88).[6] Chroniclers of the Orders made frequent reference to friars with weak health who could not go to study abroad, sufferers from recurrent fevers, those weak in mind or body who required medical treatment, and those who had to relinquish their posts of authority because of illness.[7]

[2] Humbert of Romans, 'De eruditione praedicatorum', in his *Opera de vita regularis*, ed. J. J. Berthier, 2 vols (Rome, 1888–9; reprinted Turin, 1956), 2: 373–484.

[3] Ibid., 2: 431.

[4] A. G. Little, 'Statuta provincialia provinciae Franciae et Marche Tervesinae', *AFH*, 7 (1914), p. 453, also cited in A. G. Little, 'The constitution of provincial chapters in the Minorite order', in A. G. Little and F. M. Powicke, eds, *Essays in Mediaeval History presented to Thomas Frederick Tout* (Manchester, 1925), p. 252. This rule had been dropped by 1337.

[5] 'Et cum ad dimidium miliare processissent, ceperunt oculi deficere, crura thabascere et genua infirmari a ieunio et toto debilitare corpore': *Chronica Fratris Jordani* [OFM], ed. H. Boehmer (Paris, 1908), p. 26. See also Thomas of Eccleston, *De adventu fratrum minorum in Anglia*, ed. J. S. Brewer in *Monumenta Franciscana*, 2 vols, *RS* (London, 1858), 1: 82.

[6] Humbert of Romans, *Opera*, 2: 85; Salimbene de Adam, *Cronica*, ed. G. Scalia, 2 vols, *CChr.CM*, 125, 125A (Turnhout, 1998–9), 43 (1: 45).

[7] Richard of Devon, OFM, who suffered from frequent quartan fevers; Richard Rufus of Cornwall, OFM, who was commanded to go to Paris as a lector in 1250 but obtained leave to continue his studies at Oxford owing to his weak health: Brewer, *Monumenta*, 1: 6, 330. In 1250 Stephen of Auvergne, OP, prior provincial of Provence, had to resign after being seriously hurt whilst travelling: *Acta capitulorum provincialium ordinis fratrum praedicatorum:*

The concerns for health and strength may also have been linked to the need to take other friars from their own work in order to care for invalids or to replace them at their duties.[8] Problems could be especially acute when illness struck while the friars were travelling, affecting not only the sick friar himself but his *socius* as well. On the journey home to Oxford from Lyons where they had been at the General Council in 1245, the Franciscan Adam Marsh's companion, John of Stamford, was taken ill. Following the instruction of the Rule that sick friars were not be left unless satisfactory arrangements had been made for their care,[9] Adam was duty-bound to look after his colleague. When the travellers were half-way home, as Robert Grosseteste wrote to Adam's prior provincial,

> Brother John became much weaker and Brother Adam found it impossible to take him farther or to leave him alone. Both of them have therefore remained at Mantes and I earnestly entreat you to send Brother Peter of Tewkesbury with some other friars who can stop with Brother John while Peter himself returns with Adam.[10]

It may have been inconveniences such as these which prompted the chapters to monitor the health of their candidates for admission. The sick, as Humbert pointed out, were of no use to the community, unable to perform the work expected of them, especially that most important duty of the friars, preaching for the salvation of souls.[11]

Première province de Provence, Province Romaine, Province d'Espagne, ed. C. Douais (Toulouse, 1894), p. 5, n.2.

[8] 'Ubi tamen infirmitas vel debilitas aut labor itineris seu administrationis aliud suas erit faciendum possint se a communi vita conventus, infirmi quidem et debiles quamdiu infirmitas et debilitas duraverit alio vero itineris seu administrationis laboribus fatigati diebus aliquibus separare et in aliquo congruo et honesto loco refici moderate a superfluius et excessivis expensis penitus praecavendo': Michael Bihl, 'Ordinationes Benedicti XII pro fratribus minoribus promulgatae per bullam 28 Novembris 1336, *Redemptor nostri*', *AFH*, 30 (1937), p. 339.

[9] 'If a friars falls ill, no matter where he is, the others may not leave him, unless someone had been appointed to look after him as they would like to be looked after themselves': Rule of 1221, in *St. Francis of Assisi: Writings and Early Biographies*, ed. Marion A. Habig (Chicago, 1972), p. 60.

[10] A. G. Little, 'The Franciscan School at Oxford', *AFH*, 19 (1926), p. 835.

[11] 'recuperata sanitate possit in aliquo utilis esse communitati, quod non possit esse durante infirmitate': Humbert of Romans, *Opera*, 1: 389. 'Notandum est autem quod studium non est finis ordinis, sed summe necessarium est ad fines praedictos, scilicet ad predicationes et animarum salutem operandam quia sine studio neutrum possemus. . . . Studium est ordinatum ad praedicatio ad animarum salutis quia est ultima finis': 'Expositiones super constitutiones', ibid., 2: 28.

How were medical problems identified and which ones were to be eliminated?

A panel of three Dominican friars made enquiries about the health, character, legitimacy, and education of candidates for admission and their evidence was then presented to the chapter for approval. One of the questions asked in the original Constitutions was whether the postulant had any hidden illness or physical weakness ('occultam habeat infirmitatem').[12] The earliest concerns about the admission into the religious life of those with less-than-perfect physical health were based on the text in Leviticus 21.17 which forbade service in the priesthood to those with a bodily defect: 'Whoever he be . . . that hath any blemish let him not approach to offer the bread of his God.' The sanctuary of the altar was profaned by the presence of the blind, the lame, the hunchback or the dwarf, those with broken limbs, deformity, or skin disease. The canonical prohibitions were of particular relevance to the Dominicans as priests and to the increasing numbers of Franciscans who chose, or were chosen, to be ordained, and some mechanism was required to identify these physical defects.

Genital mutilation was a particular bar to the priesthood and considered so seriously by Old Testament authors that someone so afflicted was forbidden to join the Church congregation.[13] In 325 the Council of Nicaea had recommended examination, physical or merely in the form of questioning, in order to establish proof of the presence of such mutilation in a candidate, because if it had been inflicted by others such as a surgeon, or an enemy, or one's lord, the ban on entering the priesthood might be lifted.[14] Some kind of examination certainly took place and exclusion was not automatic.

In a letter to one of his bishops, Pope Innocent I (402–17) had ruled that self-inflicted mutilation of any part of the fingers should also be a bar to ordination,[15] but Alexander III (1159–81) had permitted the ordination of a man who had lost only a part of a finger in a duel, as long as it did not interfere with the celebration of the mass.[16] A man

[12] *The Constitution of the Dominican Order, 1216 to 1360*, ed. G. R. Galbraith (Manchester, 1925), pp. 214–15.

[13] Deut. 23.1.

[14] D 55 cc.7–10: *CIC*, 1, cols 216–17.

[15] D 55 c.6: *CIC*, 1, col. 216.

[16] X 1.20.1: *CIC*, 2, col. 144.

with a missing eye could not become a priest.[17] A candidate who developed a defect of his eye ('maculam habens in oculo') was to have an eye test ('examini visum fuerit') and was permitted to be raised to the episcopate if he was not greatly deformed by his affliction.[18] In addition to the problems of genital mutilation, it was visible deformity which was particularly relevant and which any examination was primarily intended to disclose.

The mendicant Orders were obliged to consider these afflictions in new candidates and Humbert of Romans explained the problems caused by such deformity or absence which was likely to bring the office of priest into disrepute. 'People who are disfigured in this way are debarred from the Lord's service in Leviticus [21.17] and similarly the Church has banned them from public office for fear of popular scandal and ridicule.'[19] It was not possible or appropriate for a priest to undertake his duties if physical integrity was compromised. It was not only the profaning of the altar but also the honour due to the sacraments and the reputation of the Church and its priests which was at stake. The anxiety felt about the possibility that the Eucharist might be shown some disrespect by clumsy hands spilling the wine or mishandling the bread appears in several sources.[20] This may be compared with a ruling by Honorius III (1216–27) concerning the monk Thomas St Amand of Brescia who, when he was a boy, had his thumb permanently damaged by an iron bar falling on it. He was permitted to enter the priesthood as long as he was not prevented by the deformity from breaking the host ('frangendum eucharistiam').[21] For some, admission to the priesthood was not always an attractive option and the late-fourteenth-century writings of Bartholomew of Pisa contained a story of the Franciscan Thomas of Ireland who was so

[17] D 55 c.13: *CIC*, 1, cols 218–19.

[18] X 1.20.2: *CIC*, 2, cols 144–5.

[19] 'Non debet habere aliquam, nec multa notabilem, et apparentem deformitatem corporalem; sicut enim huiusmodo corpore vitiati. removento a ministerio Domini ut patet Lev. 21; 17': Humbert of Romans, *Opera*, 2: 406.

[20] 'Volo vos admonere religionis exemplis; nostis qui divinis mysteriis interesse consuestis, quomodo, cum suscipitis corpus Domini cum omne cautela et veneratione servatis. ne ex eo parum quid decidat ne consecrate muneris aliquid dilbatur': *Origène, Homélies sur l'Exode*, ed. Marcel Borret, SC, 321 (Paris, 1985), XIII.iii (p.386).

[21] 'Thomas monachus sancti Amantii de Brixia proposuit coram nobis, quod, quum in annis puerilibus esset constitutus, quaedem barra ferrea super dextrae suae pollicem fortuito casu cadens, ungulam avulsit ab eo . . . si ad frangendum eucharistiam sit in pollice ipso potens . . . propter deformitatem huiusmodi non dimittas': X 1.20.7: *CIC*, 2, col. 146.

anxious not to become a priest that he amputated his own thumb, hoping to remain unordained in the interests of humility and making his hands unsuitable to offer the host.[22]

In accordance with the canonical prohibitions on obvious skin disease which would also bring the priesthood into disrepute, signs of leprosy would no doubt have been looked for in new candidates. Evidence that friars were also excluded because of serious skin disease is given in the story of the Franciscan who was cured at the shrine of St Francis of blisters and swellings of his skin before he was able to join the Order.[23] There are indications in the Dominican Constitutions that they, like some of the monastic Orders before them, were willing to look after some of their own friars who developed leprosy, although they lived separately from the rest of the brothers.[24] It was only if the demands of the convent's work became too great that leper friars were sent elsewhere. The early stages of leprosy would not involve any serious accompanying deformity such as bone loss from the hands or face and would not therefore necessarily be a bar to admission. The Franciscans too appear to have been willing to accommodate some leprous friars, and it may have been the development of the disease after profession which allowed such friars to stay in the Order.[25]

The difficulty in establishing the presence of less obvious medical problems by questioning alone is indicated in Bonaventure's *Major Life* of St Francis, which referred to a young man, James of Iseo, who as a boy had developed a hernia. He was later inspired by the Holy Spirit to join the Friars minor, which he did, but 'never told anyone about his injury',[26] suggesting that he might not have been permitted to enter if he had confessed to such an incapacity. Salimbene, describing the illness in rather more robust terms than Bonaventure, suggested that the youth's inguinal area and genitalia had been 'totally

[22] Bartholomew of Pisa, 'Liber de conformitate', in *Analecta Franciscana*, 12 vols (Quaracchi, 1885–1983), 4: 290.

[23] 'infirmitae vesicae gravatus et tumefactus': 'Chronica aliaque varia documenta', in *Analecta Franciscana*, 4: 253.

[24] 'Fratres leprosi infra scepta sui conventus seorsum ab aliis procurentur. Quod si altitudo illius loci vel alia causa legitima non permiserit per priorem provincialem ad conventum alium nostri ordinis transferentur': Galbraith, *Constitution*, p. 211. The interpretation of *fratres leprosi* is problematical and may refer to the sick in general rather than the leprous.

[25] Bihl, 'Statuta Aquitaniae et Franciae', p. 500.

[26] Bonaventure, 'Major Life of St. Francis', in Habig, *St. Francis of Assisi*, p. 776.

destroyed',[27] which would link James's particular problem to the ruling of canon law on genital mutilation. We are not told whether the young man was explicitly asked about his health as was usual at admission and it would seem that actual physical examination did not take place in this instance or his problem would have been discovered. Was this concern for discovering hidden deformity linked to the concept that the imperfect body reflected the imperfect soul? A candidate who was so deficient in virtue that he concealed what should have been declared might have been put forward as a moral exemplum, showing his unsuitability for the life of a friar. But the topos of illness, subsequent recovery, and later sanctity was popular and, in the case of James of Iseo, despite the apparent deception over his admission, he was subsequently cured by a miracle and went on to perform wonders of his own.[28]

Several Dominican and Franciscan accounts tell of those who applied to join the Orders but were rejected because of particular illnesses. Reginald of Orleans (d.1220), gravely ill with a fever, joined the Order of Preachers only after receiving a miraculous cure through the prayers of the founder, Dominic.[29] The Franciscan candidate Gunther of Brabantia (*c.* 1248) was certain that the disease which he suffered in his leg would disqualify him from entry, but was cured after a vision of St Francis.[30] Swellings such as those of the neck glands in scrofula and other similar afflictions would be visible to cursory inspection; these diseases were also classified as 'deformities' and as such could be a reason for refusing entry. Some time before 1240 an anonymous sick man had his application to join the Franciscan Order rejected after an interview with the Minister because of a scrofulous tumour in his neck. Its identification as a 'deformity' linked the disease to canon law prohibitions. Because of it the candidate was not suitable to do the work of a friar but was advised that the performance of secular good works would be an alternative and health-giving occupation. After following this advice he was rewarded by a vision in which he was persuaded to reapply for entry and the sudden recovery of his health was given to him as a sign. The

[27] 'frater Jacobus de Yseo, qui in locis inguinaribus et membris genitalibus totaliter erat confractus': Salimbene, *Cronica*, 96 (1: 99).

[28] Ibid.

[29] Jordan of Saxony, *Libellus de principiis ordinis praedicatorum*, ed. H. C. Scheeben, Monumenta ordinis fratrum praedicatorum historica, 20 (Rome, 1941), no. 56.

[30] 'Chronica XXIV generalium ordinis minorum', in *Analecta Franciscana*, 3: 241.

chronicler went on to remark that it was God's will that friars should be able to undertake the labours required of them and to be able to travel long distances.[31] Although there was no mention that the imperfection was the result of sin, this and other exempla give some indication of the importance of health as an attribute for a friar and, by citing the miraculous removal of the deformity or illness which made a barrier to admission, its close association with the pursuit of a virtuous life.

While miraculous cures might be hoped for, more earth-bound measures were also taken with regard to health in order to follow the vocation of a friar. The emphasis in the mendicant constitutions on hidden illness may have been representative of the concern about concealed genital mutilation or may also have been intended to disclose those friars who suffered from the recurrently debilitating tertian and quartan fevers which are so much a part of any medieval medical history, episodic diseases such as epilepsy, or other unseen but incapacitating illnesses. The regulations of both Dominicans and Franciscans came to include more specific reference to the necessity for freedom from occult disease (which could not be seen), and latent illness (which had periods of inactivity), as well as from the external bodily defects or *corpore vitiati* laid down by canon law, not only to preserve the reputation and finances of the Order but also because of the effect that illness might have on the vocation of a friar and the useful employment of his time. The word of the candidate was usually sufficient to describe his state of health on admission, although the increasing use by the Orders of trained physicians for advice and medical counsel is testified to in this and other sources.[32] Medical men may also have been used to advise on admission if there were particular concerns but too frequent employment of outside physicians might harm the reputation of the Orders by possible contraventions of the vow of poverty. In instructions which echoed the Rule of St Benedict, Franciscan friars were encouraged by their Minister-general Bonaventure (1257–74) to limit their requests for special food, attentions, treatments, and medicine in illness.[33] Such diversion from the

[31] 'Chronica XXIV generalium ordinis minorum', in *Analecta Franciscana*, 3: 242.

[32] Account books from the convents of S. Domenico and S. Francesco at Bologna record payments made to physicians, surgeons, and apothecaries for medicines and treatment for their friars during the thirteenth and fourteenth centuries: Bologna, Archivio di Stato, S. Domenico, Demaniale 294/7574; Bologna, Biblioteca Comunale, MS B. 490–2.

[33] 'Ad patientam in infirmitate pertinet paucis obsequiis pauciisque remedie

convent's usual routine and the cost involved, at a time when rising living standards in the Orders still seemed to many to run counter to the demands of poverty, would make the ministers and diffinitors anxious to prevent such problems arising if they could.

Early Franciscan entrants had been admitted by the provincial minister who examined the candidate on his knowledge of the faith and the sacraments,[34] but physical standards were added later: amendments to the statutes in 1239 stated that if the candidate had any sickness which affected the quality of his body which would be burdensome to him, or he had any sort of incapacity in addition to mutilation, he could not be received.[35] The year's novitiate established for both Orders from 1254 would allow time for latent disease to become apparent,[36] and action was sometimes taken if diseases developed after admission. In the thirteenth century the Franciscan chronicler Salimbene wrote of the former soldier, Raymond Attanulfi of Hyères, who was once a Friar minor but during his novitiate was 'cast out of the Order' because he was ill.[37]

The discovery of previously undisclosed illness in a Franciscan friar could result in dismissal from the Order and the ministers placed the onus on the candidate to declare any possible incapacity. Franciscan brothers who became ill after admission were to be sent back to the place they had come from.[38] It is likely that this referred specifically to novices before profession such as Raymond Attanulfi, as the *Regula bullata* had instructed that once professed in the Order a friar could not leave. The Dominicans took a slightly different attitude. Humbert had advised that the regulations on such matters as illness, deformity, and

contentum esse, iuxta exigentium paupertatis': S. Bonaventure, 'Expositio super regulam fratrum minorum' in *Doctoris seraphici S. Bonaventurae, S.R.E Episcopi Cardinalis, opera omnia: ad plurimum codices mss. emendate, anecdotis aucta prolegomenis scholiis notisque illustrata, edita, studio et cura PP. Collegii a S. Bonaventura*, 11 vols in 10 (Quaracchi, 1882–1902), 8: 34.

[34] *Regula bullata* of 1223, in Habig, *St. Francis of Assisi*, p. 58.

[35] 'si infirmitate aliquem habeat vel praevam corporis qualitatem propter quam foret postea onerosus si membrum aliquod mutilatum habeat vel inefficax quoquomodo': Cesare Cenci, 'De fratrum minorum constitutionibus praenarbonensibus', *AFH*, 83 (1990), p. 76.

[36] 'Praedicationes et Minores infra annum probationis quemquam ad sui ordinis professionem recipere non possunt': VI 3.14.2 (*CIC*, 2, col. 1051).

[37] 'Raimundus Attanulfi . . . fuit miles in seculo et fuit in Ordine fratrum Minorum, sed in novitiatu fuit licentiatus et emissus de ordine quia infirmus erat': Salimbene, *Cronica*, 368 (1: 387–8).

[38] 'si aliquem fratrem post receptam obedientiam contigerit infirmari reputetur de loco ad quem erat iturus': Ferdinandus M. Delormé, 'Documenta saeculi XIV provinciae S. Francisci Umbriae', *AFH*, 5 (1912), p. 534.

illiteracy must be explained to a new candidate and evidence looked for by those admitting him. If such defects, which should have been identified on admission, were discovered later the friar ought not to be discharged from the Order against his will.[39]

In order to prevent illness, practical measures to keep the brothers in good health were prescribed. Convents were moved from unhealthy, insanitary sites and concern was shown for the provision of a clean water supply and protection from the dangers of fire. Humbert had advised that Dominican friars should be provided with sufficient suitable clothing in case sickness or death should result from any inadequacies,[40] and food had to be wholesome and fresh to prevent illness in those who ate it.[41] Gardens were provided for the health and recreation of the brothers, and a few days off and meat meals were granted to friars who had been working particularly long hours or travelling long distances.[42] Despite such measures, the rigours of mendicant life and the severity or chronic nature of particular illnesses made it inevitable that some friars became physically unsuited to continue in the Order. After profession a sickly friar could apply to join another Order, and transfer to a less-demanding religious life was certainly permitted in the fourteenth century. Papal letters recorded several such grants to sick friars: an ailing Franciscan was allowed to move to the less rigorous surroundings of a Benedictine monastery in 1327 'because of the various weaknesses and illnesses which frequently troubled him';[43] in 1388 a Dominican friar was transferred from the Order because of his 'horrible illness'.[44] Another Friar Minor was transferred in 1350 because 'his weak body and complexions could not sustain the austerities of the Order',[45] wording which reflected the

[39] Humbert of Romans, *Opera*, 2: 214–16.

[40] Ibid., 1: 196.

[41] 'Et super omnia cavere debet ne res corruptae vel putridae, quae sunt in periculum sanitatis, fratribus unquam dentur': ibid., 2: 283.

[42] See above, n. 8.

[43] 'Petrus de Moreto . . . propter debilitatis varias et infirmitates propriis, quibus frequentius molestaris': *Bullarium Franciscanum Romanorum pontificium: constitutiones, epistolae, ac diplomata continens tribus ordinibus*, ed. J. H. Sbaraglea and C. Eubel, 7 vols (Rome, 1759–1904), 6, no. 532.

[44] 'Laurence Ientri de Prato . . . tam propter infirmitatem horribilem': *Registrum litterarum fr Raymundi de Vineis Capuani, magistri ordinis 1380–1399*, ed. T. Kaeppeli, Monumenta ordinis fratrum praedicatorum historia, 19 (Rome, 1937), no. 234.

[45] 'Iohannes Haussy . . . qui austeritatem ordinis fratrum minorum in quo se voto professionis obstrinxerat propter corporis et complexionis debilitatem sustinere non valens': Sbaraglea and Eubel, *Bullarium Franciscanum*, 6, no. 532.

current medical thinking concerning the influence of Galenic temperaments and complexions on health and sickness. Whether these transfer requests to the pope were initiated by the friars concerned or came from their superiors is not stated, but it was apparent that the presence of physical weakness or disease meant that friars were unable to use their time in the Order to good effect. These were likely to be chronic illnesses which led friars to ask for, or be advised to retire into, a less rigorous form of religious life, or in the case of novices to leave the Order altogether.

The Orders were obliged to follow the dictates of canon law regarding the physical disqualification of priests. Particular deformities were excluded by oral enquiry and possibly on occasion by some form of physical examination. Identifying the obviously deformed, the sickly, and later those with hidden or recurrent disease would at the same time increase those friars who began their time in the Order in good or adequate health. Once admitted, the presence or onset of disease or disability could affect and influence many aspects of the friar's life and work, bringing spiritual benefits or considerable inconvenience and expense. Tasks which were usually accomplished with ease might become difficult or impossible and have to be done by others; time previously spent in useful toil or devout prayer had to be exchanged for the slow passing of the hours in the infirmary; time spent in or beside a convent sickbed detracted from the mendicant purpose of saving souls.

The care of a sick friar, though useful and dutiful, was not the ultimate aim and end of either Order; their mission demanded that their days be better spent in accomplishing the aim of universal salvation and the conquest of heresy. There is evidence that the rejection of mendicant candidates for canonically-designated deformity alone was succeeded by a keener interest in reducing and limiting the presence of those with other types of disease. The successful spiritual and practical outcomes of a friar's vocation were dependent on his physical health: he had to be fit to preach and pray. Questioning, decision-making, and advice by the Orders' ministers and diffinitors screened out unfit applicants and ensured that those who remained in the Orders were able to use their time productively. The ethic which tied bodily health to the efficient use of spiritual labour was emphasised by the Dominican Master-general, Humbert of Romans, and the Franciscan theologian, Francesc Exameneis (1327–1409). The former wrote: 'Your body is not yours alone but is deputed to the use of the community',[46] while Exameneis urged: 'Love health that with your healthy body . . . you may serve God with all your senses.'[47]

University of St Andrews

[46] 'Corporis sui, quod non solum est suo, sed communitatis servitio deputatum': Humbert of Romans, *Opera*, 1: 391.

[47] Cited in L. Garcìa-Ballester, 'Changes in the Regimina Sanitatis', in Sheila Campbell, Bert Hall, and David Klausner, eds, *Health, Disease and Healing in Mediaeval Culture* (Basingstoke, 1992), p. 120.

'LESYNG OF TYME': PERCEPTIONS OF IDLENESS AND USURY IN LATE MEDIEVAL ENGLAND

by DIANA WOOD

Then came Sloth, all be-slobbered, with two slimy eyes.
'I must sit down to be shriven,' quoth he, 'or else I shall fall asleep.
I can't stand or prop myself up, or kneel without a hassock.
If I were put to bed, no amount of bell-ringing would get me up
until I was ready for dinner – well, not unless I had to relieve myself.'

THIS is Langland's description of Sloth in *Piers Plowman*.[1] Originally a monastic vice, meaning boredom with the cell, sloth, or *accidia*, came to be applied to spiritual duties generally. By the time Langland wrote, it had also come to mean physical laziness or idleness, that is 'lesyng' or misspending of time.[2] This paper investigates some ideas about idleness and its consequences as they emerge from the spiritual and didactic literature of late medieval England. They are linked with ideas about the most detested idlers, the usurers, the money-lenders. Usurers violated time in a double sense, for not only did they misspend it, but they also made a profit from selling it. Equally vilified as idle were the clergy. The poet John Gower sourly observed that 'Slouthe kepeth the librarie' of the corrupt English clergy.[3] They will feature here only incidentally, although it is perhaps worth pointing out that some ecclesiastics profited from lending money. In the late thirteenth century a council held at Exeter had to decree the suspension from both office and benefice of usurious

[1] William Langland, *The Vision of William Concerning Piers the Plowman*, ed. Walter W. Skeat, 2 vols, new edn (Oxford, 1969), C viii, ll.1–5 (1: 167). This and all future quotations have been modernized.

[2] Ibid., B ix, l.98 (p. 272); Siegfried Wenzel, *The Sin of Sloth: 'Acedia' in Medieval Thought and Literature* (Chapel Hill, NC, 1967), esp. chs 3 and 4.

[3] John Gower, *Confessio Amantis*, in *The English Works of John Gower*, ed. G. C. Macaulay, 2 vols, *EETS*, e.s. 81–2 (1900–1), prologue, l.321 (1: 13).

clergy.[4] In the mid-fourteenth century no less a person than Archbishop Melton of York profited from lending money.[5]

God's command in Genesis (4.19) to fallen Adam, 'in the sweat of thy face shalt thou eat bread', was taken seriously in England, especially in the wake of the post-Black Death labour legislation and the growing outcry against idle but able-bodied vagrants. The Augustinian canon and preacher John Mirk (*c.* 1400), for example, related how, after the Fall, God had clothed Adam and Eve and bade Adam labour and

> eat his meat with sweat, and Eve bear her births in woe and pain, and gave Adam various tools to work with . . . From this example you should learn to labour busily; for if Adam and Eve had busied themselves in labour, the fiend would not have overcome them so quickly.[6]

Keeping busy was the only way to escape Hell:

> He that will escape the doom that he will come to at the second coming . . . must exercise his body in good works, and get his life with *swynke* [toil], and put away all idleness and sloth. For he that will not labour here with men, as St Bernard said, he shall labour for ever with the fiends of hell.[7]

The Devil found work for idle hands on earth too. Layabouts were especially vulnerable, and Chaucer's Parson outlined the sort of work that the Devil would find for them:

> An idle man is like a place that has no walls; the devils may enter on every side or close at him all unprotected by temptation at every side. This idleness is the sink of all evil and villainous thoughts, and of all gossip, trifles, and filth. Certainly heaven is given to those who labour well, and not to idle folk.[8]

[4] D. Wilkins, *Concilia magnæ Britanniæ et Hiberniæ*, 4 vols (London, 1737), 2: 146, canon 24.

[5] L. H. Butler, 'Archbishop Melton, his neighbours, and his kinsmen, 1317–1340', *JEH*, 2 (1951), pp. 54–68.

[6] John Mirk, sermon 15, in *Mirk's Festial: a Collection of Homilies by Johannes Mirkus*, ed. Theodore Erbe, *EETS*, e.s. 96 (1905), pp. 66–7. On Mirk, see W. Pantin, *The English Church in the Fourteenth Century* (Cambridge, 1955), pp. 214–18.

[7] Mirk, *Festial*, sermon 1, p. 2.

[8] Chaucer, 'The Parson's Tale', in *The Riverside Chaucer*, ed. Larry D. Benson, 3rd edn (Boston, MA, 1987), p. 312 ll.710–17.

The fourteenth-century *Book of Vices and Virtues* specifically linked 'lesyng of time' with idleness:

> idleness . . . is a sin that does much harm . . . for when a man is idle, and the devil finds him idle, he puts him to work at once, and makes him first think harmful thoughts, and then to desire foul dissipations like lechery, and thus *lese his tyme* and much good that he might have done to enable him to reach paradise.[9]

Waste of time was a sin. In *Piers Plowman*, Intelligence warned Will the Dreamer 'Lesyng of tyme – truth knows the truth! Is most hated upon earth of them that be in heaven.'[10] The author of the *Memoriale presbiterorum*, a fourteenth-century confessor's manual, included instructions about the time-wasting cleric:

> Item, he ought to confess and do penance over loss of his time, which he wasted over illicit gossiping, feasting and drinking . . . and in which he ought to have done good work, for of such it is said, 'Alas, nothing is more precious than time', but nothing is reputed more cheaply among clerics and especially among priests today.[11]

Langland lent support to this. Sloth admitted to having been a parish priest for more than thirty years[12] and boasted of how he spent every day in the ale-house enjoying scurrilous tales and slandering his neighbours, with precious little thought for the Passion of Christ, and no effort to perform the corporal works of mercy.[13]

Idleness was also a social sin, because it upset the workings of society. The idler, the waster, was a parasite living off the labour of others. The Franciscan author of the *Fasciculus morum*, an early fourteenth-century preacher's manual, compared idlers with the cuckoo, 'who does not hatch its own eggs but puts them into the nest of another bird and eats the other bird's eggs. In this way the slothful person lives off other people's labor, and what others have gained by hard and painful work, he eats up in idleness.'[14]

[9] *The Book of Vices and Virtues*, ed. W. Nelson Francis, *EETS*, o.s. 217 (1942), p. 27.

[10] *Piers Plowman*, B ix, ll. 98–9 (1, p. 272).

[11] Michael Haren, *Sin and Society in Fourteenth-century England: a Study of the Memoriale Presbiterorum* (Oxford, 2000), p. 161.

[12] *Piers Plowman*, C viii, l.31 (1, p. 169): 'I have been priest and parson passing thirty winters.'

[13] Ibid., C ix, ll.18–24 (1: 169).

[14] *Fasciculus morum. A Fourteenth-Century Preacher's Handbook*, ed. and tr. Siegfried Wenzel (Philadelphia, PA, 1989), V, i (p. 401).

More specifically, idleness could be tied to social status: it meant not labouring to maintain one's estate, not fulfilling one's social obligations. In discussing sloth, the fourteenth-century Dominican preacher John Bromyard described members of the traditional three estates, 'faithfully holding to their status' as members of God's family.

> The Devil, however, invents a fourth group, namely the slothful, who are of no order. They neither labour with the villeins, nor ride around with the merchants, nor fight with the knights, nor pray or chant with the clergy. Alas, they shall go with their own abbot, of whose order they are, namely the Devil, to where no order exists, but only eternal horror. It is not just that he whom they ought to serve should reward them.[15]

A few years later Thomas Brinton, Bishop of Rochester (1373–89) provided a variation, but with the same message. He reminded his congregation that man was naturally born to work, and that the Christian army consisted of three orders, prelates, religious, and labourers. They should be constantly occupied either in active works of mercy, or in contemplative work, or in manual labour. 'Those wretched idlers who are not occupied in any of the three grades and therefore are unfruitful deprive themselves by divine justice of the kingdom of God.'[16] Idleness could mean not just plain laziness, but also usurping the social functions of others. A Wycliffite, perhaps Nicholas Hereford, after making the familiar comparison of the Church with the body, remarked: 'and if one part neglects the work to which God has limited him, and takes the work of another part, sinful doubt is in the Church. And therefore each man must know what his estate is, and keep to the work of that estate, otherwise he sins in idleness.'[17]

How does all this apply to usury, and what was meant by it? Usury was concerned with lending, especially the lending of money, although it could be applied to anything that could be counted, weighed, or measured. Two definitions feature in Gratian's *Decretum*, both of them based on patristic texts. The first is 'expecting to receive back more than you have given' in a loan, whether of money or

[15] John Bromyard, *Summa Praedicantium*, 2 vols (Venice, 1586), A c.1 §vii (1, fol. 3ra).

[16] Thomas Brinton, sermon 20, in Sister Mary Aquinas Devlin, ed., *The Sermons of Thomas Brinton, Bishop of Rochester (1373–1389)*, 2 vols, Camden Society Publications, ser. 3, 85–6 (1954), 1: 83.

[17] *On the Seven Deadly Sins*, in Thomas Arnold, ed., *Select English Works of John Wyclif*, 3 vols (Oxford, 1871), 3: 143 (ch. 17). On the authorship see Wenzel, *Sin of Sloth*, p. 91.

anything else.[18] The second is that 'whatsoever exceeds the principal is usury'.[19] John Gower less formally called it lending a small pea and receiving back a bean.[20] In other words, any profit from a loan – what we should now call interest – was regarded as usury, and was a deadly sin, a branch of Avarice.

Usurers were idle; they did no recognizable work. Thomas of Chobham (Surrey), writing about 1216, just after the Fourth Lateran Council, pointed out that the usurer 'wishes to pursue his profit without any labour, even while sleeping, which is contrary to the precept of the Lord, "In labour and the sweat of your face shall you get your bread."'[21] He was much exercised by the comparison of usurers with prostitutes. Why, he wondered, did the Church coerce usurers more severely than prostitutes?[22] One answer was the question of labour. While moralizing that 'No one ought to labour unless they honour God through their labour', he allowed that prostitutes 'hire out their bodies for shameful use, but because they undergo bodily labour, it is lawful for them to keep what they receive for such labour.'[23] Bromyard, too, was to complain that the usurer could make a profit even in his sleep.

> The usurer is worse than the robber, because the robber usually steals at night. The usurer, however, robs by day and night, having no regard for time or solemnity, for the profit which accrues to him through a loan never sleeps, but always grows.[24]

Bromyard's three-estates entry about the slothful, under the letter A for *accidia*, was probably written about 1326. The article on usury, at the other end of the alphabet, was written about 1348.[25] Here he made explicit what was implied in the entry on sloth: the traditional three orders invented by God had become four – 'the four wheels on the chariot of Israel [II Kings 2.12, 13.14] that is, Holy Church'. The

[18] C.14 q.3 c.1: *CIC*, 1, col. 735.

[19] C.14 q.3 c.3: *CIC*, 1, col. 735. For discussion see T. P. McLaughlin, 'The teaching of the canonists on usury', *Mediaeval Studies*, 1 (1939), pp. 81–147, at p. 95.

[20] Gower, *Confessio amantis*, bk 5, ll. 4408–9 (2: 67).

[21] Thomas of Chobham, *Summa confessorum*, ed. F. Broomfield, Analecta mediaevalia Namurcensia, 25 (Louvain and Paris, 1968), p. 504 (q. 11, art. 7, dist. 6, c.4).

[22] Ibid., p. 347 (q. 6a, art. 7, c.2).

[23] Ibid., pp. 297, 296, respectively (q. 5a, art. 6, dist. 4).

[24] Bromyard, *Summa*, U c.12 §8 (2, fol. 468ra).

[25] Leonard E. Boyle, 'The date of the *Summa praedicantium* of John Bromyard', in idem, *Pastoral Care, Clerical Education, and Canon Law, 1200–1400* (London, 1981), no. 20, pp. 533–7.

merchants, 'for their usefulness in governing the state', had become a fourth order, perhaps in recognition of their increasing importance in English society. There was also a fifth wheel:

> The Devil . . . orders and devises a fifth class of people, who are like the fifth wheel added to the chariot, that is, usurers, and consequently the chariot is wrecked. Because they are not occupied in labour ordained by God, but wish to live and to profit by an art invented by the Devil, they shall not be tortured with mankind in purgatory, but by the devils in hell.[26]

The usurer's torment was to be for all time. This was his punishment not only for wasting time, but also for stealing it and then profiting from its sale. It was a medieval commonplace that time was God's time: it was ecclesiastical time, to be spent in the work God had ordained. Because, like knowledge, it was the free gift of God, it was not to be sold.[27] Time was church time, as Le Goff has shown. In practice, it was regulated by liturgical seasons and services, and its passing was sounded by church bells. One of the major changes of the Renaissance was that man slowly assumed ownership of time, as ecclesiastical values and interests gave way to secular and mercantile ones, and the mechanical clock started to regulate lives.[28] The first such clock in Europe was made in 1283 for Dunstable Priory.[29] Obviously the change was gradual. In the early thirteenth century Thomas of Chobham declared, 'The usurer does not sell the debtor something which is his own, but time, which belongs to God. It follows that because he sells something belonging to another he ought not to have any profit from it.'[30] Bromyard later complained of usurers selling both the time of daylight and the time of the night rest.[31] Avarice, in his confession in *Piers Plowman*, admitted, 'Whatever a man borrowed from me, he bought the time.'[32] The Wycliffite preacher

[26] Bromyard, *Summa*, U c.12 §1 (2, fol. 466va). Cf. Brinton, sermon 56 (Devlin, *Sermons*, 2: 259).

[27] Jacques Le Goff, *Your Money or Your Life. Economy and Religion in the Middle Ages*, tr. Patricia Ranum (New York, 1990), ch. 3, pp. 33–45: 'The Thief of Time'.

[28] Jacques Le Goff, 'Merchant's time and Church's time in the Middle Ages' and 'Labor time in the "crisis" of the fourteenth century: from medieval time to modern time', in his *Time, Work, and Culture in the Middle Ages*, tr. Arthur Goldhammer (Chicago and London, 1980), pp. 29–42, 43–52, respectively.

[29] E. G. Richards, *Mapping Time. The Calendar and its History* (Oxford, 1998), p. 58.

[30] Chobham, *Summa confessorum*, p. 504 (q. 11, art. 7, dist. 6).

[31] Bromyard, *Summa*, U c.12 §8 (2, fol. 468ra).

[32] *Piers Plowman*, C vii, l.247 (1, p. 151).

linked the sale of time with both idleness and the final reckoning of account:

> And so, since length of time and time are one and the same, he [the usurer] sells time to his neighbour, and that he is not allowed to do; for God alone is Lord of time, and wills that time should be common to all manner of creatures that dwell within it. Nor does trading of time profit any man . . . [God] freely grants man gifts of grace and gifts of nature to have for a time; and afterwards, at the end of time, he asks for an account of how each man has profited with the gifts of God. If he has profited greatly, the Lord is the better paid, and all the increase the Lord gives him, for the Lord is rich enough and damns idleness.[33]

Usury became a complicated issue in the late medieval period, because in an increasingly monetized society credit and liquid cash were essential for the workings of the economy. A number of ways of advancing money and making a profit from it which circumvented the Church's usury prohibitions became common and licit. There was a change in emphasis from the gain made by the usurer to his potential loss. The idea evolved that the lender might charge compensation – interest, as opposed to usury – for loss or potential loss.[34] The acid test for what constituted usury, however, was always intention, on the basis of 'Lend hoping for nothing again' (Luke 6.35). Enshrining a long tradition, the author of the *Fasciculus morum* proclaimed, 'Only the hope or intention creates usury' – 'sola spes sive intencio facit usuram.'[35] That apart, many of the arguments were based on time or labour. Money, barren metal, was something which was not changed by time, and therefore to lend a particular sum and to expect more to be returned after a space of time was usury. Natural things, such as crops or animals, however, were changed by time, and since they could be weighed, counted, or measured, they, too, could be loaned.

Many of the arguments arose in connection with credit sales, where

[33] *On the Seven Deadly Sins*, p. 154 (ch. 24).

[34] The best discussions of the theory of usury are G. Le Bras, 'La Doctrine ecclésiastique de l'usure à l'époque classique (viie–xve siècle)', *Dictionnaire de théologie catholique*, 15/ii (Paris, 1950), cols 2336–72; and John T. Noonan, *The Scholastic Analysis of Usury* (Cambridge, MA, 1957). On what became known as 'extrinsic titles' to interest see cols 2336–72 and pp. 100–32, respectively, and for the attitude of the canonists, T. P. McLaughlin, 'The teaching of the canonists on usury', *Mediaeval Studies*, 1 (1939), pp. 81–147; 2 (1940), pp. 1–22, esp. 1, pp. 125–47.

[35] Wenzel, *Fasciculus morum*, p. 352, l.2 (IV, vii).

merchants almost literally played for time by gambling on the future price of goods. True, they were not the same as straight loans, but it was increasingly recognized that usury – selling time – was as likely to occur in credit sales as in conventional loans.[36] The blurring of the line between them was also due to a famous decretal of Pope Gregory IX, *Naviganti* (1227–34).[37] Although it was about credit sales, it could be and was applied by many writers to loans. *Naviganti* allowed a higher price to be charged where payment was deferred over time if there was real doubt about the future price of the goods – that is, if time had altered their value or quality.

Under the heading of usury, the author of the *Fasciculus morum*, relying on *Naviganti*, discussed cases where it was licit to receive an amount beyond the principal, and specified cases of doubt:

> If someone gives you ten measures of grain, wine, or oil, so that at a later time the same amount of grain, wine, or oil may be given back to him, which then is worth more, if he is at the time of handing over in genuine doubt whether their price would go up or down, he must not be called a usurer.[38]

The author then turns to credit sales. Doubt about future value excuses someone who charges more than the current value for selling cloth, grain, or wine on credit, unless the price charged is exorbitant or the expected delay very long.[39] In the early fifteenth-century prose dialogue *Dives and Pauper* the subject is advance payment for goods, although it is discussed in terms of a loan. Pauper explains:

> If a man or woman lend ten shillings at Easter . . . to receive as many bushels of wheat in harvest and the wheat be better for that time than is the money, and it be in reasonable doubt whether the wheat shall be more worth or less in time of payment, it is not usury.[40]

[36] This was implied by William of Auxerre (1160–1229) who placed his discussion of usury under the heading of credit sales, and was taken up by Giles of Lessines (d. 1308) in his *De usuris*, the first specifically economic treatise: see Odd Langholm, *Economics in the Medieval Schools. Wealth, Exchange, Money and Usury according to the Paris Theological Tradition, 1200–1350* (Leiden, New York, and Cologne, 1992), pp. 311–12, 314–15, 388–9.

[37] X 5.19.19: *CIC*, 2, col. 816.

[38] Wenzel, *Fasciculus morum*, pp. 350–1, ll.78–83 (IV, vii).

[39] Ibid., ll.83–7.

[40] *Dives and Pauper*, ed. Priscilla Heath Barnum, 2 vols, *EETS*, o.s. 275, 280 (1976–80), 2: 196 ll.32–5 (commandment vii, ch. 24).

It is the sinful hope that time will make profitable changes which makes such transactions usurious. Pauper warns: 'If a man lend silver, corn, or wine to have again the same quantity in certain time only in hope that the same quantity shall be more worth in time of pay he doth usury.'[41]

Allowing time to take its course and effect its own changes was a lazy way of making a profit. Scholastic thinkers, however, began to realize that it was not time that made barren money breed, but labour and industry; and whereas time belonged to God, labour belonged to man. In the late thirteenth century Richard of Middleton examined the question of whether a usurer had to restore profit to the borrower which he had acquired through legitimate business, but based on the illegitimate proceeds of usury – in effect, after he had recycled his usurious profit into a respectable venture. On the understanding that money was sterile, Richard declared: 'Any profit arising from it is not the fruit of the money, but of human industry and labour. And because man is lord of his labour and industry, profit which is acquired by just business from money extorted by usury does not have to be restored.'[42] In passing, Richard seems to have anticipated Locke's doctrine of labour as a title to property. The Scottish-born Oxford philosopher John Duns Scotus was a younger Franciscan contemporary of Richard. He agreed that what made money fruitful was not time, but labour, in this case the labour of the borrower: 'Money does not from its nature have any fruit, as have other things which may germinate of themselves, but any fruit which does occur is through the labour of another, that is the user . . . therefore he who wishes to get fruit from the money wishes to have the fruit of another's industry.'[43] In tackling the question of recycled usury, Scotus agreed with Richard that legitimate profit did not have to be restored by the usurer to the borrower. After all, it had been acquired by his own industry. Unlike the original profit it could not be restored to the borrower, because the

[41] Ibid., 2: 200 ll.62–5 (ch. 25).

[42] Richard of Middleton, *Super quatuor libros Sententiarum*, 2 vols (Brescia, 1591), 2: 224b (bk 4, dist. XIV, art. 5, q. 6): 'lucrum enim de pecunia proveniens non est fructus eius, sed humanae industriae et laboris: et quia homo dominus est sui laboris et industriae, lucrum quod iusta mercatione acquisivit de pecunia extorta per usuram non tenetur restituere.'

[43] John Duns Scotus, *In librum quartum Sententiarum*, in his *Opera omnia*, 24 vols (Paris, 1891–5, repr. Farnborough, 1969), 18: 293a (IV, dist xv, q. 2): 'Pecunia non habet ex natura sua aliquem fructum, sicut habent aliqua alia ex se germinantia, sed tantum provenit aliquis fructus ex industria alterius, scilicet utentis . . . ergo ille volens recipere fructum de pecunia, vult habere fructum de industria aliena.'

borrower would then be committing usury by receiving the fruit of someone else's industry. Scotus appreciated the very real danger that this situation would encourage usury: 'magis posset homines inducere ad usuram'.[44] In effect, there was nothing beyond a guilty conscience to prevent the usurer from pocketing a rapid secondary profit before making restitution of the original.

Scotus' words serve to highlight both continuity and change in ideas about work and time. He still regarded usury as the selling of time: 'Usurers . . . sell . . . another's need and time, neither of which is theirs.'[45] That had not changed. What had changed was the idea of secular work. This was no longer confined to physical work – eating one's meat with sweat – but had expanded to include industry. This came to mean something like business acumen, as Odd Langholm has suggested.[46] Late medieval English preachers, trying to stun their audiences into repentance, still saw the usurer as a pernicious idler, intent on making an evil profit, sleeping or waking. The concern of the scholastics, however, was with the theory of usury. They raised the possibility that the money-lender might sometimes engage in honest work and reap a legitimate profit. In the mercantile atmosphere of late medieval England his life was no longer a total 'lesyng of time': on occasions he might even (in the words of John Mirk) 'get his life with *swynke* and put away all idleness and sloth.'[47]

Department for Continuing Education, University of Oxford

[44] John Duns Scotus, *In librum quartum Sententiarum*, in his *Opera omnia*, 18: 333a. Cf. Langholm, *Economics in the Medieval Schools*, pp. 417–18.

[45] John Duns Scotus, *Reportata Parisiensia*, in his *Opera omnia*, 24: 239b (IV, dist. xv, § 22).

[46] For discussion see Odd Langholm, *The Aristotelian Analysis of Usury* (Oslo, 1984), p. 102.

[47] See above, p. 108.

CHURCH TIME AND ASTROLOGICAL TIME IN THE WANING MIDDLE AGES

by HILARY M. CAREY

TIME, according to medieval theologians and philosophers, was experienced in radically different ways by God and by his creation. Indeed, the obligation to dwell in time, and therefore to have no sure knowledge of what was to come, was seen as one of the primary qualities which marked the post-lapsarian state. When Adam and Eve were cast out of the garden of delights, they entered a world afflicted with the changing of the seasons, in which they were obliged to work and consume themselves with the needs of the present day and the still unknown dangers of the next. Medieval concerns about the use and abuse of time were not merely confined to anxiety about the present, or awareness of seized or missed opportunities in the past. The future was equally worrying, in particular the extent to which this part of time was set aside for God alone, or whether it was permissible to seek to know the future, either through revelation and prophecy, or through science. In the fourteenth and fifteenth centuries, the scientific claims of astrology to provide a means to explain the outcome of past and future events, circumventing God's distant authority, became more and more insistent. This paper begins by examining one skirmish in this larger battle over the control of the future.

Towards the end of 1346, King Edward III requested that one of his chaplains, a gifted academic who had travelled with the army to France, deliver a *sermo epinicius* (victory sermon) as part of the celebrations to mark his recent success against the French at Crécy and against the Scots at Neville's Cross.[1] The sermon or, more

[1] H. A. Oberman and J. A. Weisheipl, 'The *Sermo epinicius* ascribed to Thomas Bradwardine (1346)', *Archives d'histoire doctrinale et littéraire du moyen âge*, 25 (1958), pp. 295–329 [hereafter *Sermo epinicius*], edit the text from Oxford, Merton College 180, fols 183ra–188vb. The tradition that Bradwardine was Edward III's 'confessor' as well as a regular preacher before his army is not very well attested and, although it is repeated by most modern commentators, may well rely on no more than the manuscript of the *Sermo epinicius* itself. Savile's description, for example, of the eloquent sermons Bradwardine preached and which were instrumental in their success can be explained by his acquaintance with the manuscript of the *Sermo epinicius* which he would have known

correctly, homily, since it is addressed to a text of Scripture, was delivered by Thomas Bradwardine, Chancellor of St Paul's Cathedral in London. Bradwardine was then at the height of his powers and scholarly fame, having published his most important work, the *De causa Dei contra Pelagium*, in 1344. While in France he used the opportunity to visit the University of Paris where he took part in a disputation with his fellow Mertonian, Thomas Buckingham, on his rigorous view of God's total dominion over his creation.[2] After delivering the victory sermon in English before the King and his nobles, Bradwardine responded to the request of Annibaldo de Ceccano, Cardinal Bishop of Tusculum, and wrote a fuller version in Latin to try and secure for it a wider audience.[3] This does not appear to have happened. The sermon exists in one Merton College manuscript where it is anonymous, but authorship is attested by Oberman and Weisheipl and is accepted without question by Edith Dolnikowski in her analysis of the *Sermo epinicius*.[4]

If the King had been expecting to be flattered with references to his own authority and military prowess, he is likely to have been disappointed. He may even have been rather annoyed. About the time Bradwardine was probably putting the finishing touches on the Latin version of the *Sermo epinicius*, the King was refusing to acknowledge Bradwardine's election as Archbishop of Canterbury.[5]

from the Merton library. See *Thomae Bradwardini De causa Dei, contra Pelagium*, ed. Henry Savile (London, 1618) [hereafter *De causa Dei*]. Savile and the sources he cites remain the main authorities for what is known of Bradwardine's life. For further discussion of Bradwardine's life and work see Gordon Leff, *Bradwardine and the Pelagians* (Cambridge, 1957); H. A. Oberman, *Archbishop Thomas Bradwardine; A Fourteenth Century Augustinian* (Utrecht, 1957), p. 21.

[2] For Buckingham's critique of Bradwardine, see the edition by Jean-François Genet, *Prédétermination et liberté créée à Oxford au XIVe siècle. Buckingham contre Bradwardine* (Paris, 1992).

[3] *Sermo epinicius*, p. 307: 'Set in Latino parumper ex causa diffusius prosecutus quam in Anglico dicebatur.'

[4] See n.1 (Oberman and Weisheipl); E. W. Dolnikowski, 'Thomas Bradwardine's *Sermo epinicius*: some reflections on its political, theological and pastoral significance', in J. Hamesse, B. M. Kienzle, D. L. Stoudt, and A. T. Thayer, eds, *Medieval Sermons and Society: Cloister, City, University. Proceedings of International Symposia at Kalamazoo and New York*, Fédération Internationale des Instituts d'Études Médiévales, Textes et Études du Moyen Âge, 9 (Louvain-la-Neuve, 1998), pp. 357–70.

[5] *De causa Dei*, sigs a4v–a5r. Bradwardine was elected to succeed on the death of John Stratford on 23 August 1348; however, Edward III resisted the appointment. When John Ufford died before his consecration, Bradwardine was again elected, on 19 June 1349, and travelled to Avignon to receive the pallium. After a reign of less than a month, he died of the plague in Canterbury on 26 August 1349. As a theologian with very little experience of

Nevertheless, Bradwardine was not motivated by any failure of loyalty to the King or of patriotism in addressing him so sternly. He was proud of the English victories, if we can judge by his rather matter-of-fact account of them in a letter to friends in London.[6] But using the text: *Deo gracias qui semper triumphat nos* (II Cor. 2.14), Bradwardine's main theme was not one of victory, but of denunciation, reproving those in the army who had predicted or justified the outcome by reference to astrology, fortune, chance, their sexual abilities,[7] or anything other than the will of God. Pointing to God's power over the heavenly bodies, Bradwardine began by recalling the power of God to make the sun and the moon stand, or the sun reverse itself, as was revealed to Joshua and Isaiah:

> What astrologer has foretold that this might happen? What astrologer has judged that this might happen? What astrologer has foreseen this might be? What astrologer has predicted such things? Indeed, beloved, here is a certain prediction, which is not able to fail, nor to be falsified: whatever God wishes to be or to become, that will be; whomsoever God wishes to be victorious, he will be victorious, and whomsoever God wishes to reign, he will reign.[8]

Bradwardine identifies seven groups who failed to credit the victory to its true source. In the first place were those vain astrologers who attribute all things to the seeds of men and the virtue of the stars. Secondly, there were those who gave credence to the 'Egyptian days', days of supposed good fortune based on the experiences of the wise men of Egypt. But in every battle there must be winners and losers,

government, Bradwardine's election is likely to be a reflection of the disruption of the plague years. According to Savile, the King resisted Bradwardine's appointment because he did not wish to lose so valuable a member of his household.

[6] *Adæ Murimuth, Continuatio chronicarum; Robertus de Avesbury, De gestis mirabilibus regis Edwardi tertii*, ed. E. M. Thompson, *RS*, 93 (London, 1889), pp. 201–2. This letter does not in fact indicate that Bradwardine was an 'eye witness' of the Battle of Crécy, as Oberman and Weisheipl suggest (*Sermo epinicius*, pp. 302–3). His comment on the many dead and captured, etc., suggests reports brought back to camp.

[7] *Sermo epinicius*, p. 323: 'Set dicunt, quod nullus esse poterit animosus, nisi fuerit amorosus vel diligat amorose; quod nullus se peterit gerere strenue excessive, nisi diligat excessive.'

[8] Ibid., p. 309: 'Quis astrologus pro[g]nosticasset huius? Quis Astrologus preiudicasset hec fieri? Quis astrologus talia previdisset? Quis astrologus talia predixisset? Verum, Karissimi, ecce pro[g]nosticacio una certa, que numquam potest fallere, numquam falli: quicquid Deus vult fore seu fieri, illud fiet; quemcumque Deus vult vincere, ille vincet; et quemcumque Deus vult regnare, ille regnabit.'

and if a particular day was good for the victors it must nevertheless be bad for the vanquished. The third error related to the astrological ascription of the Lot of Fortune.[9] But this was a very foolish doctrine, for in all the representations of the goddess Fortuna she is depicted as a blind woman who distributes prosperity and adversity without regard to anyone's merits. Nor was it correct to suggest that fortune was a hidden cause of any action because nothing proceeds from fortune, unless in respect to inferior causes, and all fortunate and casual events arise in the divine will.[10] The fourth error related to two views about fate. The first, which was clearly heretical, ascribed power to the three fatal sisters who disposed of human deeds. But why should the Christian offer thanks for a triumph to demonic forces rather than to God? The second view considered fate to be a form of celestial power which moderated human affairs, but many authorities rejected this.[11] Bradwardine then turned from those who attributed victory to celestial forces, to those, equally reprehensible, who gave the credit to human ingenuity, power, or sexual vigour. Here Bradwardine includes a lengthy discussion of English military tactics which is full of interest but which need not detain us. Nevertheless, all were as nothing to the one true lord of victory.

This paper uses Bradwardine's sermon to examine certain aspects of the debate about astrology in the later Middle Ages, a debate which can be characterized as a clash between two different views of time – church time and 'astrological time'. In some ways this particular argument can be seen as an episode in the long-running dialogue between faith and science, or, as contemporary philosophers would have termed it, faith and reason. The paper also argues that political events in England and France in the late fourteenth century led to a transformation in the perceived authority of astrology which led ultimately to a critical weakening of the status of church time against

[9] For the method of calculating the lot of fortune see *Abu Ma'shar. The Abbreviation of the Introduction to Astrology together with the Medieval Latin Translation of Adelard of Bath*, ed. and tr. Charles Burnett, Keiji Yamamoto, and Michio Yano (Leiden, 1994).

[10] *Sermo epinicius*, p. 312: 'Nil igitur [provenit] a fortuna, videlicet preter intencionem agentis, nisi respectu inferiorum causarum. . . . Omnia fortuita igitur atque casualia ad voluntatem divinam ascendunt.'

[11] Ibid., p. 313. See the proposition condemned in Paris in 1270: 'Quod fatum, quod est dispositio universi, procedit ex providentia divina non immediate, sed mediante motu corporum superiorum; et quod ista fatum non imponit necessitatem inferioribus, quia habent contrarietem, sed superioribus': Henri Denifle and Emile Chatelain, eds, *Chartularium universitatis Parisiensis*, 4 vols (Paris, 1889–97), 1: 543–55 (no. 195).

the demands of princes, philosophers, and laymen – including, as Le Goff was the first to point out, merchants.[12] Bradwardine's sermon was written when restraint over the use of astrological advice by princes and clerics was stretched to breaking point. Ultimately, the control of the Church was broken and astrology began two hundred years of influence over most fields of early modern thought.

In the Middle Ages, the status of astrology was the subject of prolonged and at times acrimonious debate. Was it a noble pursuit, a work of great value to both Church and State? Was it a leisure activity – somewhat reprehensible, on a par with prostitution, gambling, and drinking? Or was it simply a trifle, a game which should not distract learned or pious men, but in which there was no great harm? Was it, in short, work, rest, or play? At the beginning of the Middle Ages there would have been no trouble deciding the issue: astrology, according to Scripture, the fathers, authority, and reason, was of no value to Christians and tainted all who indulged in it with the vices of the pagans and the errors of heretics. Remarkably, by the fourteenth century this assurance was gone, and the Church was fighting a rearguard action against astrology which it was, ultimately, to lose.[13] How did this happen? Let us see if the answer to this question can be found in the fourteenth century.

In his important paper on church time, first published in 1960, Jacques Le Goff argued that a fundamental conflict arose late in the Middle Ages between the theological understanding of time and eternity and the time constraints of merchants and other clock watchers of emergent mercantilism. In addition, he suggested that a critical role in the fracturing of biblical time may have been played by the scientific speculation of the masters of Merton College, Oxford, and lesser-known scholars in Paris in the fourteenth

[12] Jacques Le Goff, 'Au moyen âge: temps de l'église et temps du marchand', *Annales*, 15 (1960), pp. 416–33, tr. in his *Time, Work and Culture in the Middle Ages* (Chicago, 1980), pp. 29–42.

[13] There is an extensive literature relating to Church objections to the practice of astrology. For discussion of the Renaissance polemic for and against the scientific and ethical status of astrology, see Eugenio Garin, *La zodiaco della vita: la polemica sull'astrologia dal trecento al cinquecento* (Rome, 1976), tr. C. Jackson and J. Allen, *Astrology in the Renaissance: The Zodiac of Life* (London, 1983). For the wider history of astrology in the later Middle Ages and the Church's ambiguous relationship to it see Jim Tester, *A History of Western Astrology* (Woodbridge, 1987); Nicholas Campion, *The Great Year: Astrology, Millenarianism, and History in the Western Tradition* (London, 1994), ch.13; and references cited in Hilary M. Carey, *Courting Disaster: Astrology and the English Court and University in the Later Middle Ages* (London, 1992), p. 168 n.31.

century.[14] Le Goff's ideas have served as an inspiration to more recent historians of astrology. Referring to Le Goff's 'pages lumineuses' on church time, Gregory advanced a far more adventurous thesis arguing that church time was pushed aside by astrological time as the physician and the prince, the merchant and the traveller, found in the skies, or at least in the astrologers' interpretation of them, the confirmation for their plans.[15] The theologian may have insisted that God alone determined the workings of the universe, but, quoting the aphorism attributed to Ptolemy, 'the wise man ruled the stars'.[16] Referring, in his turn, to Gregory, Pomian has argued that astrology presented a rival view of human and universal history which was not only different from, but opposed to, sacred history.[17] Astrology provided a means of integrating seemingly chaotic natural forces, usually referred to as secondary causes by natural philosophers, with an orderly view of the universe. It was evident that such a system could operate, potentially, without the necessary intervention of the Creator. Smoller has also argued that the clash between the two systems, which is very evident in the Paris condemnations of 1277, was in some ways inevitable.[18]

At this point, one feels the need to pause and draw breath. Was astrology really this important and significant to the mentality of the later Middle Ages? Should we take the bombast of a few self-promoters, such as Roger Bacon (who is cited extensively by Gregory),[19] all that seriously as evidence of what the wider Christian community believed? However luminously expressed, in what way could the erudite lectures given by masters in Oxford and Paris combine with the bustling concerns of the merchants of Genoa, Venice, and Lubeck (the examples given by Le Goff) to 'fracture'

[14] Le Goff, *Time, Work and Culture*, p. 42. The point is repeated in his 'Le Temps du travail dans la "crise" du XIVe siècle: du temps médiéval au temps moderne', *Le Moyen âge*, 59 (1963), pp. 597–613; also translated in *Time, Work and Culture*, p. 50.

[15] T. Gregory, 'Temps astrologique et temps Chrétien', in *Le Temps chrétien de la fin de l'antiquité au moyen âge IIIe–IIIe siècles*, Colloques internationaux du Centre National de la Recherche Scientifique, 604 (Paris, 1984), pp. 557–73.

[16] 'Vir sapiens dominabitur astris.' This widely quoted saying was usually attributed to Ptolemy, but occurs in neither the *Quadripartitum* nor the *Centiloquium*.

[17] Krzysztof Pomian, 'Astrology as a naturalistic theology of history', in Paola Zambelli, ed., *'Astrologi hallucinati': Stars and the End of the World in Luther's Time* (Berlin, 1986), pp. 29–43. Using a terminology of his own devizing Pomian notes: '[M]y purpose is to show that astrology was a coherent chronosopy and more specifically: a naturalistic theology of history opposed to and logically incompatible with its theocentric variant.'

[18] Laura Ackerman Smoller, *History, Prophecy and the Stars: The Christian Astrology of Pierre d'Ailly* (Princeton, NJ, 1994), pp. 80–1.

[19] Cited in 10 out of 45 footnotes by my count.

time? In the first part of his career, Bradwardine was, after all, one of those Merton scientists, and yet he abhorred the new currents of thought which threatened to place the natural world and its operations beyond the control of the God of providence. So it is important to stress that medieval time was not a uniform construct and many propositions, including those in astrology, formed part of a long-running debate in which there were no clear winners and losers.

Bradwardine's sermon against astrology arises in part from an Oxford Augustinianism which gave priority to an analysis of time in which the future was reserved in a special and privileged way to God alone, excluding the insights and predictions of rational determinations.[20] For medieval thinkers following Augustine, it was evident that one of the most significant features that distinguished God from man was in the differential experiences of time of the Creator and his creations. God existed outside of time and space and could experience all created moments, past, present, and future, in his eternal majesty.[21] (Working out how this could be made compatible with free will was rather more challenging, but can be put aside here.)[22] The determinism of the *mathematici* (astrologers), or the fatalism of the Stoics, was dismissed and in its place was asserted God's absolute foreknowledge and authority over all events.[23]

Against this view, natural philosophers, including some astrologers, would argue that this allowed too little space for human reason and the kind of assessment of secondary causes which formed the basis for astrological predictions, medical diagnoses, or other scientific judgements. It also appeared to impede the acceptance of prophecies which

[20] I follow here the illuminating discussion of Edith Wilks Dolnikowski, *Thomas Bradwardine. A View of Time and a Vision of Eternity in Fourteenth-century Thought* (Leiden, 1995).

[21] *Sancti Augustini Confessionum*, ed. Lucas Verheijen, *CChr, series Latina*, 27 (Turnholt, 1981) [hereafter *Confess.*], XI.xiii.16, p. 202: 'Omnia tempora tu fecisti et ante omnia tempora tu es, nec aliquo tempore non erat tempus.' These concepts of the divine were not simply physical and theological conceits. For a poetic realization of a deity existing outside time and space see Dante, *Paradiso*.

[22] For a vintage synthesis see T. O. Wedel, *The Medieval Attitude Towards Astrology* (New Haven, CT, 1920). Excellent summaries of the debate about astrology and free will are also provided by Smoller, *History, Prophecy and the Stars*, pp. 25–42, and by Jan R. Veenstra, *Magic and Divination at the Courts of Burgundy and France. Text and Context of Laurens Pignon's Contre les divineurs (1411)* (Leiden, 1998), pp. 137–200.

[23] *De causa Dei*, III.xii, pp. 688–9: 'Incipit disputare illam famosissimam quaestionem, nunquid omnia quae euenient, de necessitate euenient; & recitat opinionem Mathematicorum seu Stoicorum dicentem, quod omnia quae euenient, euenient de necessitate simpliciter absoluta.'

arise from God, such as those relating to the coming of the Antichrist. In Buckingham's challenge to Bradwardine, Buckingham insisted on the dignity and certainty of some classes of future contingents, such as prophecies relating to the Antichrist.[24] Against Bradwardine, it would seem, were the reasonable men: astrological time was precise and orderly; it provided the mechanism for the transmission of heat, light, and other celestial influences to the sub-lunar regions; with study, as scientific astrologers asserted, it could allow for the foretelling of great events, including the rise and fall of empires and religions, the coming of the Antichrist, even the end of the world. In the waning Middle Ages, whose view of time would come to prevail – the conservative view of the Church, as defended by Bradwardine, or the practical modernizers such the princes and the astrologers whose judgements they sought?

In order to answer this question what is needed is an analysis of interventions by church leaders and theologians to defend the Church's view of time against that of the astrologers. Bradwardine's sermon is an example of one such intervention, but it can be compared with two others by his compatriots, John of Salisbury and Roger Bacon.

* * *

In the *De causa Dei*, Bradwardine reinforces his attack on astrology, chance, and fate by reference to John of Salisbury.[25] This is appropriate, for John provides one of the most significant medieval syntheses of scriptural, patristic, and classical pagan objections to astrology. In the *Policraticus*, which was probably completed around 1159 during John's exile from the court of Henry II, John set aside most of the first two books to an attack on astrology and all forms of divination.[26] In the end he leaves no doubt as to the scriptural and literary authority for the condemnation of all attempts to practise divination: 'Read books, turn histories upside-down, pry into every

[24] Genet, *Prédétermination*, p. 185, affirms the question: 'Utrum credere prophecie de aliquo contingenter futuro sit meritorium creature.' Foreknowledge of the Antichrist is also Roger Bacon's justification for astrological prediction. For argument relating to the necessity of Antichrist, see *De causa Dei*, III.xv–xvii, pp. 690–2.

[25] *De causa Dei*, III.xii, p. 689; III.xxv, p. 700. Bradwardine noted that John of Salisbury's voluminous arguments against the Stoics and *mathematici* had the added endorsement of Thomas Becket.

[26] *Ioannis Saresberiensis, Policraticus I–IV*, ed. K. S. B. Keats-Rohan, *CChr.CM*, 118 (Turnhout, 1993) [hereafter *Policraticus*].

corner of the scriptures and nowhere will you find approval for the practice of divination.'[27]

It is probably reasonable to assume that John gave priority to a denunciation of astrology at such length and prominence in the *Policraticus* because he saw divination, astrology, and other nonsense as a real nuisance to the court from which he had been banished. But in close to a hundred printed pages there appear to be only two or three references to John's own experiences with the dangers of using magical means to discover hidden and/or future things. One of these concerns John's own uncomfortable introduction to divination as a child when a priest enlisted him under oath to scry in a glass for what John assumed later had to be demons.[28] He also refers to futile consultations with a certain *aruspex* (diviner) and *chiromanticus* (palm-reader) before Henry II's campaign against the northern Welsh in 1157.[29] A reliance on their predictions did nothing to forestall the death of a relative of Becket, to whom the *Policraticus* was addressed.

Apart from these sly references John provides little to support his general slur that courtiers were abandoning Christian restraint in their greed to gain advantage through astrological knowledge of the future. Yet even John was prepared to concede that it was acceptable in some circumstances to seek out the future. The two exceptions were those of God-given prophecy and medical diagnosis, if based on a reading of natural signs – and even then only if this could be accomplished without prejudice to faith or religion.[30] This was to be the back door to a transformation in mentalities, for medical diagnosis was based on astrological prediction.

* * *

Despite the impressive forces which John of Salisbury was able to array against it, astrology grew in influence and importance as Greek

[27] Ibid., II.xxvii, p. 155: 'Lege libros, reuolue historias, scrutare omnes angulos Scripturarum, nusquam fere in bona significatione diuinationem inuenies.'

[28] Ibid., II.xxviii, p. 167.

[29] Ibid., II.xxvii, p. 148: 'Cum aduersus Niuicolinos Britones regia esset expeditio producenda, in quo te consultus aruspex praemonuit? . . . Item chiromanticus adhibitus et consultus quid contulit? Nam sub eo articulo uterque, quisquis hoc egerti, consultus est.'

[30] Ibid., II.xxix, pp. 169–70: 'Licet tamen de futuris ut aliquis consulatur, ita quidem si aut spiritu polleat prophetiae aut ex naturalibus signis quid in corporibus animalium eueniat phisica docente cognouit aut si qualitatem temporis imminentis experimentorum indiciis colligit; dum tamen his posterioribus nequaquam quis ita aurem accommodet ut fidei aut religioni praeiudicet.'

and Arabic learning came to dominate the later medieval universities. It would seem in the thirteenth century that its time had come. Roger Bacon was one of the most ardent defenders of the new sciences, including astrology. Bacon was also clear that what made astrology so valuable was its capacity to provide information about the future – the realm previously set aside to God alone. In the *Opus Majus*, completed at the request of Pope Clement IV in 1267, Bacon provided an extensive justification for astrology, beginning with a ham-fisted attempt to overthrow patristic disapproval of the predictive science. Bacon claimed that the church fathers not only did not reprove true astrologers (*mathematici*), they actually gave their approval to the knowledge of the future.[31] He gave special prominence to Augustine's supposed endorsement of astrological predictions of future events in the *De doctrina Christiana*. This rather startling reference to Augustine, which can only be a wilful misreading of the text, is typical of Bacon's special pleading for scientific astrology. While Augustine does accept that astronomy could give rise to firm and certain predictions, he prefaces this with the observation that such knowledge is of little use to an understanding of Scripture and, moreover, is dangerously close to the ravings of the astrologers (*genethliaci*). It should be strictly restricted to the movements of the stars and not extended to human deeds and actions.[32] But Bacon was not to be held back by the Fathers. He wrote with passionate conviction about the value of astrology to the support of both State and Church.[33] Above all – and this was Bacon's king hit – he claimed that if sufficient attention was paid to all the evidence available, from sacred and prophetic texts, the

[31] *The Opus Majus of Roger Bacon*, ed. J. H. Bridges, 3 vols (Oxford, 1897), 1: 247: 'Et adhuc considerandum est, quod si consideremus dicta sanctorum, nos inveniemus manifeste quod non solum non reprobant mathematicos veros, sed approbant in futurorum cognitione. Quoniam Augustinus dicit libro secundo de Doctrina Christiana, quod mathematica habet futurorum regulares conjecturas, non suspiciosas et ominosas, sed rectas et certas tam de futuris quam praesentibus et praeteritis.' He goes on to illustrate the point by reference to Cassiodorus, Basil, Ambrosius, and Isidore.

[32] Augustine, *De doctrina Christiana*, ed. R. P. H. Green (Oxford, 1995), II.cxiii (pp. 108–10): 'Quae per se ipsa cognitio, quamquam superstitione non alliget, non multum tamen ac prope nihil adiuvat tractationem divinarum scripturarum et infructuosa intentione plus impedit; et quia familiaris est perniciosissimo errori fatua fata cantantium, commodius honestiusque contemnitur. . . . Habet etiam futurorum regulares coniecturas, non suspiciosas et ominosas, sed ratas et certas, non ut ex eis aliquid trahere in nostra facta et eventa temptemus, qualia genethliacorum deliramenta sunt, sed quantum ad ipsa pertinet sidera.' Augustine provided a more comprehensive critique of astrology, to which he was drawn in his youth, in *Confess.*, VII.vi–vii and *De civitate Dei*, V.ii–viii.

[33] Bacon, *Opus Majus*, 1: 253.

prophecies of the Sibyl, Merlin, Joachim, and others, as well as to the books of philosophy and history and the judgements of astrology, then it would be possible, with some or at least a greater degree of certainty, to anticipate the time of the Antichrist.[34] Bacon was convinced that the coming of the Antichrist was imminent and that the enemies of Christianity, including the Tartars, were gaining the ascendancy because they had the good sense to listen to the forecasts of their astrologers.[35]

* * *

Towards the end of the thirteenth century, driven partly, it is to be suspected, in response to excesses of the kind revealed in Bacon's aspirations for a new world order based on the scientific principles including those of astrology, the Church struck back. At both Paris and Oxford, the presiding ecclesiastical authorities issued condemnations of suspect doctrines. Of the 219 propositions condemned in 1277, a significant number related to astrological principles such as the Great Year, the heavenly intelligences, the nature of the relationship between divine providence, fate, and the celestial bodies, and the way in which the celestial influence operated from the moment of birth to incline men toward particular causes of action.[36] Bradwardine refers to both the Paris and Oxford condemnations in the *De causa Dei*.[37] There were also political restrictions and trials of some of the more flagrant practitioners of magic and judicial astrology, particularly at the papal court at Avignon.[38] However, practising astrologers seem to have quickly evaded the ban on all but the most proscribed activities. Scientific astrology was resuscitated along with the more rigorous investigation

34 Ibid., 1: 268–9: 'Nolo hic ponere os meum in coelum, sed scio quod si ecclesia vellet revolvere textum sacrum et prophetias sacras, atque prophetias Sibyllae, et Merlini et Aquilae, et Sestonis, Joachim et multorum aliorum, insuper historias et libros philosophorum, atque juberet considerari vias astronomiae, inveniretur sufficiens suspicio vel magis certitudo de tempore Antichristi.'

35 Ibid., 1: 400: 'Et ideo Tartari procedunt in omnibus per viam astronomiae, et in praevisione futurorum et in operibus sapientiae.'

36 Denifle and Chatelain, *Chartularium*, 1: 543–55. Pierre Mandonnet, *Siger de Brabant et l'Averroïsme latin au XIIIme siècle*, 2nd edn (Louvain, 1911), pp. 175–91. My description follows Mandonnet's thematic grouping of the propositions he numbers 93–107.

37 *De causa Dei*, III.xxiii, p. 697 (twice), and passim.

38 Jean-Patrice Boudet, 'La Papauté d'Avignon et l'astrologie', in *Fin du monde et signes des temps: visionnaires et prophètes en France méridionale*, Cahiers de Fanjeaux, 27 (Toulouse, 1992), pp. 257–93.

of Aristotelian natural philosophy.[39] Astrology had become necessary for a reasoned understanding of the way the world worked. Celestial influence was accepted as a vehicle for the flow of secondary causes which gave rise to mundane events.

Overall, there appears to have been something of a truce declared by the middle of the fourteenth century. At the same time as Bradwardine was denouncing the reliance on astrology or fortune in relation to the English victories at Crécy and Neville's Cross, his one-time colleague at Merton, John Ashenden, was preparing a detailed analysis of two series of conjunctions which he was later to allege predicted not just the English victories, but the coming of the plague.[40] Also contemporary with Bradwardine, Jean de Murs was attempting to secure from the pope closer attention to the scientific significance for governance of astrology. Boudet has edited a remarkable letter written by Jean de Murs to Pope Clement VI sometime between 1345 and 1352.[41] In this letter (if it is genuine) Jean de Murs sought to warn the Pope of the dire consequences for Christendom and France of two conjunctions in 1365 and 1357. No-one was more prudent or better placed to secure some remedial action to avoid the coming danger than him, for what was seen as impossible or inevitable for others was possible and achievable for him.[42] This was not blasphemous presumption, but true science which the Church should embrace. It is not known if the Pope made any response.

* * *

[39] This is best illustrated by the popularity of the text known as the *Speculum astronomie*, attributed to Albertus Magnus, which can be read as a defence of astrological science against theological rigorists. See Paola Zambelli, ed., *The Speculum astronomiae and its Enigma: Astrology, Theology, and Science in Albertus Magnus and his Contemporaries* (Boston, MA, 1992).

[40] Ashenden was Bradwardine's contemporary at Merton and the major English astrological writer of the later Middle Ages. Keith V. Snedegar has completed a fine study of Ashenden, including an edition of his analyses of the conjuctions of 1345–68, which unfortunately has remained unpublished: 'John Ashenden and the *Scientia Astrorum Mertonensis* with an edition of Ashenden's *Pronosticationes*' (University of Oxford, D.Phil. thesis, 1988). See esp. ch.7 on problems of faith and science.

[41] Boudet, 'La Papauté d'Avignon', pp. 258–60.

[42] *Epistola magistri Johannis de Muris ad Clementem sextum* (BN, MS lat. 7443, fols 33r–34v), ed. Boudet, 'La Papauté d'Avignon', pp. 283–4: 'Cum igitur dicat Ptholomeus in principio *Almagesti*, quod vir sapiens dominabitur astris, et in *Centilogio*, quod effectus stellarum sunt inter neccessarium et contingens, possunt enim per homines prudentes declinari sepius et auctoritati, nullusque sit inter mortales presentes Sanctitate Vestra prudentior in sensu, nec potentior in effectu, prefatis imminentibus periculis occurrere velociter, et succurrere efficater intendatis, que enim apud alios impossibilia seu neccessaria estimantur, apud Vos possibilia et levia merito reputantur.'

It is now time to return to Thomas Bradwardine and the historical context in which he delivered the *Sermo epinicius*. Nowhere is the potential tension between church time and astrological time realized more starkly than in the *Sermo epinicius*. As noted above, Bradwardine touches on astrology in the *De causa Dei* in chapters repudiating pagan worship of the celestial bodies, fate, or chance. These topics are something of a stalking horse for those who, in his view, restricted the unrestrained action of divine will.[43] The argument is from the usual authorities and has none of the rhetorical flair or sense of contact with the community which is so evident elsewhere in the sermon. While the *Sermo epinicius* is therefore much his most elaborate statement on astrology, it is interesting to speculate on whether, had he lived, he might have written more fully on the subject. With hindsight, Bradwardine would seem to be one of the last defenders of a decaying temporal order. It no longer seemed natural to assume God's control of the universe, or even of a battle; it required a thunderous sermon to insist upon it.

The supposed success of astrologers in predicting the plague gave great authority to their predictions and, according to Veenstra, the fourteenth- and fifteenth-century French and Burgundian courts swarmed with astrological advisers.[44] Veenstra's conclusions are supported by historians who have considered astrological influences at other late-medieval courts, including that of the Avignon papacy.[45] In the fifteenth century, in the waning Middle Ages, Pierre d'Ailly came to argue that the scientific principles of astrology might be married with faith to create a noble discipline, a Christian Astrology. Recalling the fevered hopes and creative use of authorities of Roger Bacon, d'Ailly argued that astrology could allow the prediction of great events in Christian history, including the time of Antichrist, the Second Coming, or the end of the world.[46] For d'Ailly the papal schism (which he was to play a leading part in healing) was a sign of the end times and in his work Christian astrology was married, with powerful effect, to Joachimite prophecy.[47]

[43] *De causa Dei*. For astrology, fate, and chance see: I.i, corol. 12, p. 8 (Contra adoratores Solis vel Lunae, Martis vel Iouis, cuiscunque signi caelestis); I.xxviii, p. 264 (De Fato); I.xxix, p. 267 (De Casu & Fortuna); III.xii, pp. 688–9 (Mathematici).

[44] Veenstra, *Magic and Divination*.

[45] Maxime Préaud, *Les Astrologues à la fin du moyen âge* (Paris, 1984).

[46] Smoller, *History, Prophecy and the Stars*, p. 23.

[47] Ibid.

On the whole this is not the pattern we see in England. The rise of astrology is slow and the control of the Church over the domain of the future remained tight. While belief in political prophecy flourished and features in chronicle writing, there is little evidence of a surfeit of astrological advice to English rulers. On the other hand, at a popular level there is surprisingly little evidence that the Church sustained the patristic objection to astrology as both an offence against the second commandment, and an abuse of leisure which should be spent on more profitable things. The medieval history of leisure, unlike, it could be said, the history of unleisure (work), is only in its infancy.[48] But from a search of moralizing literature, including sermons and treatises on the Ten Commandments and the vices and virtues, it would seem that moralists were too busy condemning the more base forms of divination to worry about the elite practice of astrology.

John Myrc's *Instructions for Parish Priests* advises clergy to live chaste lives, stay out of taverns, be wary of women, and follow after virtue.[49] Among practices which are anathematized, some clearly relate to witchcraft: 'all that maken experimentes or wichecrafte or charmes with oynementes of holy chirch, and all þat leben on hem.' Priests were to ask themselves and their parishioners:

> Hast þow lafte goddes name,
> And called þe fend in any grame? . . .
> Hast þow made any wych crafte,
> For any þynge þat þe was rafte;
> Hast þow made any sorcery
> To gete wymmen to lyge hem by?[50]

Bradwardine was insistent that even so much as consulting the *pars fortune* to assess the outcome of battle was tantamount to paganism. But at the level of the parish confessional, Bradwardine's scruples about astrology were clearly much too sophisticated for ordinary folk. In the later Middle Ages, such matters were largely of concern to

[48] With the laudable exception of Le Goff, *Time, Work and Culture*, the English literature is dominated by books for a general readership, including Compton Reeves, *Pleasures and Pastimes in Medieval England* (Stroud, 1995). Reeves includes astrology in the chapter on religious pastimes, pp. 182–7.

[49] John Myrc, *Instructions for Parish Priests*, ed. Edward Peacock, *EETS*, o.s. 31 (London, 1868), pp. 2–3.

[50] Ibid., pp. 23, 30.

courtiers. John of Salisbury, as we have seen, condemned the reliance on magic and astrologers as part of the time-wasting frivolity which distracted the prince from his proper attendance to matters of state and religion.

For those at both the top and the bottom of society, divination, gambling, and other sallies with the future were not classed among those few privileged forms of leisure honoured, in the tradition of Horace, as a proper part of the ennobling pleasures of *otium*.[51] It was just something which distracted the clergy from their duties and the laity from paying proper attention to the sermon. Bromyard sneered that the diviner (*sortilega*) speaks about those things which lead to the damnation of souls, and attracted a large audience. But Christ speaks, and his ministers and people ask: 'Who is this?'[52] Diviners were also condemned for sinning in pride. For example, in the English translation of the *Somme le Rois* of Lorens d'Orleans, diviners are allied with witches and such that use charms and work by the devil's craft.[53] The use of dice for gambling or games of chance was particularly frowned upon, because it was by the casting of lots that the soldiers decided who would receive the garment of the crucified Christ.[54] But astrology seems to have escaped the general anathema.

I do not wish to suggest that Bradwardine's view exerted an influence over the practice of astrology beyond his grave. There is nothing even to suggest that other astrologers or princes read it. There is no reference to the *Sermo epinicius* or Bradwardine's hostility to judicial astrology (except maybe parenthetically) even in the massive compendium of John Ashenden, written after Bradwardine's death and, like the *De causa Dei*, dedicated to the fellows of Merton. So little did Bradwardine establish a reputation as an opponent of astrology that Symon de Phares, writing in 1498, even claimed that he had cast the

[51] Brian Vickers, 'Leisure and idleness in the Renaissance: the ambivalence of otium (Part II)', *Renaissance Studies*, 4 (1990), pp. 107–54.

[52] Bromyard, *Summa Praedicantium*: 'Loquitur trufator, loquitur vetula, loquitur detractor, loquitur sortilega de hiis quae ad damnationem pertinent animarum, et multos habent auditores; . . . loquitur Christus, et ejus ministri . . . et dicunt "quis est hic?" (Eccl.13).' Quoted by G. R. Owst, *Preaching in Medieval England: an Introduction to Sermon Manuscripts of the Period c.1370–1450* (Cambridge, 1926), p. 71 n.3. See also G. R. Owst, 'The people's Sunday amusements in the preaching of medieval England', *Holborn Review*, 68 (1926), pp. 32–45.

[53] *The Book of Vices and Virtues*, ed. W. Nelson Francis, *EETS*, o.s. 217 (London, 1942), p. 15.

[54] W. L. Braekman, 'Fortune-telling by the casting of dice: a Middle English poem and its background', *Studia Neophilologica*, 52 (1980), pp. 3–29.

nativity of Edward III and predicted the plague.[55] We can say with certainty that this was not the case.

Nevertheless, on repeated rereading, the steely authority of Bradwardine's victory sermon remains deeply impressive in its rejection of all sources for Edward III's victory except God alone. Bradwardine has been seen as something of an extremist, a radical determinist who allowed insufficient space in the conduct of human affairs for the admission of free will. Yet I believe he had considerable insight into the temptation of astral determinism to the members of the English and French military classes whose world he was briefly able to view. Bradwardine's sermon can be seen, with hindsight (a facility which does not impugn the all-seeing providence of God), as one salvo in what was to prove a long-running battle. The Church's failure to resist the claims of astrology over the realm of the future in the fourteenth and fifteenth centuries reflects the continuing prestige of Aristotelian natural philosophy, of which astrology was a significant branch. It was not until Aristotelianism and scholasticism were overthrown that the outcome was to be any different. Until then, the Church was rendered more or less impotent as a critic of both the science and the ethics of seeking, by human reason, to foreknow through astrology.

University of Newcastle, New South Wales

[55] Symon de Phares, *Recueil des plus célèbres astrologues et quelques hommes doctes*, ed. Ernest Wickersheimer (Paris, 1929), p. 210: 'En ce temps florit en Angleterre Thomas Bradvardin, singulier homme et grant astrologien. Cestui predist et prenostica plusieurs choses des differans des princes et composa en astrologie ung traicté qui se commence: «Omne motum successivum alteri». Cestui prenostica au roy d'Angleterre, sur la revolocion de sa nativité, d'une grande maladie qui lui advint, dont il fut moult apprecié et estimé des plus grans.' While it might seem silly for Simon to have described Bradwardine's treatise on momentum as a work of astrology, I note that the electronic version of the old *DNB* currently lists Bradwardine's fields of interest as theology and occultism.

TIME AND THE TESTATOR, 1370–1540

by JUDITH MIDDLETON-STEWART

THERE were many ways in which the late medieval testator could acknowledge time. Behind each testator lay a lifetime of memories and experiences on which he or she drew, recalling the names of those 'they had fared the better for',[1] those they wished to remember and by whom they wished to be remembered. Their present time was of limited duration, for at will making they had to assemble their thoughts and their intentions, make decisions and appoint stewards, as they prepared for their time ahead; but as they spent present time arranging the past, so they spent present time laying plans for the future. Some testators had more to bequeath, more time to spare: others had less to leave, less time to plan. Were they aware of time? How did they control the future? In an intriguing essay, A. G. Rigg asserts that 'one of the greatest revolutions in man's perception of the world around him was caused by the invention, sometime in the late thirteenth century, of the mechanical weight-driven clock.'[2] It is the intention of this paper to see how men's (and women's) perception of time in the late Middle Ages was reflected in their wills, the most personal papers left by ordinary men and women of the period.[3]

Most of the wills to which reference will be made here come from Suffolk, the 'other half' of the old diocese of Norwich, but there are,

1 Norwich, Norfolk Record Office [hereafter NRO], Norwich Consistory Court wills [hereafter NCC], Robinson 55, John Baret, Halesworth (1519).

2 A. G. Rigg, 'Clocks, dials and other terms', in D. E. Gray and E. G. Stanley, eds, *Middle English Studies Presented to Norman Davies in Honour of his Seventieth Birthday* (Oxford, 1983), p. 255.

3 The wills cited here were proved at the Prerogative Court of Canterbury, the Norwich Consistory Court, and the Archdeaconry Courts of Suffolk and Sudbury, the three tiers of Church courts which represented varying levels of movable estate within the diocese of Norwich. For the historian, wills reveal family ramifications, circles of friends, trade associations, parish communities, lines of patronage, and clerical influence. They also shed light on the individual's personal wishes and intentions for the distribution of the 'loose change' of the estate, but not the implementation of those desires. Wills can be full of interest or barren, and need to be used judiciously and with caution. For comment see C. Burgess, 'Late medieval wills and pious convention: testamentary evidence reconsidered', in M. A. Hicks, ed., *Profit, Piety and the Professions in Later Medieval England* (Gloucester, 1990), pp. 14–33. As ever, my work on East Anglian wills owes much to Peter Northeast.

too, a few references from Norfolk. Suffolk was heavily populated in the late Middle Ages, with a great number of small, independent farmers farming the land of 'High Suffolk', the backbone of Suffolk's prosperity.[4] To the south of the county were the great weaving centres along the river Stour, and to the east lay the fishing ports and towns which traded with the European mainland. This was by no means a poor county – but its make-up lacked the great magnates of the shires, and so the county represented a mixture of trade and agricultural and maritime pursuits, pursued by good, honest, but ordinary citizens.

The years 1370 to 1540 can be seen as a discreet period at the beginning of which the first surviving late medieval wills appear in East Anglia. This period of 170 years, while showing an overall growth in the number of wills, had an internal rhythm of its own, reflected in an increase in bequests to churches and their fittings which peaked around 1500, followed by diminution towards the end of the period. Within this rhythm there are subtle changes in the fashion of intercessory prayers, but changes are also apparent in testaments, not only in their dating but also in their format and language. Wills from the Prerogative Court of Canterbury and the Norwich Consistory Court survive from 1370, though not in any great number at this time, and around 1440, the wills from the archdeaconries of Suffolk and Sudbury appear. From then on, the number of wills steadily increases, as does the diversity of bequests.[5] By 1540, the testators were responding to the prohibitions of the Crown, yet the number of wills held steady. By 1540 the reformation of the English Church was well under way and many traditional observances had been prohibited. Wills from this period show that saints' days had been reduced and that pilgrimage, the veneration of relics, and offerings to images had been banned. Some of the most popular smaller bequests in wills had been for lights to burn before certain images, but these were now snuffed out and were reduced to a light before the rood, one before the holy sacrament, and one above the sepulchre.

These same 170 years, however, when set against a much wider background, are the latter part of the period when 'modern' time, as

[4] D. MacCulloch, *Suffolk and the Tudors: Politics and Religion in an English County, 1500–1600* (Oxford, 1986), pp. 13–19.

[5] For example, in the deanery of Dunwich, the largest deanery in late medieval Suffolk, the number of wills which have survived from the decade 1440–9 is 65. In the following decade, 1450–9, the number of wills is almost quadrupled, at 229.

we now know it, first impinged on the consciousness of the common man. The history of 'modern', 'merchant', or 'public' time began in the fourteenth century when, as Mollat said, 'the use of bells to regulate the course of the working day became increasingly common'; and, at the same time, the first mechanical striking clock appeared – in Milan.[6] Time had been when time was measured by the moving shadow, and later the shadow was measured against a dial, but only during the daytime. Time could also be measured by water, using the *clepsydra* of the ancient Egyptians, which enabled time to be measured at night; or it was measured by sand in the hour glass, or by the wax burning on a calibrated candle.[7] Mass dials were scratched on hundreds of parish churches but they were unreliable and they, too, needed the sun; and as all these early time-pieces were referred to as *horologia*, their specific histories are obscured by the use of this one word.[8] The canonical hours, which had been tolled seven times daily by the monastery bell, were by the fourteenth century too imprecise in a time which sought accuracy, albeit the bells sounded God's time.

The modern system of hour reckoning and the public clock originated in the Italian cities, Milan the first to be 'securely documented' in 1336.[9] Nearer home, Dunstable priory had a mechanical clock in 1283; and by 1322 Norwich cathedral priory had a large astronomical clock with fifty-nine automata and a procession of monks.[10] There is, however, no evidence that these were striking clocks, as was the clock in the tower of St Gottardo in Milan. At York in about 1360, during the building of the cathedral, one clock called the people to prayer, another got the workforce on the job: God's time

[6] R. W. Symonds, *A History of English Clocks* (Harmondsworth, 1947), pp. 9–10; M. Mollat, *The Poor in the Middle Ages: an Essay in Social History* (New Haven, CT, and London, 1986), p. 208; G. Dohrn-van Rossum, *History of the Hour: Clocks and Modern Temporal Orders* (Chicago, 1992), pp. 108, 112.

[7] R. Dale, *Timekeeping* (London, 1992), pp. 12–18.

[8] F. A. B. Ward, *Handbook of the Collection Illustrating Time Measurement, part 1: Historical Review*, 4th edn (London, 1958), pp. 11–15.

[9] Dohrn-van Rossum, *History of the Hour*, pp. 112, 128, 130; C. M. Cipolla, *Clocks and Culture 1300–1700* (London, 1967), p. 40. Cipolla states that during the fourteenth century mechanical clocks became progressively more numerous in Europe and were soon equipped to strike the hours. He gives the date for Milan as 1309 (which does not tally with Dohrn-van Rossum), Beauvais 1324, Cluny 1340, and Chartres 1349.

[10] Dale, *Timekeeping*, p. 20; G. H. Baillie, C. Ilbert, and C. Clutton, eds, *Britten's Old Clocks and Watches and Their Makers: a History of Styles in Clocks and Watches and Their Mechanisms*, 9th edn (London, 1982), p. 5; J. Geddes, 'Iron', in J. Blair and N. Ramsey, eds, *English Medieval Industries: Craftsmen, Techniques, Products* (London and Rio Grande, OH, 1991), pp. 178–9.

and merchant's time, as Le Goff described it.[11] By the end of the 1300s, whereas time had previously been counted by the canonical hour or 'at daybreak', 'before dusk', or 'after curfew', time now became known by the hour as we use it today. John Almyngham of Walberswick used it, too, when he left instructions for a priest to say Mass daily between five and six in the summertime and between six and seven during the winter, adding 'and when he is not disposed to say it, he to go to one to do it'.[12] Another change which can be noticed in early wills is the modernization of time in the dating of documents. When Richard Micklefield wrote his testament at Blyford in 1408, it was in Latin and dated 'on the Sunday before the feast of St Martin'. His last will followed, in French, dated the Saturday before the feast of St Katherine the Virgin. Thirty years later his son, William, dated his Latin testament 20 September 1439, and wrote his last will, in English, on 7 November.[13] By the end of the century, most testaments and last wills had merged and were written in English.

Time had an effect on church architecture. The increasing size of bells, necessitating a substantial internal framework, meant the rebuilding of towers, many towers in East Anglia dating from the fourteenth century. Suffolk wills reveal bequests to towers from 1370, reaching a peak between 1425 and 1475. Bell 'projects' peaked between 1450–1500.[14] Such work was vastly expensive, and an assortment of individual bequests reveals on-going commitment. St Peter Mancroft, the great market church at Norwich, provides some of the earliest and lengthiest testamentary evidence. The first bequest 'to the new tower' was dated 1391. In 1410, the bell tower received a bequest and, in 1431, 8*d*. was paid to 'the new bell'. In 1454 the patron paid for bell-ropes, and in 1507 the steeple was being leaded.[15] Here the construction of the tower can be envisaged stage by stage in a building programme which probably involved the destruction of a central Romanesque

[11] J. Le Goff, 'Merchant's time and church time in the middle ages', in his *Time, Work and Culture in the Middle Ages* (Chicago and London, 1980), pp. 29–42.

[12] Ipswich, Suffolk Record Office [hereafter SROI], IC/AA2/4, fol. 68, John Almyngham, Walberswick (1500).

[13] NRO, DN/Reg.4, liber 7 (1407–15), fols 70–1, Richard Micklefield, Blyford (1408); NRO, NCC, Doke 145–6, William Micklefield, armiger, Blyford (1439).

[14] I owe this information to Peter Northeast, taken from his work on pre-Reformation church building projects found in Suffolk wills.

[15] NRO, NCC, Harsyk, Thomas de Ryslee, Norwich (1391): Lambeth Palace Library, Reg. Arundel 2, fol. 51; NRO, NCC, Surflete 78, John Herryes, Norwich (1431); F. Blomefield, *Essay Towards a Topographical History of Norfolk*, 11 vols (Fersfield, 1805–10), 4: 186; NRO, NCC, Spyltymbre 42, Henry Wilton, Norwich (1507).

tower and certainly meant a total but piecemeal rebuilding of the church.[16]

John Baret of Bury St Edmunds left a will dated 1463 which reveals that the sight and sound of time was, at that time, of prime importance.[17] Baret's chantry was to be celebrated in the Lady Chapel and he continued,

> I will that John Elys search surely and oversee the chimes at St Mary's altar, and the chimes in the steeple, there to make a new barrel which is ready and to make plumbs of lead and new lines and ropes and all things that [be]longeth thereto and substantially wrought to endure. And I require my executors to spare no cost that this be do.

At Baret's year day, the bellmen were to have 'fourpence to go yearly about the town . . . for my soul'; the sexton to have 'twelvepence so he ring well . . . and each year, what time my year-day falleth, that of twelve of the clock at noon before my dirge he do the chimes'. The sexton was to be paid eight shillings yearly 'to keep the clock, take heed to the chimes, wind up the piece and the plumbs . . . so that said chimes fail not to go through the default of the said sexton'. The Baret family originated at Cratfield in East Suffolk. The Cratfield clock bell was a gift of William Aleys, churchwarden in the 1490s, and the bell inscribed 'Prey for the sowle of William Aleys' still stands in Cratfield's vestry. The clock-keeper in 1535–6 was John Smyth, the gild priest, who was paid a wage of 16*d.* 'till the feast of the Purification of Our Lady'; and the clock for which he was responsible now stands in the tower.[18] Neighbouring Laxfield, a parish of roughly three hundred souls, housed five 'great' bells and a clock in its church tower, the clock benefiting from a 40*s.* bequest for its new bell.[19] At Halesworth, the 'Mary Baret' was bought with ten marks left to the people of Halesworth in 1493, and although re-cast in 1624, she still

[16] F. Woodman, 'The rebuilding of St Peter Mancroft', in A. Longcroft and R. Joby, eds, *East Anglian Studies: Essays Presented to J. C. Barringer on his Retirement* (Norwich, 1995), pp. 290–4.

[17] Bury St Edmunds, Suffolk Record Office [hereafter SROB], Hawlee 95, John Baret, Bury St Edmunds (1463), printed in S. Tymms, ed., *Wills and Inventories from the Registers of the Commissary of Bury St Edmunds and the Archdeacon of Sudbury*, Camden Society, 1st ser., 49 (1850), pp. 15–44.

[18] W. Holland (ed. J. J. Raven), *Cratfield: a Transcript of the Accounts of the Parish from AD 1490 to AD 1642, with Notes* (London, 1895), pp. 18, 65.

[19] NRO, NCC, A. Caston 139, John Noloth, Laxfield (1482).

hangs – and rings.[20] A more personal bequest came from William Gage, a cleric from Woolpit, who in 1500 left two astrolabes to the library of St Peter's college in Cambridge, and his clock to Roger Blownfeld, a witness to his will.[21] At Mount Bures, four bells were recorded in the steeple, and there were two hand-bells and another little bell in the chancel, these perhaps being a sacring bell rung to alert people at the elevation of the Host during Mass, and a bell to accompany the priest when carrying the *viaticum* to the dying, small objects which were sometimes purchased through a testator's generosity.[22]

Most testators knew, or were advised, how to regulate bequests by remote control to ensure that work would be completed. Stage payments could also be exercised by executors releasing money when the parish got around to doing the work, but neither method was always successful. At Helmingham, in Suffolk, a Norfolk mason, Thomas Aldrych, undertook to build a tower of knapped flint to a height of sixty feet.[23] The contract was dated 1487. The tower was to be finished within ten years and the townsfolk agreed not to hang any bells for four years after completion. Nevertheless, in 1538, the battlements were still unfinished. On Lavenham's tower, the corner pinnacles never have been finished. William Chapman left ten marks for the repair of Mildenhall's 'great' bell in 1464 but, within two years, the townspeople had brought an action for breach of contract against Richard Brasyer, the Norwich bell-founder, because he had failed to recast it. Was the bell still awaiting attention in 1535, when Henry Pope bequeathed £3 10*s.* towards its making, adding philosophically 'whensoever the town go about the making thereof'?[24] Running repairs to bells were frequently covered by bequests, including one and a half stones of hemp bequeathed for new bell-ropes to ten named churches;[25] and the churchwardens at Boxford and Walberswick

[20] NRO, NCC, Caston 169, Geoffrey Baret, Halsworth (1493); see J. J. Raven, *The Church Bells of Suffolk* (London, 1890).

[21] NRO, NCC, Cage 92, William Gage, clerk, Woolpit (1500).

[22] 'Church Goods in Suffolk, no. XXVII', *The East Anglian, or Notes and Queries*, n.s. 2 (1887–8), p. 56. These figures come from the inventory of 1552.

[23] L. F. Salzman, *Building in England down to 1540: a Documentary History*, rev. edn (Oxford, 1967), pp. 547–9.

[24] SROB, Baldwyne 379, William Chapman, Mildenhall (1464); L. F. Salzman, *English Industries of the Middle Ages* (Oxford, 1923), pp. 154–5; SROB, Poope 51, Henry Pope, Mildenhall (1535).

[25] NRO, NCC, Briggs 28, Margery Howton, Mildenhall (1515).

recorded countless similar repairs.[26] At Walberswick ropes, clappers, knepylls, bell-frames, and bell-wheels were all renewed, a skin for the baudrick costing 10*d.*[27] In 1469, Walberswick's bells were hallowed. This cost the churchwardens 25*s.* 8*d.*, implying there were several bells to hallow; but gifts as well as two specific bequests had been received towards the hallowing, which was a dedication ceremony similar to baptism.[28] Salzman tells of the hallowing of 'Harry', the great bell of St Lawrence, Reading, which ceremony cost the parishioners 6*s.* 4*d.*, 'Sir William Symys, Richard Clich and Mistress Smyth being Godfather and Godmother at the consecracyon'.[29]

Time was capricious, the hour of death uncertain. Not all wills were written at the last moment. John Baret survived his will by several years and other testators had other reasons for writing 'before their time'. Richard Camplyon emphasised the uncertainty of time in 1491, asking to be buried at Stowmarket 'if it happen me there to yield the ghost'.[30] Agnes Wrestler was proposing to set off on pilgrimage to St James of Compostella in 1479; and Herry Fleccher, a yeoman, was journeying far afield in 1513, 'taking upon me the chance of this wretched world going with the kings grace and my master this new voyage in to France'.[31] Mariners and fishermen referred to journeys about to be undertaken which might be one-way only. Robert Pylgryme, 'being in the parties of Iceland', wrote his will in July 1516. When the ship returned home with its catch of cod in November, probate was granted to his executors. A traditional deathbed scene, on the other hand, presents an ordered death. Margery Lowis, 'being sick, lying upon a bed in a parlour . . . in Lowestoft' made her will with the principal actors arranged in order of appearance as on an East Anglian seven-sacrament font.[32] The bell which accompanied

[26] P. Northeast, ed., *Boxford Churchwardens' Accounts 1530–1561*, Suffolk Record Society, 23 (Ipswich, 1982).

[27] R. W. M. Lewis, ed., *Walberswick Churchwardens' Accounts A.D. 1450–1499* (privately printed, 1947), pp. iv, 26, 129, 139. In his introduction, Lewis suggested Walberswick had a total of five bells. By the Reformation, there were only two, and a sanctus bell: see 'Church goods in Suffolk, no. XLIV', *East Anglian*, n.s. 3 (1889–90), p. 131.

[28] Lewis, *Walberswick*, p. 26.

[29] Salzman, *English Industries*, p. 150.

[30] SROB, Hervye 453, Robert Camplyon, Stowmarket (1491).

[31] NRO, NCC, Aubrey 113, Agnes Wrestler, Lowestoft (1479); SROI, IC/AA2/8, fol. 9, Herry Fleccher, Wissett (1513).

[32] An excellent example of this can be seen at the church of St John the Baptist, Badingham, Suffolk. The panel depicting extreme unction on the seven-sacrament font shows five figures which include the priest anointing the temple of a dying man, and a grieving woman standing at the foot of the bed.

the *viaticum* was now silent.[33] As Margery lay *in extremis*, it was the church bell which tolled slowly, protecting her soul from the machinations of the devil, and at the time of her death the passing-bell would ring 'in tokenyng of calling to God for help', as one Norfolk testator expressed it.[34] Margery would have awaited her end in the accepted position, supine, *gisant*, face turned towards Heaven, her position in these final moments of life prefiguring the effigy after death.[35] The last confession made, the cool chrism would be applied by the priest to her temple, breast, and wrists before she received the *viaticum*.

For all Purgatory may have been timeless, time on earth was short, and the swifter the soul achieved amendment, the sooner purgation was completed. A testator from Aldeburgh demanded 'to have, as hastily as it may be had after my decease, a trental *songyn* for my soul'.[36] Thomas Fuller asked that twelve friars in Thetford should have twelvepence to celebrate twelve masses in one hour immediately after his death, while a priest from Lavenham wanted prayers to be said 'in as possible haste after my death as is goodly' for himself and his friends.[37] The good offices of relatives and friends on earth coupled with the prayers of the faithful departed, who had an indefinable and inaudible part to play in this, ensured that everything had been accomplished to speed the soul. The funeral took place as soon as possible, as much to implement the prayers of suffrage as to dispose of the rotting flesh. The liturgy began with *Placebo* on the eve and *Dirige* with *Commendatio animarum*, the Commendation, followed on the day of the funeral. The Requiem Mass and interment came next, the place of burial frequently intimated in the will.[38] Additional masses could be included on burial day, the Mass of the Five Wounds to be celebrated at

33 SROI, IC/AA2/3, fol. 23, William Leveriche, Dunwich (1483); P. Ariès, *The Hour of Our Death* (Harmondsworth, 1983), p. 173; C. W. Dugmore, *The Mass and the English Reformers* (London, 1958), p. 67.

34 R. Houlbrooke, *Death, Religion and the Family in England 1480–1750* (Oxford, 1998), pp. 115, 149.

35 P. Ariès, *Western Attitudes towards Death: from the Middle Ages to the Present* (London, 1976), p. 8.

36 SROI, IC/AA2/3, fol. 196, Thomas Waller, Aldeburgh (1496).

37 SROB, Hervye 349, Thomas Fuller, Mildenhall (1484); NRO, NCC, Gelour 238, Robert Hervey, priest, Lavenham (1479).

38 R. C. Finucane, 'Sacred corpses, profane carrion: social ideals and death rituals in the later middle ages', in J. Whaley, ed., *Mirrors of Mortality: Studies in the Social History of Death* (London, 1981), pp. 40–60.

Henstead for Margaret Doke, 'the priests that shall sing to have every of them 8*d*.'[39]

Divisions of time, common to everyday life, were employed to bring a temporal discipline to Purgatory for, to the dying, purgatorial time must have seemed of indefinite duration, intransigent and uncompromising. To those familiar with the 3,000 years indulgence granted for each Mass of the Holy Name to be celebrated over thirty days, as described in an early fifteenth-century missal from Norwich diocese, Purgatory erred on the lengthy side.[40] The continuum of time after death became more comprehensible if worldly time, to which testators were well attuned, was used to advantage in the planning of post mortem intercessions. Prayers were divided and subdivided as necessary or as financially expedient and were tied back to the earthly calendar or the liturgical year, for this was the measure of time the dying knew well. Prayers to be said in the first days of mourning included the popular seven-day and thirty-day celebrations, celebrated at the end of the first week after death and at the end of the first month.[41] John Speed of Mildenhall specified in 1438, 'to each chaplain present at my obsequies on the day of my death fourpence, and 7 day and 30 day.'[42] Speed, however, exerted his own subtle control of events by continuing, 'If the vicar will allow Mass of Requiem to be celebrated on the three days specified, then threepence be offered at Mass but, if not, only 1*d*.' Joan Foote was twice widowed and a woman of some wealth. She omitted the seven-day celebrations but left instructions for Placebo, Dirige, and Mass of Requiem by note to be performed every day 'for thirty days next immediately after my burying day with all the priests then dwelling within the said town [of Melford]'. Priests, clerks, two holy water clerks, the sexton, two children acting as servers to be named by her executors and supervisor, and poor men and women within the town were all to attend and were all to be paid and fed at her expense.[43]

The natural culmination of the seven- and thirty-day celebration was the anniversary or obit, also called year-day, year-tide, year-mind, or earth-mind, the solemn occasion being celebrated with not a little ceremony as it relived the funeral service which had taken place

39 NRO, NCC, Cooke 99–100, Margaret Doke, Henstead (1540).
40 R. W. Pfaff, *New Liturgical Feasts in Later Medieval England* (Oxford, 1970), p. 63.
41 NRO, NCC, Puntyng 162, Margaret Bumble, Wissett (1540).
42 NRO, NCC, Doke 67, John Speed, Mildenhall (1438).
43 PRO, Prob. 11/9, fols 94r–v, Joan Foote, widow, Melford (1517).

precisely at the same place and time the year before.[44] Sir Edmund Jenney, who dated his will the Friday before the Nativity of the Blessed Virgin Mary as late as 1522, asked for his year-day to be kept for ten years, 'willing, charging and trusting alway that my heirs after my will performed shall and will continue the same by the space of an hundred years and longer.'[45]

Perpetual chantries, or service chantries running for as long as the ninety-nine years specified by John Garneys in his will of 1524, rarely appear in these wills;[46] but the intercessions which appear to have become increasingly popular, to the disadvantage of the seven- and thirty-day and anniversary commemorations, were the service chantries administered by feoffees, who hired a priest to 'sing for the soul' of the deceased for a year or two, paying him an annual stipend of around £6. In Norwich, Tanner found these services tended to run from one to four years; while Burgess suggested that the majority in Bristol ran for one or two years, occasionally for five or ten.[47] These could be divided and even subdivided. Harry Dixon requested 'a priest by half a year for me and my wife and for my friends';[48] and an extract from the executors' account of Robert Shepparde, reflecting Robert's testamentary choice of intercessions, reads, 'Item paid unto the Greyfriars for a trental 10*s*., Item for a priest for a quarter service 30*s*.'[49]

Financial outlay over time was of immediate importance to these testators for death, to many of them, meant leaving orphans, widows, widowers, parents, dependent neighbours, servants, and friends. Whatever personal requirements were recorded in their wills, they tried to maintain a certain control over the future, for testators were now accustomed to hearing the hours ringing out in measured, accurate strokes, and they knew that time equalled money. As the cost of the prayer varied directly with its duration and timing, intercessions could be had for a set fee and where bequests were made with the barest information, the cost invariably represented the type of intercession required. An *Agnus Dei* cost 4*d*. A certeyn (or sangrede as it was often

[44] SROB, Hervye 10, Roger Fuller, Melford (1473).

[45] NRO, NCC, Briggs 108, Edmund Jenney, knight, Knodishall (1522).

[46] NRO, NCC, Briggs 138, John Garneys, Kenton (1524).

[47] N. P. Tanner, *The Church in Late Medieval Norwich*, Pontifical Institute of Mediaeval Studies, Studies and Texts, 66 (Toronto, 1984), p. 101; C. Burgess, 'Strategies for eternity: perpetual chantry foundation in late medieval Bristol', in C. Harper-Bill, ed., *Religious Belief and Ecclesiastical Careers in Late Medieval England* (Woodbridge, 1991), p. 3.

[48] SROI, IC/AA2/3, fol. 55, Herry Dixon, Aldeburgh (1487).

[49] SROI, IC/AA1/2/5/14.

called in Suffolk) cost 4*s.* 4*d.*, and involved the reciting of the testator's name from the bede roll. In 1483, John Coket asked that the curates or parish priests of seven named churches in Norfolk and Suffolk should 'have yearly, during the space of seven years, 4*s.* 4*d.*, to this intent: that every of the said curates or parish priests, every Sunday during the said years, openly in the pulpit, when he biddeth the bedes, to pray for my soul'; and according to the will of Almeric Molows in 1461, it was also possible to have a certeyn of masses.[50] Margaret Borhede paid the curate 12*d.* to keep her name on the bede-roll for eight years after her death, and although it is not known how long a name would remain enrolled, that probably ensured a longer commemoration than a smaller payment would have purchased.[51] A fee of 10*s.* represented a trental, a group of thirty masses for the repose of the soul to be said on a single or on successive days, very often requested to be undertaken by friars: 'to Friar John Tesard of the order of Preachers in Yarmouth, doctor, to celebrate for my soul and for the soul of Agnes, my late wife, a trental of masses of St Gregory: 10*s.*'[52] A half-trental would cost 5*s.*

The passage of time, however, took its toll of bells and intercessory prayers as testators responded to edicts of the Crown. Within a few years of 1540, the prayers had ceased. No longer did the bellmen alert the parishioners of Bury to pray for John Baret on his year-tide. Bequests to towers and bells faltered. At Gorleston in 1547, it was said that the initial sale of plate 'brought in £14 four years since, the which is bestowed upon a new bell-frame to the bells and a new battlement to the steeple for four years past.'[53] Yet the fate of sacring bells and bells carried to the dying was sealed as churchwardens acceded to the crown commissioners. The ringing for the dead on All Saints' night

[50] PRO, Prob. 11/7, fols 170v–172r, John Cocket, Ampton (1483); SROB, Baldwyn 287, Almeric Molows, Wattisfield (1461).

[51] SROI, IC/AA2/11, fol. 120, Margaret Borhede, Henstead (1531); J. C. C. Cox, *Churchwardens' Accounts from the Fourteenth to the Close of the Seventeenth Century* (London, 1913), pp. 61, 159. Donors' names on the bede-roll were recited at Christmas, Michaelmas, and every Sunday. The bede-roll was later called the Bidding Prayer, i.e. bidding the congregation to pray for the souls of the benefactors.

[52] NRO, NCC, Aubrey 72, Everard Wrestler, Lowestoft (1486). See also E. Duffy, *The Stripping of the Altars: Traditional Religion in England, 1400–1580* (New Haven, CT, and London, 1992), pp. 293–4; R. Pfaff, 'The English devotion of St Gregory's trental', *Speculum*, 49 (1984), pp. 75–90. The total cost of a full trental of St Gregory, called 'le grete trental' should have been 12 marks (£8) or 5*s.* 4*d.* per mass, celebrated on the feasts of the Nativity, Epiphany, Purification, Annunciation, Easter, Pentecost, Trinity, Assumption, and Nativity of the Virgin Mary, repeated three times within the ten octaves. Testators, however, consistently bequeathed 10*s.* for St Gregory's trental in a truncated and cheaper version.

[53] 'Church goods in Suffolk, no. VII', *East Anglian*, n.s. 1 (1885–6), pp. 102–4.

was banned, the passing-bell was restricted to 'a short peal before the burial and one after' and, apart from one bell to be rung before the sermon, the general ringing of bells on Sunday was 'utterly forborne'.[54] But the clocks remained, their rhythmic ticking a reminder of merchants' time; for by now God's time was a thing of the past.

University of East Anglia

[54] R. Hutton, *The Rise and Fall of Merry England: the Ritual Year, 1400–1700* (Oxford, 1994), pp. 80, 84; Houlbrooke, *Death, Religion and the Family*, p. 266; Duffy, *Stripping of the Altars*, p. 452.

ORGANIZING TIME FOR SECULAR AND RELIGIOUS PURPOSES: THE *CONTEMPLACION OF SINNERS* (1499) AND THE TRANSLATION OF THE BENEDICTINE RULE FOR WOMEN (1517) OF RICHARD FOX, BISHOP OF WINCHESTER

by BARRY COLLETT

THE career of Bishop Richard Fox was marked by his dedication to hard work and his obsession with the organized management of time. Fox was born about 1448 into a Lincolnshire yeoman family, was educated at local grammar schools and Oxford, was subsequently ordained, and later became a doctoral student at the University of Paris. In 1484 he joined the entourage of the exiled Henry Tudor, who recognized his ability and gave him considerable responsibility in negotiating with the French government and planning the 1485 invasion of England.[1] After Bosworth, Fox became Lord Keeper of the Privy Seal and a member of the royal council with particular responsibility for foreign affairs.[2] He was appointed bishop successively of Exeter, Bath and Wells, Durham, and Winchester. In 1516, he founded Corpus Christi College, Oxford, retired from politics, and returned to Winchester, where he died in 1528.

Fox was the epitome of secular efficiency, working about seventy hours each week, in accordance with his belief that those who bore responsibilities should, in discharging those responsibilities, strive after 'better, straighttar and spedyar wayes . . . mor diligence and labour . . . duties and profitz'. Such efficiency must be based upon clear understanding of the objectives and outcomes: 'every person ought to knowe the thyng that he is bounde to kepe or accomplisshe . . . the thyng that he is . . . bound to do and execute.'[3] Francis Bacon, using government archives nearly a hundred years after Fox's death, admired his accurate appraisal, careful planning, and co-operative effort, and described him

[1] M. V. C. Alexander, *The First of the Tudors: A Study of Henry VII and his Reign* (London, 1981), p. 24.

[2] Peter Iver Kaufman, *The 'Polytyque Churche': Religion and Early Tudor Political Culture, 1485–1516* (Macon, GA, 1986), p. 23.

[3] *The Letters of Richard Fox, 1486–1527*, ed. P. S. and H. M. Allen (Oxford, 1929), pp. 83, 86–7.

as 'a grave counsellor for war or peace' who worked with Henry 'as it were an instrument with the workman'.[4] Insofar as efficiency was instrumental in the survival of Henry VII's government – a disputed view – Fox was probably the royal servant most responsible for Tudor political stability. His efficiency is also obvious in the management of his dioceses and episcopal estates during long absences in London – especially his choice of suffragans and stewards such as West, Incent, Nykke, and other capable administrators in the pre-Reformation English Church, some of them trained in law at northern Italian universities.[5]

Organized time was a crucial element of Fox's efficiency. His letters and papers show that he adapted 'merchants' time' to his political work in ways that might aptly be summed up as 'civil service' time, showing itself in three characteristic modes. Firstly, time was used as an instrument of planning for routine daily tasks. Secondly, time was organized to plan an entire career: once education was completed no time should be wasted in leaving the schools and beginning a career, for as Fox once said, it was 'sacrilege for a man to tarry any longer at Oxford than he had a desire to profit'.[6] The emphasis upon this long secular view of time was probably shared by the increasing numbers of career civil servants under the Tudor regime. The third characteristic was that he applied 'civil service time' to all social levels, not merely to senior civil servants, but also to archdeacons, abbesses, stewards, carpenters, or anyone else with responsibility for particular tasks. The organized use of time was an instrument in the hands of all capable persons who had responsibilities to discharge.

Fox's attitudes are mostly embedded in his letters, routine memoranda, and instructions issued in the busy working life of an executive. Despite his considerable literary talents he expounded the theme of time only twice, in the two books which are the subject of this study, each written during a period of crisis in his career. The first work, the *Contemplacion of Synners*, was published in 1499 at the end of his difficult time as Bishop of Durham.[7] As Henry VII's regional chief executive in Northern England, he organized military defences and negotiated with the Scots on military matters and on the marriage of

[4] Francis Bacon, *The Historie of the Raigne of King Henry VII* (London, 1622), p. 49.

[5] C. J. Drees, *Authority and Dissent in the English Church* (Lewiston, 1997), p. 72; Kaufman, *'Polytyque Churche'*, p. 202.

[6] William Harrison, *Description of England*, quoted in *DNB*, 20, p. 150.

[7] Westminster, 1499. Cited hereafter as *Contemplacion*.

Henry's daughter Mary to King James IV, and also tried to control the extremely unruly landed families of the border country who were giving the English and Scottish governments great trouble during the 1490s with their disregard for the law of both countries.[8]

> For theef and robber ye wyll be aduocate
> Whiche is more synne and shamfull confusyon.[9]

This was a period in which Fox became reflective about social disorder and the kinds of social and ecclesiastical reform necessary to achieve the smooth and effective functioning of society. His experiences at Durham followed by the Cornish unrest during 1497–8 brought him to the conclusion that good government and stability required not only that the monarch exercise power efficiently, but that it was necessary for the governed to co-operate actively with governance, through a heightened sense of their social morality. Coincidentally, Nicolò Machiavelli, then a senior civil servant in Florence, was considering similar questions about the necessity for civic *virtù*. The political questions troubling these contemporary bureaucrats were not new, but the problem for both men was how to reach practical conclusions. Fox's solution was to relate virtuous behaviour to the fulfilling of vocational responsibilities (as mirror-for-princes literature had always done), but to this formula he added two radical elements. First, he defined the process of fulfilling both worldly and religious vocations in the same terms – that of efficiency and the proper use of time. Second, the requirement of practical efficiency, common to both worldly and spiritual vocations, was extended to all people who exercised responsibility and authority at whatever level. The management of time was the key to personal efficiency, which in turn ensured the well-being of all individual souls and the community. 'God's time' and secular time (or 'merchants' time') were two sides of one coin, the proper use of which sustained the health both of souls and societies.

[8] Anthony Goodman, 'Religion and warfare in the Anglo-Scottish Marches', in Robert Bartlett and Angus MacKay, eds, *Medieval Frontier Societies* (Oxford, 1989), pp. 245–66, esp. 259–61. The border problem is neatly summarized by E. F. Jacob, *The Fifteenth Century* (Oxford, 1961), p. 637: 'The problem of order in the north was not simply one of defence against the Scots, but of providing adequate civil administration.'

[9] *Contemplacion*, sig. Cvi^{r}; J. A. F. Thomson, *The Early Tudor Church and Society, 1485–1529* (London, 1993), p. 78; Drees, *Authority and Dissent*, pp. 74, 78; Kaufman, *'Polytyque Churche'*, pp. 121–2; Alexander, *First of the Tudors*, p. 158.

The first literary fruit of his thinking was the *Contemplacion of Synners*, originally composed by a Scottish Franciscan as a manual of daily biblical and patristic readings in Latin, intended for the devotional use of friars.[10] Fox probably first saw the manual in Durham or during a diplomatic visit to Scotland. He revised and published it during his last year at Durham, adapting its monastic devotions for the laity. The original appears to have consisted of seven themes – one for each day of the week – with readings in Latin from the Bible and the fathers for each day. Each day's theme has been supplemented with meditations and verses in English, thus broadening the readership to include the literate laity and those to whom it could be read. Fox was therefore seeing the themes of worldly uncertainty (Monday), the need for enlightenment (Tuesday), sin's effects (Wednesday), judgement and penance (Thursday), Christ's Passion (Friday), the pains of hell (Saturday), and the joys of heaven (Sunday), as a basis for preaching his own view of responsibility and the use of time. He then wrote a prologue: 'desyrynge gretly all vertue to encreace and vyce to be exyled, hath caused this booke to be enprynted to the entente that oft redynge this booke [the reader] may surely serche and truely knowe the state of his conscyence.'[11] The completed monastic–lay manual was printed by de Worde at Westminster, its colophon giving the date of 10 July 1499.

The *Contemplacion* began with the commonplace exhortation to realize how precious is time. Because life is short and death is close, time is a commodity in short supply, not to be used casually or wastefully, but profitably in an organized manner. 'Therefore sythen our tyme is but short and uncertayne, and for dyuerse Impedymentes ryght daungerous, it sholde be prouffytably spended. For as saynt Bernarde sayth, there is no thynge commyted to the dysposycyon of man more precyous than is tyme.'[12] Present time must be used systematically in the contemplation of future time and mortality: 'To thynke hoe deth by dulfull dyffeueraunce Out of this worlde for euer shall you exclude.'[13] Within this meditation on the use of time we have a brief glimpse of a deep and sophisticated concept of hell seen in terms of personal frustration: because death ends all available time in

[10] C. S. L. Davies, 'Richard Fox', forthcoming in the *New DNB*. Dr Davies has kindly shown me the typescript of his article.

[11] *Contemplacion*, sig. Aii^r.

[12] Ibid., Prologue, sig. Aiii^r.

[13] Ibid., sig. Fvi^r.

which to make changes, the timeless pains of hell include the suffering of impotence and frustration. This frustration – to have no time when tormented by the urgent need for 'reformacion' – constitutes

> The furyious fyre and paynes Infernall
> . . . of a thousand myllyon yeres the slydyng
> . . . is but a begynning.[14]

Fox urged that meditations upon time and eternity should be stimulated more by life's experiences than by abstract pious exhortations. Thus news of the death of others, whether the well-publicized funeral of a prince or the death of a neighbour, should stimulate all people to meditate upon the passage of time and the need for swift, diligent action:

> Sythen but retorne thou drawes daye by daye
> To deth and dome, dress the with dylygence
> And thy misdede amende without delaye.[15]

Having grasped the preciousness of time, the next task for thoughtful sinners was to understand how to use their remaining time. First, they should 'prouffytably spend' it systematically reading this devotional treatise, 'often redynge' and 'dyscrete[ly] glosynge', day by day and week by week, until through their reading and annotating they came to understand clearly the state of their souls and the requirements of their vocations 'with often redynge of mysty maters myght folowe a new intellygence & a more clere understandynge. Wherfore I commende for conclusyon to the reders of the same treatyse that theyr dyscrete glosynge may prevayle.'[16]

Having cogitated upon passages from Scripture, the fathers, and Fox's additional meditations, the contemplative sinner was next to read other exemplary literature to acquire the 'new intellygence & a more clere understandyng' of worldly affairs.

> And though for the prouffytable dyspensacyon of our precyous tyme ryght spedefull it be to all estates & condycyon of men to rede or here dyuerse scryptures & compylacyons of books, in

[14] Ibid., sig. Mviii^{r}.
[15] Ibid., sig. Giii^{r}.
[16] Ibid., sig. Avi^{r-v}.

> whiche are conteyned noble hystoryes moral techynges, & ryall examples of men of vertue by the whiche we may eschue vyce & chese vertue.[17]

The passage reveals the connection between the spiritual and the worldly realms. People moved from spiritual clarity to worldly understanding by continuing to read Scripture, and also by reaching out to include edifying exemplars and 'moral techniques' – use of that term was characteristic of Fox and describes his book. This meant that the spiritual and the worldly realms were part of a single spectrum of human activities in which time was to be 'profitably dispensed'. Time spent in acquiring 'the seed of vertue and sapience', 'a new intellygence & a more clere understandying' brought people a double harvest – spiritual and worldly – from 'theyr precyous tyme, in the whiche they myght gete scyence & soule helthe.' Moreover time was not to be merely a measure for this or that event in the routines of God's time or merchant's time, but was to be used as an instrument of planning – to be 'profitably dispensed'. Thus, properly organized, time brought both spiritual and worldly understanding which in turn brought competence to worldly vocations and benefited the common good.[18]

The meditation on Zachariah, set for Tuesday, expounded the obligations of leaders to implement justice and peace and to set a good example to the populace. This was essential to social harmony and a healthy society: 'The comen people may stande in to good state, Whan that the hedes are ruled by reason.'[19]

> Now to you kynges I crye with compassyon
> That of your state ye take Intellygence
> Thynke on your bonde, and hygh professyon
> How ye sholde kepe with duly dylygence
> Peas in your people, thrugh Justyce and prudence.[20]

Monarchs and other leaders often mismanage their task by falling into the 'spiritual cowardness' of exercising their authority for political advantage and out of 'drede for Mannes Indygnacyon'. In acting thus 'theyr wytte & strength they spende in perdycyon, And to do Iustyce

17 *Contemplacion*, sig. Aiii^r.
18 Ibid., sig. Aiii^r.
19 Ibid., sigs Eiii^r, Hvi^v–Iiv^v.
20 Ibid., sig. Biii^r.

they are effemynate.'[21] They fail to exercise their responsibilities for those people affected by their care; if they become 'vycyous and infatuate, Than falle the comens to folyche confusyon.'[22] Of course, rulers eventually answer for such failures of responsibility: 'A connynge kyng may then knowe sodenly, He may of god drede ferefull Jugement.'[23]

Tuesday's passages may appear to be yet another conventional mirror-for-princes exhortation to virtue; but an analysis of *Contemplacion* shows that they were part of a larger message about the efficient exercise of authority, based upon the management of time. Fox defined princely 'virtue' only briefly in terms of pious attitudes, yet much more in terms of good governance and the smooth and orderly running of society, combining moral virtue with clear-eyed and rational action. 'Justice' in governance was expanded into practical advice for kings and nobility on the need to delegate, communicate, and manage employees skilfully, and to avoid corruption and negligence:

> Fyrst to drede god, and loue aboue all thynge
> Syne of his persone haue generall gouernynge
> And see his offycers be true, and dylygent
> . . . In weyghty maters gyve personall presence,
> In smaller accyons, geuynge commyssyon,
> To men of fayth, good fame, and sapyence,
> Iustyce to kepe, without excepcyon,
> As they wyll answere to god and to your crowne,
> And take in queste how Justly they procede,
> But fede, or fauour, or clockyd correccyon,
> Then gyue theym dome accordynge to theyr dede.[24]

The *Contemplacion for Synners*, superficially a commonplace tract of moral exhortations, has been given a bureaucratic twist towards the obligations of authority at all levels, the techniques of exercising authority, the importance of time for both understanding and practical implementation.

Fox's meditations on the exercise of authority were then addressed beyond the political elite, to the lower orders, 'all estates and

21 Ibid., sig. Fiv^{v}.
22 Ibid., sig. Eiii^{r}.
23 Ibid., sigs Cv^{r}, Fiv^{v}.
24 Ibid., sigs Bv^{r-v}.

condycyon of men', who must similarly be informed by Scripture and moral tales. The egalitarian implications in this treatment of authority place the book beyond a mere religious discourse intended to control the beliefs and social behaviour of the lower orders. His hierarchical sense of authority was extended to 'all estates and condycyon of men' who also have responsibilities to exercise and who also need to manage time well in their own personal spheres, in both their worldly and spiritual work.

At first sight this bishop-bureaucrat's emphasis upon the systematic implementation of virtue seems like an example of semi-Pelagian doctrines which the Reformers later pilloried as the prime defect of the pre-Reformation Church, that the sinner merits salvation through good works made in co-operation with the grace of God.[25] The *Contemplacion*, however, suggests that Fox's semi-Pelagianism, if it existed at all, was considerably modified by his Pauline and Augustinian allusions to prevenient grace. Moreover, in *Contemplacion*, Fox's concern about 'time misspent' reveals a specific perception of the bondage of the will. There is a lengthy passage in which Fox implies that once the stage of youthful innocence has passed, it is almost impossible to move towards meritorious behaviour because the efficacy of free will has been crippled by its social context.

> But now allas grene youthe and Innocence,
> To vyce and vertue whiche is indyfferent,
> So sonped[26] is in synne and Insolence,
> Thrugh euyll ensample and lack of techement.
> Thus of chyldehode the tyme is so myspent,
> That though men wolde theyr lost lyfe refounde,
> Euyll blage[27] maketh so grete Impedyment
> It wyll not be but yf grace more habounde.[28]

Grace is present at all times, but young people are led away from that grace by the bad example of their elders. 'So now all states of grace lacke the lyght, Both spyrytuall, temporall and men of religyon, The

[25] Strictly speaking semi-Pelagianism is the doctrine that the beginning of faith is made independently of God's grace, and that subsequently the sinner merits salvation through good works made in co-operation with divine grace.

[26] Sumped: in a morass, sodden.

[27] Blague: pretentious falsehood.

[28] Ibid., sig. Dv^{v}.

daye of vertue tornynge in the nyght, Thrugh synne are blynded and worldly abusyon.'[29] This suggests that grace is at all times present, but through blindness caused by 'euyll ensample and lack of techement' people deliberately turn away from God's grace and salvation rather than accepting it (almost an inverse of semi-Pelagianism). Fox's recognition of the power of social constraints on virtuous behaviour acknowledged an incapacity of the will to act justly – a socially conditioned negation of the freedom of the will. The antidote to this socially conditioned crippling of free will was for the young to overcome this hindrance, first by the recognition of God's grace and then to accept the gift of grace by not wasting time but preparing themselves (as should kings, nobles, and common people), for the efficient discharge of their responsibilities:

> . . . to forbere
> The seed of synne, of sloth, & neglygence
> And sowe the seed of vertue and sapience.[30]

Fox's view on the incapacity of the will through social conditioning was not a precursor of Luther's theological teachings on free will; but is evidence that eighteen years before the posting of Luther's theses an English bishop, expounding what seem to be semi-Pelagian doctrines of merit and salvation, was nevertheless aware of the problem of the incapacity of free will, and was trying to grapple with that problem both in terms of theological doctrine and human behavioural responses.

* * *

In 1517 the same themes reappeared in Fox's second book, the translation of the Benedictine Rule for nuns.[31] Fox was then nearly seventy, growing blind, disenchanted with the court of Henry VIII from which he had just retired, and regretful for his neglect of his diocesan responsibilities for which he feared 'the damnacion of my

29 Ibid., sig. Bii^{r}.

30 Ibid., sig. Dv^{r}.

31 London, 1517; cited hereafter by the incipit, *Here begynneth*. The translation of the Rule is analysed and set in context in B. Collett, 'The civil servant and monastic reform: Richard Fox at Winchester, 1516', in J. Loades, ed., *Monastic Studies: the Continuity of Tradition* (Bangor, 1991), pp. 211–28.

saule and many other sawles wherof I have the cure'.[32] When he returned to Winchester amongst his first actions was a review of spiritual zeal in religious houses, both male and female. After discussions with abbesses and prioresses he concluded that some nuns did not do their job properly through ignorance of their work: 'the yonge Nouices may first knowe and understande the sayde Rule, before they professe them to it, So that none of them shall mowe [now] afterward probably say, that she wyste nat what she professed, as we knowe by experience that somme of them have sayd in tyme passed.'[33] Three conventual heads asked him to translate the Benedictine Rule into English for nuns who did not read Latin. Fox did so, expanding the sparse Latin and adding his own commentaries.

As he had done in the *Contemplacion of Synners*, he extended the original material to emphasise the fleeting nature of life and the closeness of death. What may be translated as 'keep death daily before one's eyes', Fox rendered more forcefully: 'allweyes suspecte deth, & have it dayly in remembrance as though it were present and continualy byfore your [e]yes.'[34] Almost all expressions of time were elaborated in translation. What may be rendered in English as 'at all times' and 'always' he translated as 'at all hours' and 'every houre'. He inserted references to time where the Rule had none: what may be rendered as 'God sees one everywhere', he translated as 'all myghty god allwayes, And continually ouer looketh seeth & heereth you, youre werkes, wordes, and thoughtes, in every place and tyme.' He also translated expressions of time to emphasise long and short term commitment: at 'every houre' for constant day by day commitment, whilst his use of 'continually . . . in every place and tyme' and 'seasons' implied long-term commitment and organization.[35]

Fox expounded monastic time in terms of the efficient use of secular time. If nuns spent time hearing the Rule in Latin without understanding it, they not only wasted time but failed to learn from the Rule how to use time productively in the future. They therefore 'nat only lese their tyme, but also renne into the euident daunger and perill of the perdicion of their soules'. Even when the Rule was understood there were other impediments to the effective running of the

[32] Letter to Wolsey, 23 April 1516: Allen and Allen, *Letters of Richard Fox*, p. 83.

[33] *Here begynneth*, Prologue.

[34] Justin McCann, ed. and tr., *The Rule of Saint Benedict* (London, 1952), p. 29; *Here begynneth*, sig. Biv^{v}.

[35] McCann, *Rule*, pp. 20, 29; *Here begynneth*, sig. Biv^{v}.

monastery. Time was wasted by sluggishness and slowness to act, so what may be translated as 'Not somnolent; not slothful',[36] Fox greatly expanded: 'ye be not slepy and slugysshe nor moche yeuen to slepe . . . ye be not slewthful, heuy, or slow to doo your office or duete.' A worse problem was idleness. The concise Latin of the Rule's chapter 48 translated as 'idleness is the enemy of the soul', but he enlarged it into the more vigorous 'Idlenes is an vtter and extreme enemy of the sowle'.[37] The emotional turmoil aroused by malice, anger, and complaining wasted time and must be removed quickly, so he greatly expanded the sparse Latin translatable as 'Not to yield to anger. Not to nurse a grudge'. His comments made three references to long-term malice and anger: 'be neuer thurghly nor longe angry, & if it fortune you to be angry, that then ye execute not your yre or anger, nor to do that thyng that your yre moueth you to. . . . you bere no malyce longe in your mynde, thynkynge in tyme to wreke your angre, or to auenge you.'[38] The admonition is that of the Benedictine Rule, but the additional language and emphasis is Richard Fox's application of secular efficiency to God's time.

Finally, Fox himself 'derected, composed & ordred' some uncertain details of the Rule to improve routine organization. He specified the placing of the sixth hour for English nuns: 'From the holy feeste of Easter unto witsontyde, the susters shall goo to dyner at the .vi. houre of the daye whiche is after the Englyshe rekenyng abowtes an houre before the mydday.' Similarly, for the sake of precise arrangements, he adjudicated in the matter of wine. Although nuns ought not to drink wine at all, he acknowledged that modern young women would resist the prohibition (as the Rule said about men a thousand years earlier), therefore they could have wine or ale provided they 'drynke not to our full and saciate, but scarcely and soberly'. He determined that the Rule's measure, a 'hemina', an ancient measure and the subject of some dispute, should be one English pint, 'nygh abowtes a mydes in the Italion toonge, a pynte in the frenche, and the Englysche toonges (which be nyghe by all oon measure) suffyseth to every person in wyne for oon daye.'[39] This exact placing of the sixth hour, the measure of

[36] McCann, *Rule*, p. 29, amended; *Here begynneth*, sigs Aii^{r}, Biv^{v}.

[37] McCann, *Rule*, p. 111; *Here begynneth*, sig. Fi^{r}.

[38] *Here begynneth*, sig. Biv^{r} (nos xxii and xxiii of the instruments of good works); McCann, *Rule*, p. 27.

[39] *Here begynneth*, sigs Eiv–v.

wine, and other details, removed uncertainties within the regulated monastic life.

The preface which he added to chapter 4 (on the instruments of good works) reminded nuns that the monastic vocation depended, in common with lay vocations, on having clear aims, being organized, managing time well, getting things done efficiently in order to have a successful outcome 'bothe in this p[re]sent lyfe, may honestly & after the pleasure of god be derected, composed & ordred & also after the same lyfe, they may blessedly reigne with christ in heuen.'[40] The words 'directed, composed and ordered' were the language of structured vocations, and at the heart of his methodical and business-like approach to religion. Time was to be used in clarifying what he had described in 1499 as 'scyence and soule helthe', through which came clear understanding: ordered piety for individual spiritual health, and pious order for institutional perfection.[41] Fox was a pre-Reformation reforming bishop using the Benedictine Rule's regulated daily round to expound to the nuns of his diocese the importance of clarity, organization, and purposeful accomplishment; but behind the reforming approach of *Here begynneth* lay the cast of mind of a bishop-bureaucrat obsessed with methodically improving – indeed perfecting – both spiritual and worldly affairs through clarity, the ordered use of time, and continually getting things done: *semper reformanda*.

Fox's emphasis upon time and order for 'both spiritual, temporal, high estate, and low' crossed boundaries between 'spiritual' and 'worldly' values. Fox undoubtedly accepted the superiority of spiritual values, and he believed that involvement in worldly affairs was a distraction in the pursuit of holiness for, being a political prelate, he knew the dangers of mingling the two: 'We are so blundred in worldly besynes, Both spyrytuall, temporale, high estate, & lowe . . . We selle our soule for vayne prosperityee', he had written in *Contemplacion*.[42] Now, in *Here begynneth*, what might have been translated more concisely from the Rule as 'avoid worldly conduct', Fox translated as 'ye medle not nor talke, speke, nor commune, in worde, werke, or deed of any worldly maters or busines, but them utterly & extremely refuse and renounce so that in all your affections ye be utterly alienate from the worlde.'[43] This translation, however, was made for cloistered nuns

40 *Here begynneth*, sig. Biii^{r}.
41 *Contemplacion*, sig. Aiii^{r-v}.
42 Ibid., sigs Biii^{r-v}.
43 *Here begynneth*, sig. Biv^{r} (no. xx of Instruments of good works); McCann, *Rule*, p. 27.

whose complete withdrawal from 'worldly maters or business' was the vocation of only a privileged few. Withdrawal apart, both worldly and religious vocations, at all levels of responsibility, needed the properties of organized time, clarity of thought, and skilful, efficient action, to see that things get done well and to achieve stability within the soul and across the whole community. Fox therefore held an integrated view of the spiritual and the secular, in which the 'religious' in the cloister and the laity in 'the world' were quite separate, yet operated upon the same practical principles of clarity and efficiency.

Was Fox a 'worldly' prelate? Fox's views on time-management are a key to reassessing whether he was guilty of a 'scandalous example of neglect' because he gave much greater attention to politics than to his ecclesiastical duties. In return for service to the king, Fox held a number of sees, Exeter, Bath and Wells, Durham, and Winchester, each wealthier than the last; a clear example of how Henry VII used ecclesiastical promotion to reward his ministers and tie the episcopate to the business of government.[44] On the part of Fox, this was not worldliness in the sense of being indifferent to spirituality, which he clearly was not, or falling into excessive ambition or acquisition. It could perhaps be called worldly in the simple sense of the bishop's working time being occupied in political rather in episcopal duties, but this view rests upon an anachronistic bipolar distinction between political work and its moral purposes, which ignores the interdependence of the two – a mingling neatly encapsulated by Kaufman's description of Fox as one who 'thought administratively about religion and religiously about administration'.[45] Another interpretation could be that Fox's theological-social beliefs were directed towards ensuring worldly social conformity of the populace through control by the governing classes. His beliefs, however, had this purpose only indirectly, for they were principally addressed to the more basic question of how a community, whether a small institution or an entire society, can function with as much stability, equity, and prosperity as possible.

Moreover, Fox's idea that at all levels worldly and religious vocations overlap and use the same processes of management was potentially empowering to all social classes. In that respect Fox goes

[44] J. R. Lander, *Government and Community: England, 1450–1509* (London, 1980), pp. 124–5; R. H. Britnell, *The Closing of the Middle Ages? England, 1471–1529* (Oxford, 1997), p. 152; Drees, *Authority and Dissent*, p. 71.

[45] Kaufman, *'Polytyque Churche'*, p. 120.

some way towards providing both the theory and the practice of 'meritocracy', a concept which deserves closer investigation in this period. These ideas, expressed in 1499 and 1517, had the same liberating potential as Luther's more effective attack of 1520 upon the separation of the spiritual from the worldly, and his consequent assertion of the spiritual condition of 'the world'. Fox also had his version of Luther's corollary that the State had the right to reform the Church, not in doctrine but certainly in the organization and behaviour of the clergy:

> Thus myght that kyng in fame & mede increase,
> And cause the clergye to kepe good obseruance,
> And brydell many fro blynded bruckylnesse,
> . . . And though a kyng haue no correcyon
> On spirytuall state, yet may his hygh prudence
> In to the chirche cause reformacyon.[46]

Fox's concern for the organized use of time, his definition of vocation, his belief that the health and survival of an institution depended upon the smooth working of all its members, with all ranks doing their job properly through the organized use of time; all these ideas could not only perhaps give purpose and status to the lower orders, but were also meant to improve the morale and the working efficiency of small societies and organizations. In *Here begynneth* the small perfect societies were monasteries, but his ideas applied also to other institutions. They are clearly reflected in the statutes of Corpus Christi College, Oxford, which Fox himself drafted in 1516, and he applied similar thinking to estate management, confraternities, and the work of builders and master carpenters. Moreover, there are indications that from the 1490s Fox believed that the efficient and smooth working of such small societies provided blueprints for larger institutions – government, Church, universities, and English society at large.[47]

Fox's ideas on time and management in *Here begynneth* also give the appearance of a semi-Pelagian programme of organized merit to achieve salvation. A closer examination, however, reveals this to be

[46] *Contemplacion*, sig. Ci^{r}.

[47] James McConica, 'The rise of the undergraduate college', in idem, ed., *The History of the University of Oxford, vol. III: the Collegiate University* (Oxford, 1986), pp. 17–29; John Newman, 'The physical setting: new building and adaptation', ibid., pp. 607–11.

even less the case than with *Contemplacion.* The Benedictine Rule frequently asserts entire reliance upon God's grace, attributing all good acts and virtues to God's grace rather than to merit. Fox's own views are suggested by the considerable vigour with which he translated the Rule's several passages on prevenient grace, particularly on the theme that works did not merit salvation but were a response to the gift of salvation through the grace of 'he whiche hath vowched safe to accept us as in the nomber of his chosen children':[48] 'what so euer goodnes or vertue ye thynke to be in you . . . repute and knowe well that it co[m]meth oonly of god and not of your selfe, ne of your merytes nor deseruynge.'[49] The implication of the Rule, given greater strength by Fox's translation, is that God's grace is already and always present, a point repeatedly made by monks during the Reformation controversies.[50]

Fox's use of time in his two books gives us windows into pre-Reformation spirituality in at least five overlapping respects. First, his assertion of common ground between the secular and the spiritual, in that both required clarity of thought, efficiency, and skills of management, diminished the distinction between 'spiritual' and 'worldly'. Second, piety was connected to doing one's job properly; and since this required that time be organized, the way in which time was used was crucial in his doctrine of vocation – both spiritual and worldly. Third, Fox extended this notion to all who, at whatever level, were obliged to do their jobs properly; that is, to exercise responsibility with the organized and efficient use of time. Embedded in this idea are the outlines of contemporary theory and practice of the concept of meritocracy.[51] Fourth, the outcome of time management and piety was that communities such as monasteries, confraternities, and colleges, were enabled to fulfil their functions as small perfect societies. Fifth, his ordered approach to spiritual life, treating it as an exercise in efficiency and time-management, may appear as an example of crude

[48] *Here begynneth*, sig. Aiii^{r}.

[49] Ibid., sig. Biv^{v}.

[50] An excellent example is the Italian Benedictine monk Isidoro Chiari, of the Congregation of Santa Giustina of Padua, a Pauline scholar who addressed this question at length in his *Adhortatio ad concordiam* of 1536: *Isidori Clarii . . . Epistolae ad amicos . . . accedunt duo opuscula alia* (Modena, 1705), p. 197.

[51] For a discussion of merit and authority, some Italian influences, and Fox's views, see B. Collett, 'British students at the University of Ferrara, 1480–1540', in M. Bertozzi, ed., *Alla corte degli Estensi: filosofia, arte e cultura à Ferrara nei secola XV e XVI: atti del convegno internazionale di studi, Ferrara, 5–7 marzo 1992* (Ferrara, 1994), pp. 125–46.

semi-Pelagianism attacked by the Reformers (and, later, Dominicans); but this judgement would be misleading, for Fox was not advancing a doctrine of salvation through merit but an affirmation that God's work must be well done. In thinking through this objective, and how it would be achieved by the efficient use of time, Fox developed ideas on the bondage of the will, the acceptance of God's grace, vocation, the exercise of both spiritual and secular authority by all Christians, and the ideals of ordered piety and pious social order, all of which are similar to themes in Luther's almost contemporary teachings. The paradox of a 'semi-Pelagian' pre-Reformation prelate thinking in similar terms to the Reformers means that historians must look again at the ideas of both the pre-Reformation Church and the Reformers themselves, and at the way that 'worldly' perceptions stimulated and shaped theological ideas. Moreover, it is time for polarities to be set aside whilst paradoxes are grasped more fully. The common understanding of the value and use of time would be a useful starting point.

University of Melbourne

TIME FOR PRAYER AND TIME FOR WORK. RULE AND PRACTICE AMONG CATHOLIC LAY SISTERS IN THE DUTCH REPUBLIC

by JOKE SPAANS

> One shall rise at five in the morning and go to communal prayers at six. After prayer and meditation one shall read the first three canonical hours: matins, lauds and prime – but those who do not have the leisure can also do this over their work.[1]

THIS is how the Rule of a community of seventeenth-century Dutch Catholic lay-sisters started. Theirs was a very flexible rule, designed to accommodate both wealthy sisters, who could spend much of their time in their devotions, and poorer ones, who had to work for their living. Their Rule provides a good illustration of attitudes towards the use of time among pious Christians in the seventeenth century.

The community whose life and devotional routines are considered here was one of semi-religious women. These Catholic lay-sisters lived in Haarlem, one of the larger towns of Calvinist Holland. They called themselves *kloppen*, a word of unknown etymology and thus untranslatable.[2] They belong to a well-known type, however. They chose to live a celibate and sober life, in obedience to a father-confessor, but without taking any formal vows. They devoted themselves to both contemplation and works of piety in the service of the Church. The Counter-Reformation produced a series of Orders and congregations of this kind, some male but most female. They carried out an active apostolate of teaching, nursing, and works of mercy, under clerical supervision. Whereas the Church had always

[1] Utrecht, Library Rijksmuseum Het Catharijneconvent [hereafter Library Catharijneconvent], collection 'Parochie St Joseph' [hereafter St Joseph], MS 102 (*Regel en onderwijsing der Maaghden*, hereafter cited as *Rule*), fol. 7r.

[2] Most informative on the Haarlem *kloppen* is Eugenie Theissing, *Over klopjes en kwezels* (Utrecht, 1935); more general on *kloppen* in the Dutch Republic, Marit Monteiro, *Geestelijke maagden. Leven tussen klooster en wereld in Noord-Nederland gedurende de zeventiende eeuw* (Hilversum, 1996); Elisja Schulte van Kessel, *Geest en vlees in godsdienst en wetenschap. Vijf opstellen over gezagsconflicten in de zeventiende eeuw* (The Hague, 1980), chs 2–3, pp. 51–115.

been rather shy of female religious who were active in the world, in the course of the seventeenth century these groups came to be valued and encouraged.[3]

The congregation of *kloppen* in Haarlem began around 1580. From the start it existed in an officially Protestant environment. The sisters do not seem to have considered themselves a direct continuation of earlier types of semi-religious, even though there were contacts with the members of beguinages in Haarlem and other Dutch cities, and they took over certain characteristics of the Sisters of the Common Life such as the writing of Lives and the composition of *rapiaria*, collections of devotional texts for private use. They most closely resemble the Counter-Reformation non-contemplative female congregations.[4] It will be argued here that the *kloppen* should be seen as a link in the tradition of semi-religious communal life, bridging the gap between the late medieval beguines and Sisters of the Common Life on the one hand and the Counter-Reformation Orders and congregations on the other. After describing the religious niche these Catholic women filled in Protestant Holland and the tradition in which they stood, attention will move on to how they regarded themselves, and how the appreciation of the religious life changed in the later seventeenth century.

* * *

In the Dutch Republic the Catholic Church was formally outlawed. Catholics enjoyed freedom of conscience only. Any form of exercise of their religion was formally forbidden and from 1580 penal laws of increasing severity were devised. These laws were never as draconian as those in force in England at the time, and moreover were never fully enforced, but they did limit Catholic religious practice to the private sphere. In this situation semi-religious could render their Church

[3] Generally, Ruth P. Liebowitz, 'Virgins in the service of Christ. The dispute over an active apostolate for women during the Counter-Reformation', in Rosemary Ruether and Eleanor McLaughlin, eds, *Women of Spirit. Female Leadership in the Jewish and Christian Traditions* (New York, 1979), pp. 131–52; Ronnie Po-chia Hsia, *The World of Catholic Renewal 1540–1770* (Cambridge, 1998), pp. 33–41, 138–51; on specific communities Anne Conrad, *Zwischen Kloster und Welt. Ursulinnen und Jesuitinnen in der katholischen Reformbewegung des 16./17. Jahrhunderts* (Mainz, 1991); Elizabeth Rapley, *The Dévotes. Women and Church in Seventeenth Century France* (Montreal, 1990); M. de Vroede, *Kwezels en zusters. De geestelijke dochters in de Zuidelijke Nederlanden in de 17e en 18e eeuw* (Brussels, 1994).

[4] Most Counter-Reformation female congregations were founded later than the *kloppen*. On chronology see Conrad, *Zwischen Kloster und Welt*; Rapley, *Dévotes*; De Vroede, *Kwezels en zusters*, pp. 95, 115–18.

eminent service.[5] The remaining priests in the Republic had to work within a rudimentary church organization. In 1622 the Pope had declared that the traditional hierarchy had collapsed and that consequently this area was a mission field. Vicars apostolic co-ordinated the work of secular and regular priests, who were technically missionaries. These priests had to gain the confidence and tacit approval of local magistrates in order to be able to carry out their ministry.[6]

The penal laws against the Catholics were based on the suspicion that some of them remained loyal towards the Spanish enemy. Priests were closely watched for signs of seditious activity, especially when these were foreigners or regulars, who necessarily stood under the direction of superiors residing abroad. Jesuits were suspected above all others. Among indigenous secular clergy there were also strong and generally known feelings of resentment towards the Protestant establishment. The first two Vicars Apostolic, Sasbout Vosmeer and Philip Rovenius, condemned any accommodation of Catholics to the institutions of the officially Protestant Republic, from civil marriage to service in the army. This forced upon Dutch Catholics a division of loyalty between their Church and the civil authorities, and made pastoral work, for which priests needed the tacit approval of these same authorities, something of a balancing act.[7]

Soon after the religious alteration it became common for Catholic priests, both secular and regular, to gather groups of *kloppen* around their person. These women kept house for the priest, swept the church, sewed and embroidered vestments and linen for the altar, enlivened church services with vocal and instrumental music, taught the catechism, engaged the faithful in pious conversation, collected alms for the needy and contributions towards the education of candidates for the priesthood, cared for the sick, kept watch over the dying, and prayed for the souls of the departed. As they often were the daughters of local Catholic families of some social standing they

[5] John Bossy, *The English Catholic Community 1570–1850* (London, 1975), p. 282, suggests that female semi-religious, by mediating between Catholic clergy and the 'matriarchal' familial religiosity in recusant families, could have helped the English Catholic community grow.

[6] On Dutch Catholicism in the seventeenth century, L. J. Rogier, *Geschiedenis van het katholicisme in Noord-Nederland in de zestiende en zeventiende eeuw*, 3 vols (Amsterdam, 1945–7); W. P. C. Knuttel, *De toestand der Nederlandsche katholieken ten tijde der Republiek*, 2 vols (The Hague, 1892–4).

[7] M. G. Spiertz, 'Pastorale problemen in de Noordnederlandse katholieke kerk van de zeventiende eeuw', *Kleio*, 20/iii-iv (1979), pp. 42–8.

provided the priest with a dense network of local connections, that protected him, but at the same time ensured that he would not provoke the local magistrates by overstepping the boundaries set on Catholic religious activity. In this way they both supported and domesticated the clergy.[8]

* * *

Such semi-religious women have not been very extensively studied. Moreover, any scholarly interest has mainly focused either on the late medieval or on the Counter-Reformation periods.[9] Communities of semi-religious women emerged in Western Christianity from the twelfth century onward, as with the growth of the cities lay religiosity developed new forms. The highly urbanized Low Countries were rich in semi-religious, as were the Rhine valley and Northern Italy. Women who could not afford the dowries required for entering a convent, or who had family responsibilities that prohibited leaving the world, but still wanted to lead a religious life, entered communities of beguines or Sisters of the Common Life or affiliated with an established religious Order as tertiaries. These alternatives were cheap, and did not necessarily mean leaving the family home. This does not mean however that this middle state, between monastic and lay, was seen as second-best to entering a convent as a professed nun. Many seem to have been attracted to the relative freedom it offered. The pressures that the ecclesiastical hierarchy eventually brought to bear on these groups to transform them into enclosed monastic Orders were often resented.[10]

The Church, often presented as somewhat inimical to these lay initiatives, also had an interest in them. It has been convincingly argued that semi-religious groups emerged mostly in periods of change. The middle state, with its lack of strict rules and its flexible organization, offered the opportunity to experiment with new devotional styles. The eventual transformation of these experimental communities into

[8] Cf. Hsia, *World of Catholic Renewal*, p. 84.

[9] Separate historiographical surveys in Kaspar Elm, '*Vita regularis sine regula*. Bedeutung, Rechtsstellung und Selbstverständnis des mittelalterlichen und frühneuzeitlichen Semireligiosentums', in Frantisek Smahel, ed., *Häresie und vorzeitige Reformation im Spätmittelalter* (Oldenburg, 1998), pp. 239–73; De Vroede, *Kwezels en zusters*, pp. 7–15.

[10] De Vroede, *Kwezels en zusters*, p. 75, Florence Koorn, 'Women without vows. The case of the beguines and the Sisters of the Common Life in the Northern Netherlands', in Elisja Schulte van Kessel, ed., *Women and Men in Spiritual Culture. A Meeting of North and South* (The Hague, 1986), pp. 135, 141.

monastic Orders can be seen as a natural evolution, a stabilization of newly developed forms, adapted to new situations. Canon law was stretched in order to accommodate semi-religious groups, uneasily at first, but with growing confidence as time progressed. By the beginning of the sixteenth century some theologians defended the position that the middle state more closely followed the example of the early Church than the monasticism developed in the course of the Middle Ages. In the heyday of humanism with its reverence for the pristine purity of the apostolic and patristic Church, it could be presented as the highest Christian vocation.[11]

The Counter-Reformation Church was at first highly ambiguous about semi-religious women. The Council of Trent prescribed strict claustration for women religious. With these rulings the hierarchy of the Church not only protected male clerical prerogatives, but also responded to social pressures. Women who entered religious communities without strict vows had the right to return to the world, marry, and demand their dowries. A daughter or sister who did not leave the world for good by taking solemn vows and confining herself behind convent walls could prove a financial liability to her relatives.[12] On the other hand the Catholic reform movement favoured an active apostolate. Hesitatingly at first, but from the middle of the seventeenth century wholeheartedly, the Church came to see semi-religious female congregations as a valuable asset in its outreach to the faithful.[13]

The period from the Council of Trent to around 1630 appears to have been one of experimentation. Only a few groups, those who with full support of the local bishop proved themselves valuable to the introduction of reforms, were exempted from the general rule of enclosure. The Dutch *kloppen* of the late sixteenth and early seventeenth centuries were among these, together with the Ursulines after their reorganization by Cardinal Borromeo and before their transformation into an enclosed Order, and also some more local communities in Italy, the German Empire, and the Southern Netherlands.[14] The forms of lay apostolate developed in these communities would be

[11] Elm, '*Vita regularis*'.

[12] Leibowitz, 'Virgins', pp. 140–2; Rapley, *Dévotes*, pp. 38–41.

[13] Rapley, *Dévotes*; Kathryn Norberg, 'The Counter-Reformation and women: religious and lay', in J. W. O'Malley, ed., *Catholicism in Early Modern History* (St Louis, MO, 1988), pp. 133–46.

[14] Schulte van Kessel, *Geest en vlees*, pp. 95–110; Rapley, *Dévotes*, pp. 48–56; De Vroede, *Kwezels en zusters*, pp. 85–94; Conrad, *Zwischen Kloster und Welt*, pp. 95–102.

taken up in the great flowering of active female congregations from the second half of the seventeenth century.

* * *

The Haarlem community of *kloppen* has left a wealth of documents from which to determine their own appreciation of the middle state. The most important of these are a collection of over two hundred Lives, the Rule, and about sixty volumes of sermons and devotional texts.[15] The Rule, in combination with material from the Lives, gives an insight into the sisters' views on the use of time. About rest and play we can be very short: the Rule recommends an hour of recreation after lunch, which the sisters seem to have used for a stroll in the garden, to sing spiritual songs or chat. Good cheer was considered important. The spiritual directors ordered celebratory banquets twice a year: indoors at Carnival and a garden party in the summer. Similar festivities came to be held when new *kloppen* were received into the community. These occasions for merriment are only mentioned in passing in a few Lives, and it is clear that older sisters considered them frivolous innovations.[16]

The main interest of the sisters was the cultivation of their spiritual lives through prayer, meditation, reading of devotional literature, and not least the sacraments of the Church and the sermons of their directors. Only the richer sisters, however, could spend much of their time at their devotions. Quite a number of *kloppen* had to work for their living. The Rule gives extensive prescriptions for the techniques through which secular preoccupations like work could be turned into prayer. These techniques were not specific to the *kloppen*, but can be found among many semi-religious groups, from the Sisters of the Common Life to the Counter-Reformation *dévotes*.[17] They were devised to discipline the minds of those who did not partake in the safe and regular liturgical

[15] All of this in Library Catharijneconvent, collections St Joseph and 'Preciosa Warmond' [hereafter Warmond].

[16] Life of Machteld Bickers (†1624), Library Catharijneconvent, Warmond, MS 92 B 13, fol. 159r, of Apollonia Areians (†1628), ibid., fol. 234v, and of Annetge Sixtus van Emingha (†1632), MS 92 B 14, fol. 84v, cf. Theissing, *Over klopjes en kwezels*, p. 95. For criticism of frivolity see the Life of Tryn Jansdr. Oly (†1651), MS 92 C 10, fols 431r, 435v.

[17] A. G. Weiler, 'Over de geestelijke praktijk van de Moderne Devotie', in P. Bange et al., eds, *De doorwerking van de moderne Devotie, Windesheim 1387–1987* (Hilversum, 1988), pp. 29–45; Louis Chatellier, *The Europe of the Devout. The Catholic Reformation and the Formation of a New Society* (Cambridge, 1989), pp. 33–8.

rounds of monastic timetables, but led a religious life in the world, whether in a community or individually.

The sisters were to formulate a pious intention for everything they did. Getting up early in the morning should remind them of the trumpets that will raise the dead from their graves at the Resurrection, or of the women who went to the grave where Jesus was buried early on Easter morning. While dressing themselves they had to contemplate how the first humans had been as if dressed in righteousness, a virtue lost by their disobedience.[18] The work they did was to be dedicated as a sacrifice to God. Not only the priest sacrificed, although he alone was authorized to officiate at the Mass. Everyone could sacrifice, remaining in the state in which she had been called. Each according to her status had to do what needed to be done, keeping her thoughts fixed on God, to avoid them straying into vain matters. Quick prayers, renewal of the pious intention, meditation on the sermon or lecture of the day, or other pious materials could help in this. Also they were advised to let the actual work they did inspire them to pious thoughts. Making clothes or anything that would serve as an ornament to the body should remind them of the virtues that adorn the soul; cleaning or repairing utensils of renewal of the spirit or attaining perfection; serving others for a meagre salary of what to do to deserve the heavenly reward that God promises the faithful.[19]

The Life of Magdalena van Dam (†1634) describes in great detail how she kept the schedule prescribed by the Rule. She was moderately well off, so she could spend relatively much of her time in the church, attending Mass, hearing sermons, and meditating. She was not a purely passive listener, but also sang in the choir and played the violin during services. With some other wealthy sisters she spent part of the day doing the sewing and mending for the sisters who had to go out to work for their living and did other charitable work. Yet all her time was dedicated to prayer and meditation. She had devised pious exercises for each of the twenty-four hours of the day and the night. For each hour she took into consideration a moment from the life of Christ, his hidden life during the night, and his public life during the day, and meditated on certain aspects of that episode. Also she invoked certain saints. At night, when suffering from sleeplessness, she kept these exercises, and for those she had missed while asleep she made up

[18] Library Catharijneconvent, St Joseph, MS 102, fols 8v–20v.
[19] Ibid., fols 98v–105r.

on waking again. When during the day she was unable to keep to her schedule, she relied on the saints she would normally invoke to do her exercises for her. In this way she was with her Bridegroom always, but also could do her work without worrying about neglecting her devotions.[20]

Interestingly, the same Rule has a very exalted view of the virtues of work. It very explicitly states that as there is a time for prayer, there also is a time to work, because prayer alone cannot produce holiness. Contemplation should always be accompanied by some useful work. This is proved by two main arguments. The first is that mankind was created to work, and if any would not work, neither should he eat. The second asserts that human nature of itself is too prone to the temptations of the world to be able to sustain a life of prayer only.[21]

The Rule starts by proving the first point from the order of creation. According to St Augustine, even before the Fall Adam was obliged to cultivate the Garden of Eden. In his pristine state of sinlessness this task was both easy and rewarding. It was only after the Fall that labour became a punishment. The Rule continues by pointing out that Scripture does not contain any exemplary lives of pure contemplation. Jesus himself left heaven to spend his first thirty years on earth as a carpenter. Mary and Joseph, although they were in the company of the Son of God continuously, both worked. The Apostles, after being granted the vision of the glorified Christ on Mount Tabor, returned to their fishing; and Paul, who had been transported to the third heaven, repeatedly indicates in his letters that he will not live from gifts or alms, but that he and his companions will work for their living day and night. It is not denied that pure contemplation is the most perfect state, but only God, his angels, and the saints in heaven can remain in this state of perfection continuously. Therefore the founders of the first monastic communities prescribed work as a fixed part of the daily routine of their monks. The Desert Fathers, Augustine, Chrysostom, Jerome, and Cassian, are all quoted as defenders not only of a modicum of manual labour, but actually of monasteries as self-supporting communities. They moreover condemned the accumulation of wealth in monasteries. The early

[20] Library Catharijneconvent, Warmond, MS 92 B 14, fols 182r–217r (Life of Magdalena van Dam); for the 24-hour schedule of devotions, fols 200r–205r.

[21] What follows is a paraphrase of the chapter 'On work' in the *Rule*: Library Catharijneconvent, St Joseph, MS 102, fols 81r–105v.

monks were exemplary in that they lived a sober life, taking from the fruits of their labour only their daily needs. Surplus wealth was given to the poor and not accumulated.[22]

The medieval monasteries, which exempted their monks from the biblical commandment to work for their living, are presented as having lost the perfection of this early simplicity. They lived from the endowment of their house or from begging. This set the monks free to spend their time in contemplation – and after the foregoing argument that only the denizens of heaven were entitled to pure contemplation this appears definitely presumptuous. But this is not the only criticism contained in the Rule. Idleness led the medieval monks to inconstancy, disquietude, and evil greed. The ambition to build large estates in order to draw fat revenues led them to flattering the rich and powerful and involved them in continuous litigation. All this involved them in the world, and made them dependent on creatures, instead of setting them free.[23]

The second argument in favour of work was that human nature is too weak to sustain a life of prayer and meditation only. Work alone could keep away the evil temptations that beset the praying soul. Pure contemplation is not wholly impossible for mere humans, but it is given only to the very few, and usually only in the form of temporary transports. The leaning towards creation instead of the Creator is the effect of original sin, an effect that cannot be eliminated except by the divine grace that is the reward for those who during many years have striven for perfection in the middle state, that is a life of both prayer and work. Just as a blacksmith mixes iron with other metals, because pure iron is weak, the founding fathers of the monastic Orders prescribed a mixture of prayer and some useful work, either manual labour, study, or teaching. This was even more necessary for virgins and widows, because of the weakness of the female nature. Jerome himself knew from experience that even fasting and prayer in the solitude of the desert could not isolate the human spirit from the seductions of the created world. It was the study of the Hebrew language that restored his peace of mind.[24]

In the end, work is the only certain way to deny the devil access to the heart. As long as David was a warrior he did not have time for

22 Ibid., fols 81v–86v.
23 Ibid., fols 86v–87v.
24 Ibid., fols 87v–90v.

adultery or murder; and as long as Solomon was busy building the Temple he did not succumb to idolatry. Judas became a traitor to Jesus because even years of discipleship could not cure his excessive sloth. Without work spiritual progress is impossible and holiness out of reach. Even those with independent means, who did not have to work for a living, should work, if only to give the results of their handiwork or their earnings from it to the poor. And this part of the Rule ends, as it had started, with the injunction that after death one would be held accountable for one's use of time. Time after all was God's gift, and only those who had spent it productively could die with a quiet conscience.[25]

* * *

The views of the Haarlem *kloppen* on the relative importance of prayer and work concurred with a number of more general currents of ideas in the sixteenth and early seventeenth centuries. Their criticism of the lifestyle of monks and nuns reflects reforming ideals, both in Protestantism and within the Catholic Church of the early sixteenth century. In the 1530s, while the preparatory negotiations which would lead to the convocation of the Council of Trent were under way, the Pope established a committee of four cardinals to formulate a list of reforms. In their report, the *Consilium de emendanda ecclesia* of 1535, the cardinals were critical of monastic life. They boldly proposed to abolish the contemplative Orders.[26] The new religious Orders, first of all the Jesuits, show new, reforming ideals. They focused on missionary activity, both to bring the faith to the heathen and to reinvigorate that same faith among Christians – that is, as long as it involved male Orders. Female religious participation in this mission of teaching came a bit later, as we have seen.

There was also a wider hostility, from the early sixteenth century, towards a life without work. In this period all over Western Europe reform of the system of poor relief and the repression of begging was being discussed. In these discussions also the Pauline text on the necessity for man to work in order to eat was prominent. Criticism was directed not only against able-bodied beggars and lazy vagabonds, but

[25] Library Catharijneconvent, St Joseph, MS 102, fols 90v–105r.

[26] Text-edition in *Concilium Tridentinum: diariorum, actorum, epistolarum, tractatuum nova collectio*, 13 vols (Freiburg im Breisgau, 1901–50), 12: 131–45; introduction and German translation by Luther (who must have had a field day) in J. K. F. Knaake et al., eds, *D. Martin Luthers Werke: kritische Gesamtausgabe*, 67 vols (Weimar 1883–1997), 50: 288–308.

in general against all those who lived from accumulated wealth and called it Christian living. The most radical of the sixteenth-century reformers may have been Vives, who held that it was plainly wrong to accumulate funds and endowments, even for the support of the poor. He expressly rejected hospitals. Of course the honestly indigent were entitled to charity, but this ought to be living charity. If all would give alms, according to their wealth and according to the actual need of the moment, the poor could be provided for in their own homes more efficiently and in a more Christian manner than by admitting them into an endowed hospital. Hospitals corrupted all those involved: they fostered greed in those who had to administer their funds and laziness in the poor.[27] These very same arguments are levelled against monasteries by the Rule of the Haarlem *kloppen*. The proposals for welfare-reform are still sometimes considered inherently Protestant,[28] but they also reflect social views very generally held in the sixteenth century, in all confessional camps.

Prayer alone would not make one holy. For the *kloppen*, as for earlier and contemporary semi-religious, work was necessary: mankind was created to work, and would be morally corrupted without it. Work and prayer were not mutually exclusive; on the contrary, a whole array of techniques was available to dedicate all one's time to devotion, and make work into prayer. These assumptions made it possible in the sixteenth century for people from a wide spectrum of social backgrounds to live a religious life while staying in the world. From the middle of the seventeenth century this seems to change, at least in the Dutch Republic. Piety, a devout lifestyle, increasingly became something for the well-to-do, for Protestants as well as for Catholics.

* * *

The answer to Question 43 in the *Heidelberg Catechism* states that believers should offer their lives as a sacrifice to God. The doctrine of the priesthood of all believers implied that each church member, staying within his or her calling, could lead a dedicated life of piety, pleasing to God. Interconfessional polemics accordingly portrayed Protestantism as a religion for weavers, cobblers, and women, reading

[27] Ludovicus Vives (ed. Armando Saitta), *De subventione pauperum* (Florence, 1973); on hospitals see pp. 70–2.

[28] Cf. Ole Peter Grell, 'The Protestant imperative of Christian care and neighbourly love', in Ole Peter Grell and Andrew Cunningham, eds, *Health Care and Poor Relief in Protestant Europe, 1500–1700* (London, 1997), pp. 43–65.

and discussing the Bible over their daily business, and Protestants rather gloried in this image. With the emergence of pietistic strains in Dutch reformed Protestantism, this egalitarianism faded. Pietists themselves acknowledged that those who had to work for their living could not lead a religious life.[29] True piety demanded leisure time, to read, pray, examine one's conscience, and cultivate the spiritual life in the meetings of pious conventicles. Work had come to be regarded as a distraction.

A similar shift in perspective seems to have affected the Dutch Catholic semi-religious. After the middle of the seventeenth century the typical *klop* was a woman from a good family, who lived alone, or with one or two others. Communities, like the one in Haarlem, in which richer sisters subsidized the poorer members, disappeared. These later *kloppen* took their guidelines for an individual spiritual life from printed manuals.[30] Where in Catholic countries the religious aspirations of poorer women could be channelled into teaching and nursing,[31] in the Protestant Republic there was no place for semi-religious in these fields. This was so not only because they could not openly act as Catholic religious, but mainly because the Republic boasted extensive public systems of both education and welfare, in which, increasingly so from the middle of the seventeenth century, provision was made for dissident religious groups.[32] *Kloppen* hardly took part in this. Here only the model of the solitary, well-to-do *dévote* remained.

University of Amsterdam

[29] Peter van Rooden, *Religieuze Regimes. Over godsdienst en maatschappij in Nederland, 1570–1990* (Amsterdam, 1996), pp. 69–70.

[30] F. Smit, 'Klopjes en klopbroeders binnen de clerezie', in idem, *Batavia Sacra* (Amersfoort, 1992), pp. 39–62. The *kloppen* described by Schulte van Kessel (*Geest en vlees*) and Monteiro (*Geestelijken Maagden*) may be examples of this later type. In the Dutch Republic printed manuals appeared mainly from the second half of the seventeenth century: Monteiro, *Geestelijke Maagden*, pp. 355–60.

[31] Cf. Rapley, *Dévotes*, pp. 69, 83–94, 113–16; De Vroede, *Kwezels en zusters*, pp. 135–79.

[32] Joke Spaans, *Armenzorg in Friesland, 1500–1800. Publieke zorg en particuliere liefdadigheid in zes Friese steden. Leeuwarden, Bolsward, Franeker, Sneek, Dokkum en Harlingen* (Hilversum, 1998).

DANIEL'S PRACTICE: THE DAILY ROUND OF GODLY WOMEN IN SEVENTEENTH-CENTURY ENGLAND

by ANNE LAURENCE

GODLY women from noble, gentry, mercantile, and clerical families were much commemorated at their deaths in funeral sermons. Apart from preaching on a suitable text, ministers commonly gave an account of the life of the deceased, describing, amongst other things, how she passed her time. Godly lives from sermons for men outlined the course of their careers, stressing their public activities, the manner in which they took religion out into the world and engaged with worldly matters; those for women followed a formula describing the deceased's childhood, virtuous education, marriage, performance as wife, mother, mistress of servants, hospitality (especially if the woman was the wife of a minister), and charitable work, and enumerated her merits in these roles. Instead of recounting the events of their whole lives, ministers dwelt upon the women's daily routine of pious practices, with variations for the Sabbath or days on which they took communion. The convention of *de mortuis nil nisi bonum* was strictly observed, but the edificatory nature of the life was also an important element in the telling of it. Sometimes sermon titles acknowledged this, otherwise they referred to the good death of the deceased or, if they were published to improve the career prospects of the preacher, they referred to the text upon which he had preached.

Women were praised for following Daniel's practice, the practice for which he was thrown into the lions' den. This was to kneel upon his knees, three times a day, and pray and give thanks before his God.[1] In the early years of the seventeenth century, Mrs Mary Gunter, companion to Lettice, Countess of Leicester, 'resolved upon Daniels Practice'. 'Besides Family duties, which were performed twice every day, by the Chaplain . . . And besides the private Prayers which she daily read in her Ladies Bed-Chamber, she was thrice on her Knees every day before God in secret.'[2] Lady Elizabeth Langham's 'constant

[1] Dan. 6.10.

[2] Samuel Clarke, *The Lives of Sundry Eminent Persons in this Later Age* (London, 1683), part 2, p. 137. For a discussion of this work, see Jacqueline Eales, 'Samuel Clarke and the "Lives" of godly women in seventeenth-century England', *SCH*, 27 (1990), pp. 265–76.

retirements' for her devotions in the 1660s 'were answerable to Daniels thrice a day'.[3]

Others went further and followed David's practice, 'Seven times a day do I praise thee because of thy righteous judgements.'[4] Elizabeth Langham, from three times a day, 'more than doubled that proportion even to David's seven times a Day' after the death of her much-loved sister-in-law.[5] Thomas Ken, preaching in 1682 at the funeral of Lady Margaret Mainard, described her devotions as following David's example 'as far as her bodily Infirmities and necessary Avocations would permit'. Not surprisingly, he also commented that 'her Oratory was the place, where she principally resided, and where she was most at home.'[6] The royalist Anne Halket 'divided the 24 hours into three parts, allocating five for Devotion, ten for necessary refreshment, nine for Business'. The five hours dedicated to devotion were from 5 to 7 a.m., 1 to 2 p. m., 6 to 7 p. m., and 9 to 10 p. m.[7] Mrs Eleanor Murden supposedly spent 'half her time in Praying and Reading, her circumstances allowing her leisure for it'.[8]

While funeral sermons naturally tend to stress the virtues of the deceased rather than their imperfections, diaries and autobiographies are more revealing about the success of efforts to observe the discipline of the godly timetable. As explicit exercises in spiritual accounting, they required the acknowledgement of personal failings. The Countess of Warwick was said to pass two hours a day 'in Meditation and Conversing with the Invisible World'.[9] However, she confessed in her diary that, especially when she was in London, she found the religious life difficult.[10]

The terms in which female godliness and the devout management of time are described have little to do with their religious or political allegiances. Margaret Houghton was the widow of a royalist M.P., but Isaac Ambrose, who preached her funeral sermon and whose prefer-

[3] Clarke, *Lives*, 2, p. 200.

[4] Ps 119.164.

[5] Clarke, *Lives*, 2, p. 200.

[6] Thomas Ken, *A Sermon Preached at the Funeral of the Right Honourable Lady Margaret Mainard* (London, 1682), p. 24.

[7] *The Life of the Lady Halket* (Edinburgh, 1701), p. 55.

[8] Thomas Reynolds, *A Funeral Sermon upon the Death of Mrs Eleanor Murden* (London, 1713), p. 25.

[9] Anthony Walker, *Leez Lachrymans sive Comitis Warwici Justa* (London, 1673), Epistle Dedicatory.

[10] *Memoir of Lady Warwick: also her Diary*, Religious Tract Society (London, 1847), p. 90.

ment to the vicarage of Preston she had assisted in 1649, was a well-known Presbyterian who lost his living in 1662. Lady Capel was the widow of Arthur Lord Capel, who had objected to ship money but had refused to rebel against the King. Elizabeth Langham was the wife of a royalist gentleman with a recent mercantile fortune, but more significantly she was the daughter of the Earl of Huntingdon, a royalist family but with a strong tradition of Puritan godliness. The Countess of Warwick was the wife of a strongly parliamentarian and Puritan man, and the daughter of the equivocally royalist Earl of Cork.

Their devotional regimes, even if imperfectly observed, imposed a considerable discipline on these women's lives, and one which biographers did not see as competing with their duties as wives and mothers. 'The perfection of a Lady that has a great Family, consists not in being all day upon her knees, but in dividing her time so well, as to set apart a proportion for prayers, and the rest for the affairs of her Family.'[11]

However, time management was an important matter, and conduct manuals and manuals of personal devotion, virtually always written by men, gave advice on organizing the day around religious devotions. It is common to find authors emphasising the need for different kinds of religious activity – family prayers, private reading, meditation, and study – but being noncommittal about the actual hours at which these activities should take place. The Puritan Isaac Ambrose believed that 'No time can be prescribed to all men; . . . it is enough that we set apart that time wherein we are aptest for that service.'[12] The godly had a duty not only to God but to others. The nonconformist Samuel Slater advised that private prayer had to take its place alongside other duties. 'Know, O man, thou sinnest if thou art in thy Closet, when it is thy duty to be in thy Shop; or thou, O woman, when thou oughtest to be employed about the affairs of thy Family; and thou, O Servant, when thou shouldest be doing thy Master's or thy Mistris's business.'[13]

Theophilus Polwheile, another Puritan divine, giving *Choice Directions How to Serve God*, advised adaptability. 'Let nothing interpose [between you and your private prayer] unless some special business

[11] Edward Panton, *Speculum Juventutis: or, a True Mirror; Where Errors in Breeding Noble and Generous Youth, with the Miseries and Mischiefs that Normally Attend It, are Clearly Made Manifest* (London, 1671), p. 278.

[12] Isaac Ambrose, 'Of the Nature and Kinds of Meditation', in *The Compleat Works of that Eminent Minister of Gods Word Mr Isaac Ambrose* (London, 1674), p. 182.

[13] Samuel Slater, *A Discourse of Closet (or Secret) Prayer* (London, 1691), p. 173.

accidentally come to be considered of', and if at such times there was 'occasion to speak (as having a bed-fellow, or any other company with you) let your discourses be suitable'.[14] Likewise, when going to bed he gave advice on meditating while undressing: 'Let your speeches (if there be company) be spiritual.'[15] But he also advised his readers not to leave work undone in order to have time for religious duties, but rather 'to dispatch your work that you may have time'.[16]

This reticence is in marked contrast to the manuals of huswifery which showed no hesitation in laying down most detailed timetables for the performance of household tasks. Elizabeth Burnet, third wife of the bishop, combined the advice of a devotional manual with more practical advice in managing a household and offered such stern injunctions as, 'Allow no more Time for sleep than Health requires. . . . Six or Seven Hours is enough for most Constitutions.'[17] But she was refreshingly direct about the difficulties, 'if needless Scrupulosity is indulged, it will become tedious, and more superstitious than profitable.'[18]

Different regimes were considered to be appropriate to different orders of people. Polwheile believed that servants should perform their religious duties in their own time, not their masters', for 'God does not allow that'.[19] Married and single women were expected to conform to Paul's advice that 'The unmarried woman careth for the things of the Lord, that she may be holy in both body and in spirit: but she that is married careth for the things of the world, how she may please her husband.'[20] This belief gave rise to comment that Elizabeth Langham, at her marriage, 'abated not of her Devotion, and

[14] Theophilus Polwheile, *Choice Directions How to Serve God, every Working, and every Lords Day* (London, 1667), p. 79.

[15] Ibid., p. 106.

[16] Ibid., p. 93. Robert Russell, preaching on the duty of prayer, drew a nice distinction between work and non-work: 'for People to go on and pour out their Souls to God in Secret, confess their own particular Sins and daily Infirmities, bemoaning their Case to God, bewailing their inbred Corruption, lamenting over a hard Heart, a blind Mind, a dead and dull Spirit, a hearty begging for Pardon, for Deliverance from Sin, for Power against Corruption, for Strength against the evil Lusting of the Flesh, Begging for Grace and a new Nature, and a new Life: now this Work, together with frequent Meditation, and Self-Examination, these Duties the Devil opposeth with all his Might': Robert Russell, 'The Saint's Duty and Exercise', in *Seven Sermons*, 29th edn (London, 1719), pp. 59–60.

[17] Mrs Burnet, *A Method of Devotion*, 2nd edn (London, 1709), p. 3.

[18] Ibid., 26.

[19] Polwheile, *Choice Directions*, p. 93.

[20] I Cor. 7.34.

thereby rendered herself a singular instance of exception, to the difference which the Apostle St Paul puts between a Wife and a Virgin.'[21] Margaret Mainard both 'retained her accustomed devotion which she practis'd when a Virgin', and successfully 'united Martha and Mary together, took a due care of all her domestick Affairs, and manag'd them with a wise frugality, with a constant deference, to God's merciful providence.'[22]

By the later seventeenth century such religious devotion was seen as primarily a female activity. The poet laureate Nahum Tate wrote in 1693, that 'it must be confessed, and ascribed almost wholly to the female sex, that religion at this day is anything more than a name. . . . We are too busy for contemplation, and leave it to the women as having more leisure to observe the punctilios in religion.'[23] For men, time spent on private devotion was secondary to their main occupation. Sir George Dalston, who died in 1657, gave himself to religion and devotion having divested himself of secular employment, but only after forty years as an M.P.[24] The young John Harington, who died at the age of twenty-two, was exceptional in leading a life disciplined by godly exercises. Needing only six hours sleep, he would often wake at four or five in the morning, read a chapter of Scripture, pray with his servants in his chamber, spend an hour reading some holy treatise such as Calvin's *Institutes*, share a psalm, chapter, and prayer with his family before dinner and supper, and conclude the day with prayers after supper. In addition, there was private prayer in his closet, three or four hours study and meditation on a sermon after dinner, and writing his diary after the prayers after supper. Before finally going to sleep someone in his chamber read him a couple of chapters of the Bible.[25] The account of his life inspired the young Elizabeth Langham to her regime of pious practices.[26]

A life of religious discipline might be regarded as work, occupying women's days with what could be a punishing timetable. This 'work'

[21] Clarke, *Lives*, 2, p. 200.

[22] Ken, *Sermon*, p. 35.

[23] Nahum Tate, *A Present for the Ladies, being an Historical Account of Several Illustrious Persons of the Female Sex*, 2nd edn (London, 1693), pp. 84–5.

[24] J[eremy] T[aylor], D.D., *A Sermon Preached at the Funerall of that Worthy Knight Sir George Dalston* (London, 1658), p. 33.

[25] Samuel Clarke, *The Marrow of Ecclesiastical History, The Second Part* (London, 1775), pp. 59–60.

[26] Simon Ford, *A Christian's Acquiescence* (London, 1665), p. 116.

was contrasted with leisure, on the one hand, and idleness on the other. Some women's devotions amounted to work, in the sense of being their principal employment. The terms 'task' and 'holy Work' were used of Elizabeth Langham's activities.[27] It was said of Lady Capel that 'prayer [was] the first work she went in hand with every morning.'[28] Elizabeth Wilkinson was said to be 'much busied in prayer, meditation and selfe-examination'.[29] Lady Anne Waller, wife of the parliamentary general, was, according to the Puritan divine Edmund Calamy, 'one who made Religion her business, not (as some Ladies do) her Idle hour, but her daily labour'.[30] Margaret Mainard's 'chief employment, was Prayer, and Praise'.[31]

A favourite text was Ephesians 5.16: 'Redeeming the time because the days are evil'. Not wasting time was an essential part of the discipline of the godly life. Isaac Ambrose's sermon on this text for Lady Margaret Houghton in 1657/8 claimed that 'Well she had learnt that idleness was the rust and canker of the soul, the Devils cushion, pillow, chief reposal.'[32] Lady Capel was 'a zealous abhorrer and hater of idleness' and it was said of Elizabeth Langham that she took care to spend the time when she was not at prayer or religious duties 'in profitable converse' and that she

> did buy Time out . . . of the Hands of those Wasters of precious Minutes, which buy it all up, even from the most Religious imployments, to lavish it out in Pass-times and Recreations . . . she never allowed herself to see any maskes, Interludes or Plays; or to play at Cards or the like Games.[33]

The Countess of Warwick was said by the preacher of her funeral sermon in 1678 not to play any games, judging them 'great wasters of

27 Clarke, *Lives*, 2, pp. 200–1.

28 Edmund Barker, *A Sermon Preached at the Funerall of the Right Honourable and Most Excellent Lady, the Lady Elizabeth Capell, Dowager, together with some Brief Memorialls of her Most Worthy Life and Death* (London, 1661), p. 34.

29 Edmund Staunton, *A Sermon Preacht at Great Milton in the County of Oxford Decemb: 9 1654 at the Funerall of that Eminent Servant of Jesus Christ Mrs Elizabeth Wilkinson, late Wife to Dr Henry Wilkinson, Principall of Magdalen Hall; Whereunto is added a Narrative of her Godly Life and Death* (Oxford, 1659), p. 24.

30 Edmund Calamy, *The Happinesse of Those who Sleep in Jesus* (London, 1662), p. 28.

31 Ken, *Sermon*, p. 24.

32 Isaac Ambrose, 'Redeeming the time. A sermon preached at Preston in Lancs January 4th 1657', in Ambrose, *Works*, p. 14.

33 Barker, *Sermon*, p. 37; Clarke, *Lives*, 2, p. 200.

precious time, of which she was always very thrifty'.[34] In her autobiography she referred to her conversion resulting in her days being 'almost quite taken up in reading, meditation and prayer, being then very solicitous to redeem my former misspent time'.[35] Her experience of conversion gave her 'inexpressible comfort', 'which did make me to hate and disrelish all my former vain and idle pleasures'.[36]

Religious discipline required every minute of the day to be filled. One of Lady Capel's virtues was that she was 'a strict accountant' of time, 'even to small parcels: beshrewing and grutching [grudging] every hour, which was otherwise spent, than either in the actual service of her God, or at least in some proportion and tendence thereunto'.[37] Lady Alice Lucy used every available opportunity to offer prayer and 'never removed out of one Room into an other, but she used some short Ejaculations, with lifting up her Eyes and hands to God'.[38]

For some women, private religious activities expanded to fill what they perceived as the amount of leisure available to them. Elizabeth Burnet's biographer reported that 'when she would divert herself with Work [that is, needlework], she had generally some Persons to read to her.'[39] She herself used the word 'leisure' to indicate periods of time when extra devotional activities might be added, suggesting, for example, that those who had the leisure should reflect on the virtues they found particularly difficult.

Even leisure needed to be occupied constructively. Margaret, Duchess of Beaufort, daughter of Lady Capel, was known for spending that time 'that many other ladies devote to the tiresome pleasures of the town . . . virtuously and busily employed in her garden. . . . [H]er servants assured us, that excepting the times of her devotions, at which she was a constant attendant, gardening took up two thirds of her time.'[40] Elizabeth Burnet's biographer refers to her spending much of

[34] Anthony Walker, *Eureka, Eureka. The Virtuous Woman Found, Her Loss Bewailed* (London, 1678), p. 58.

[35] Mary Rich, Countess of Warwick, *Autobiography*, ed. T. Crofton Croker, Percy Society, 22 (London, 1848), p. 23.

[36] Ibid., p. 22.

[37] Barker, *Sermon*, p. 37.

[38] Clarke, *Lives*, 2, p. 141 (ejaculation meaning short extempore prayer).

[39] Burnet, *Method of Devotion*, p. vii.

[40] Stepher Switzer, *The Nobleman, Gentleman, and Gardener's Recreation* (London, 1715), p. 54.

her time at her devotions and in reading when she lived in the country 'where she had much leisure'. After the death of her first husband, she 'had more Time and Leisure' to spend on them.[41]

The Duchess of Beaufort and Mrs Burnet, wife of the bishop, were wealthy and well-connected women. Indeed, almost all the examples quoted hitherto are of women of gentry or noble status, from prosperous if not wealthy circumstances which allowed them, and other women like them, to carry out their schedules of prayer and meditation. Two women of more modest circumstances, both wives of ministers, provide counter examples; they could scarcely afford to pray three times a day, let alone seven. Katherine Clarke, after her religious duties and household tasks, 'at leisure times imployed her self in knitting stockings for her self and grand-children'.[42] Another clergyman's wife, Mrs Crook, evidently sacrificed her own leisure to her husband's, for she was 'carefull, to free and ease him of all emergent occasions, avocations, and businesses of ordinary concernment, that so he might with the more freedom follow . . . his divine imployments, and enjoy himself, and friends in his necessary relaxations'.[43]

Leisure was something to be used profitably and idleness was to be avoided. Lady Capel's chaplain inveighed against idleness as

> a vice, grown of late years the common fashion and distinction, of too many of her [Lady Capel's] rank and quality; who, because the plenty and abundance of their estates, do advance them beyond the necessity of working for a livelihood, do therefore look upon themselves as priviledged and mark't out unto a life of Idleness; not considering that God Almighty, who hath given Ladies hands as well as others, doth also expect work and action from them (in proportion to their rank and quality) as much as from any people.[44]

His patron was herself

> careful to be continually busying her self about some good employment or other . . . so in case her spiritual enemy should

[41] Burnet, *Method of Devotion*, pp. vii, x.

[42] Samuel Clarke, *A Looking-Glass for Good Women to Dress Themselves by* (London, 1677), p. 26.

[43] Samuel Clarke, *A Collection of the Lives of Ten Eminent Divines* (London, 1662), p. 32.

[44] Barker, *Sermon*, p. 37.

> come suddenly thrusting upon her at any time with his temptations, she might have her answer ready, viz. That she had other work in hand and was not at leisure now to attend him.[45]

But for women of high social status, employment was not necessarily much more than the practice of ladylike accomplishments. Anne Halket declared that her childhood lessons in writing, speaking French, playing the lute and virginals, dancing, and needlework, showed that she was 'not brought up to an idle life'.[46] Idleness was addressed in the conduct literature with advice to allow 'no temptation [to] find opportunity to fix upon your wandering thoughts'.[47]

Idleness was equated with pointless amusements and with spending excessive time on unworthy ends. Dressing in the morning might provide the occasion for wasting time. Elizabeth Burnet advised, 'Lose not the Morning, by being too long in eating your Breakfast and Dressing.'[48] But it would be wrong to think that personal appearance was not of concern to the godly. They decried vanity and the mutability of fashion; nevertheless, a comely countenance and dress appropriate to the wearer's status were very important, and time spent on it was significant. Susanna, Countess of Suffolk, who died at the age of twenty-two in 1649, was said to have 'the least affection' for 'her Attire and Dressing' for herself 'but only for those who were related to her, that she might not seem mean or unworthy [of] their allyance or affections'.[49]

Dressing was plainly a process that took a substantial amount of time even for those who were not particularly concerned with their appearance, so it provided the occasion for reflection. Elizabeth Burnet counselled that 'While Dressing, at least before engaging in worldly Business or Study, employ your Thoughts on such Reflections as these: If any Sin has been committed since your last Examination, if you have indulged Sloth beyond the Rules of Health, or the like'.[50] Such considerations were not restricted to the manuals. Elizabeth

[45] Ibid., p. 38.

[46] John Loftus, ed., *Memoirs of Anne, Lady Halkett and Ann, Lady Fanshawe* (Oxford, 1989), p. 10.

[47] *The Whole Duty of a Woman: or a Guide to the Female Sex from the Age of Sixteen to Sixty . . . Written by a Lady*, 2nd edn (London, 1696), p. 3.

[48] Burnet, *Method of Devotion*, p. 100.

[49] Clarke, *Lives*, 2, p. 212.

[50] Burnet, *Method of Devotion*, p. 7.

Langham's memorialist was at pains to explain that, though she spent so long on meditation in her closet, she did not neglect her appearance, bestowing on it 'so much time and pains (after the necessary concerns of her Soul) as decency required, tho haply not so much as curiosity . . . would have called for'.[51] The Countess of Warwick's diary suggests that she spent as little time as possible in dressing, while Lady Lane had her children read passages from the Scriptures to her while she was dressing.[52]

By the later seventeenth century advocating and, indeed, holding up as a good example a life dedicated to religious observance carried less weight, perhaps because of fears of religious enthusiasm. The preacher of Lady Newland's funeral sermon in 1690 acknowledged that it was remarkable that, though she spent two hours in the morning at prayer and at least another hour before retiring at night, 'this severe and abstracted kind of Life, which she led, and which in others is too commonly attended with some very bad consequents, with Moroseness and Peevishness, Pride and Censoriousness . . . in her . . . produc'd quite the contrary.'[53] The Countess of Orford, who died in 1702, was said to have been 'ever constant to the prayers, service and sacraments of the church, at which her behaviour was devout and solemn, decent, natural and unaffected, and showed she was not acted by unaccountable fits and transports of devotion'.[54] Elizabeth Burnet advised moderation in devotional activity, but perhaps more from an apprehension that setting one's sights lower might in the end achieve more than from fear of enthusiasm. She advised that the portions of Scripture read as a basis for meditation should not be long, and that study should be governed by whether 'your Inclinations dispose you, and your outward Circumstances admit much Reading'.[55] However, she warned that ''tis a Sin and shame to give hours to dressing and to think half an Hour long in Prayer.'[56]

There was little to choose between high Anglican and Puritan regimes, and advice given to Catholics was very similar to that of Protestant manuals. There is the same stress on organizing time,

[51] Clarke, *Lives*, 2, p. 200.

[52] *Memoir of Lady Warwick*, pp. 73, 74, 81; Nathaniel Taylor, *A Funeral Sermon Occasioned by the Death of Lady Lane* (London, 1699), p. 32.

[53] John Scott, *A Sermon Preached at the Funeral of the Lady Newland* (London, 1690), p. 16.

[54] Samuel Barker, *A Sermon Preach'd at the Funeral of the Right Honourable the Countess of Orford* (London, 1702), p. 6.

[55] Burnet, *Method of Devotion*, pp. 80, 95.

[56] Ibid., p. 104.

meditating, and examining one's conscience.[57] Likewise, Catholic *vies édifiantes* served a very similar function to the lives of Protestant women, as we may see in the life of Margaret Clitherow, for example.[58]

It is clear that those women with the time, money, and inclination took with great seriousness religious injunctions to use their time profitably. However, the most voluminous source for their conduct, the funeral sermon, is not easy to construe. Funeral sermons were explicitly dedicated to praising the deceased; in some of them no hyperbole is spared. They also had an exemplary function, providing a model for Christian life. The details of the deceased's life were set out, with an account of her parents, marriage, and children, and of her virtues as mistress of servants and benefactor, then her daily round from rising in the morning to going to bed at night. The auditor or reader might be supposed to wish to model her life on this example.

This formula had a further function. It is a kind of trope, a trope which is used both for the time of day and the place in the house (from which it ought perhaps to be called a topos rather than a trope). It offered an aide-memoire for what was required of the good Christian. Such timetables imposed discipline and order on religious life, ensuring that the duties which had to be performed got done. The location in time and place served as a reminder of the kind of religious activity that was required. But this was a discipline for wealthy and leisured women. These women were praiseworthy for passing their days diligently and not in frivolous activities. Few women had a funeral sermon preached extolling their virtues as wage-earners. So the discipline of Daniel's practice provided occupation for the leisured class rather than a pathway to heaven for the righteous.

The Open University

[57] *A Daily Exercise, and Devotions, for the Young Ladies, and Gentlewomen Pensioners at the Monastery of the English Canonesses Regular of the Holy Order of S. Augustin, at Bruges* (Douai, 1712), pp. 5–6, 40, 43.

[58] Quoted in Claire Cross, 'The religious life of women in sixteenth-century Yorkshire', *SCH*, 27 (1990), pp. 318–19.

CATHOLIC AND QUAKER ATTITUDES TO WORK, REST, AND PLAY IN SEVENTEENTH- AND EIGHTEENTH-CENTURY ENGLAND

by MICHAEL A. MULLETT

SINCE its publication in 1904–5, Max Weber's *The Protestant Ethic and the Spirit of Capitalism* has provided a paradigm for assessments of the attitudes to the profitable use of time among different branches of Christianity, emphasising the sanctification of work and thrifty care for time allegedly found in pronouncedly Protestant religious groups. This paper tests further assumptions made by Weber and his school by considering attitudes espoused within the two religious groups in early modern England which are often taken to epitomize the stereotypical extremes of Weberian hypotheses: on the one hand the Catholics, on the other the Quakers.

* * *

The English Catholic community between 1558 and 1829 was led by and, it might be assumed, took many of its collective social assumptions from, a landed aristocracy of gentry and titled nobility. That Catholic aristocracy formed a 'leisured class'[1] in the sense that its members were denied the working public functions – as justices of the peace, militia officers, members of parliament, and so on – that normally belonged as of right to the country's landed classes: as the first Marquess of Halifax (1633–95) observed, 'The laws have made them men of pleasure, by excluding them from public business.'[2] Fr Hughes wrote that

> the whole system of exclusion from the national life, from the army and navy, from the professions, from the national culture, from Parliament and from all civil and political affairs obtained, and in the social ostracism that was its sequel the English Catholics

[1] Thorstein Veblen, *The Theory of the Leisure Class*, 1st edn (New York, 1899; reprinted with additions by Augustus M. Kelley, Fairfield, NJ, 1991), ch. 3. Veblen spoke (p. 41) of the 'honorific' nature of abstention from labour in traditional societies, though in early modern England exertion in public office was regarded as deeply honourable.

[2] Halifax, cited in J. A. Hilton, *Catholic Lancashire: from Reformation to Renewal, 1559–1991* (Chichester, 1994), p. 43.

> lived as contemplatives in some enforced but gladly accepted cloister.

Therefore, '[m]any a Catholic squire lived . . . a life regularly ordered with its daily appointed devotions faithfully followed, while in his life's externals he managed his estate, drove, shot and hunted socially with his neighbours.'[3]

If the genus of Hughes's enforcedly leisured 'Catholic squire' were to be incarnated, no more exact epitome might be found than the Lancashire recusant gentleman Thomas Tyldesley of Myerscough, who compiled a diary for the years 1712–13. Developing as a kind of enlargement of an account book of expenditure, Tyldesley's journal might strike us as a slightly odd compilation, since it seems to record, with something of the compulsive time-accountancy of a Samuel Pepys, time largely wasted, though the hours and days frittered away are interspersed with due religious devotion, with 'prayers' being code for Mass and 'X' for Confession. Tyldesley's opening entry, the first day in the old calendar of the new year 1712 and the feast of the Annunciation – one of the many holidays of obligation that were to exercise at least one seventeenth-century English Catholic in his quest for a revized work ethic – sets the tone for a chronicle of mild piety decorating long days of ambling idleness: 'Went with Ms. to Booke [Bulk, near Lancaster], to prayrs, and home to dinr. Afterwards wentt a fowling to Lancr and Aldcliffe marces, and to see Ashton gardens.'[4] Day after day passed in such *dolce far niente*: 'Alday in town, a bussy in improving ye dame garden.'[5] Squire Tyldesley's version of 'bussy', though, meant in point of fact getting and paying others to do the actual hands-on work for him; yet even then a day's gardening involving the labour of three men (paid as much in ale as in money wages) could still leave the squire 'werieded'.[6] Gardening apart, time was expended in going to view items of modest interest – 'Went to see Will Bracon's mare'[7] – and in seeking distractions: 'to ye Recorders [in Lancaster], where we had some diversion in seeing 2 wimen and a man

[3] Philip Hughes, *The Catholic Question 1688–1829: a Study in Political History* (London, 1929), pp. 133–4.

[4] Joseph Gillow and Anthony Hewitson, eds, *The Tyldesley Diary. Personal Records of Thomas Tyldesley (Grandson of Sir Thomas Tyldesley, the Royalist) During the Years 1712–13–14* (Preston, 1873), p. 15.

[5] Ibid.

[6] Ibid.

[7] Ibid., p. 18.

examoned as wagrents.'[8] Hunting in season raised the levels of physical exercise within a regime of *otium*: 'Went a hunting with cos. Butler . . . killed a brace off hares . . . killed a hare with fine sport . . . Hunted all day.'[9] However, a day concerned with alcohol – 'gave Evan Williams 8 duble botles to ffil with brandy' – might well precede indisposition: 'Alday in the house, not very well.'[10] Family and other social visits soaked up time: 'In ye eivening I went to garden, and affterwards Mrs. and I went to see yonge cos. Tom Carus and his wiffe.'[11] What, though, strikes the modern reader perhaps most forcefully is the sheer length of daytime hours that were whiled away in socializing, for here was care neither for time, nor for work discipline, nor, perish the thought, for industrial capitalism:[12] 'Went with Mr. Robtt Lawson to ye coffy house, and stayed ffrom 9 to twelve . . . Affter dinr Jo Clarke came and satte with me 3 howrs.'[13]

Even so, if we are attempting to construct Thomas Tyldesley's life of leisure in conformity with stereotyped expectation about how only Catholic elites led their lives in vain pursuits (more or less interspersed with the habits of piety), it might rightly be objected that rest and recreation were generally expected to be, to say the least, major components in the lifestyles of the privileged in early modern England. As Viscount Conway remarked, 'We eat and drink and rise up to play and this is to live like a gentleman; for what is a gentleman but his pleasure?'[14] Indeed, the careers of the well off could often be, as was Parson James Woodforde's later life, virtually empty of productive effort of any kind.[15] For Catholic Tyldesley, though, his exclusion from the kind of public business in which a man of his rank might normally be expected to engage was a specific legal effect of his Catholicism.

Lancashire Protestant gentry were renowned for their conviviality, a central focus of which was the mock corporation of Walton-le-Dale near Preston. However, they could also take life and its duties seriously,

8 Ibid., p. 19.

9 Ibid., pp. 60–1.

10 Ibid., p. 22.

11 Ibid., p. 18.

12 E. P. Thompson, 'Time, work discipline and industrial capitalism', *P&P*, 38 (Dec. 1967), pp. 56–97.

13 Gillow and Hewitson, *Tyldesley Diary*, p. 18.

14 Conway, cited in Lawrence Stone, *The Crisis of the Aristocracy 1558–1641* (Oxford, 1965), p. 27.

15 John Beresford, ed., *The Diary of a Country Parson: The Reverend James Woodforde*, 5 vols (Oxford, 1968), 5, *passim*.

as did Tyldesley's acquaintances, the politically and legally active high sheriff for 1712, William Rawsthorne of Newall and his successor in office in 1713, William Farington of Shawe Hall. While such Protestants, known to Tyldesley, enjoyed county influence, power, and prestige, Catholic Tyldesley was never more than a social bystander in the entertainments which accompanied the wielding of real authority by such men: 'I suped with ye Sheriffe. . . .'[16] At the Lancaster recorder's office in 1712, it was Tyldesley's role, not to be involved as a justice in examining vagrants, but to *watch* the examination as an idle spectator, frittering away his morning.

Yet it is far from clear that what was, on the face of it, Tyldesley's aimless life, was entirely congenial to him, and there are signs that when the opportunity to do something constructive arose (as happened, for example, in the discussion with the Lancaster Castle governor in which he was involved at Christmas 1713 of 'what method to take about the goale'),[17] Tyldesley responded eagerly to the challenge and opportunity of any public function that was on offer. So, too, did his co-religionist Lancashire acquaintance, Nicholas Blundell of Crosby, who saw no difficulty in holding one – onerous – public position that was, oddly, open to him, as churchwarden of the parish church of Sefton in which he could not in conscience worship (though in law his position obliged him to delate other recusants).[18]

The evidence grows to the effect that, as the largest and most important county Catholic elite in Stuart and Hanoverian England, Lancashire's recusant gentry, who had responded in impressive numbers to James II's invitation to them to take part in the strenuous and dangerous business of shire and borough government in 1687–8, were far from being by any natural, or, more specifically, confessional, inclination more prone to ease than to effort.[19] Indeed, it is perfectly possible that a motive for the Jacobite activism that characterized such Lancashire Catholic gentry as Thomas Tyldesley's son in 1715 was that of being given the opportunity, in a second Stuart restoration, of operating in the time-consuming and honour-conferring roles in

16 Gillow and Hewitson, *Tyldesley Diary*, p. 15.

17 Ibid., p. 128.

18 Michael A. Mullett, *Catholics in Britain and Ireland, 1558–1829* (Basingstoke and London, 1998), p. 85.

19 Michael Mullett, 'Recusants, Dissenters and North-West politics between the Restoration and the Glorious Revolution', in John C. Appleby and Paul Dalton, eds, *Government, Religion and Society in Northern England, 1000–1700* (Stroud, 1996), pp. 199–209.

public business to which men of gentry class normally had a hereditary claim.[20]

Nicholas Blundell's grandfather, the pious William (who recalled that Thomas Tyldesley's father had followed 'his business close, to the end that he might the more enjoy his pleasures')[21] set down his thoughts in his observations entitled 'Oeconomia'. Here he examined the implications of Catholicism for a life of work, paying particular attention to the common charge that the proliferation of feast-days in the Catholic liturgical year reduced working days in such a way that, as the Protestant economist Sir Peter Pett, writing in the same decade that Blundell reflected on 'Oeconomia', put it, 'the greater part of persons engaged in trade and traffic . . . hate ceremonies in general and what does unnecessarily take up time.'[22] Yet it was the devout Catholic Blundell who directed sharp criticism at his own faith's tendency to steal time away from work. His analysis closely resembled the assumptions and methods of his contemporary, the economist Gregory King,[23] who pioneered a labour theory of value and who came up with grand totals of the gross national product remarkably close to Blundell's. Blundell identified a clear link between festal Catholicism and reduced work output:

> A.D. 1683 Christmas began on Tuesday, so that we had at that time eight holydays altogether, Sunday being included therein. Immediately before that Christmas, we had six days beginning on Wednesday 19th, whereof five were fasting-days, one holyday, and one Sunday; so that there were at that time fourteen days altogether, which were all of them either holydays or fasting days. . . . I was at Paris in July 1680, and found there that the 26th of that month (St. Anne's day) was not kept holyday, neither was the 24th kept as a vigil either by fasting or abstinence.[24]

20 Colin Haydon, *Anti-Catholicism in Eighteenth-Century England, c. 1714–80: a Political and Social Study* (Manchester, 1993), p. 81.

21 T. Ellison Gibson, ed., *Crosby Records: A Cavalier's Note Book. Being Notes, Anecdotes & Observations of William Blundell of Crosby, Lancashire, Esquire, Captain of Dragoons under Major-Gen. Sir Thos. Tyldesley, Knt., in the Royalist Army of 1642* (London, 1880), p. 121.

22 Pett, cited in Jacob Viner, *Religious Thought and Economic Society: Four Chapters of an Unfinished Work*, ed. Jacques Melitz and Donald Winch (Durham, NC, 1978), p. 163.

23 George E. Barnett, ed., *Two Tracts by Gregory King: (a) Natural and Political Observations and Conclusions upon the State and Condition of England; (b) Of the Naval Trade of England at 1688 and the National Profit then Arising Thereby* (Baltimore, MD, 1936), p. 30.

24 Ellison Gibson, *Crosby Records*, pp. 122–3.

Blundell's specific observations on holy days arose out of a larger discourse on work and leisure which assumed a direct relationship between annual gross numbers of days worked and a nation's prosperity: 'If there be four million of working people in a country who are each able to earn *6d.* per diem, the work of one day will amount to 100,000 *l.*'[25] Feast days, then, cost a nation money by prohibiting work, 'So that the difference of working and not working of the people of a whole nation is no small thing as to civil and political respects. Note the different consequences of industry and idleness by comparing the present state of Spain and the lazy old Irish.'[26] However, in Blundell's view the difference between industrious nations and indolent ones lay not on a confessional line but rather on differentiation based on a country's proneness or otherwise to take lots of holidays in the form of holy days. Whereas the profusion of the latter linked Catholic England with Blundell's work-shy and non-thriving Spanish and with the 'lazy' Irish, Catholic Flanders (which Blundell took to be prospering) and Catholic France were bracketed with Protestant Holland, the very model of economic success in the minds of analysts within the period – and all because these countries curbed feasts which otherwise cut into work-time: France, which Blundell knew first-hand, was singled out for commendation as a land that accorded priority to wealth creation by severely rationing cultic days off.[27]

In the course of the seventeenth century France became a model of the sober, ascetic Catholicism that emerged out of the Council of Trent to inspire the Catholic Reformation in early modern Europe. The prophet of the new French spirituality was François de Sales, whose guide for lay people aiming to live piously, the *Introduction à la vie dévote*, was first published in 1609 and had a profound influence in the Catholic world, not least in England. There it was especially influential through the mediation of the eighteenth-century Vicar Apostolic Richard Challoner.

The work's significance for the creation in early modern Europe of a distinctive set of Catholic values – cautious, abstemious, directed at endeavour rather than at pleasure – is partly evident in the very orderly layout of the text. In its systematic scheduling of the devout life the

25 Ellison Gibson, *Crosby Records*, pp. 122–3.
26 Ibid.
27 Ibid.

Introduction breathes an unmistakeable flavour of method which in itself can be seen as conducive to orderly habits of work:[28] the treatise's underlying message might indeed be summed up in the words that de Sales offers to his spiritual client Philothée – 'Soyez donc soigneuse et diligente en toutes les affaires que vous aurez en charge.'[29] An entire grave, calm, wise way of proceeding through the business of life is commended from the familiar trope of Martha and Mary: 'Recevez donc les affaires qui vous arriveront en paix, et tâchez de les faire par ordre, l'une après l'autre.'[30] Within its methodical framework, the *Introduction* is much concerned, perhaps not centrally with inculcating a work ethic, but rather with dispelling a pleasure principle. Dances, for example, are 'ces impertinentes récréations [qui] sont ordinairement dangereuses . . . A même temps que vous étiez au bal, plusieurs âmes brûlaient au feu d'enfer, pour les péchés commis à la danse . . . Les jeux des dés, des cartes et semblables . . . sont simplement et naturellement mauvaises et blâmables.'[31] It is particularly significant that de Sales disparages the gains that may accrue from gambling, for these by their very nature cannot qualify to be the 'prix de l'industrie';[32] while at the same time the fretting associated with gambling shatters that calm and balanced approach to life that he commends as its key.[33] Far more than its rival for popularity amongst devout readers, à Kempis's *Imitation of Christ*, the *Introduction* forms not so much a guide to an attempt at monastic life within the world as a code for an authentic Christian and also authentically lay way of living and working.

That said, the English devotional writer John Gother, in his *Instructions for Particular States and Conditions of Life*, first published in 1689, borrowed the model and metaphor of the regular orders as his example for 'laborious and working Christians' who should form

> a Kind of religious Order, in which God himself has instituted their Rule: he has expressly commanded that they shall eat their Bread in the Sweat of their Brows; and if, in Submision to this Command, they undertake their Work, it is certain that their daily

[28] *Introduction à la vie dévote par S. François de Sales*, intro. Henry Bordeaux (Paris, 1937), pp. 33–58.
[29] Ibid., p. 171.
[30] Ibid., p. 172.
[31] Ibid., pp. 254, 251.
[32] Ibid.
[33] Ibid., p. 252.

> lives will be as much an Act of Religion and Obedience, as what those do, who live in a Cloyster, and observe the Rules of their Founder.[34]

Gother's most popular successor as a devotional writer for the English Catholic community, the Vicar Apostolic Richard Challoner, incorporated in his durably popular handbook of the devout life in the world, the *Garden of the Soul* (first published in 1740), a morality of work deep within the regime of absolution in the Sacrament of Penance and the Examination of Conscience that was necessary to achieve the full confession on which that sacrament's efficacy in part depended. 'Have you neglected your work or business to which you were hired, or by contract obliged?', the penitent is to ask of himself or herself.[35] A nightly moral accountancy, 'An Examination of Conscience for Every Night', asks 'in what manner you have acquitted yourself of the duties of your calling';[36] while 'An Universal Prayer for All Things Necessary for Salvation' contains the invocation 'Grant that I may ever be . . . *diligent* in my employments.'[37] The universality of the obligation to work, alongside a sense of varied vocations throughout the social fabric, was iterated in Challoner's insistence that 'God almighty most certainly appoints to every one in his family his respective employment.'[38]

A doctrine of the calling there set out is accompanied by Challoner's stress on the need to carry out one's work in a calm and organized manner: 'Take care to mortify that over-great eagerness with which you sometimes find yourself set upon your work, and do all with calmness and peace.'[39] That might sound like the sort of code of method adopted by one of R. H. Tawney's puritan archetypes – one who 'disciplines, rationalises, systematizes his life'[40] – until we realize that that spirit of calm is also the one breathed by Challoner's mentor, François de Sales. The Vicar Apostolic's lengthiest exordium on work as a virtue comes in his survey 'Of the Ordinary Actions of the Day', in

[34] Gother, cited in Mullett, *Catholics in Britain and Ireland*, p. 93.

[35] The Garden of the Soul. A Manual of Spiritual Exercises and Instructions for Christians who Living in the World, Aspire to Devotion (London, n.d.), p. 227.

[36] Ibid., p. 173.

[37] Ibid., p. 121.

[38] Ibid., p. 181.

[39] Ibid., p. 182.

[40] R. H. Tawney, *Religion and the Rise of Capitalism. A Historical Study* (London, 1936), p. 201.

which, like Gother, Challoner invokes the scriptural divine mandate to labour:

> Often call to mind that sentence laid upon all mankind, Gen. iii, 19, *In the sweat of thy brow thou shalt eat thy bread*.... In consequence of this sentence, submit yourselves to the labours of your calling.... Fly idleness as the mother of all mischief; and if your condition of life does not oblige you to any work or employment by way of seeking your bread, yet chuse always something of this nature for your soul's sake, that the devil may never find you idle.[41]

It goes without saying that Challoner's sense of the omnipresent duty of labour was driven by moral considerations along the lines of avoiding the mischief that the tempter prepares for indolent hands, and also profoundly centred on God: 'Perform all your works with due care to do them well, not as pleasing in the eyes of men, but the eyes of God; in whose presence, and for whom you ought to do all that you do.'[42]

Challoner's view of God as the Great Foreman conditioned his understanding of the primacy of religion and its obligations before work itself: it was inconceivable that his model Catholic Christian should make of work a surrogate cult, as did Tawney's 'Puritan' for whom 'mundane toil becomes itself a kind of sacrament'.[43] The fact that work was carried out at the Almighty's mandate of necessity required that 'when by his will you are call'd away from your work, as you are to be willing to do it for him, so you must be willing to leave it for him.'[44] In the earlier seventeenth century the number of days on which Catholics were supposed to 'leave [work] for him' – on which 'the Catholick Church commands all her children, upon *Sundays* and *Holidays*, to be present at the great Eucharisticke Sacrifice which we call the Mass, and to rest from servile work on those days, and to keep them holy'[45] amounted to almost forty, with variations around the country. By 1777, a rough century after the penning of Blundell's complaint about the drain of feast days away from labour, and within Challoner's Vicariate Apostolic, a papal decree had rationed the feast

41 Challoner, *Garden of the Soul*, p. 199.
42 Ibid., p. 181.
43 Tawney, *Religion and the Rise of Capitalism*, p. 199.
44 Challoner, *Garden of the Soul*, p. 181.
45 Ibid., p. 22.

days to twelve, or ten, if the Vicars Apostolic exercised their powers to permit work on two summer harvest days.[46]

The point about the harvest days needs further commentary. The traditional cycle of feasts and fasts in Catholicism found much of its meaning in a natural and seasonal rhythm based to a large extent on solar and lunar patterns. The liturgical year, to which Challoner paid a perhaps nostalgic tribute by tabling it in all its amplitude, with its twenty-nine days of devotion and its Ember Days,[47] moved in tandem with the seasons. The sombreness of the November commemoration marked the death of the year with the month of the departed holy souls; then the Advent season of the shortest days and the great late-autumn harvest festival, Christmas, and a series of festivals of light in a dark time of year – Christmas itself and Epiphany through the Candlemas feast of the Purification and on to the longer days; while the great fast of Lent, lovingly observed by devout English Catholics, coincided with a time of natural dearth between winter and the arrival of new crops. Finally the joys of spring and renewed life and fertility found their sacral correspondence in the Easter days, life returning after death. By Whitsun a half year of sacred observances had taken place, marching alongside and interpreting the chords of nature, light, climate, and the seasons.

The traditional festal regime was profoundly harmonious with a rural seasonal schedule – and profoundly disruptive of an urban, commercial, or industrial one. In a pre-industrial and agrarian economy an extended twelve-day Christmas, a festal hibernation spread over the shortest and agriculturally least active days of the year probably did little harm, and up to the Restoration English Catholics tended to celebrate it in a style of which Sir Toby Belch would have approved.[48] William Blundell's criticism of the extended cessation of work over those many days comes, though, from the pen of a Catholic who was not only an amateur political arithmetician and intellectual admirer of Sir Josiah Child, but also a pioneer of provincial banking, a money-lender to neighbouring gentry of sums of £50 at 6 per cent (despite traditional Catholic prohibitions by theologians Blundell dismissed as 'casuists').[49] It was his business instinct that led

[46] John Bossy, *The English Catholic Community 1570–1850* (London, 1975), pp. 116, 120; Hilton, *Catholic Lancashire*, p. 73.

[47] Challoner, *Garden of the Soul*, pp. 19–21.

[48] Bossy, *English Catholic Community*, pp. 119–20.

[49] Ellison Gibson, *Crosby Records*, p. 76.

him to deplore the disappearance of series of potentially lucrative days into a black hole of capriciously disruptive holidays culled from a rustically rooted seasonal cultic system which had little to do with the brisk business affairs of Blundell's neighbouring town of commercial Liverpool, in whose dramatic rise he took such a keen interest. Catholic Squire Blundell condemned the everlasting Christmas of 1683 because he was a commercialist with a driving work ethic and a strong sense of economic timetabling.[50]

His orientation towards a town, a place of commerce, of work ideally carried on according to fixed schedules interrupted, on the whole, only by the predictably recurrent weekly Sabbaths of Protestantism, presaged the growing urban orientation of Catholics in England during the century between Blundell's condemnation of the excesses of the festal cycle and the papacy's drastic reduction of them. The traditional rural bases of post-Reformation English Catholic life – the estate villages of central and western Lancashire – were increasingly losing their inhabitants to Manchester, Liverpool, Preston, and Wigan, whose collective Romanist populations rose five-fold in the thirty years between 1780 and 1810.[51] Concomitant with this shift in the demographic centre of the English Catholic community was a turn towards a pronouncedly bourgeois social leadership, in the hands of men bred into a reverence for work (though, as we have seen, Blundell was no stranger to those values either). As early as the aftermath of the 1715 Rebellion we can see evidence of a social shift in the nature of the men who rose to prominence in the recusant community. Then, for example, the damage done to the extensive coal-bearing estates of the Catholic Lord Widdrington as a result of his active Jacobitism was muted by the industrious efforts of the professional, middle class, and intensely hard-working managers, Joseph Dunn and Albert Silvertop – the latter described by Leo Gooch as the epitome of the 'hard-headed businessman who was taking over from the old gentry'.[52]

Later in the century Lancaster saw the rise of the furniture business of the Gillow family, who exercised leadership in their Catholic

[50] Ibid., p. 275.

[51] W. J. Sheils, 'Catholicism from the Reformation to the Relief Acts', in Sheridan Gilley and W. J. Sheils, eds, *A History of Religion in Britain: Practice and Belief from Pre-Roman Times to the Present* (Oxford and Cambridge, MA, 1994), pp. 248–51.

[52] L. Gooch, '"Incarnate Rogues and Vile Jacobites": Silvertop *v.* Cotesworth, 1718–1723', *Recusant History*, 18 (1986–7), pp. 277–81.

community, providing an informal chapel on their factory premises but also running a business as a model of industrial efficiency, with little sign of rest, play, or feast. Robert Gillow, a Catholic whose father was a joiner from Great Eccleston in Lancashire, was a man determined to supplant London's hold on the furniture trade. 'Ingenious', driven, inventive, and an active partner in a group of local Protestant merchants, Gillow comes over as a kind of Weberian archetype, especially in his relentless search for further profit, for example by packing the empty drawers and cupboards of exported furniture with saleable items.[53] The Gillow firm was supremely indifferent to denominational differentiations and sold on a healthy inter-faith basis to Catholics, Quakers, members of the Church of England, and what have you. A business and work ethic indeed dominated this enterprise and is revealed above all in its trading account books which enshrine an admirable clarity and method of book-keeping and also record a rolling programme of industrial production and delivery that ran on impervious to traditional Catholics cycle of feasts and fasts: Blundell would, no doubt, have been impressed.[54]

Did the rise of an English Catholic work ethic in the age of Gillow and Challoner represent the cultural conquest of the community's attitudes by a set of values essentially derived from prevailing English Protestantism? Or perhaps it was the case that a rising rate of Protestant conversions into Catholicism in the course of the eighteenth century[55] resulted in the importation into the Catholic community's value system of an outlook on work and wealth essentially derived from a Protestant background. Or, to take another tack (and if Weber was right to argue that a predestinarian soteriology may foster a value-system and life-style conducive to wealth creation through the dominance of a culture of work), then the undoubted prominence of Jansenism in Catholic circles in eighteenth-century Britain may indeed have introduced into those same circles the sort of personality traits – thriftiness, prudence, dedication to labour, care for time, regularity of work patterns – which, it is often claimed, helped Calvinists to prosper in early modern Europe (and America). Such

[53] Melinda Elder, *The Slave Trade and the Economic Development of 18th-Century Lancaster* (Halifax, 1992), pp. 121–3.

[54] Lancaster, Lancaster University Library: British Museum Microtext 4/0361 (Gillow of Lancaster, The Lancaster Archives, 1731–1932: Day Book, 1763–68, Journal, 1769–74).

[55] Eamon Duffy, '"Poor protestant flies": conversion to Catholicism in early 18th-century England', *SCH*, 15 (1978), pp. 292–304.

people were induced to give proof of their salvific election by their worldly labour and success in it:

> a duty to attain certainty of one's election and justification in the daily struggles of life. . . . [I]n order to attain that [soteriological] self-confidence intense worldly activity is recommended as the most suitable means. It and it alone disperses religious doubts and gives the certainty of grace. . . . Thus the Calvinist . . . himself creates his own salvation.[56]

In fact, though, it will be argued here that the prevalence of an ostensibly 'Protestant' work ethic amongst Catholics in Georgian England derived from the intellectual, devotional, and spiritual resources of Tridentine Catholicism itself. In particular, it is not necessary to examine the predestinarian resonances of Jansenism to explain the strident work ethic of which Gother and Challoner were the leading – and durably influential – spokesmen, and Gillow the archetypal practitioner. The influence of St Augustine on Challoner, on the Council of Trent, on Bishop Cornelius Jansen, in the source-book of Jansenism (*Augustinus*, published in 1640), was profound and pervasive. This was the Augustine who praised the accomplishments of human work, 'all . . . grand and fully deserved by mankind . . . those who want to be spiritual only, and not labor with the body, reveal their indolence.'[57] However, unlike Jansen, Challoner did not bring away a predestinarian message from Augustine, but rather an emphasis on the salvific role of good works enacted in (limited) free will. Challoner, the supreme mentor of English Catholicism between the mid-eighteenth and mid-twentieth centuries, may have taken his confidence in the Christian's ability to contribute a measure to his or her redemption from de Sales, who insisted, in his depiction of election, on the use of the key voluntaristic verbs, 'choose' and 'accept'.[58]

Challoner was indeed a disciple of Augustine, one who translated the *Confessions*, but he was not a predestinarian Augustinian.[59] In a short essay on election within the *Garden of the Soul*, he used, as de Sales

[56] Max Weber, *The Protestant Ethic and the Spirit of Capitalism*, tr. Talcott Parsons, intro. Anthony Giddens (London, 1976), pp. 110–15.

[57] St Augustine, cited in Albert Hyma, 'The economic views of the Protestant Reformers', in Robert W. Green, ed., *Protestantism and Capitalism: the Weber Thesis and its Critics* (Boston, MA, 1959), p. 100.

[58] *Introduction à la vie dévote*, p. 55.

[59] Challoner, *Garden of the Soul*, p. xii.

did, the verbs of volition: 'I accept, I choose.'[60] In this he was doing no more than remaining within the modified Augustinian consensus declared by the Council of Trent and reiterated with admirable succinctness in the bull *Caelestis pastor* of 1687: 'Humana activitas ad salutem et perfectionem necessaria.'[61] If a gospel of work may arise – as Weber argued it had arisen – out of Christian doctrines of redemption, is it not likely to have evolved out of a soteriology that stressed the role of 'activitas' in our souls' fate, and thereby to have created a generalized climate of personal endeavour? A theology of works thus engendered a gospel of work in the heart of post-Reformation Catholicism. The new religious Orders of the sixteenth century, the clerks regular, with their abandonment of lengthy collective and contemplative prayer in favour of practical and social endeavour in the world, were symptoms and effects of a mounting work dynamic in post-medieval Catholicism. Best known of those new orders, and driven by the ferocious cult of work of their founder Loyola, the Jesuits typified and taught an evangel of labour caught by one of the best-known of Jesuit preachers, Louis Bourdaloue. If we seek a doctrine of work, of the lay calling (as in Gother), of the duties of one's 'state' in life linked to salvation (and to perfectibility, sainthood, and indeed, predestination) we find it in this seventeenth-century Jesuit teaching:

> Il faut s'avancer dans la perfection de son état, pourquoi? parce que c'est ce que Dieu veut de nous, parce que c'est uniquement pour cela qu'il nous a préparé des grâces, parce que c'est en cela seul que consiste notre sainteté, et à quoi par conséquent notre prédestination est attachée . . . que chacun de nous . . . se sanctifie dans l'état où il a été appelé de Dieu.[62]

It would, I believe, be difficult to conceive of a more ample and doctrinally grounded statement of a Catholic work ethic.

* * *

Historiography sees Quakers, of course, as the standard-bearers of a Protestant and Puritan cult of labour, of the calling, thrift, care for

60 Challoner, *Garden of the Soul*, pp. 63–4.

61 *Caelestis pastor* (1687) in Januarius Bucceroni, S.J., ed., *Enchiridion morale complectens: Selectas decisiones Sanctae Sedis et Sacrarum Romanum Congegationum quae professoribus theologiae moralis et confessariis magis usui esse possunt* (3rd edn, Rome, 1900), p. 5.

62 'Sur l'Etat de Vie, etc.', in L. Bourdaloue, *Chefs-d'oeuvre oratoires de Bourdaloue* (Paris, [1910]), pp. 389, 393.

time, and, it goes without saying, of economic success. Weber firmly included them in his schedule of minorities driven 'through their voluntary and involuntary exclusion from positions of political influence . . . with particular force into economic activity' (he did not mention English Catholics). Especially striking was 'the connection of a religious way of life with the most intensive development of business acumen' and their 'otherworldliness' was 'as proverbial as their wealth'.[63] More modern commentaries emphasise features of Quaker thought and action that seem to have guaranteed to members of the denomination overall worldly, material, and economic success; notably the absence of a pursuit of pleasure and play. James Walvin, for example, cites the early Friends' counsels that they should 'avoid all such conversation as may tend to draw out their minds into the foolish and wicked pastimes with which this age aboundeth',[64] eschew 'sports, plays and all such diversions',[65] and steer clear of 'amusing themselves with the pernicious works of stage-authors, and romances; which strongly tend to excite irregular passions, and to introduce them into the giddy pursuits and pollutions of a degenerate age.'[66] Both the traditional alehouse culture of leisure and the ancient observance of festival days were condemned by the official central censor of the collective behaviour of the Society of Friends, the London Yearly Meeting. In 1691, the Meeting instructed them 'to avoid unnecesary frequenting taverns, alehouses, all looseness, excess, and unprofitable and idle discourses, all mis-spending their precious time and substance, . . . and that Friends keep to their wonted example and testimony against the superstitious observation of days.'[67] The alehouse, for centuries the central domain of gregarious English pleasure-seeking, certainly continued to be a subject of moral warning from the Friends' higher circles. In 1768, for example, the Yearly Meeting exhorted 'all in profession with us, against the unnecessary frequenting of public houses, and those places of resort which are too often used as occasions of intemperance, dissipation, animosity and the baneful spirit of party.'[68]

[63] Weber, *Protestant Ethic*, pp. 39, 44.

[64] James Walvin, *The Quakers: Money and Morals* (London, 1997), p. 36.

[65] Ibid., p. 37.

[66] Ibid., p. 51.

[67] *Epistles from the Yearly Meeting of Friends Held in London to the Quarterly and Monthly Meetings in Great Britain, Ireland, and Elsewhere; from 1681 to 1857, Inclusive*, 2 vols (London, 1858), 1: 56.

[68] Ibid., 1: 353.

However, the more innocent diversions of the age that saw the invention of the novel also came under condemnation. In 1720 it was 'also seriously advised, that no Friends suffer romances, play-books, or other vain and idle pamphlets, in their houses or families, which tend to corrupt the minds of youth; but instead thereof, that they excite them to the reading of the Holy Scriptures and religious books.'[69] In 1772 'the pernicious works of stage-authors, and romances' were condemned.[70] Meanwhile, over the course of the eighteenth century, as a range of affordable pleasures and leisures was commodified and expanded, the official central London Yearly Meeting commensurately widened the scope of its condemnations, to take in 'sports, plays, and all such diversions'.[71] In 1739, for example, advice was elaborated to the effect that Friends in general and their youth in particular 'avoid all such conversation as may tend to draw out their minds into the foolish and wicked pastimes with which this age aboundeth; particularly balls, gaming-places, horse-races, and playhouses; those nurseries of debauchery and wickedness'.[72] In 1778 they were warned once more 'against spending their time, and the substance of their hands, unprofitably, by resorting to places of vain, irreligious, and dissipating entertainment; also against high and expensive living, or an affectation of pomp and figure'.[73] As affluent Friends were drawn into the net of those with time and means to hunt, so the Meeting turned to

> the practice of some members [of the Society] of hunting and shooting for diversion. We clearly rank these practices with vain sports, and we believe the awakened mind may see that even the leisure of those whom Providence hath permitted to have a competence of worldly goods is but ill filled up with these amusements . . . let our leisure be employed in serving our neighbour, and not in distressing the creatures of God for our amusement.[74]

The Quaker behavioural discipline set out in these injunctions represents what is surely the most formidable anti-pleasure casuistry

[69] Ibid., 1: 221.
[70] Ibid., 1: 227.
[71] Ibid., 2: 12.
[72] Ibid., 2: 35.
[73] Ibid., 1: 157–8.
[74] Preston, Lancashire Record Office: Lancaster Friends' Meeting House Archive, Yearly Meeting Papers, 1694–1819, 1, No. 108.

established by any of the Christian churches: in the end, the recreation allowed to the individual Quaker was 'the relief of distress; and his chief delight, to promote the knowledge, and to exalt the glory, of his Heavenly Master; and this is most effectually done, under his holy influence, by a life of faith, purity, and general benevolence'.[75] The most influential author of a Quaker code of practice for daily life, Robert Barclay, had taught a doctrine of perfectibility and set out an absolute 'inner-worldly asceticism' from which all those particular rulings of the Yearly Meeting (backed up by any number of re-affirmations from regional bodies such as the Quarterly and Monthly Meetings) took their rise. Barclay wrote: '*That it is not lawful to use Games, Sports, Plays, nor among other Things Comedies among Christians, under the Notion of Recreations, which do not agree with Christian Silence, Gravity, and Sobriety: for Laughing, Sporting, Gaming, Mocking, Jesting, vain Talking &c. is not Christian Liberty, nor harmless Mirth.*'[76] Alongside the ascetic principle of avoidance of pleasure was, as might be expected, some moral encouragement of work. Children, above all, were to have a work ethic instilled into them. Barclay enjoined 'that Friends of all degrees take due care to breed up their children in some useful and necessary employments, that they may not spend their precious time in idleness'.[77]

William Stout, the Georgian Quaker merchant of Lancaster, lived out Barclay's principles of abstinence from leisure and pleasure as legislated by the Quaker Yearly Meeting. He was a paradigm of Puritan rigour, even before he became a Friend, in the time when, 'active in the shop, where, out of necessary business, I passed my time in reading; or improving my self in arethmatick, survighing or other mathamatikall sciences, which I was most naturally inclined to'.[78] Stout, indeed, begins to look like Barclay's pupil, self-improving, studious, and profoundly serious, as well as essentially solitary:

> And in the spring got up as it was day, and in sumer at sunrising, and took a walk a mile out of town by myself each day of the week. And in the evnings after nine, took a walk upon the green

[75] *Epistles from Yearly Meeting*, 2: 106.

[76] Robert Barclay, *An Apology for the True Christian Divinity, Being an Explanation and Vindication of the Principles and Doctrines of the People Called Quakers*, 8th edn (Birmingham, 1765), p. 452.

[77] *Epistles from Yearly Meeting*, 2: 106.

[78] J. D. Marshall, ed., *The Autobiography of William Stout of Lancaster 1665–1752* (Manchester and New York, 1967), p. 3.

> Aire, alone, if fair. Otherways, when out of busnes, passed my time in reading religious books, or history, geography, surveying or other mathamatical sciences.[79]

He prayed, successfully, to avoid the pleasure over which Barclay had not much expatiated: 'I . . . was very sensible that my neighbour to the street side, whose lodgings with myne were in common up one pair of stairs, took all opertunetys in conversation and other insinuations to alure me to her bed, or to introduce her selfe into myne.'[80] He knew, though, that such liberties arose when men and women 'entertain each other in a bantering way in such terms as could only tend to beget evil thoughts and excite to lewdness', and he was aware that debauchery 'is mostly the effect or consequence of excessive eating and drinking of both men and women, and want of lawful exercise'.[81] Solitude and sobriety were solutions to the temptations of sociability – and perhaps of sex:

> I did now, after supper, walk an hower or two in my gardin in a solid retirement; when, at the same time, it was the custom of my neighbours of the same imploy to sit together in an aile house, entertaining them selves in vain conversation or impertinant reflections on the privet affairs of their neighbours, or on publik afairs of state.[82]

A rising figure in the Society of Friends who had attended Yearly Meetings, Stout was obviously familiar with the Yearly Meeting rubrics of 1691, cited above, which laid out the rationale for avoiding the alehouse, rules whose actual terms he himself seems quite consciously to have observed. Indeed, his presence at the Yearly Meeting was part of a rising and heavy commitment of time to his religious Society that left him with a less than obsessive focus on his business. Stout was in fact a contemplative quietist rather than an ardent entrepreneur, a naturally introverted and largely anti-social being whose serious, withdrawn nature was drawn to the Society of Friends within which he was aware of 'the comfortable presence of God, sealing the same to me in solid retirement'.[83] Admittedly he was a

79 Marshall, *Autobiography of William Stout*, pp. 80–1.
80 Ibid., pp. 84–5.
81 Ibid.
82 Ibid., p. 96.
83 Ibid., p. 98.

hard worker who 'kept close to my trade'; though that too was a facet of his solitude, for it enabled him to go 'without much conversation with any, further than my ocations required'.[84] And all along, Friends' business, protracted over several days at Yearly Meeting time, took up Stout's attention, for it embraced such varied topics as: 'their suffrings for tyths, and for refusing an oath in sevrall courts, and others [*sic*] testamonys; and the nessesety of the suffrers, and the releif [of] the poor, and many other occurances incident among them respecting to good order and a truly Christian deportment in life and conversation'.[85]

As his Quaker career unfolded, Stout undertook (and held for thirty-eight years) the demanding and time-consuming roles of clerk and treasurer of the Lancaster Friends' Monthly Meeting. This involved him in ecclesiastical administration, especially concerning matters of record, in a wide area of north Lancashire. He was further deeply occupied in onerous administrative duties with the Friends' Quarterly Meeting for Lancashire from the 1690s and through the greater part of the first half of the eighteenth century, as well as travelling in the executive ministry of the Society to Yearly Meetings in the north and in London. His meticulous keeping of the records of Friends' 'sufferings' on the account of tithes form a further permanent record of his assiduous dedication to the running of a religious denomination, so that if one were to speculate it would be to the effect that his commitment of work time to his faith's business far outweighed any demands made on a typical Georgian lay Catholic by the oft-alleged distractions of 'feast-days'. He did not get rich.

In fact, in giving his time and attention to the meetings and the Society, Stout was neglecting his business – his calling and his work – and was doing so in the properly approved Quaker manner. For Quaker authorities, from Barclay through the Yearly Meeting minutes – the authentic voice of the Society's collective conscience decade after decade – insisted that work must be relegated to its place, a place so minor in his thinking that Barclay, in his Proposition XV (on the application of Quaker doctrine to aspects of daily life), and for all his fulminations against enjoyment, had nothing of substance to write about work. His condemnation of pleasure, in fact, took off from his resentment at its incursions on God's time rather than on work time: in

84 Ibid., pp. 103–5.
85 Ibid., p. 131.

'*Dancing* and *Comedies*, *Carding* and *Dicing* . . . there is nothing to be seen but *Lightness* and *Vanity*, *Wantonness* and *Obscenity*, contrived to draw men from the *Fear* of God . . . to make them forget *Heaven*, *Death*, and *Judgment*, to foster *Lust*, *Vanity*, and *Wantonness*.'[86] Thus Barclay held a strict and censorious attitude to sensual pleasure and play, as found in the rigorous condemnation of such activities by de Sales, with an echo of his strictures against cards and dice, but none of de Sales' – or Bourdaloue's or Gother's or Challoner's – work imperative.

Yearly Meeting, too, was diffident about work. True, Friends were encouraged by the London Yearly Meeting of 1824 to 'cherish a disposition to honest industry'.[87] However, we may read an at best lukewarm attitude to labour in such observations as that of 1797: 'We are not about to condemn industry, which we believe to be not only praiseworthy, but indispensable.'[88] Equally back-handed were the comments of 1815: 'We are far from wishing to discourage honest industry. . . . We are not insensible, that the situation of many of our members is such as renders necessary to them a diligent attention to the concerns of this life.'[89]

If we wish to read into the last-cited observation the tone of voice of a body by this time made up to an extent of leisured *rentiers*, speaking as it were *d'en haut à bas* to the harsher economic needs of a rank-and-file membership, then we should recall that from a relatively early point in time spokesmen of the Society had looked to work, and if necessary enforced work, primarily as the sovereign antidote to poverty. The work-schemes of the Quaker John Bellers, such as his *An Essay for Imploying the Poor to Profit* of 1723, are full of the abstruse calculations of political arithmetic. That *Essay*'s mathematically unimpeachable optimism is reminiscent of nothing so much as Blundell's scheme for making money by abolishing Christmas: 'Therefore 2 Millions and a half got or saved yearly by a suitable Imployment of the Poor on Manufactures and Husbandry would in that proportion in 58 Years, come to ONE THOUSAND TWO HUNDRED AND FIFTY MILLIONS Sterling.'[90] However, Bellers's great design to create work (which has a parallel, for example, in a proposal put to Lancaster

86 Barclay, *Apology*, pp. 472, 475–6.

87 *Epistles from Yearly Meeting*, 2: 100.

88 Ibid., 2: 170.

89 Ibid., 2: 207.

90 George Clark, ed., *John Bellers: his Life, Times and Writings* (London and New York, 1987), p. 242.

Monthly Meeting in 1701 for 'settling a college of industry for the maintenance of the poor Friends of this county')[91] had nothing to do with creating a Quaker work mentality – of whose Catholic equivalent de Sales, Gother, Bourdaloue, and Challoner were the architects – and had everything to do with the classic early-modern English project of setting the poor on work, for their benefit and the nation's profit. Accordingly, 'in 58 years time such a Body as our present idle Poor, if they were imployed about it, would be able to turn all our wast and unimproved Lands . . . into fruitful Fields, Orchards, and Gardens, and their mean Cottages into Colleges, and fill our Barns with plenty of Bread, and our Store-houses with Manufacture.'[92] Yet there is no morality of work *per se* here, and no sense of the calling in these prescriptions which read as both ruthless and deranged, for work, as the minutes of the Yearly Meeting so far cited indicate, was viewed as a sheer economic necessity and no more than that – a raw necessity, to be kept in its place and confined in the demands it made on time by the pursuit of frugality in the expenditure to which work was dedicated and by the always prior exigencies of religion.

Above all, the demands of Quaker worship – all the greater because Friends conducted their own liturgy rather than had services conducted for them – both dominated the Sabbath, and invaded the week. Quaker casuistry insisted that members must give precedence to meetings for worship, and that their work must make way for them. In 1791 the Yearly Meeting urged: 'be not discouraged by the smallness of numbers in any place, from attending with diligence your week-day meetings. We need to have our spiritual strength often renewed.'[93] A question that expected an answer in the negative was voiced in the 1797 Yearly Meeting: 'Should we therefore suffer the things of this world to prevent our attending at the times appointed for [God's] worship; whether on the day generally set apart for that purpose, or on other stated days of the week?'[94] What 'diligence' meant in Friends' religious thinking, then, was in the first instance attention to the calls of piety. 'Indolence', meanwhile, implied a kind of accidie:

[91] Michael Mullett, '"The Assembly of the People of God": The social organisation of Lancashire Friends', in idem, ed., *Early Lancaster Friends* (Lancaster, 1978), p. 19.

[92] Clark, *John Bellers*, p. 242.

[93] *Epistles from Yearly Meeting*, 2: 83.

[94] Ibid., 2: 100.

> Indolence with regard to religion, whether it relates to the welfare of our own souls or to our usefulness in the church, is a dangerous state of mind, and offensive in the sight of God. . . . Our spiritual progress is greatly aided by frequent retirement from the cares of this life, for a longer or shorter time, to wait in reverence and fear upon the Most High.[95]

If eighteenth-century English Catholics show signs of having developed a sanctification of work, Friends, traditionally considered prime exponents of a Protestant work culture,[96] exalted (above all in their eighteenth-century pietist-quietist phase) an other-worldly spirit of contemplation and a suspicion of labour insofar as it made incursions on spirituality. While this is not the place to consider some of the actual consequences for economic success of the religio-moral life-values that we have been considering, it remains the case, as Arthur Raistrick showed, that within a world in which Nonconformists outshone non-Nonconformists in economic performance, Quakers even stood out amongst their Dissenting brethren in all fields of measurable achievement, from the sciences to trade and manufacture. There are two possible ways of explaining Quaker secular success in terms of a mainstream Quaker religiosity and spirituality that in effect relegated labour to a secondary role. The first is that Quakers abode by principles of restraint and perspective in their work lives, prioritizing the spiritual and thereby gaining the stillness and balance which in fact operated as the bases of achievement in the world. The second is that, in order to get on in the social world, Friends had to disregard their inhibiting religious principles.

In his thoughtful 'Summary and Conclusions' summarizing his findings of the notable success of Quakers in the sciences and trade and manufacture,[97] Raistrick laid no stress on the cult of work as an explanation for Quaker economic and professional accomplishment. Rather, he emphasised that Quakers taught themselves 'time and time again, that the claims of business and the responsibilities of wealth must not be allowed to encroach upon the time the individual ought to devote to his religious duties, the work of the Society, and his share

[95] *Epistles from Yearly Meeting*, 2: 226.

[96] Ann Prior, 'Friends and business: the interaction of business and religion within the Society of Friends, 1700–1830' (University of Lancaster, Ph.D. thesis, 1995), ch. 2.

[97] Arthur Raistrick, *Quakers in Science and Industry; being an Account of the Quaker Contribution to Science and Industry During the 17th and 18th Centuries* (Newton Abbot, 1968), pp. 335–49.

in Social amelioration'. Quaker networking, Quaker education and, even, paradoxically, a Quaker indifference to profit as such, resulted in the accumulation of the celebrated or notorious Quaker profits. Quakers were not work-fetishists, nor did they succeed and prosper because they were. The alternative possibility is that at least some Friends drove their business lives with a high disregard for the Society's moral strictures on the need for detachment and rest. The Lancaster Quaker merchant Daniel Eccleston conducted his business affairs in the early 1780s with the single-minded passion and irreligion of a modern commodity-dealer, sending out a flood of business letters, all entirely post-Christian in tone and content but full of prices, orders, customs duties, sailings, cargoes, and the rest. For him a 'beautiful adventure' was not the Foxian mystical rhapsody, or Barclay's contemplative raptures, but a cotton sale.[98] His strong work drive in fact violated Quaker principles, while his attendance at meetings may have been induced by motivations more mundane than those commended by the Society's guiding elite: 'As I'm on the lookout for a wife I came by Penrith and was at the yearly meeting there.'[99] Rest and play, though, were firmly in place alongside Eccleston's devoted concentration on business: 'On Tuesday [a party] in all Eight in number, took a walk to Glasson [Dock] after Dinner, to see the new pier there. We got to drinking Liverpool Ale on board the old Hulk, and did it pretty freely, but not satisfied with that, must call at Conder Green in coming home, where several *trials* ensued.'[100] Like William Stout, Eccleston clearly enjoyed a walk, though his partying marathon from Glasson Dock was neither solitary nor sober: his stroll on that occasion in fact wound up riotously in Conder Green where Catholic Thomas Tyldesley had done his drinking earlier in the century.

Moral edicts notwithstanding, it may have been the case, then, that the practical conduct of rest and play by many a Quaker was more human than conformable with prescription. The public house and the race-course against which Quaker officialdom thundered so stentoriously exercised their magnetism over Quakers too, even if in some cases their hyper-puritan consciences may subsequently have dulled the edge of those pleasures. One such was

[98] Janet Nelson, typescript: *Correspondence of Daniel Eccleston*, p. 11.
[99] Ibid., p. 36.
[100] Ibid., p. 24.

> Thomas Haresnape of Aughton in the County of Lancaster, tailor, [who] having for a season frequented the Meetings of the people of God called Quakers, and having also likewise made profession of being led and guided by the light of Christ Jesus which enlighteneth every man that cometh into the world . . . yet for want of faithfulness to it did lend an ear to the subtle temptations of my soul's enemy and hearkened to the persuasions of some young men . . . and thereby was drawn from my lawful employments to go to see a horse race which was at Crosby the second day of the fifth month last past, and as I came homeward from thence I went in the company of the said young men into an alehouse and there was drawn to quarrelling and fighting, which I knew was contrary to the profession I did make.[101]

* * *

The censuring, or self-censuring, of play and pleasure enshrined in poignant terms in Haresnape's admission of failure is part of a vast on-going regime of disciplinary control in seventeenth- and eighteenth-century English Quakerism, a system of oversight and enforcement through the ultimate use of excommunication ('denial', 'disownment') which undoubtedly helped to keep Quaker numbers low. Even though, as the citation indicates, the Quaker disciplinary apparatus was 'internalized' in some individuals over the course of time, still a vast input of ecclesiastical effort was invested into the disciplinary processes needed to keep most Quakers Quakerly as to rest and play. And at the higher end of the social scale from the provincial tailor Thomas Haresnape, the elegant worldliness and cosy pleasure-seeking of the Quaker Gurneys of Earlham confirm that rest and play continued to exercise powerful human currents of attraction in even this most austere of English Christian sects; the recollections of the Gurneys' protégée Elizabeth Fry capture a world light-years away from Barclay's angry disparagement of the dance, the theatre, 'vanity', and rank: 'I took a lesson in dancing. . . . I called on Mrs. Siddons . . . I was painted a little . . . I own, I do love grand company.'[102] In the face of pleasure-loving Quakers urged by their

[101] Michael A. Mullett, *Radical Religious Movements in Early Modern Europe* (London, 1980), p. 123.

[102] Augustus J. C. Hare, *The Gurneys of Earlham*, 2nd edn (London, 1897); *Memoir of the Life of Elizabeth Fry: with Extracts from her Journal and Letters*, 2 vols (London, 1847), 1: 38–9.

religion to back off from work and of puritanical, work-driven, pleasure-mistrusting Catholics, our few remaining beloved categorical clichés in the social history of religion seem now to stand in the severest disrepair.

University of Lancaster

'THE SABBATHS . . . SPENT BEFORE IN IDLENESS & THE NEGLECT OF THE WORD':[1] THE GODLY AND THE USE OF TIME IN THEIR DAILY RELIGION

by DAVID L. WYKES

HISTORIANS have long been aware that during the sixteenth and seventeenth centuries the intensely religious were especially strict in their observance of the Sabbath, in their rejection of amusements and diversions, and their dedication of the day to public duties and religious exercises. The godly did not restrict their religion to the Sabbath nor indeed to public exercises, for they attempted to maintain a daily regime of family worship and private study or devotion. Yet the godly were distinguished not only by the seriousness of their religious observance, but also, out of fear of neglecting their religious duties, by their attempts to discipline their day and regulate their time.

* * *

The focus of the godly week was the Sabbath, a day sanctified to God's use and set apart from the common engagements of the week. Whilst the Sabbath was a day free from secular work, it was not a day for pleasure and idleness, but rather for public duties and exercises, for hearing the Word read and expounded, attending on public prayer, and for receiving the Sacraments. Susanna Reynell honoured the Sabbath as 'the best Portion of her Time: She Welcom'd its Approach, and went to the House of God with exceeding great Joy. . . . How Reverend, Serious, and Attentive was she in the Solemn Worship of God!'[2] Strict Sabbath observance was in many respects the defining characteristic of the godly. With the injunction of the Fourth Commandment, 'Remember the sabbath day to keep it holy'

[1] Leicester, Leicestershire Record Office [hereafter LRO], Records of the Great Meeting Unitarian Chapel, Leicester, N/U/179/50, 'Declaration of Communicants', 1711–32/3, William Marshall (8 May 1712). I am grateful to the Chairman and Vestry of the Great Meeting Unitarian Chapel for permission to use and quote from the volume. The contractions in the quotations used in this paper have all been silently extended, and in some cases slightly modernized.

[2] Isaac Gilling, *A Sermon preach'd at the Funeral of Mrs Susanna Reynell, who Departed this Life Novemb. 21. 1703* (Exeter, 1704), p. 48.

(Exodus 20.8), the concern of the godly with breaches of the Sabbath was two-fold: firstly the profanation of the Sabbath itself, and secondly that such pleasures took away time that should have been devoted to religious duties. Ralph Thoresby, the Leeds antiquarian, admitted once going to a play in London, where 'curiosity carryed me but fear brought me back, it was the First & I hope must be the last time I shal be found upon the devels ground, blessed be God that preserved me from danger & kept me from being in love with that great devourer of time.'[3] Samuel Price, in a sermon preached in June 1725, deplored the neglect of the Sabbath which was all too common, but 'it is very rarely that Persons stop here, when they have gone thus far, they usually proceed to more Ungodliness.'[4]

For the godly, religious duties did not cease with the Sabbath. Their whole week was devoted to religion, and for those with households or families there was a particular responsibility to maintain a stated religious worship in their families. Lady Clinton, a member of Edmund Calamy's Prince's Street Meeting in Westminster, ensured that in her household family prayers were performed every morning and evening, 'when it was expected that all should attend, as her Ladyship constantly did'. 'This was her Practice every Day.' Besides religious worship in her family, Lady Clinton set apart time, morning and evening, for secret prayer, 'a thing so essential to a Heaven-born Soul, that it can no more live without it, than the Body can without Breath.' In the privacy of her closet she used her private retirement for 'setting her Soul in order, and conversing with her God'.[5] Peter Huson, a London merchant who was a member of Benjamin Grosvenor's Presbyterian meeting in Crosby Square, used his time in private worship 'to dress and prepare [his] Soul for a better' World. 'In these things he had a very spiritual Relish.'[6]

The godly were above all distinguished by the seriousness and

[3] Leeds, Yorkshire Archaeological Society [hereafter YAS], MS 21, Diary of Ralph Thoresby (2 Sept. 1677–31 May 1683), p. 139 (21–6 June 1680). I wish to express my thanks to the Council of the Yorkshire Archaeological Society for permission to use and quote from the Thoresby correspondence and diaries.

[4] Samuel Price, *A Sermon preach'd to the Societies for Reformation of Manners, at Salter's-Hall, on Monday, June 28, 1725* (London, 1725), p. 11.

[5] Samuel Rosewell, *The Sentence of God, and his Servant's submission. A Sermon preach'd at Westminster, Nov. the 23d, 1707. Upon Occasion of the Death and Funeral of the Right Honourable the Lady Clinton: who Dyed at Bath the preceding October the 30th* (London, 1708), pp. 27–8. Rosewell was Lady Clinton's chaplain.

[6] Benjamin Grosvenor, *Dying in Faith. A Discourse upon Occasion of the Death and Funeral of Mr Peter Huson, who Departed this Life December 29. 1711* (London, 1712), p. 34.

intensity of their private religious duties. Thomas Sharp, minister of the Mill Hill Presbyterian meeting at Leeds, reminded his congregation in 1680 that 'it is not enough to be a common Christian, God looks for something extraordinary from us.'[7] Although this reminder was made at a time when nonconformists feared renewed persecution, it was intended as a general exhortation to his congregation to live out their lives according to the exacting standards of the godly Christian. Susanna Reynell, a member of a gentry family, was described by her minister, the Presbyterian Isaac Gilling, as 'a very Mortify'd Christian', who 'far from Affecting or Delighting in Pomp and Finery' leaned perhaps too far to the other extreme, and was 'ready to scruple what was Lawful, and Suitable to her Condition and Rank'. Her heart 'was not set upon any thing of this World; no, 'twas fix'd upon the upper better World'. He went on to admit she perhaps allowed too little time for society so that she might benefit from more communion with God. 'She was loth to be hinder'd of her Hours for Retirement. How often hath she deny'd her body Sleep and Refreshment, and prevented the Dawning of the Morning, that she might early Address herself to God?'[8] The demanding nature of the religious exercises of the godly Christian was the result of a fear of sin and a desire for a life of righteousness. It was this intense fear of sin which led the godly to regulate their lives and search their hearts, for theirs was an experiential religion where the godly Christian felt the love and wrath of God immediately and directly.

* * *

Ralph Thoresby's manuscript autobiography and diary survive and therefore offer an opportunity to examine in detail the seriousness with which the godly undertook their religious duties and attempted to regulate their lives. After a visit to Halifax Church viewing monuments and inscriptions with the antiquarian John Briercliffe (*c.* 1609–82) in January 1680, Thoresby wrote 'but alas all this while little done for my Soul, duty either totally omitted or sleightly performed'.[9] A few months later he noted 'too much time spent in doing little of moment tho with sober company'. He excused in part

7 YAS, MS 21, p. 109 (7 March 1679/80).
8 Gilling, *Sermon . . . Susanna Reynell*, pp. 46–7.
9 YAS, MS 21, p. 55 (25 June 1679).

his unprofitable use of time as being 'compelled for healths sake'.[10] Following a Lecture Day, in April 1680, he acknowledged

> my own miscarriage this evening in mispending too much precious time fondly & idly if not sinfully; . . . in the night lay waking 2 if not 3 howers which tho troublesome to the body I hope thro the mercy of God may be an advantage to my Soul by a serious consideration of my multiplyed & aggravated sins, this in particular of spending so much precious time vainly & that after the Opportunity of hearing such an excellent Sermon.[11]

Despite attempts to reform his own behaviour, a month later he spent the day out on business, 'even to the omission of both private & family prayer, and in the evening performed too too slightly'.[12] In November 1680, determined 'to redeem my time from sleep', he entered into a resolution

> to redeem more time particularly to retrench my sleeping time, & getting an Alarm put to the Clock & that set at my beds head, to arise every morning by 5 & first to dedicate the morning (as in duty obliged) to the service of God, by reading a chapter in an old Bible I have with Annotations & then after prayer.

Typically, in making this resolution, he decided to spend some of this time in writing and collecting remarks on the lives and deaths of 'the Saints & Servants of God' in every age with the intention of providing an account of 'all the Heroes both spiritual & temporal, since the very first planting of Christianity in this our Island'.[13] And it is clear that Thoresby's interest in such lives was predominantly religious, for in requesting from Joseph Hill 'an account of some of the many remarkable occurances of your life', he continued that he was 'exceedingly delighted & I hope profited by the example of memorable providences in the lives of eminent persons.'[14] Yet because of his love of books and his antiquarian interests he came to neglect the principal purpose of these studies. In December 1680,

[10] YAS, MS 21, p. 104 (16 Feb. 1679/80).
[11] Ibid., pp. 118–19 (12, 14 April 1680).
[12] Ibid., p. 128 (14 May 1680).
[13] Ibid., p. 177 (1 Nov. 1680).
[14] YAS, MS 12, Ralph Thoresby to Mr Joseph Hill, minister at Rotterdam, 5 March 1696.

> upon a serious review of this week past I am ashamed of the mispending of so much precious time, much in doing of nothing or what is perhaps as insignificant as nothing at all, & much in doing that which is worse than nothing even in sining against God, but how little if any has been spent in his service, tho that was the chiefe end of my coming into the world.[15]

A year later, in October 1681, after reading Camden's *Britannia*, he came to the realization that

> alas, alas tho I can make a shift to give some times a tollerable account of the spending of my time as to temporal affairs or recreation rather, as reading History writing – yet alas but very slender as to the main, the one thing necessary is too much neglected & but litle spent about that for which the whole was given, how little in prayer & meditation & selfe examination which are either sometimes totally omitted, or too carelessly performed.[16]

In his autobiography, begun in August 1710 on his fifty-second birthday, 'Having devoted this day in a more especial Manner to self-examination & reflection' he reviewed his spiritual life, noting the 'mispence of my time hitherto'.[17] He was moved to write of his fear that 'an immoderate love to books should entrench upon the more practical dutys of Religion'.[18] Thoresby's autobiography and diary reveal his anxiety that his worldly concerns were crowding out his religion. Such anxieties, it is clear, were shared by the godly business-man, thus raising questions relevant to the long-standing debate about the relationship between dissent and business.

* * *

The most celebrated attempt to link religious beliefs to economic success was made by the German sociologist Max Weber, who, in his essay 'The Protestant Ethic and the Spirit of Capitalism', laid the foundations of the modern debate.[19] Weber, as a sociologist, was

[15] YAS, MS 21, p. 186 (3 Dec. 1680).
[16] Ibid., pp. 301–2 (1 Oct. 1681).
[17] YAS, MS 26, Autobiography of Ralph Thoresby to 1714, p. 1.
[18] Ibid., p. 40.
[19] Weber's essay, originally published in two parts in 1904 and 1905, was translated from the German by Talcott Parsons as *The Protestant Ethic and the Spirit of Captitalism* (London, 1930).

primarily concerned with the transformation of general attitudes rather than with the outlook and behaviour of particular individuals. Nonetheless, it was the application of his concept of a 'psychological sanction' driving ascetic Protestants to economic success that captured the imagination of many economic historians, since it seemed to offer a means of explaining why a small number of businessmen who were religious Dissenters apparently proved very much more successful than most of their contemporaries. Few modern historians accept Weber's thesis.[20] Nonetheless, there have been a number of attempts to advance the hypothesis. In one of the most important, Cohn argued that evidence of God's love drove the saint to work while in turn its absence initiated efforts to regain it. Cohn therefore reversed Weber's emphasis, claiming that the saint was drawn not driven, but, like Weber, he did not examine the businessman nor prove that experience did in fact follow doctrine.[21] What then was the attitude of the godly to work and business success?

It is true that the desire to separate from sin (a sign of grace) instilled a self-conscious striving for personal discipline and restraint, as historians have claimed, but if seen in its proper religious context it is difficult to perceive any practical value for business activity. The godly feared that the temptations of the world would lead them to ignore their spiritual duties; they were therefore encouraged to equate worldliness (especially the neglect of the Sabbath) with sin, and not only to condemn all recreations and pleasures as vanities of the world, but to see worldly activity in general as a danger to religion. Peter Huson, 'when he found himself in Circumstances to do it, he laid aside his Trade, and follow'd the Improvement of what God had bless'd him with', his soul. 'As Riches encreas'd, he was very much afraid of setting his Heart upon them'; for as Benjamin Grosvenor, his minister, wrote in Huson's funeral sermon, 'I often find in his Diary, Prayers and Expostulations against the Intanglements and Love of this present World.' Even when he was 'in the midst of all Avocations of Business, and Attendances on his Worldly Affairs', he still had 'a strict Regard to his Duty, to his Walk with God and his own Soul'.[22] Grosvenor was

[20] For a good survey of the inconsistencies in Weber's argument, see F. Parkin, *Key Sociologists: Max Weber* (Chichester, London, and New York, 1982), ch. 2.

[21] C. L. Cohn, *God's Caress: The Psychology of Puritan Religious Experience* (New York, 1986), pp. 112–33; D. Zaret, *The Heavenly Contract: Ideology and Organisation in Pre-Revolutionary Puritanism* (Chicago and London, 1985).

[22] Grosvenor, *Dying in Faith*, pp. 36–7, 34–5.

anxious to stress in the case of another wealthy member of his congregation, John Deacle, that 'Providence had thrown a great deal of this World into his Possession, as it were to shew, that a great Estate does not always spoil the Man that comes to it.' Deacle, who unsuccessfully contested Aylesbury in 1713 before being returned to Parliament for Evesham in 1715, had inherited £50,000 from his uncle John Deacle (d. 1709), a wealthy London woollen draper.[23] John Newman in his funeral sermon for Richard Mount, another successful London merchant, was willing to make the link between Mount's success in business and God's blessings.

> He had a considerable Genius for Trade, and as he was diligent and faithful in the Duties of his Secular Calling, God did bless his honest Endeavours with considerable Success: He was very willing to own, with Thankfulness to God's Providence, how he had made him greatly to encrease, finding by Experience that the Blessing of the Lord upon the diligent Hand make Rich.[24]

Edmund Calamy's account of Michael Watts, citizen and haberdasher of London, might also seem to support a link between a work ethic and godliness. 'He was diligent in his Worldly Business out of regard to God, who he knew had made his Being so, his Duty'; but, Calamy continued, he

> was careful so to manage himself in it, as that it might not be an Hindrance to him in his greater Concern as a Christian. He would secure a considerable time for Converse with God by serious Prayer, and Meditation, and Reading the Holy Scriptures, every morning in his Closet: and yet would visit his Ware-house as soon as others.[25]

[23] B. Grosvenor, *A Sermon on Occasion of the Death and Funeral of John Deacle, Esq; Who Departed this life, Oct. 29. Preached at Crosby-Square, Nov. 10, 1723* (London, 1723), p. 16; *The History of Parliament: The House of Commons, 1715–1754*, ed. R. Sedgwick, 2 vols (London, 1970), 1: 607–8.

[24] John Newman, *A Sermon Occasioned by the Death of Mr Richard Mount, Who Departed this Life June the 29th, in the 67th Year of his Age; Preached at Salter's-Hall, July 8, 1722: to Which is Added, some Advice to his Children* (London, 1722), p. 34.

[25] Edmund Calamy, *A Funeral Sermon Occasion'd by the Decease of Mr Michael Watts, Citizen and Haberdasher of London; Who Departed this Life on February the Third, 1707/8. Ann. Ætat. 72. Preach'd at the Meeting-House in Silver street the next Lord's-Day after his Interment* (London, 1708), p. 32.

In other words, by rising early and redeeming time Watts allowed sufficient time for his private devotions, without encroaching on the time demanded by his business affairs.

The evidence provided by funeral sermons suggests that the wealthy godly gentleman or businessman sought to prevent his worldly affairs from encroaching on his religious duties. Caution, however, is necessary in using evidence from funeral sermons; their purpose undoubtedly dictated their content. Matthew Clarke admitted 'Funeral-Commendations . . . gather'd out of the Spoils of Truth, are neither to the Honour of them on whom they are bestow'd, nor to the Reputation of those by whom they are given.'[26] Fortunately, a small volume of spiritual testimonies survives for the early eighteenth century.[27] Made by the Presbyterian members of the Great Meeting, Leicester, before their admission to the Lord's Supper, the volume allows what is possibly an unique opportunity to investigate the religious concerns and priorities of a group of ordinary men and women. Although individual accounts of religious experience are not uncommon in private diaries and autobiographies, collections of public testimonies are extremely rare, and only a handful appear to have survived. The Great Meeting volume is also unusual as the testimonies date from the early eighteenth century, a period for which no other collections are known, and they were given by Presbyterians rather than Independents. In all, 162 testimonies were made between August 1711 and the end of 1725, with a further entry for April 1726 (a median of ten a year), after which date the entries became a record of admissions only.[28] A few early testimonies are highly detailed accounts of individual spiritual pilgrimages, but the majority are descriptions of the means or signs of grace.

What do these testimonies reveal about attitudes to religious duties and work? In some respects the results concerning businessmen are disappointing. Only about a third of the narratives were by men and few of the leading businessmen who were members of the Great Meeting are included in the volume. Status is difficult to determine

[26] Matthew Clarke, *A Funeral Sermon on the Death of the Late Reverend Mr Thomas Michell. Who Died, Jan. 9. 1721* (London, 1721), p. 34.

[27] LRO, N/U/179/50, 'Declaration of Communicants', 1711–32/3 (unpaginated). For further details, see D. L. Wykes, 'The autobiographical account of a Leicester apothecary: Samuel Statham, *c.*1673–1732', *Leicestershire Historian*, 3, no. 8 (1990), pp. 6–16.

[28] A few individuals gave a second testimony, e.g. Eliza Groce (22 Aug. 1711, 4 May 1721), and Joseph Bentley (2 Nov. 1711, 4 June 1720).

because for most entries the only biographical details provided are names. But three-fifths of the men making testimonies were freemen, almost equally divided between craft and the wealthier trade or manufacturing occupations, a somewhat higher proportion than for the general population.[29] Nonetheless, it is likely that the majority of testimonies were made by the humbler members of the congregation, since most of the leading supporters are not included.

If the testimonies themselves are examined then it is clear that all the communicants, businessmen included, were preoccupied with spiritual matters. Bethia Belton found that after the death of her mother she was 'sometimes drawn away by the world to the neglect of her duty and the neglect of her prayer'.[30] William Marshall, whose father was a prominent mercer and a leading member of the Great Meeting, was led to see

> the Vanity & Emptiness of all these Enjoyments . . . & the Sabbaths he spent before in Idleness, & the neglect of the word he can now take Delight in, & has found Some Communion with God in the word Preacht, which makes him more diligent in working out his own Salvation . . . . he would herein yield himself up to God to be his for ever.[31]

The great majority of communicants made no reference to secular matters, but Joseph Bentley, one of the leading mercers in the town and a trustee of the congregation, was an exception. It is clear, however, he was concerned that his business commitments had led him to neglect his spiritual duties. In November 1711, after describing his religious condition and the means of obtaining grace, he expressed the desire to continue faithful in God, 'notwithstanding what ever opposition he may meet with from a Lazy, worldly, backward heart, or from an alluring or Terrifying world.' Unusually for the volume he made a second testimony, and in June 1720 he admitted that he has been kept off from this ordinance 'by the troubles of the world'. Similarly, the hosier, Henry Rice, 'says that it was good for him that he has been afflicted, and to be taken off from the Thouts and Business of the World.' Poorer members found the conflict even stronger because

29 See D. L. Wykes, 'Religious dissent and the trade and industry of Leicester, 1660–1720' (University of Leicester, Ph.D. thesis, 1987), pp. 84, 114–18.

30 LRO, N/U/179/50, Bethia Belton (23 May 1713).

31 Ibid., William Marshall (8 May 1712). Cf. John Cowdell (6 Sept. 1718); Rebekah Cook (11 Feb. 1711/12); Frances Ward (2 Nov. 1711).

of the practical problem of having to earn a living. Susannah Richardson was brought to conviction, 'But then she was Poor, & must mind her Work, & so was diverted from Prayer.'[32]

It is significant that these are the only references to work and economic attitudes in the volume. Moreover, in the examination of the heart, worldly commitments were, even for the leading businessmen, a source of anxiety not assurance. Admittedly, businessmen are not well represented in the volume, and undoubtedly many did not respond positively to an intense godly religion. Thoresby's father noted that although there were 'numerous & attentive auditorys on the Lords days' in Leeds during the 1670s for both conformists and nonconformists, there was only 'a very slender appearance at a week days Lecture'. This, he thought, was the result of 'too great intenseness upon busyness in some, but a blameworthy supineness in others'.[33] It should also be noted that the purpose of the testimonies, like funeral sermons, undoubtedly determined their preoccupation with religious matters. They were after all designed to record the spiritual state of the communicant. It is, therefore, not surprising that secular matters were largely ignored. Even so, on the rare occasions that worldly issues did surface it was because of the fear that they were crowding out religion. Thoresby's manuscript diary, which provides a much more extensive and detailed account of his spiritual state, portrays very similar sentiments.

None of the evidence discussed identifies any clear link between the spiritual state of the godly and a desire to succeed at business. Whilst the surviving testimonies and biographies confirm that the godly experienced a deep anxiety over salvation and the desire for conviction and assurance, there is nothing to support Weber's thesis that this sense of anxiety drove individuals by means of a 'psychological sanction' to ceaseless, systematic labour in order to obtain a sign of God's grace, which only worldly success could provide. Indeed the evidence from Thoresby's diary, funeral sermons, and the Great Meeting volume suggests the reverse: that individuals were concerned rather that their preoccupation with business and other worldly matters would lead them to neglect their spiritual duties. An examination of the best collection of seventeenth-century American testimonies led the editors

[32] LRO, N/U/179/50, Henry Rice (12 Jan. 1715/16); Susannah Richardson (24 April 1714). Cf. Elizabeth Carver (20 Aug. 1717).

[33] YAS, MS 26, p. 13.

to conclude that despite the wealth of some church members, no direct correlation between worldly estate and visible sainthood could be established.[34] Explanations for the level of involvement of Dissenters in business therefore lie elsewhere.[35]

* * *

In the everyday world, it was the seriousness with which the godly took and applied otherwise orthodox doctrine to their own lives and experiences that distinguished them from ordinary churchgoers; churchgoers who, in the words of Thomas Sharp, 'spend their days in voluntary Ignorance, thinking that if they go to church for an hower on the Lords day, God is Beholden to them'.[36] By contrast, the godly in their anxiety to live out the gospel were encouraged to bring the affairs of the world under the rule of Christ and act out everyday life as part of their religious duties. As a result they attempted to keep the Sabbath holy and maintain a daily regime of public and private religious exercises. Their anxiety that they might misuse their time, or worse sin, led them to discipline their day and regulate their time, and to avoid even sober company and lawful recreation for fear of extravagance and temptation.

Dr Williams's Trust and Library, London

[34] G. Selement and B. C. Wooley, eds, *Thomas Shepard's Confessions*, Publications of the Colonial Society of Massachusetts Collections, 58 (1981), p. 4.

[35] For a discussion, see D. L. Wykes, 'Religious dissent and the penal laws: an explanation of business success?', *History*, 75 (1990), pp. 61–2.

[36] YAS, MS 21, p. 135 (2 June 1680).

'THE BANE OF INDUSTRY'? POPULAR EVANGELICALISM AND WORK IN THE EIGHTEENTH CENTURY

by JOHN WALSH

'WORK while it is day; the night cometh wherein no man can work': John Wesley's liking for John 9.4 will not surprise a modern student of evangelical history.[1] That there was a Weberian elective affinity between Methodism and diligence has become something of a truism among sociologists examining the cluster of values comprising the Protestant ethic and social historians probing the psychological roots of industrialization in England. Thanks to a famous chapter in E. P. Thompson's *Making of the English Working Class*, countless students perceive Methodism primarily as an agency of time-work discipline, internalizing a gospel of work in the pre-industrial labourer and recasting him, by way of the fiery mould of a conversion experience, into the submissive factory worker.[2]

Thompson's version of the thesis is extreme. Nevertheless, one does not have to look far to find early evangelical writers who exalted work as a divine ordinance. Among the topics noted as themes in Whitefield's early preaching was that of 'abhorring all idleness and working diligently with the hands or head'.[3] John Wesley was a supreme embodiment of a Christian ethic of work, the most relentless of activists. 'Leisure and I have now taken leave of each other', he had announced in 1727, 'I propose to be busy as long as I live', and throughout his life he exemplified diligence and the husbandry of time to a remarkable degree.[4] He delivered his first sermon at 4 a.m. and went to bed at 9.15 p.m., having cut down his sleep to the absolute minimum; he even instructed his people to sing their hymns more

[1] *The Letters of J. Wesley*, ed. J. Telford, 8 vols (London, 1931), 6: 74.

[2] E. P. Thompson, *The Making of the English Working Class* (London, 1963); idem, 'Time, work discipline, and industrial capitalism', *P&P*, 38 (Dec. 1969), pp. 86–9.

[3] *Four Letters taken from the Weekly History* (Edinburgh, 1743), p. 18.

[4] *The Works of John Wesley, volume 25: Letters, I, 1721–1739*, ed. F. Baker (Oxford, 1980), p. 223. This excellent but as yet incomplete edition of the letters is cited in this one instance because it corrects an error in the Telford edition used elsewhere.

quickly, so as not to waste time.[5] Wesley intended industriousness to be built into the fabric of his Connexion. The Methodist society rules laid down that idlers were to be expelled; members of the 'bands' were to be 'patterns of diligence and frugality'.[6] Christians should be busy in order to counter the power of original sin which beset them in their idle moments, 'for grace flies a vacuum as well as nature, and the devil fills whatever God does not fill'.[7] Labour for Wesley had of course a far more positive role than this and he saw a close conjunction between the Pauline injunction to work out our salvation and the demands of a secular occupation: both tasks should be carried out with a similar sense of accountability, with the 'utmost earnestness of spirit, with all possible care and caution . . . with the utmost diligence, speed, punctuality and exactness'.[8] Work should be undertaken in the spirit of devotion: it was prayer, it was worship, a sacrifice offered up to God. The sacrificial theme is caught up in Charles Wesley's hymns, in which the toil and sweat of labour becomes a kenotic figuration of the way that almighty God, in an act of stupendous self-emptying, had been incarnated as a humble manual worker to effect the salvation of humanity. By offering up his labour, the devout worker entered mystically into the salvific, sacrificial work of Christ on the cross:

> Son of the Carpenter, receive
> This humble work of mine;
> Worth to my meanest labour give,
> By joining it to Thine.[9]

Nor was the gospel of work merely a matter of precept. Methodist biographies suggest that Wesley's teaching frequently fell on receptive ears. In some fervent society members, conversion seems to have overcome the sense of quotidian toil as mere drudgery and replaced reluctant compliance by a willing, inward disposition towards labour. 'Worldly business was a burden to me', Joseph Marshall confessed to

[5] *The Works of J. Wesley*, ed. T. Jackson, 14 vols (London, 1872) [hereafter Wesley, *Works*], 13: 230.

[6] Ibid., 7: 31; 8: 129, 274. Other Methodist groupings had similar rules: see, for example, *The History, Constitution, Rules and Confession of the Calvinistic Methodists of Wales* (London, 1827), p. 48.

[7] Wesley, *Works*, 11: 439.

[8] Ibid., 6: 510.

[9] *The Poetical Works of J. and C. Wesley*, ed. G. Osborn, 13 vols (London, 1868–72), 1: 172.

John Wesley, 'but He whom my soul loveth has . . . removed that . . . and keeps me in perfect peace while . . . employed.'[10] It is more than likely that many were drawn into the movement by its ethic of purposeful activity. Thomas Payne, for example, stationed unhappily with the army in St Helena, joined a Methodist society because it promoted 'cleanliness, industry, frugality and economy'.[11] Local histories of Methodism abound with examples of members who became upwardly mobile, if only modestly so. It was often observed how some converts prospered materially after adopting a value system which brought a reorientation of the will from fecklessness towards industriousness, an ethic collectively sustained by the group discipline and scrutiny of the society and the class meeting. 'True religion developed his powers' is a theme in obituary notices.[12] Methodists were frequently said to make reliable servants, apprentices, overseers, and foremen – 'send it to Bentley; for he is never known to fail.'[13] Wesley could point to the many instances in which his movement had raised the lives of whole families out of squalor. As he travelled round the country he noted with mingled satisfaction and apprehension how the 'diligence and frugality' of his people had brought them prosperity.[14]

It comes as a surprise, therefore, to find eighteenth-century Methodism denounced as 'the bane of industry'.[15] In the great volume of anti-Methodist literature of the century, in episcopal charges, parochial sermons, tracts, squibs, plays, novels, newspapers, few allegations are more persistent than that the Methodists of all kinds did not inculcate habits of industriousness but actually undermined them. They were 'enemies to diligence'.[16] Alderman Horncastle of Nottingham spoke for many of his generation when he told the preacher John Nelson, who had been carried to his house by a hostile crowd, 'What, do you expect us to take your part, when you take people from their work?'[17]

10 *The Arminian Magazine* [hereafter *AM*], 9 (1786), p. 396.

11 *The Lives of the Early Methodist Preachers*, ed. J. Telford, 5 vols, 3rd edn (London, 1866), 2: 288.

12 B. Smith, *Methodism in Macclesfield* (London, 1875), p. 214.

13 *AM*, 39 (1806), p. 27; *Wesley Banner*, 2 (1850), p. 114.

14 J. Wesley, *Journal*, ed. N. Curnock, 8 vols (London, 1938), 4: 417, 5: 30, 82; Wesley, *Works*, 7: 289–90.

15 *The Norwich Mercury*, 18 Jan. 1752.

16 H. F. Burder, *The Life of the Revd. G. Burder* (London, 1833), p. 41.

17 Wesley, *Journal*, 3: 240.

How can we account for this remarkable discrepancy between modern and eighteenth-century assessments of Methodist social behaviour? To a large extent, those who perceived early Methodists as work-shy, improvident fanatics were transposing familiar stereotypes of religious deviance on to a new movement. There was little new in the portrayal of unpopular religious bodies as enemies to diligence and sappers of economic prosperity. The charge was a staple of anti-Catholic propaganda which had long contrasted the sober, purposeful energy of Protestantism with a superstitious Romish piety that encouraged lethargy and indolence. And not only Catholics but also over-zealous Protestants could easily be tagged as enemies of work. Some Puritans and Calvinist Dissenters had already come under fire for diverting labourers away from their worldly callings, while the illuminism of religious 'enthusiasts' was commonly held to make them unfit for sustained labour: eccentric sectarians like the French Prophets in Anne's reign were blamed for reducing families 'to an abject, melancholy state' by undermining the will to work.[18] Even before his evangelical conversion John Wesley, still a rigorist High Churchman in Georgia, had been accused by planters of undermining the strength of the new colony by diverting settlers from their labours through the multiplicity of his church services, and so encouraging a 'spirit of idleness'.[19] The speed with which these charges were applied to the early Methodists suggests that they were in many ways clichés.

The force of this line of religious polemic was greatly amplified by its congruity with an archetypal prejudice now strongly reinforced by economic theory. Through the eighteenth century it was a widely held axiom that the unremitting toil of the poor was the primary source of the nation's wealth and strength. Any diminution of the will to work among the labouring masses was perceived as a threat to the body politic.[20] If the poor were offered a choice between earning more and working less, they would choose the leisure option; as Mandeville put it with characteristic bluntness, 'nobody will do the dirty slavish work that can help it'.[21] Almost any recreational activity that might seduce

[18] T. Balguy, *Discourses* (Winchester, 1785), pp. 59–60; J. Thomas, *Two Letters to the Rev. T. Coke* (London, 1777), p. 9; A. Boyer et al., *The Political State of Great Britain*, 56 (1738), pp. 145–6.

[19] P. Tailfer et al., *A True and Historical Narrative of the Colony of Georgia* (Charleston, SC, 1741), p. 41.

[20] E. S. Furniss, *The Position of the Labourer in a System of Nationalism* (Boston, 1920).

[21] B. de Mandeville, *The Fable of the Bees*, ed. F. B. Kaye, 2 vols (Oxford, 1924), 1: 302.

the labourer from toil was potentially suspect: theatre-going, cricket, wakes, the hubbub of parliamentary elections could be feared as distractions which might undermine labour discipline, 'enervate industry', and (in modern jargon) promote a backward-leaning labour supply curve. That a religious movement which made heavy demands on the time and energy of its followers should fall under suspicion is hardly surprising. Methodism could easily be viewed not as the carrier of a strenuous work ethic, but as an insidious temptation to leisure preference.

If the 'bane of industry' charge was often formulaic, it was nonetheless often firmly accepted. The critics of Methodism on this score included not only Grub Street hacks or simple-minded country parsons, but commentators who were intelligent and well-meaning. The keynote of the critique was struck early in the Revival by Joseph Trapp, Oxford Professor of Poetry, in a famous sermon delivered in 1739 on the text 'Be not righteous overmuch' (Ecclesiastes 7.16). In a word, the Methodists were guilty of supererogation. There were many virtues, Trapp observed, which if pushed to excess became vices, and religiosity – 'over-strain'd piety' – could well become one of them. However well intentioned it might be, Methodism pushed piety to extreme limits. It was fanatical in its otherworldliness.[22]

The theme of supererogation was embroidered for many decades, especially by clerical writers. To align strenuous religious devotion with other time-destroying recreations might appear to demand some ingenuity, but it was a task seriously and vigorously undertaken. Thomas Church earnestly warned John Wesley, 'Nor ought even the care of our souls, confessedly most necessary, to be pressed as to forget the care of our families and affairs.' The poor, he urged, should be told that it was 'bad to be always engaged in spiritual exercises' and reminded that labour was also a primary Christian duty. Sunday was the appropriate day for worship by poor people and the parish church was the appropriate place for it.[23] Another pamphleteer compared the dangerous proliferation of Methodist devotional occasions with the sensible practice of the Church of England which normally limited its services to 'one day of the week, that people whose subsistence depends on their industry, may have an opportunity properly to discharge their

[22] J. Trapp, *The Nature, Sin and Folly of being Righteous Overmuch*, 2nd edn (London, 1739), pp. 4, 7–8.

[23] T. Church, *An Explanation and Defense of the Church of England* (London, 1739), p. 54.

several duties'.[24] A number of divines urged the action of the Deity himself as an example in this context. Thus, in a vigorous sermon on *The Religion of Labour* (1740), Robert Clayton, Bishop of Cork, noted that 'God when he created the world, selected only one day in seven which he blessed and sanctified, but appointed the remaining six days for us to labour in.'[25] The Sabbath should be a day of rest, observed a writer in 1805, but for Methodists it was the reverse: 'it now imposes on the little mechanic, servant and labourer of this persuasion, the hardest day's work he performs in the whole week.' All that God actually required of the labouring man on a weekday was 'a short prayer, offered up on the pillow of rest'; 'larger devotions' were expected only from the leisured classes.[26]

In the opening years of the Revival it was news of the vast numbers turning out to hear Whitefield's open-air oratory that most struck the imagination of critics. The elision of Methodist preaching with time-wasting popular entertainments did not seem absurd to those who read about the huge crowds that assembled to hear him, many travelling from a distance and arriving hours before the preaching to create a holiday atmosphere resembling that of some great fair or public spectacle.[27] If Methodism encouraged mass absenteeism on this scale, surely it would damage the national economy? 'The industry of the inferior people in a society', observed a newspaper editor, 'is the great source of the prosperity and wealth of it. If one man . . . should have it in his power by his preaching to detain 5 or 6,000 of the vulgar from their daily labour, what a loss, in a little time, may he bring to the public?' The turnout of local colliers to the preaching would cause 'a prodigious rise in the cost of coals' around Bristol.[28] The arithmetically-minded Scot, Sir John Clerk of Penicuik, calculated the loss to the nation of a single day's work in the week by those who turned out to hear Whitefield as eight million sixpences.[29]

The domestic effects of this sermon-gadding were an insistent

[24] *An Earnest Appeal to the Publick* (London, 1739), p. 10.

[25] R. Clayton, *The Religion of Labour: a Sermon* (Dublin, 1740), p. 20.

[26] *A Letter to a Country Gentleman on the Subject of Methodism* (Ipswich, 1805), pp. 29, 33.

[27] [A. H. C. Seymour], *The Life and Times of the Countess of Huntingdon*, 2 vols (London, 1844), 1: 92.

[28] *The Gentleman's Magazine*, 9 (1739), p. 257, quoting *Common Sense*, 19 April 1739.

[29] *Memoirs of the Life of Sir John Clerk of Penicuik*, ed. J. M. Gray, Publications of the Scottish History Society, 13 (Edinburgh, 1892), p. 248.

theme in anti-Methodist literature. 'In every thousand men who are running after him [Whitefield] some hundreds of families must thereby suffer the want of bread' warned one observer.[30] Sixty years later the Revd Richard Fellowes described with pathos the effects of Methodism on devotees who neglected 'their proper calling' by attending too many services: they were to be seen 'covered in rags, incrusted with filth or wasting with disease'.[31] Methodists were said to spend two or three hours a day on their religious exercises. On weekdays, after their day's toil, labourers were exhausted by the need to attend emotionally draining class meetings at night. They had so many services on Sunday that it became the most exhausting day of the week.[32] To compound all this, by their puritanical hatred of 'innocent diversions and recreations' the Methodists denied their people the opportunity to rest between bouts of labour and replenish their energies.

In varied ways the Methodists were said to have 'impoverished the poor' and stripped households of the fruits of their industry. They spent far too much on charity and went in for 'irrational liberalities' to the indigent.[33] By their many collections they drained away the savings of whole families. Their itinerant preachers were spiritual mountebanks, very like the mendicant friars of legend: they too grew fat on 'the mite of helpless widows and the bread of weeping and deluded orphans' and travelled the country to 'swindle the unsuspecting country people, and bring away with them cheese and bacon'.[34] Their terrifying preaching drove bread-winners to frenzy, madness, and even suicide, throwing households on to the parish. Evangelicalism was seen as especially disruptive to the domestic economy because of its emotional appeal to women, deemed more susceptible than males to 'enthusiasm'. The Revd John Buller of Bristol painted a dismal picture of colliers' wives abandoning their homes to gad after the preachers, leaving infants 'soaking in their own piss and wallowing in their dung . . . most loudly and lamentably crying, pinched with hunger, benumbed with cold.' When told by angry husbands 'ye are

30 *Earnest Appeal to the Publick*, p. 8.

31 R. Fellowes, *Religion without Cant* (London, 1801), p. 31.

32 *Letter to a Country Gentleman*, pp. 29–30.

33 J. White, *A Letter to a Gentleman dissenting from the Church*, 2nd edn (London, 1745), p. 98.

34 J. Free, *Rules for the Discovery of False Prophets* (London, 1758), p. 29; G. Barratt, *Recollections of Methodism in Lincoln* (Lincoln, 1866), p. 75.

idle, ye are idle', they had replied 'we must serve the Lord, and save our souls.'[35]

It was a truism that religious 'enthusiasm' could produce profoundly unsettling states of mind which upset not merely social but also economic relationships. Converts who believed themselves in direct communication with the Holy Ghost were not inclined to accept orders from masters set over them. They became unruly, restless, censorious. They had ideas above their station and would not sit easily under the yoke of a work discipline administered by those whose values they despised. After hearing the Methodists, claimed one observer, labourers became noticeably less content with their wages and more likely to 'murmur'.[36] In coffee-houses the gossip was that Whitefield would 'spoil all the poorer sort of people and servants'.[37]

There were probably many to agree with William Cobbett that labouring men had frequently 'become preachers because it was pleasanter to preach than to work'.[38] According to this perception, Methodism encouraged men to abandon their menial, inherited occupations and launch out on to a new career in a freer, more exciting and wider world as itinerant evangelists. By arousing dangerous aspirations for social and spatial freedom, Methodism undermined a work-discipline which depended on an unthinking acceptance of drudgery and staying put. In Methodism, complained John Whitehead, one saw people 'brought up in laborious employments . . . miners, weavers, carriers, clothiers, soldiers, petty schoolmasters and such like' deserting their proper callings; men 'lately poor despised and unknown' who were now well-dressed and comfortably off, travelling about on horseback 'followed, caressed and almost adored by the deluded populace, in every town and village in their circuit'.[39] Methodist preachers attracted social jealousy like that now directed at pop stars and football heroes.

The doctrinal content of Methodist preaching gave grounds for disquiet to those who worried about the maintenance of work discipline. This was especially the case with the evangelical representation of justification by faith alone. Anglicans were obliged to accept this as a doctrine implanted in the Thirty Nine Articles, but most

[35] J. Buller, *A Reply to Mr Wesley's Address to the Clergy* (Bristol, 1756), pp. 25–6.

[36] *Letter to a Country Gentleman*, p. 41.

[37] *The True Character of Mr Whitefield* (London, 1739), p. 17.

[38] W. Cobbett, *Cobbett's Political Register*, 35 (27 Jan. 1820).

[39] J. Scholes, *Edward Whitehead* (Bolton, 1889), p. 18.

clerics saw it as one needing very careful exegesis: when interpreted by fanatical or semi-literate preachers it could offer a dangerous disincentive to labour. To suspicious minds, the solifidianism of evangelical teaching, with its stress on the unconditionality of grace and its denial of any efficacy for works in justification, had resonances which could extend far beyond the sphere of theology. Methodists appeared to depreciate the necessity of strenuous effort and obedience in the religious life. Their notion that grace was immediately accessible to those who had hitherto lived lives of idleness or evil, their belief that unproductive characters like prostitutes and thieves could instantaneously be accounted righteous by a literal *coup de grace*, appeared fraught with alarming consequences. Like the papists with their easy pardons and light penances, evangelicals seemed to offer a grace that was not so much free as cheap; a salvation that was morally undemanding and encouraged passivity or fecklessness. They taught that all that was required was faith – an instant faith, that was all too often only presumption. One could become 'a saint on easy terms'.[40] This was a message that the improvident lower orders seemed all too eager to hear. John Green, future Bishop of Lincoln, complained that 'every thing is represented to be done for them by the all-sufficient merits of a Saviour, little or nothing is understood to remain that can be properly done by themselves. Obligations of duty are in a great measure suspended.'[41] It was not difficult to see parallels between the theological depreciation of good works and the secular downgrading of good work. What, for instance, might simple minds make of a hymn like Toplady's 'Rock of Ages':

> Not the labours of my hands
> Can fulfil Thy law's demands?[42]

Evangelical teaching on the theme of 'walking by faith' looked dangerously otherworldly. What would happen if too many ploughboys and day-labourers were encouraged blindly to follow the perceived leadings of Providence and interpret literally the dominical injunction to take no thought for the morrow? They might well, as

40 R. Graves, *The Spiritual Quixote*, ed. C. Tracy (London, 1967), p. 235. See *The Works of G. Whitefield*, 6 vols (London, 1771–2), 5: 370: 'I have offered you salvation on as cheap terms as you could desire.'

41 J. Green, *The Principles and Practices of the Methodists Considered* (London, 1760), p. 25.

42 A. M. Toplady, *The Works of Augustus Toplady*, 6 vols (London, 1794), 6: 422.

Foote suggested in his play *The Minor*, abandon their callings, expecting the Lord to provide:

> With labour, toil, all second means dispense
> And live a rent charge upon providence.[43]

It was a constant source of complaint that evangelical preaching dwelt almost exclusively on high soteriological and experiential themes, ignoring the 'common duties' of everyday life, including work, which it was a minister's obligation to emphasise. Thus in 1794 Samuel Clapham complained that 'Christianity is not considered by the Methodists as having a sufficiently intimate relation with this world. For Virtue they substitute Holiness.' As many parish clergymen saw it, Methodist worship did not conform to an ideal establishmentarian pattern in which a dutiful flock listened to homilies on good works, duty, and diligence: on the contrary, its devotions were not rational and ethical but enthusiastic and emotional, given over to 'tedious prayers . . . sudden raptures and . . . gloomy meditations'.[44]

In many ways these allegations were absurd, often the product of unreasoning prejudice or polemical rhetoric. Yet – whether the critics of Methodism realized it or not – there were aspects of evangelical spirituality which did not easily comport with the simple stereotype of the Methodist as an unqualified devotee of worldly labour.

Evangelical theologians, like many of their seventeenth-century predecessors and not a few contemporaries, set limitations on the gospel of work. In their hierarchy of values the prosecution of a worldly calling was subordinate to the aims of pursuing salvation and promoting the Church of Christ. The ethic of secular labour was held in tension with an exacting evangelical doctrine of holiness with whose demands there was a potential for conflict. Wesley urged the necessity of industry, but like many other divines he saw clearly the danger of allowing work to become an obsession, a fetish, almost a rival religion – a lesson spelled out eloquently by William Law in his *Serious Call*, which had been the *vade mecum* of the Oxford Methodists.[45] In his Holy Club phase Wesley had recognized this danger in himself: 'deliver me O God', ran his prayer, 'from too intense an application

[43] S. Foote, *The Minor. A Comedy*, 2nd edn (London, 1760), p. 90.

[44] S. Clapham, *How far Methodism is Conducive to the Interests of Christianity* (Leeds, 1794), pp. 16–17.

[45] W. Law, *A Practical Treatise upon Christian Perfection* (London, 1726), p. 72.

even to necessary business.'[46] In his early evangelical ministry Whitefield had urged diligence on his hearers, but he also preached a vehement sermon entitled 'Worldly Business No Plea for the Neglect of Religion' in which he warned (in language strikingly reminiscent of Law's) that 'though business may assume an air of importance when compared with other trifling amusements, yet when put in the balance with the loss of our most precious souls, it is equally frivolous. . . . The most lawful callings cannot justify our neglect with the grand concern of religion.'[47] For the dedicated Methodist, as for the Puritan, the doctrine of the 'calling' possessed a binary character which modern social historians are apt to ignore. Christians had indeed a 'particular calling' to pursue the occupations by which they earned their daily bread, but they also had a 'general calling' to pursue their own salvation, and there was no doubt which had priority.[48] It is noteworthy that Wesley held up for imitation the primitive Christians who subordinated their trades to 'the one thing needful' and sought out callings which allowed the fullest scope for spiritual development.[49] Secular work must be the dutiful servant of piety, not the tyrannical master. And it was not the only form of labour. In this context it is notable that in the evangelical vocabulary the word 'work' was constantly applied to religious as well as to secular labour. Thus the promotion of revival was assisting 'the work of God': a preacher would be described as extending 'the work' in Yorkshire or Wales. Time spent in devotional exercises, in preaching, visiting the sick – this was work, and work of a higher order than that of a secular calling.

There was a potential clash between the demands of sanctification and those of daily toil. How could the Christian divide his time and energy between them? Even though secular work was prayerfully offered up to God, there might nonetheless be situations in which the pursuit of holiness involved a diminution or even suspension of labour. This subordination of work to the business of sanctification acquired an added intensity in Wesleyan Methodism through its founder's passionate devotion to the doctrine of Christian perfection, which in his view was 'the grand depositum which God has lodged with the

46 Wesley, *Works*, 11: 207.

47 Whitefield, *Works*, 5: 302–3.

48 For a modern comment on the 'calling' see E. Morgan, *The Puritan Family*, pbk edn (New York, 1966), pp. 66–78.

49 [C. Fleury], *The Manners of the Antient Christians, extracted from a French Author* [by J. Wesley] (Bristol, 1749), p. 13.

people called Methodists'.[50] With great daring (though limited success) Wesley tried to transpose into the world of labourers and housewives the quest for the perfect love of God which for centuries had been the preserve of monastic communities in the tranquillity of the cloister. 'Intramundane asceticism' found in him a strong champion. Wesley maintained with characteristic optimism that daily toil and a dedication to the attainment of the pure love of God were not at all incompatible. When the question was posed in his 1745 Conference whether one who was sanctified would be 'incapable of worldly business'? the answer was curt and firm: 'He would be far more capable of it than ever, as going through all without distraction.'[51] If offered up to God, labour would promote, not hinder, sanctification. The worker who trod the high and austere path towards perfect love would 'intermix prayer, especially the prayer of the heart, with all the labour of his hands'.[52]

It was not always as easy as that. The thirst for spiritual purity could easily become all-absorbing. Constant introspection and the expenditure of time and emotional energy on private devotion might make it hard to concentrate on the routine business of life. This could be true of evangelical piety in general; it was even more the case with those Methodists who followed 'the more excellent way' towards perfection. One notes that those with whom Wesley corresponded most intimately and easily about the quest for holiness were often female, leisured, and enjoying a degree of domestic seclusion which provided the scope for intense interior spirituality. Others, in the hurly-burly of a competitive, industrializing world, might find perfection very much harder to pursue. John Morris, who had been given the 'second blessing' of entire sanctification, lost it when he suffered a series of trials and losses in his business life.[53] Anna Reynalds, a Truro Methodist re-experiencing 'perfect love' after forfeiting it, confided to her diary that she was tempted by the thought that 'It will be impossible to retain this heavenly frame seeing such and such business and transactions must be attended to, which will necessarily call forth all the powers of the mind (I had many intricate concerns on hand).'[54]

[50] Wesley (ed. Telford), *Letters*, 8: 238.
[51] *Minutes of the Methodist Conferences* (London, 1833-), 1: 10.
[52] Wesley, *Works*, 7: 31.
[53] *AM*, 18 (1795), p. 124.
[54] Truro, Cornwall County Record Office, X210: Anna Reynalds, Diary for 6 Jan. 1817.

Methodist biography shows many society members who refused advancement, reduced their work load, or actually retired from work in order to advance their spiritual growth. Thus in 1793 William Smith told a correspondent 'I believe no part of my [life has] been so happy or so useful as the present. I have been thankful every day these three years that I got out of the commercial world, though in doing it I met with difficulties. I now devote my time, my strength and fortune to God and his people.'[55] John Furnace rearranged his daily schedule, only allotting a mere 'sufficiency' of time to business, so that he could husband the remainder for the reading of devotional books.[56] The Cornishman William Carvosso, praised by his son for being 'unambitious' and 'anti-speculative' (he refused to invest lucratively in local mines), 'sought nothing more than a moderate competency of this world's goods', and retired early to spend more time on religion.[57] John Wesley, who dissuaded a convert from giving up his business entirely, since this was 'a talent God has entrusted him with', nonetheless advised him to contract it 'that he may have more leisure for business of greater importance'.[58]

There were other points on the spiritual path where a devout evangelical might be hampered from pursuing a secular calling at full throttle. In the pangs of conversion some of those who were 'awakened' experienced phases of anxiety or joy so intense that they became incapable of mental concentration and almost incapacitated from daily labour. In his classic *Treatise on Growth in Grace* (1795) the evangelical clergyman Thomas Scott noted that:

> a defect in judgement, while love is very fervent, often produces a disproportionate zeal and earnestness: so that attention to one part of a man's duty swallows up, as it were, all due regard to others. Thus love to public ordinances, or Christian conversation, frequently misleads professors to neglect their families and necessary worldly business . . . and this brings reproach on the word of God.[59]

[55] Manchester, John Rylands University Library, Methodist Archives, Lamplough Collection: MS letter of W. Smith to J. Benson, 24 June 1793.

[56] *AM*, 25 (1802), p. 348.

[57] *The Efficacy of Faith exemplified: a Memoir of W. Carvosso* (London, 1836), p. 61.

[58] Wesley (ed. Telford), *Letters*, 5: 257.

[59] *The Works of T. Scott*, 5 vols (Buckingham, 1805–8), 4: 369. See too J. Newton, *Works*, 6 vols (London, 1808–9), 2: 571.

Several case histories bear this out. The Calvinist preacher William Huntington observed of his own long drawn out awakening, 'I now found that my rationality was sometimes amazingly impaired, insomuch that I was hardly capable either of labour or conversation.'[60] Captain Anthony Landers for a time felt so overwhelmed by the divine presence in his soul that he became alarmed that if the experience went on much longer he would have to give up work.[61] Examples were especially visible in the emotional turmoil of the more incandescent local revivals. The remarkable series of narratives produced by the Scots Cambuslang revival of 1742, partly set in motion by Whitefield, gives several instances. 'For six weeks', wrote Sarah Strong, a sixty-five-year-old widow, 'I was obliged to leave off everything by which I used to win my bread, and I could not apply myself to any worldly business at all.'[62] Protracted revivals which went on not only for days but even weeks gave cause for anxiety, even to Methodist leaders. While in progress, a revival could be physically exhausting – Thomas Coke mentions a service in 1791 which lasted for sixteen hours.[63] In Cornwall, where revivals were famous for their emotional intensity, 'business was suspended' at Redruth in 1814, and ten years later the local authorities threatened to close the Wesleyan chapel because another revival had disrupted work and commerce. Reporting the latter event, a correspondent of Jabez Bunting described how some converts were 'a little deranged, and indeed considering their distress, their agony in prayer, and bodily exertions, added to their want of rest for nights together, and the consequent inability to attend business, it was no wonder.'[64] Occasionally the excitement aroused by a nineteenth-century revival led to the temporary closure of factories, as in Northern Ireland in 1859 or South Wales in 1905.[65]

The news of a spiritual outpouring drew people (often young people) from great distances, to the potential detriment of their work. During the Bradford revival of 1793 Jonathan Saville travelled miles to

[60] W. Huntington, *Works*, 20 vols (London, 1811), 1: 132.

[61] *A Narrative of the Travels and Voyages of Capt. A. Landers* (London, 1813), p. 11.

[62] Edinburgh, New College, W. McCulloch MSS: 'Examination of Persons under Spiritual Concern at Cambuslang during the Revival in 1741–2', 1: 112.

[63] T. Coke, *The Life of J. Wesley* (London, 1792), p. 468.

[64] Manchester, John Rylands University Library, Methodist Archives, NAM PLP 17.42.2: J. Burgess to J. Bunting, 3 March 1824. See D. Luker, 'Cornish Methodism, Revivalism and popular belief' (Oxford University D.Phil. thesis, 1988), pp. 42, 309–10.

[65] W. Gibson, *The Year of Grace* (London, 1860), p. 45; D. Jenkins, *The Agricultural Community in South-West Wales* (Cardiff, 1971), p. 235.

prayer meetings after work, came home at midnight, slept in the raw wool at the mill which employed him, and then began his day's labour.[66] The duration of revival meetings caused adverse local comment, not least among the magistrates, and led some senior Wesleyan leaders to try to reduce their length, despite anxieties that this might quench the work of the Holy Spirit.[67] Even the fervent Hugh Bourne feared that his Primitive Methodist revivalism was interfering with the work patterns of miners, and ordered the curtailment of over-long prayer-meetings.[68]

Such intensity of feeling was seldom maintained at full stretch for long and the dislocations caused by revivals were necessarily brief. Indeed, it could be convincingly argued that in the long term they increased rather than diminished the will to work, promoting regularity and diligence in some of those brought for the first time into the orbit of chapel life. More long-lasting (at times) were the damaging effects on personal work-patterns of regular, scheduled Methodist piety, if it became overheated or especially demanding. The temptation was always there. Especially in the 'heroic' early decades of the Evangelical Revival, membership of a Methodist society was frequently an exacting business. Meetings proliferated, and were often held at awkward times. The itinerants on their circuits frequently preached early in the morning, before work began. Class meetings often took place at night, after the day's work was over. Sunday was potentially an exhausting day, since in Wesley's lifetime Methodist worship was supposed to be supplementary to services in the parish church, which society members were urged also to attend. There was some truth as well as impish satire in James Lackington's account of his Methodist routine in London in 1774, before he lapsed. He told his wife (he said) that he had no intention of getting rich at his trade as a book-seller. Instead he was resolved

> to keep our minds as spiritual as we can, we will always attend our class and band meetings, hear as many sermons etc. at the Foundery on week days, as possible, and on sabbath days we will mind nothing but the good of our souls: our small beer shall be fetched in on Saturday nights, nor will we dress even a potato

[66] F. W. West, *Memoirs of Jonathan Saville of Halifax*, 4th edn (London, 1857), p. 3.
[67] *AM*, 17 (1794), p. 650.
[68] H. Bourne, *History of the Primitive Methodists to the Year 1823* (Bemersley, 1835), p. 5; D. Valenze, *Prophetic Sons and Daughters* (Princeton, NJ, 1985), p. 84.

> on the Sabbath. We will still attend the preaching at five o'clock in the morning; at eight go to the prayer meeting; at ten to the public worship at the Foundery; hear Mr Perry at Cripplegate at two; be at the preaching at the Foundery at five; meet with the general society at six; meet in the united bands at seven, and again be at the prayer meeting at eight; and then come home and read and pray by ourselves.[69]

Whitefield's Calvinistic Methodists in London and Bristol and the Countess of Huntingdon's flock in Bath provided similar opportunities for supererogation.[70] To be sure, such lively metropolitan centres had more associational activity than was on offer for rural congregations, but even small societies could take a heavy toll of a member's energy. Wesley himself was surprised in 1753 to find the little society at Trewalder in Cornwall meeting every night and morning.[71] Night meetings might be 'prolonged to an unseasonable hour'.[72] Methodist biography abounds with examples of members trudging long distances to attend preaching – like George Escrick who often walked the twelve miles from Bolton to Manchester to hear the 5 a.m. preaching and then walked home for breakfast before work.[73] A host of local preachers, working men who combined a part-time ministry with their secular callings, tired themselves out on a Sunday by plodding off to gruelling preaching appointments in far-off chapels. One spiritual athlete in the Chester circuit walked thirty-two miles on a Sunday and preached three times.[74] Of his Sabbath day of rest, Thomas Olivers remarked 'I was commonly more wearied than on any other night of the week.'[75] The high membership turnover in early Methodism may well be related to the demands that it imposed on its members. How many drop-outs resembled Francis Coxon, who left the Biddick society in 1782 because it 'took up too much of his time'?[76]

Evangelical authorities were well aware of the potentially damaging effects of intense devotion on work and family life and sensitive to the adverse comment this provoked from employers. The issue arose most

69 J. Lackington, *Memoirs* (London, 1792), p. 220.
70 E. Welch, ed., *Two Calvinistic Methodist Chapels* (London, 1975), pp. 14–15.
71 Wesley, *Journal*, 4: 79.
72 *An Account of the Revd. J. Fawcett* (London, 1818), p. 12.
73 Methodist Magazine, 31 (1808), p. 128.
74 F. Bretherton, *Early Methodism in Chester* (Chester, 1903), p. 268.
75 *AM*, 2 (1779), pp. 129–30.
76 *AM*, 8 (1785), pp. 197–8.

obtrusively in rural areas during the harvest times for hay and corn, when meeting times often had to be adjusted to allow for the long hours of summer labour.[77] Wesley's Conference tried to regulate devotion so that society members should not be diverted from necessary labour or their due quota of sleep. There should be no late preaching – that is, after seven p.m. – except in harvest time. Lovefeasts (the more ecstatic of which lasted all night) should not exceed an hour and a half, and should leave time for everyone to get home by nine o'clock. Local preachers should not preach more than twice a day on weekdays.[78] In his *Directions to Class Leaders* in 1804, James Wood admitted the excessive length of meetings and urged a two-hour limitation: members should give their attention to the classes, but also spend more time quietly at home in their domestic devotions. 'The public means of grace are so numerous', he warned, 'that it is absolutely impossible for our people to have leisure for family and private duties, unless they be very careful to redeem every moment of the time.'[79] The repetition of such injunctions suggests that they were hard to enforce. Curtailing a long drawn-out meeting on which the Holy Ghost was descending with power could seem a deeply culpable quenching of the Spirit.

No doubt evangelical religion brought a great many converts into the range of moderate prosperity by helping them to structure their lives in orderly ways and imbuing them with a sense of purpose. At the same time some, while becoming spiritually richer, became financially poorer. The expenses of piety and generosity to the cause were far from negligible. William Cobbett was probably exaggerating wildly when he reckoned that by Methodism 'a labourer's family is, one way or another, taxed to the amount of as much as would bring up a child', but he had a point, since membership of a society entailed a subscription as well as pressure to subscribe to special collections.[80] Especially for poorer members, the expense involved in putting up a travelling preacher or other religious visitors could make inroads on the domestic budget. The burden of chapel debt imposed great anxiety, while dedication to the cause led humble people to borrow money, sell furniture, pawn wedding-rings, and even precipitated an occasional bankruptcy. In rural areas, much physical toil went into the erection of

77 R. Robinson, *Posthumous Works* (Harlow, 1812) p. 284.

78 *Minutes of Conferences*, 1: 51, 94.

79 J. Wood, *Directions to the Methodist Class Leaders* 2nd edn (London, 1804), pp. 10, 14–15.

80 *Cobbett's Political Register*, 35 (27 Jan. 1820).

new chapels, a labour of love indeed, but still demanding – in Wensleydale John Madern gave 100 days to the task.[81]

Finally, against the case-histories of Methodists who gained work because of their earnestness should be set those who lost it for the same reason. Wesley warned his people that they might very well forfeit their businesses and employment and end up poorer than they were when they joined his societies.[82] Methodists who left off Sabbath trading, like barbers, milk sellers, and many hawkers, were particularly hard hit, and might well be tempted to backslide.[83] Not all Methodist servants fell unreservedly into the category of the much-admired 'treasure'. A memorialist noted of Jonathon Thompson that 'his master acknowledged . . . he was one of the most trusty and faithful servants he ever had – but he hated his religion; and because he refused to work on the Lord's Day, and continued to reprove sin, he dismissed him from his service.'[84] Employers made very different assessments of the impact of Methodism on their labour force. Some employers welcomed early Methodism because they were convinced that it would instil self-discipline into their work force, but others (like West Country farmers or Caribbean planters) bitterly opposed evangelical preaching or Sunday Schools because they gave labourers ideas above their station.

Modern social historians, especially when theory-driven and mesmerized by a selective reading of Max Weber, tend to focus their gaze on the 'methodical', quasi-Calvinist elements of Methodism and find in it the work-inducing characteristics of economic rationality, iron self-discipline, and intra-worldly asceticism. Many eighteenth-century critics began from the very different assumption that Methodism was a species of 'enthusiasm' and as such given over to irrationality, temperamental volatility, and a religiosity that encroached on the time and energy necessary for productive work. Both cases could be plausibly maintained by a careful cherry-picking of examples; neither is absurd, for each reflects, if in an exaggerated form, a trait of

[81] Adam Taylor, *A History of the General Baptists*, 2 vols (London, 1818), 2: 58–9; W. Daniell, *Warminster Common* (Warminster, 1850), p. 103; W. Jessop, *An Account of Methodism in Rossendale* (Manchester, 1880), p. 86; D. M. Evans, *Christmas Evans* (London, 1863), p. 136.

[82] Wesley, *Works*, 8: 356.

[83] *AM*, 22 (1799), p. 490; 8 (1785), pp. 197–9; *An Account of T. Hawkes* (St Albans, 1817), p. 11; Lackington, *Memoirs*, p. 259.

[84] C. Atmore, *The Methodist Memorial* (Bristol, 1801), pp. 423–4.

spirituality discernible within evangelical Protestantism itself, which can easily contain (and sometimes oscillate between) disciplined asceticism and a charismatic freedom of the Spirit. It is unlikely, however, that either stereotype comes remotely close to covering the varieties of social and spiritual experience to be found among those touched by the power of evangelical religion in an industrializing England. It is doubtful whether many Methodist society members felt inclined slavishly to copy John Wesley in his unrelenting industriousness, or obey his precepts in all their austerity, and this was probably even more the case with the mass of less committed Methodist 'hearers' who outnumbered the members by perhaps three to one. The evangelical ethic of work had always to be adjusted to fit huge variations in spiritual dedication, in patterns of work, and in domestic circumstance.

Jesus College, Oxford

ESCAPING THE COMMON LOT: A BUCHANITE PERSPECTIVE OF THE MILLENNIUM

by JILL SÖDERSTRÖM

ON the day of the 'May' or 'Cow Fair' in 1784 the main streets of Irvine, one of the principal towns in Ayrshire, were crowded to excess with those who had come to take part in the fair.[1] It was not unusual for the streets of this busy seaport to be filled with noise and activity. Whilst Irvine was not a prominent manufacturing town it was, as a royal burgh, a major port for local and foreign trade.[2] Consequently its streets often reverberated with noise from the many carts which transported coal and other merchandise to and from the docks. The town was also a busy commercial centre with banks, a town house, merchant houses, shops, and street markets. Home to some fifty vessels, over three hundred sailors,[3] and thirty-eight taverns, it was a 'town of crowds – meal mobs, redcoats, pressgangs, smugglers, fairs, and the Buchanites'.[4]

At about noon on this particular fair day the local 'Bailies' charged with the task of evicting Elspath Buchan from Irvine were finding it difficult to clear a path through the crowds.[5] The 'Bailies' were followed by a strange procession. In the lead, in a cart, sat Buchan, dressed in a scarlet cloak, together with the Revd Hugh White, former minister of the Irvine Relief Church, and John Gibson, a wealthy master-builder.[6] On foot followed some forty women, children, and men. An eye-witness described the procession as mostly comprising 'clever chiels and bonny spankin, rosy-cheeked lasses' in their teenage

[1] There were five fairs in Irvine each year and over two hundred in Ayrshire annually. Their primary focus had been economic but by the end of the eighteenth century they had become popular social events. John Strawhorn, *The Scotland of Robert Burns* (Darvel, 1995), p. 73.

[2] Ibid., pp. 73, 80–1; Sir John Sinclair, ed. (ed. Donald J. Withrington and Ian R. Grant), *The Statistical Account of Scotland 1791–1799; vol. 6 Ayrshire*, rev. edn (East Ardsley, 1982), pp. 244–6.

[3] Ibid., p. 245; James Edward Shaw, *Ayrshire 1745–1950: A Social and Industrial History of the County* (Edinburgh, 1953), p. 25.

[4] John Strawhorn, *The History of Irvine* (Edinburgh, 1985), p. 95.

[5] Edinburgh, National Library of Scotland, Innes MSS, Train Papers (MS 1166 Acc 6683) [hereafter Train Papers], fol. 35.

[6] Joseph Train, *The Buchanites from First to Last* (Edinburgh, 1846), p. 61.

years, with the girls dressed in the simple garb of peasant maids of the lowlands of Scotland.[7] John Galt, a five-year-old child at the time, was amongst those who ran behind them, intrigued by their joyful singing as they passed through the main streets heading towards the Kilmarnock road.[8]

In contrast to the joyful departure recorded by Galt, Andrew Innes, one of those in the procession, recalled a hostile crowd and the way in which the holiday atmosphere of the fair day fuelled the sport to be had from witnessing the eviction of 'Luckie Buchan', the notorious witch-wife.[9] Despite the tumult around them, Buchan and her disciples were resolved upon complying with their personal vision – an imminent return of Christ at which they would leave the earth and meet with the Lord 'in the air'.[10] Whilst the eviction order had been issued against the Buchanite leader, her disciples felt compelled to leave with her.[11] Their 'daily expectation of personal translation' created an urgency which over-ruled prevailing notions of time and created an expectation of its end so profound it eclipsed other considerations.[12] Whereas the people of Irvine were angry and confused at the sudden decision by some of their respectable citizens to leave behind their homes and business,[13] the disciples were preoccupied with taking up their place, alongside Buchan, as a chosen, end-time people.

Such was the Buchanite exodus from Irvine. Only one year earlier, Buchan[14] had been extended a warm welcome by the Irvine Relief

[7] Train, *Buchanites*, p. 61.

[8] John Galt, *The Autobiography of John Galt*, 2 vols (London, 1833), 1: 6–7.

[9] Train Papers, fol. 35.

[10] The Buchanites believed they would not die; at the second coming of Christ they would be instantly changed into immortal beings. Those 'sleeping in Christ' would also be raised and together they would return to the earth to reign with Christ for 1,000 years. The millennial reign of the righteous preceded the resurrection of the wicked and the final judgement. Hugh White, *Number Second of the Divine Dictionary; or, a Treatise Indicted by Holy Inspiration* (Edinburgh, 1786), p. 81.

[11] They left 'with such precipitation that some of them never shut the door behind them; one left a washing on the green, another a cow bellowing at the crib without food or anyone to mind her': Robert Burns to his cousin James Burness in J. De Lancey Ferguson, ed., *The Letters of Robert Burns* (Oxford, 1931), p. 16.

[12] Train, *Buchanites*, p. 149.

[13] To leave 'without lawfull call' and 'ruin your poor families, by leaving house and all': Anon., *Satan's Delusions: A Poem on the Buchanites* (Kilmarnock, 1784), p. 13.

[14] Elspath Buchan née Simpson, the daughter of an inkeeper in Banff, was born in 1738. Brought up in the Scottish Episcopal Church, she married a Burgher Seceder. Glasguensis Mercator, 'Account of the Buchanites', *The Scots Magazine* (Nov. 1784), p. 589.

Church after its minister, the Revd Hugh White, had told the members of her remarkable ability to expound Scripture.[15] Buchan, the wife of a potter at the Broomielaw Delftworks in Glasgow, and mother of three children, had heard White preach at a Sacrament in Glasgow in December 1782 and entered into correspondence with him.[16] Whilst Buchan believed she was the recipient of special insights from God from as early as 1774, she had received little encouragement from the ministers she had approached to share her 'mind'.[17] In a letter to White, dated January 1783, she lamented that she had been more 'stumbled and grieved by ministers than by all the men in the world'.[18] White, however, was to be an exception in that she considered him to be purposed by God to share in her heavenly commission.[19]

The spiritual mantle proffered by Buchan was willingly taken up by White. When challenged by the Managers and Elders of the Irvine Relief Church over 'erronius doctrine' and his refusal to send Buchan away,[20] White declared he would 'sooner cutt off his right arm' than separate himself from her.[21] His refusal, however, to desist from preaching both publicly and privately a doctrine which, in their view, contravened both Scripture and the Westminster Confession of Faith, brought about a decision in October 1783 to bar him from holding office.[22]

If it was envisaged that White's expulsion would bring the so-called Buchanite 'delusion' to an end, this was not to be the case. Although no longer able to support his wife and two young children as a minister of the Relief Church, he proceeded with Buchan, now known as 'Friend Mother in the Lord', to form a Society of the Buchanites.[23] Their

[15] Train, *Buchanites*, p. 20.

[16] The 'power of God wrought so wonderfully upon all my senses, that it overcame the flesh so much, that I could not make use of earthly food for some weeks': H. White, E. Buchan, and J. Purves, *Eight Letters Between the People called Buchanites and a Teacher near Edinburgh* (Edinburgh, 1785), pp. 38–41.

[17] Ibid.

[18] Train, *Buchanites*, p. 17.

[19] According to Buchan, White had, in the same way as the prophet Jeremiah, been sanctified in the womb and would, because of his wisdom, become 'very high in righteousness': ibid., p. 21.

[20] Edinburgh, Scottish Record Office [hereafter SRO], Irvine Relief Church Session Minutes, CH.3/409/1, 7 May 1783.

[21] Ibid., 20 April 1783.

[22] Ibid., Oct. 1783.

[23] It was hoped that his loss of income would persuade him to return to his position. Whilst at New Cample, Mr Bell 'the relief minister of Glasgow', invited White back at the request of the people of Irvine but he 'dispised' the offer. Train Papers, fol. 38.

meetings, held in private dwellings, were well attended and attracted public curiosity – not all of which was favourable. Once their unusual doctrine and enthusiastic manner of worship became known they were often disturbed by hecklers and angry townspeople.[24] Buchan came under particular attack and numerous attempts were made to disperse her Society.[25] Public outrage, together with pressure from the town's respectable burgesses and the Relief Church, brought about a ruling from the magistrates to expel the Buchanite leader.[26]

Whilst it was widely held that Buchan had used 'black art' to cause her followers to 'instantly forget all earthly concerns' and go with her, Innes asserted that their 'confident hope of a speedy translation to heaven without tasting death' was behind their decision to leave.[27] This apocalyptic expectation transcended all other realities. Time, no longer incalculable, was now encapsulated within an eschatological framework which necessitated a reshaping of conventional realities. Within the context of this new temporal consciousness the Buchanites' decision to leave behind 'worldly' concerns and focus 'wholly on objects above' was considered by them as neither foolhardy nor excessive.[28]

Buchanite doctrine centred around a notion that God's Spirit had been absent from the earth since the passing of the last of the apostles. It was not that God had removed his Spirit but that the 'world' had destroyed the last of those who possessed it. Without a messenger indwelt by God's light the possibility of salvation had been removed.[29] Buchan's role, as the woman of Revelation 12, was therefore crucial in that she was to restore God's light and salvation.[30] Within this paradigm her special purpose was to prepare a people for the second coming of Christ. Whilst the exact day and hour of Christ's return was

[24] Buchan passed on the spirit by breathing on her disciples: White et al., *Eight Letters*, p. 37. '[S]he pretends to give them the Holy Ghost by breathing on them, which she does with postures & practices that are scandalously indecent': Robert Burns to James Burness (Ferguson, *Letters of Robert Burns*, p. 19).

[25] Train Papers, fol. 34.

[26] J. Cameron, *A History of the Buchanite Delusion: 1783–1846* (Dumfries, 1904), p. 28.

[27] Train, *Buchanites*, pp. 2, 7.

[28] White et. al., *Eight Letters*, p. 6.

[29] 'Why this earth has been without a person of holy inspiration, since the murder of the last of the apostles, until this present generation . . . From the time that there has not been on earth a person with the inspiration of Christ and his apostles, there has not been one grain of salvation-work carrying on in this world': White, *Number Second*, p. 79.

[30] Hugh White, *The Divine Dictionary; or, a Treatise Indicted by Holy Inspiration* (Dumfries, 1785), p. 35.

known only to God it was believed that Buchan's prophetic role as the woman of Revelation 12 provided a last opportunity for the world to hear and repent.[31] As for those who questioned the validity of Buchan's role as an end-time female prophet, White remarked that it was 'better to follow a divine spirit in a woman to heaven, than Satan's spirit in a man leading to hell'.[32]

The departure of the Buchanites from Irvine was significant in that it functioned as a catalyst which ushered in their existence as a millenarian sect. Their forced exodus severed ties with their past and facilitated the introduction of a new order.[33] The slow pilgrimage through Auchinleck, New Cumnock, and Thornhill to New Cample Farm in Closeburn Parish in Dumfriesshire provided time to adjust to new circumstances. On reaching their final destination the Buchanites had determined an alternative way of living. Marriage was no longer recognized and they adopted a celibate lifestyle, living together as brothers and sisters. Seeking to separate the evil 'lusts of the flesh' from the purity of the Spirit, they required married women to separate from their husbands and revert to their single state.[34] They formed a community and held all monies and possessions in common. Paid work was forbidden. Whereas before they had devoted their efforts to trade and business, they were now exhorted to give no thought to tomorrow but live at the 'Lord's expense'.[35] To work to provide for their material needs was to conform to the values of the 'children of this world' who depend on 'their own industry and activity'.[36]

The Buchanites based themselves at New Cample Farm by necessity rather than by choice. The hasty departure from Irvine had thrown the business interests of some members into disarray. The wealthiest amongst them, Patrick Hunter, a coal merchant and lawyer, was stopped just outside Thornhill by a troop of constables holding a warrant for his return to Irvine. Fearing a similar fate, several others also returned with him to settle their affairs. The remainder, loathe to proceed without their 'most zealous and wealthy members', decided to

[31] Buchan wrote to a clergyman in England 'this is the last time we have on prophecy': White et al., *Eight Letters*, p. 44.

[32] White, *Number Second*, p. 109.

[33] Buchan stated that they 'never left any place till the persecution was so hot, that the place could not bear us any longer; and so had to flee for our lives, according to the Scriptures': White et al., *Eight Letters*, p. 43.

[34] White, *Number Second*, p. 70.

[35] Train, *Buchanites*, p. 29.

[36] White et al., *Eight Letters*, p. 6.

await their return and procured lodgings in an empty barn at New Cample.[37] Although this was to be a temporary arrangement, the Buchanites stayed on as the farm tenant, Thomas Davidson, offered them land on which to build the house which later became known as 'Buchan Ha'.[38] Davidson's generosity went in the face of increasing local hostility towards the Society,[39] but he was undoubtedly content with their ability to pay up-front for all their requirements as well as their willingness to work without payment. Whilst the Buchanites were often accused of spending their days in idleness,[40] they continued to work, but 'not for the same end as before'.[41] Work now provided the means to share their beliefs and was not directed towards earning money.[42] After all, the immediacy of their translation rendered the need to conserve wealth meaningless.

The Buchanite view was that the second coming of Christ had not taken place because there had been none who were worthy and would wait for his return.[43] As White noted in a letter to James Purves, a school teacher in Edinburgh,[44] he had travelled over 20,000 miles around the globe but had not, prior to 1783 and meeting Buchan, seen a single person waiting for the coming of Christ.[45] Nominal Christians might profess a belief in a second coming of Christ, but their continued involvement with worldly concerns belied the genuineness of their faith.[46] For those truly born of God every available moment could only be focused upon waiting and preparing themselves and others for the day of Christ's return.[47]

Within this paradigm, for the Buchanites time had a specificity

[37] Train, *Buchanites*, p. 65.

[38] Ibid., p. 104.

[39] SRO, Church of Scotland, Presbytery at Penpont Minutes, CH2/298/8, p. 105.

[40] Ferguson, *Letters of Robert Burns*, p. 19.

[41] White et al., *Eight Letters*, p. 43.

[42] 'My working with my hands to help the needful in their necessities, is a divine operation: if I have no other views in so doing, except to get an opportunity to convince them, that their ways of working are against God. However, if I take wages, I do no more than the heathens': White, *Number Second*, p. 84.

[43] Ibid., p. 7.

[44] Discussion on the timing of the millennium was popular at the end of the eighteenth century. James Purves was a schoolteacher and pastor of a 'fellowship society' and author of books on biblical prophecy. White, Buchan, and Purves exchanged a number of letters. Le Roy Edwin Froom, *The Prophetic Faith of our Fathers: the Historical Development of Prophetic Interpretation*, 4 vols (Washington, DC, 1946–54), 2: 695.

[45] White et al., *Eight Letters*, p. 15.

[46] Ibid., pp. 15–16.

[47] Ibid., p. 43.

which excluded concerns beyond their vision. The preaching of their gospel assumed a vital role and it was said that White preached almost daily to large assemblies of people.[48] Whilst Buchanites claimed there could be no better 'use of God's time' than coming to 'where the light of God is' in order to 'receive of that divine light',[49] many came only to mock or deride.[50] The efforts at spreading the Buchanite gospel met with some success, however, and they were, during the period leading up to the translation attempts of 1786, joined by followers from England and Scotland, bringing the total membership to around sixty. As the expected time of their translation approached, their efforts intensified, and lagging recruits were exhorted to hurry as 'the Spirit of God would not remain on earth on account of worldly business'.[51]

The various attempts at translation were to be critical to the continued existence and character of the millenarian sect. The initial experience, which took place sometime between April and July 1786, was greeted with great excitement. Responding to what they believed to be a loud voice coming from the clouds the members gathered together clapping, dancing, and singing, 'Oh! hasten translation, and come resurrection! Oh! hasten the coming of Christ in the air!'[52] They cast aside their jewellery and watches, the last of their 'earthly entanglements'; but the moment passed without translation being realized.[53] Buchan, however, was undaunted, and attributed the cause of their failure to her followers being insufficiently prepared.[54]

This first attempt was followed by a forty-day fast to ensure a level of spirituality sufficient for translation in much the same way as Elijah fasted for forty days before he ascended into heaven.[55] It was thought that 'as the blood receded from their veins, the Holy Spirit would occupy its place' and elevate them to a higher spiritual state.[56] They

48 Train, *Buchanites*, p. 74.

49 White, *Divine Dictionary*, p. iii.

50 Glasguensis Mercator, 'Account', p. 590.

51 They calculated the date as being 1,260 days after the woman of Rev. 12 gave birth to her man-child, i.e. the days which elapsed after the spiritual birth of White as Buchan's man-child. A specific date appears, however, to contradict the notion that they could hasten the day of translation by being spiritually prepared. Train, *Buchanites*, p. 244.

52 Ibid., p. 105.

53 Ibid., pp. 106–7.

54 Ibid., pp. 108–9.

55 Innes also refers to Moses fasting before approaching the Lord's presence on the 'Nau Mount' and Jesus remained 'fortey days after he arose from the Grave in a steat of fasting so we inclined to be like them': Train Papers, fol. 64.

56 Train, *Buchanites*, p. 109.

locked themselves away from the 'outside world' and accepted only a little hot water and treacle from 'Friend Mother' when necessary. News of the fast became known in the surrounding districts and caused alarm amongst local people and relatives who feared Buchan would starve her followers to death.[57] Not all of those, however, who embarked on the fast stayed until the end of the forty days, and a number either quit voluntarily or were forced to leave.[58]

On the expected day of their translation, just before sunrise, the hopeful Buchanites, pale and emaciated, ascended Templand Hill, a small hillock nearby Buchan Hall.[59] They placed themselves on wooden platforms, with Buchan on a higher elevation so she could be seen, and extended their arms and faces towards the rising sun. They had cut their hair short, except for a tuft on the top for the angels to catch them by when drawing them up.[60] White had dressed in his full canonicals,[61] and Buchan, who had continued to eat so that she would not become 'too transparent' to her followers, stood with her unbound hair flowing over her 'hillocks of rosy flesh'.[62] They sang as they waited in anticipation. But instead of being transported to meet Christ in the air, a gust of wind caused their platforms to capsize and they were thrown to the ground.[63]

Time now changed for the members of the Society. Contrary to their expectation of its end it became apparent they were not to be translated. The dejected Buchanites returned to New Cample. Disappointment was soon followed by disenchantment with Buchan and White's apocalyptic claims, and members started to leave. For some this meant a return home impoverished, as they had handed over all

[57] Train, *Buchanites*, p. 109.

[58] Mrs Hunter was able, with the help of a magistrate, to remove her children and husband from the Society prior to the completion of the fast and return with them to Irvine: Train Papers, fol. 67.

[59] The description of the Templand Hill translation attempt was forwarded to Train by the Revd D. Mundell, rector of Wallace Hall Academy. The account was corroborated by an eye-witness, Mr James Hossack of Thornhill: Train, *Buchanites*, pp. 125, 213. Innes refutes the Templand Hill attempt. He did not, however, complete the fast as he was forced to leave once it became known he had got Katherine Gardner with child. In later years Innes made every attempt to play down negative accounts of Buchan and the Society: Train Papers, fol. 153.

[60] John Mactaggart, *The Scottish Gallovidian Encyclopedia* (London, 1824; repr. Strath Tay, 1981), p. 98.

[61] R. M. F. Watson, *Closeburn (Dumfriesshire) Reminiscent Historic and Traditional* (Glasgow, 1901), p. 209.

[62] Train, *Buchanites*, p. 127.

[63] Mactaggart, *Gallovidian Encyclopedia*, p. 98.

their personal wealth to the Society. Hunter, who had returned to Irvine prior to the Templand Hill translation attempt, had discharged any claim to the money he had spent on the Society's behalf, but this was not the case with others. James Gibson, who also returned to Irvine and resumed his business as a master builder, sought to recoup the money he had spent by taking out a warrant which placed Buchan and White in Dumfries gaol.[64] Once it became known that their numbers and financial resources were dwindling, Buchan and White came under the scrutiny of Closeburn kirk session who were, amongst other things, concerned that the remaining Buchanites would become a burden on the parish.[65] Despite assurances that some members still had money which they would share, the matter was placed in the hands of the county magistrates at Brownhill, who determined that the Society should leave Dumfriesshire before 10 March 1787.[66]

The Buchanites relocated in May 1787 to a poor moorland farm known as Auchengibbert in the parish of Urr in Galloway. Their resources were now depleted and they were forced to accept payment for their work as well as secure credit to purchase their basic needs. In Irvine and Closeburn they had lived in daily expectation of the millennium. Their finite understanding of time had excluded the need to acquire or conserve wealth and they had been free to live according to the dictates of their vision. Their failure to achieve translation, however, required them to adjust their paradigm to take into account an extended sojourn in the world. Whereas previously they had taken every opportunity to broadcast their beliefs, they now sought to establish good relations with their neighbours and avoided speaking of religion.[67] White, according to Innes, quickly acquired a hunger for worldly wealth and was diligent in securing 'ready money' for their work.[68] They supported themselves by taking in cattle for grazing, contracting themselves out for shearing, manufacturing tin products and spinning wheels, and by spinning factory yarn.[69] Buchan, however, did not readily accept the changes and continued to hold fast to her vision and to share her beliefs freely. Tenaciously she clung to the conviction that Christ would return, and persisted in taking her

64 Train, *Buchanites*, p. 135.
65 SRO, Closeburn Kirk Session Minutes, 1780–1805, CH2/1233/2, 15 Sept. 1786.
66 Train, *Buchanites*, p. 144.
67 Ibid., p. 149.
68 Ibid., p. 156.
69 Privado, 'The Buchanites', *The Castle Douglas Miscellany*, 27 Feb. 1826, p. 257.

followers to a hilltop where they would wait, yet again, for their translation.[70] White, meanwhile, became increasingly impatient and placed restrictions on Buchan leaving the farm or speaking to strangers. Disillusioned, he threatened to leave both Buchan and the Society, but his tarnished reputation as a minister made it difficult for him to do so.[71] White's disapproval of Buchan was now easily discernible and he no longer deferred to her spiritual insights. Buchan, forced to withdraw, became increasingly isolated and dejected and suffered ill-health. On 29 March 1791, she died.

Buchan claimed on her deathbed that, as the Spirit of God, it was not possible for her to die – she would only appear to do so. After six days, ten or fifty years, she would return, depending on the purity of their faith. Her failure, however, to rise after six days presented to the Buchanites, perhaps for the first time, the realization they too would die.[72] Already forced to accept that Christ had not returned for them, it was ultimately Buchan's death which precipitated a crisis in their continued existence as a millenarian sect. Once again compelled to reconsider their position, they modified their eschatological world-view to incorporate not only their continued existence in the world but also the fact they would remain there until death.

This final adjustment to the Buchanite temporal paradigm brought White and those aligned to him to a point where they abandoned their apocalyptic beliefs and accepted a return to ordinary life. White distanced himself from his earlier writings and Buchan's message and took over leadership of the Society.[73] He also resumed care of his wife and children and encouraged other members to marry. He was not, however, able to gain the support of that minority of members who continued to affirm the veracity of Buchan's teaching, and the Society was eventually disbanded. On 11 June 1792 White and some thirty others left for America. The remaining fourteen or so members resolved to continue as a community, and leased a farm at Larghill in the hill country behind Crocketford in the parish of Urr.[74]

These remnant Buchanites applied themselves to transforming

[70] Privado, 'The Buchanites', *The Castle Douglas Miscellany*, p. 257.

[71] Train, *Buchanites*, p. 158.

[72] Archibald Chalmers, 'The Buchanites and Crocketford', *Dumfriesshire and Galloway Natural History and Antiquarian Society Transactions and Journal of Proceedings*, 3rd ser., 1 (1912–13), pp. 293, 297.

[73] Train, *Buchanites*, p. 181.

[74] Chalmers, 'Buchanites and Crocketford', p. 294.

Larghill, once a barren sheep farm, into a profitable business. They became famous throughout the south of Scotland for their spinning wheels and their finely spun yarn, attracting customers from nobility and gentry.[75] From these profitable ventures and their farming they were eventually able to purchase five acres of land in Crocketford, where they built houses and gardens worth in excess of £900.[76] The Crocketford Buchanites, whilst maintaining their distinctiveness, became known as a kindly, quiet, and hardworking people. They were respected not only for their industry but also for their charity and their medical expertise, which they offered freely. The derision and hostility which had followed their provocative existence during the early apocalyptic period was now replaced by quiet acceptance. The adoption of an 'unobtrusive religious system' had been successful in laying to rest any residual concerns over earlier fanaticism.[77]

In January 1846 the last survivor, Andrew Innes, died. The Buchanites had incorporated a garden cemetery at 'Newhouse', their Crocketford home. Here they buried their dead, maintaining a physical separateness from wider society until the end. Innes, the last of their number to die, was buried together with Buchan's remains. Her corpse, which had been buried under the hearthstone at Auchengibbert, in an open chest at Larghill, and in a room next to Innes at Newhouse, was finally laid to rest.[78] In accordance with Innes's final wishes she was buried beneath him to ensure he would wake should she rise.[79]

It is clear that any attempt to measure contemporary perceptions of the value and use of time in late eighteenth-century Scotland must take into account a diversity of world-views. Popular and minority perceptions existed alongside, and in juxtaposition to, dominant religious cultures and the expectations of commercial enterprise. One such minority view existing at the popular level was the Buchanite apocalyptic paradigm which provides an insight into the 'Buchanite world'.[80] Governed by their vision, the Buchanites cast aside the pursuit of worldly gain and spurned any notion of carnal pleasure. Their transitory attitude towards time transcended prevailing temporal

75 Privado, *Castle Douglas Miscellany*, 6 March 1826, p. 265.

76 Train, *Buchanites*, p. 190.

77 Chalmers, 'Buchanites and Crocketford', p. 295.

78 Innes continued to converse with Buchan's spirit every day: Train, *Buchanites*, p. 225.

79 Privado, *Castle Douglas Miscellany*, 6 March 1826, p. 265.

80 The Buchanites and their place as a millenarian sect in eighteenth-century Scotland will be discussed in my forthcoming Ph.D. thesis.

notions. Their eschatological paradigm, whilst dominated by an impending apocalypse and translation, required and sustained a recasting of conventional values. It was left to the failure of their apocalyptic paradigm to effect their re-entry into the realities of ordinary society.

Murdoch University

THE GOSPEL OF WORK AND THE VIRGIN MARY: CATHOLICS, PROTESTANTS, AND WORK IN THE NINETEENTH CENTURY

by JANE GARNETT

WHEN, in 1904–5, Max Weber published his famous essay on 'The Protestant ethic and the spirit of capitalism', he set out to explore the reasons for an affinity, the existence of which was a commonplace in large parts of Europe and North America. Whilst the literature on the strengths and weaknesses of Weber's thesis is vast, much less attention has been paid to the contours of the mid to late nineteenth-century debate out of which his interest developed.[1] Yet the neglect of that context has continued to foster over-simplified views of the world with which Weber's argument originally engaged. His essay forms part of a much more extensive discourse on the role of religious belief in economic life. This paper discusses one particular nexus of that debate: the way in which British Protestants shaped their economic ethic by reference both to their ideas of Catholicism and to perceived oversimplifications of Protestant virtue; and the way in which Catholics in Italy responded to the promotion by secular liberals of what was seen by them as 'puritan' economics – that is, the maxims of British classical political economy. To compare the British and Italian contemporary literatures on this theme helps to draw out and to clarify some significant complexities in nineteenth-century thinking about the relationship between economics and morality. Underpinning each religious critique in Britain and in Italy was an emphasis on the necessary closeness of the relationship between attitudes to work and attitudes to the rest of life. In each case this implied an assertion at the philosophical level that economics had a metaphysical dimension which needed to be justified, and at a practical level that time spent both working and not working was devotional. Because each was engaging with a popularized model of political economy there were in fact methodological affinities between

[1] A recent and stimulating set of essays which addresses the contemporary (principally German) context as well as the reception of Weber's work is H. Lehmann and G. Roth, eds, *Weber's Protestant Ethic* (Cambridge, 1993).

their respective positions in this context, little though each would often have liked to acknowledge it. These have been obscured by obvious distinctions of cultural and political development which have in turn produced different historiographical traditions. Moreover, the predominance, since the early twentieth century, of a supposedly 'objective' model of economics which tacitly denies its metaphysical dimension has meant that nineteenth-century Christian economic thought has been discussed rather as part of the multiple stories of denominational social action than as what it more crucially set out to be: that is, a radical intellectual challenge to the premises of mainstream economic assumptions.

* * *

In 1855 British readers were introduced to a book, translated in that year from the French, which offered a series of stereotypical images which, for many Protestants, both then and since, have seemed to offer an explanation for the diverse economic fortunes of Protestant and Catholic parts of the world in the nineteenth century. The book was Napoléon Roussel's *Catholic Nations and Protestant Nations Compared in their Three-fold Relation to Wealth, Knowledge and Morality*. This very detailed account of the economic and social development of selected Protestant and Catholic nations, designed to show the superiority of Protestantism, was commended to their readers' attention by British evangelical journals. There were several aspects to Roussel's argument. First, emphasis was laid on the fact that there was an inverse relationship between natural resources and industrial and commercial success. Protestant countries or regions had overcome obstacles by greater effort and will. Catholic areas, by contrast, became indolent in their lands of plenty. This could be illustrated by reference to the contrast between North and South America, Ulster and the rest of Ireland, and (especially) Protestant and Catholic cantons in Switzerland. Then, a specific link was made between the abhorrent devotional life of the Catholics and their economic degeneracy. Houses in Catholic Switzerland were painted like the inside of chapels: 'Jesus Christ, the Virgin, and St Christopher and the Holy Spirit may there be seen mingled with *cordeliers*, *capucins*, and hermits; the usual means adopted by Catholicism to attract towards earthly saints the respect and adoration which is due only to the God of Heaven.' The taste for processions, pilgrimages, and other acts of '*useless* devotion introduced by the monks' had encouraged a spirit of idleness. By contrast, in

Protestant Zurich the spirit of learning predominated, as did honest trade: at Zurich there are 'neither comedians, mountebanks, nor newsmen'. Roussel's description of the canton of Vaud, the best cultivated area in Switzerland, makes the landscape and activity of the fields the reflection of Protestant order. The terms used make clear the type of Protestant regime to which he aspired, in which balance would create a sense of security and of harmony: a rest which was not the antithesis but the apotheosis of work.

> What agreeable ideas of repose and retirement are given to the agitated traveller by those rustic residences so well placed near those clumps of elms, those orchards, and those fertile meadows.... Luxury and opulence do not reign in the towns which you traverse, but neither do rags and misery give pain there to the friends of the poor and of equality.... The cultivation of the land and the anxieties of commerce have not so absorbed the Vaudois as to make them negligent of the lofty wants of intelligence. Everyone reads, but they are still happy to work.[2]

This type of characterization, produced in the context of Ultramontane revival in France, was reinforced in 1875 by the Belgian economic theorist Émile de Laveleye in his *Le Protestantisme et le catholicisme dans leur rapports avec la liberté et la prosperité des peuples.* This pamphlet was immediately published in English with a preface by Gladstone, to whom it provided corroboration of his concern (heightened by the First Vatican Council) about the stultifying effects of papal power. De Laveleye was widely read on the Continent, and in Italy his argument related closely to that of many liberal commentators on the prospects for Italy's economic progress. Unsurprisingly, and especially since he himself was still nominally a Catholic at the time of this publication, his approach was roundly condemned by Catholics. More interestingly, it was also attacked in Britain by John Ruskin, to whom De Laveleye had sent a copy of his essay, for its perpetuation of a misguidedly polarized view of confessional differences in relation to economic energy and morality. Ruskin took De Laveleye to task for reviving 'the miserable question of a schism between Catholicism and Protestantism ... and taking no note whatever of the true and eternal schism, cloven by the very sword of Michael, between him that serveth

[2] N. Roussel, *Catholic and Protestant Nations Compared in their Three-fold Relation to Wealth, Knowledge and Morality* (London, 1855), pp. 138–9, 146–7.

God, and him that serveth Him not'.[3] Ruskin passionately attacked his own society for purporting to live by Protestant principles, without reflecting that the laws of political economy were in fact rooted in a diametrically opposite ethic. To argue that the single-minded pursuit of wealth could be analysed as an autonomous exercise, the conclusions of which might then be modified by moral considerations, was absurd self-delusion. The pursuit of material prosperity for its own sake could too easily become a hegemonic goal. Key economic terms like wealth, value, labour, needed to be given more rigorous philosophical attention to show how painfully narrow and reduced their conventional meanings had become.

In fact, in the period between the 1850s and the 1870s, a more nuanced Protestant debate had developed in Britain, which addressed what a Protestant ethic should mean if it was to be dynamic and self-sustaining. It was not a way of living which could merely be assumed, and there were real dangers in the over-ready identification of Britain's success with her Protestantism. James Anthony Froude, so often taken as a straightforward apologist for British Protestantism, in fact repeatedly tried to expose its complacencies. In his 1871 address to the students of St Andrew's University on Calvinism, he likened current pursuit of the laws of political economy to Egyptian worship of the sun: 'Where Nature is sovereign, there is no need of austerity and self-denial.' In the contemporary reaction against dogmatism and the simultaneous elevation of happiness as the ultimate human goal, a gulf had opened up between opinion and morality. 'We have learnt, as we say, to make the best of both worlds, to take political economy for the rule of our conduct, and to relegate religion into the profession of orthodox doctrines.'[4] It was too easy to forget that goodness was not synonymous with a certain kind of material happiness.

An extensive evangelical literature developed in nineteenth-century Britain in order to identify the features of a proper Protestant engagement with the modern economic world. In its predominant appeal to a middle- and lower-middle-class world, it stressed the virtues of steady application, a balanced approach to work which left time for family, church, intellectual pursuits, and civic and philanthropic activity. The British might be proverbially hard-working, but

[3] E. T. Cook and A. Wedderburn, eds, *Works of John Ruskin*, 39 vols (London, 1902–12), 28: 402–3.

[4] J. A. Froude, *Calvinism: An Address delivered at St Andrew's* (London, 1871), pp. 23, 58.

they were also capable of exalting mere drudgery, and of sacrificing too much at the shrine of the goddess of industry. An evangelical journal which campaigned for shorter hours of work attacked the spiritual and moral shallowness of Sir Edward Lytton Bulwer's confident statement that 'We have been a great people because we have always been active; and a moral people because we have not left ourselves time to be vicious.'[5] Thomas Carlyle had exalted work as man's protection from the doubt caused by inactivity; but here again, the evangelical literature identified a danger.[6] Too much emphasis had been placed on setting barriers against idleness and not enough on establishing the appropriate moral status of work. After all, Cain was an industrious and successful man, 'the memory of sin stifled and buried in the daily occupations of life'.[7] Hyperactivity and overwork seemed to be more characteristic of the mid-nineteenth century than idleness, and in fact, to present a more complex set of moral problems. In this context the biblical doctrine of rest was articulated: as the gift of God in the sense of being a support *in* the labours of life, rather than a relief from them.

It was in this light that the Sabbath should be seen as God's respite of the sentence of labour. This security would relieve that fretting anxiety which could so easily dominate working life, and would encourage a foresight which could make work a positive part of life as a whole. Only work done in the right spirit was sanctified, and only such work could interact productively with recreation.[8] At the same time, more attention was paid to recreation, and some nonconformist ministers criticized Puritan dread of amusement and indifference to beauty.[9] Moreover, whilst observance of the Sabbath was fundamental,

[5] *Early Closing Advocate and Commercial Reformer*, no. 6 (June 1854), p. 97. Cf. ibid., no. 3 (March 1854), p. 38; T. H. Tarlton, 'The right way of resting', *Excelsior*, 2 (1854–5), pp. 273–4.

[6] T. Carlyle, 'Labour', *Past and Present* (London, 1843), pp. 264–6; idem, 'Reward', ibid., pp. 270–1; J. H. Hinton, introductory discourse to *Baptist Manual* (1857), p. 89.

[7] J. W. Reeve, 'The activity of worldliness in the last days', in *Present Times and Future Prospects* (London, 1854), p. 38.

[8] A. M. Pollock, *The Object of Life* (Dublin, London, and Edinburgh, 1859), pp. 16, 21; T. Binney, 'Salvation by fire', *Sermons Preached in King's Weigh House Chapel 1829–69* (London, 1869), p. 153; *London Quarterly Review*, 6 (1856), pp. 167–77; *Church of England Monthly Review*, 1 (1856), pp. 100–3; H. R. Reynolds, 'Rest in the Lord', *Notes on the Christian Life. A Selection of Sermons* (London, 1865), esp. p. 137; A. Maclaren, 'Anxious care', *Sermons Preached in Union Chapel* (London, 1859), p. 276.

[9] *Baptist Magazine*, 50 (1858), p. 406; ibid., 54 (1862), p. 547; R. W. Dale, 'Amusements', *Weekday Sermons* (London, 1867), p. 251; J. B. Brown, 'Recreation', *The Home Life in the Light of the Divine Idea* (London, 1866), p. 187. See also J. Garnett, 'Nonconformists, economic ethics and the consumer society in mid-Victorian Britain', in A. Kreider and J. Shaw, eds, *Culture and the Nonconformist Tradition* (Cardiff, 1999), pp. 99–107.

and commended for its regularity by contrast to the irregular rhythms of Catholic saints' days, it was yet dangerously possible to divide weekday and Sunday so sharply that people could imagine distinctions between weekday and Sunday morality.[10] These writers urged a proper integration of work, leisure, and worship.

A significant context in which these sorts of distinctions were pursued was in the burgeoning mid-century genre of Protestant exemplary biography, especially of men involved in industrial or commercial life.[11] This genre, which itself enjoyed a wide circulation, was developed in response to the oversimplifications of the immensely popular success and self-help literature which proliferated from the 1840s. In 1845 Samuel Smiles gave a series of talks to a Mutual Improvement Society in Leeds, which was the genesis of *Self-Help*, published fourteen years later. Smiles's own point of departure had been that people needed some practical evidence of the working of a secure moral order, but he did not see the potential ambiguities in his version of the Protestant ethic, which could seem to promote as a moral imperative the selfish predicates of classical political economy, and not to distinguish between right and wrong uses of qualities which in themselves were morally neutral. At the opening of the chapter in *Self-Help* on 'Energy and Courage', he quoted, with no qualifying remark, an old Norseman, 'thoroughly characteristic of the Teuton': '"I believe neither in idols nor demons", said he, "I put my sole trust in my own strength of body and soul".'[12] In the Preface to his revised edition of 1866 he did acknowledge, however, that the very title of the book – *Self-Help* – had proved unfortunate in its implications of human autonomy.[13]

Promoters of economic modernization in Italy, meanwhile, in the search for ideological models, drew strongly on the British literature of self-help, which was in many cases assimilated to a form of social darwinism. *Self-Help* itself was translated in 1865, with the title *Chi si aiuta Dio l'aiuta* (*God Helps Him Who Helps Himself*), and had gone into

[10] J. Pickard, *The Sabbath, Its Origin, History and Obligations* (London, 1856), pp. 38–44; L. Wiseman, *Things Secular and Things Sacred* (London, 1856), p. 23.

[11] E.g. W. Arthur, *The Successful Merchant; Sketches of the Life of Mr. Samuel Budgett, late of Kingswood Hill* (London, 1852); B. Gregory, *The Thorough Business Man: Memoirs of Walter Powell* (London, 1871); P. Lorimer, *Healthy Religion Exemplified in the Life of the late Mr. Andrew Jack, of Edinburgh* (London, 1852); J. Stacey, *A Prince in Israel: Sketches of the Life of John Ridgway* (London, 1862).

[12] S. Smiles, *Self-Help; with Illustrations of Character and Conduct* (London, 1859), p. 151.

[13] Ibid. (1866 edn), preface, pp. iii–iv.

sixteen editions by 1877. *Character* was published in Italy in 1872, and had reached fourteen editions by 1907. In 1867 the Minister for Foreign Affairs set up a competition for the publication of a book which would provide examples from Italian life on the model of Smiles's work in order to promote a sense of national character. The book which won – *Volere è potere* (*To Will is to Achieve*) by Michele Lessona – rapidly became a bestseller. Strafforello, the first translator of Smiles, produced his own version of heroes of labour for The Library for the Education of the People, a publishing initiative in Turin inspired by the British Society for the Diffusion of Useful Knowledge.

Dell'ozio in Italia [*Idleness in Italy*] was published in 1870–1 in the same series by Carlo Lozzi, who referred to *Self-Help* as an *opera santa*.[14] Without a trace of irony he referred to the marvellous activity of the Anglo-Saxons as being like perpetual motion.[15] Alongside the positive stereotype of Teutonic energy, Lozzi predictably placed a negative stereotype of Latin Catholicism. According to Lozzi, the fundamental problem of the Italians was idleness. He was embarrassed by the fact that the phrase *dolce far niente* had been carried untranslated into the vocabularies of other countries, thus fixing it as a quintessentially Italian vice.[16] He argued that religious feasts were originally instituted to reinvigorate people's strength and to keep alive thoughts of the divine and the dignity of human nature. The Sabbath of Genesis was not rest, but change of labour. However the pontifical regime, by allowing the number of feasts to multiply, had encouraged the love of idleness. Workers were deprived of sober and industrious habits and lived on superstition. Catholic devotional practice was ridiculous and in fact confused the sacred and the profane: at a Neapolitan mass, donkeys laden with grain had been brought into church and presented to the Madonna; artisans had then in their turn brought plates of steaming macaroni. To their practitioners, of course, such practices expressed the seamless interrelationship of work and worship. To Lozzi, however, they typified the lack of a proper Italian industrial spirit. According to him and to other Italian liberal commentators, a purge of feast-days and a change to keeping only the Sabbath were urgently needed. The only feasts which were wholesome were civil

14 C. Lozzi, *Dell'ozio in Italia*, 2 vols (Turin and Naples, 1870–1), 1: 379.
15 Ibid., 1: 153.
16 Ibid., 1: 14–15.

exhibitions (with prizes) of industrial, scientific, or agricultural progress, or military festivals – in other words, precisely the sorts of event which the liberal state was already trying to promote in place of religious celebrations. Such events would crown the promotion of education defined as useful knowledge. A religious sense was necessary as the foundation of moral order, but this was to be (in Hegelian terms) essentially a principle of action. George Washington, Savonarola, Daniel O'Connell, Gioberti, and Cavour were cited in support of an alliance between liberty and religion – but this was a religion implicitly purged of most essential elements of Catholicism in order to make it progressive.[17]

Such an emphasis continued to be promoted, although it was felt even by some liberal commentators that there were respects in which it was dangerously uncritical of one particular Protestant model. In his illuminating social survey *L'Italia vivente* (1873), the Jewish Italian Leone Carpi argued that in Northern Europe there had been an over-rigid application of economic liberty supported by the 'puritan economists': 'Se il Dio *stato* è un assurdo, il Dio *individuo* è la negazione di Dio e della morale.'[18] If religious education under the aegis of the papacy had been responsible for the failure of Italians to develop masculine virtues, devotion to Smithian dogmas had contributed to the work of demolition rather than creation of energy of spirit. For Carpi the answer was not to lurch to what he saw as the opposite extreme of the German 'socialism of the chair', but to regain confidence in a native Italian tradition of inductive economics which could avoid these extremes.[19]

Seeing the greatest prospects for the future as lying with the middle classes, he recognized the continued inspiration of Catholic religious life and practice – the daily saying of prayers, the attendance at processions and at evening benediction. Regarding such public devotion largely in external terms as the appreciation of spectacle, he held out the hope that a morally uplifting secular theatre might eventually transcend it. But though he might have hoped for it, there was no theatre yet to equal it, nor did the negative goal of dismantling religious tradition in pursuit of progress seem either necessary or

[17] C. Lozzi, *Dell'ozio in Italia*, 1: 342–5, 167–76.

[18] 'If the deification of the state is an absurdity, the deification of the individual is the negation of God and of morality': L. Carpi, *L'Italia vivente* (Milan, 1878), p. 61. See also A. M. Banti, *Storia della borghesia italiana. L'età liberale* (Rome, 1996), pp. 227–8.

[19] Carpi, *L'Italia vivente*, pp. 290–6.

desirable.[20] Many Italian political economists had seen Adam Smith's work as being morally framed by Scottish Calvinism, and had praised the spirit of John Knox which underpinned the respectability of Scottish banks.[21] But they had not followed through the implications of translating into another culture economic dogmas shorn of the religious and moral system which provided the original context for reading them. In his much more polemical *Tirannide borghese* [*Bourgeois Tyranny*], Pietro Ellera asserted that the liberal state had shown itself to have no other means of inspiration than to turn money-making into a religion. Anticipating Huizinga's *Homo Ludens*, he saw the substitution of the *festa nazionale* for the traditional pre-Lent carnival as part of bourgeois *tristesse*, a crushing of joy on an English model.[22] The Italian liberal critique of Catholic culture was thus not without its own sharp critics.

In Britain the first phase of Protestant engagement with classical political economy on a popular level had laid overwhelming stress on the affinities between natural theology and economic laws; it was this which led to exaggerated confidence in the automatic working of Providence. But the inadequacies of this approach, on both a philosophical and a practical level, were comprehensively exposed in the mid-century debate, which was itself nourished by awareness of increasing economic complexity. In Italy the evolution of a Catholic economic ethic was complicated by several factors: the political role of the papacy; the issue of national unification; the generally limited level of industrialization; and the extreme unevenness of economic development within the Italian states.

From the 1830s a popular Catholic literature began to be produced, which was to be reprinted and elaborated well into the last quarter of the century. A series of books written by Cesare Cantù, *Il galantuomo* [*The Honest Man*], *Il giovanetto drizzato alla bontà* [*The Young Man Directed to Goodness*], *Il buon fanciullo* [*The Virtuous Youth*], all published in 1837, and later works such as *Buon senso e buon cuore* [*Good Sense and a Good Heart*] of 1870 and *Portafoglio d'un operajo* [*A Worker's Pocket-Book*] of 1871 all emphasised the positive ethical aspects of work – defined as both duty and sacrifice. Cantù, who had been imprisoned in 1833–4 for his involvement with Young Italy, was part of the so-called

20 Ibid., pp. 305–7.

21 'Associazione pel progresso degli studi economici: verbale dell'Adunanza del Comitato di Padova, 13 febbraio 1875', *Giornale degli economisti*, a. 1, 1 (Padua, 1875), p. 28.

22 P. Ellera, *La tirannide borghese*, 2nd edn (Bologna, 1879), pp. 414–15, 443–44.

neo-Guelph group which wished to stress the potential for the alignment of Catholic principles with the progress of the nation. He proposed his models of economic behaviour as an Italian corrective to the moral failings of what was perceived stereotypically as the British ethic of success, reflected in the self-help literature. Cantù saw the need to replace embarrassment about Italian backwardness with a positive view of the potential for a new way forward rooted in Catholic principles. In affirming the interlocking religious and economic virtues of loyalty, reciprocity, generosity, and altruism in place of the individualistic, utilitarian, competitive dogmas of Protestant political economy, he was trying to recapture the traditions of Catholic philosophy interrupted by Protestant rationalism. In the *Portafoglio d'un operajo* the enlightened paternalist cloth manufacturer Alessandro Rossi was given a voice with which to denounce economic theory and morality predicated on a new and pernicious logic of human nature.[23] This literature remained at a more abstract and generalized level than the equivalent advice literature in Britain, but in some respects it served a comparable ideological function. In Italy the enemy to be combated was *not* the over-ready *assimilation* of religious and economic ethics, but the polemical denial that there *could* be a Catholic foundation for successful economic progress. As in Britain, although for different reasons, the model offered was underpinned by a fundamental denial of the adequacy of purely secular criteria of success.

One aspect of both the secular and the Protestant critiques of the fitness of Catholicism to sustain economic progress was the assertion that Catholic devotional practice was inimical to economic discipline. This was a context in which Catholic opinion could strike back most effectively at what were in fact assaults on Catholic religious identity as a whole. *La civiltà cattolica*, the extremely influential Jesuit journal established in 1850 to reinforce the intellectual identity of Catholic culture, raised the challenge from the beginning. At a moment when the proposal of the regime in Piedmont to reduce the number of feast-days was being debated, and was raising principles relevant to the rest of Italy, the Catholic press asked whether it was not more important to sanctify feasts rather than abolish them. Feasts were a fundamental part

[23] C. Cantù, *Portafoglio d'un operajo* (Milan, 1871), pp. 254–8. For discussion of Rossi's view of the negative consequences of the pursuit of liberal economic theory in Britain, see G. Baglioni, *L'ideologia della borghesia industriale nell'Italia liberale* (Turin, 1974), pp. 254–61.

of the social order because they engaged individuals not as isolated entities but as part of a community. They were important in underpinning civil society, as they evoked the equality of all in the face of God. They should be days of joy and bright colours, as far removed as possible from the sobriety of the Judaizing Sabbath of the Protestants. To justify cutting down the number of feasts on the ground that labour was sacred was to fall into the most common contemporary vice – to latch on to a catch-phrase, and then to invoke it without any sense of context. Labour was sacred because it was sanctioned by God, and so were feast days; indeed the sanctification was inherently inter-relational.

Another criterion used without any real examination of what it meant was utility. A focus on the disutility of devotion – obviously an old *topos* – was presented with renewed confidence under the banner of a political economy which concerned itself solely with the production of market value.[24] An American visitor to Paris in the 1840s had been shocked by the number of ornaments draped as gifts and ex-votos on the various altars of Notre Dame, and commented that the gold and silver *squandered* on the Madonnas of this Church would alone be enough to construct a railway line from Paris to Le Havre.[25] Such terms of reference were all too typical. A formulaic invocation of usefulness lay behind the closure of the contemplative Orders, criticism of the consumption of candles in churches, or again the attack on religious feasts.[26]

In 1861 the Società della santificazione delle feste was established in Turin, and soon spread to other parts of Italy. Its patron was St Joseph, the emblematic worker-saint whose cult was becoming increasingly popular in the nineteenth century. It had three categories of member: ordinary members, promoters, and commercial members of both sexes. It was to act as a practical pressure group within local communities and also to be an agent of education about the devotional inter-relationship between work and repose. It was the spearhead of a critique of the values of liberal capitalism, but also part of the positive cultivation of a

[24] 'I dì festivi', *La civiltà cattolica*, ser. 1, a.1, 1 (1850), pp. 385–403; 'L'ordine nella beneficenza privata', ibid., ser. 5, a.13, 4 (1862), p. 45.

[25] G. de Bertier de Sauvigny, *La France et les français vus par les voyageurs américains 1814–1848*, 2 vols (Paris, 1985), 2, p. 180. The American visitor was John Sanderson, who travelled to Paris in 1835, and published his comments in his *Sketches of Paris, in Familiar Letters to his Friends, by an American Gentleman*, 2 vols (Philadelphia, PA, 1838).

[26] Cf. 'Della economia sociale alla moderna', *La civiltà cattolica*, ser.1, a.3, 8 (1852), p. 256.

Catholic associational life. It established links with similar associations in other countries, and publicized news of international developments.[27] Intellectually its trump card was the fact that it promoted the better keeping of Sunday as well as other feast days; and it was able to point to the fact that those countries which kept Sunday most religiously were both the most liberal, politically and religiously, and the most industrious and economically advanced: Britain and the United States. Thereby it turned admiration for Anglo-Saxon liberalism on its head. Gladstone and Proudhon were frequently cited to make an effective contrast: Protestants, rationalists, and unbelievers recognized the need for Sunday rest, whereas Catholic Italy lagged behind.[28] Some secular reformers tried to rescue the Sunday question from the Church, by separating it from the issue of feasts and by arguing that the need for a weekly day of rest was more an economic than a religious question.[29] But for the state the whole question was inherently a religious one, and hence any legislative change was resisted.[30]

Of all the regions of Italy, Sunday was observed most assiduously in Liguria, and a liberal writer in 1883 used this to support his point that there was a clear relationship between industriousness and the keeping of Sunday.[31] Liguria, a flourishing commercial and industrial area in the north-west of Italy, was held to be the hardest-working part of the country. An industrial suburb of Genoa, the local capital, was known as 'the Manchester of Italy'. But this liberal commentator also wanted to argue that the maintenance of feast days was an anachronism. He argued that now that every city had theatres, shops, and a cornucopia of offerings for the spectator, ordinary private diversions had – quite properly – succeeded public and religious ones. Here, however, Liguria would precisely have destroyed his case. Carpi had commented that apart from the very south of Italy the most fantastical and elaborate religious spectacles were to be found here.[32]

[27] *La settimana religiosa*, a.2, no. 24 (16 June 1872), pp. 203–4; ibid., a.4, no. 26 (28 June 1874), pp. 222–3; ibid., a.5, no. 2 (10 Jan. 1875), pp. 14–15.

[28] *Annali cattolici*, a.1, 1 (1863–4), p. 45; 'L'Uomo macchina', *La civiltà cattolica*, ser.13, a.38, 8 (1887), pp. 135–6; 'Il riposo festivo e la legislazione', ibid., ser.17, a.48, 1 (1898), pp. 400–1.

[29] L. Papa d'Amico, 'Il riposo domenicale e le pubbliche manifestazioni a Milano e a Palermo', *Nuova antologia*, ser. 2, 41 (1883), pp. 724–44.

[30] See C. Jannet, 'French catholics and the social question', *Quarterly Journal of Economics*, 7 (1892), p. 141 for similar inhibitions in France; cf. R. Beck, *Histoire du dimanche de 1700 à nos jours* (Paris, 1997), pp. 260–1.

[31] Papa d'Amico, 'Il riposo domenicale', p. 741.

[32] Carpi, *L'Italia vivente*, p. 399.

This was true not just in remote rural parishes, but in the modern commercial city of Genoa. In Genoa, also the home of Mazzini, conflicts between secular and religious authority were often violent in the second half of the nineteenth century. Catholic practice remained strong and widely diffused; members of Mazzinian workers' associations carried crosses in processions as members of religious confraternities. But there was also significant anti-clericalism, and the municipal authorities repeatedly banned religious processions on key feast days on the ground that they represented a threat to public order.[33] Even the procession for the feast of John the Baptist, the city's patron, was for several years confined within the cathedral.[34]

The Catholic press took pains to publish regular accounts of parish processions for a host of local feast-days which took place peacefully, with large crowds attending.[35] In 1637 the Genoese Republic had crowned the Virgin Mary as their queen, and Liguria remained profoundly devoted to the cult of Mary.[36] In response to anti-clerical attacks, the Catholic press made effective rhetorical use of the fact that during the republican period (down to the end of the eighteenth century), the state authorities participated in processions to key Marian sanctuaries to pray for her intercession or to give thanks for graces granted. Now under a liberal constitutional monarchy she was neglected by the state, which instead tried to promote secular feasts like the anniversary of the *Statuto*.[37] This anniversary of the granting of the constitution in Piedmont was made obligatory in 1861, and was scheduled to take place in early June – near the feast of Corpus Domini, which it was hoped the new anniversary would supersede. In fact its focus on gymnastic displays and the award of medals for scholastic and military achievement never caught the popular imagination, and in the 1890s the Catholic press gleefully reported workers demanding the right to work on that day.[38] A front-page illustration in the Catholic *L'Eco d'Italia* in January 1892 showed a long line of

[33] *L'Eco d'Italia*, a.2, no. 173 (1884), p. 2; ibid., a.6, no. 125 (1888), p. 2.

[34] *La settimana religiosa*, a.8, no. 14 (7 April 1878), pp. 150–1; *L'Eco d'Italia*, 44, no. 111 (1892), p. 3.

[35] *L'Eco d'Italia*, a.6 (1888), nos 129, pp. 2–3, 130, p. 2, 131, p. 3.

[36] See N. Lanzi, *Genova città di Maria Santissima. Storia e documenti della pietà mariana genovese* (Pisa, 1992), passim; especially pp. 9–17, 42.

[37] See, e.g., *L'Eco d'Italia*, a.2, nos 209–10 (1884).

[38] *La civiltà cattolica*, ser.17, a.48, 1 (1898), p. 743, cited in I. Porciani, 'Lo Statuto e il Corpus Domini. La Festa Nazionale dell'Italia liberale', *Il Risorgimento*, a.47, nos 1–2 (1995), p. 173.

faceless hungry workers, a factory in the background, the words *Lavoro e Pane* (Work and Bread) in the sky. The caption was: 'Processioni antiche e Processioni moderne: Dopo che col *progresso* settario sono proibite o molto inceppate le processioni religiose si vedono ben di frequente altre processioni più numerose ed anche più . . . pericolose.'[39]

In the same year of 1892 a huge Columbus anniversary exhibition was held in Genoa, of crucial importance for reinforcing the city's international commercial image. In preparation for it, the city authorities planned an ambitious programme of urban transformation – the creation of wide avenues à la Haussmann – to replace still extant medieval streets and religious buildings. In the seventeenth century a statue of the Virgin had been placed on each of the city gates. One of these gates – with its statue – was scheduled for demolition in the run-up to 1892, the argument used by the municipal authorities being that it was aesthetically unattractive, and that visiting foreigners would be embarrassed to see the statue of Mary. It would undermine the modern image of the city. The Catholic campaigners used this claim as yet another example of the state's failure to take the moral context of modernity seriously. They asserted that foreigners might be impressed to see a city maintaining its religious and moral identity.[40]

Genoese Catholics were to the forefront of the nineteenth-century devotional revival. New pilgrimages to the many Marian sanctuaries were recommended for May – the month of Mary – as well as on other key dates in the annual Marian calendar. They adopted with energy the renewed cult of St Joseph, centred on March, and created new forms of devotion. The liturgical year was full.[41] This Marian emphasis only accentuated another aspect of criticism of time spent on devotion which related to its economic implications for the image of the nation as a whole, the charge that it was feminizing. Even some Catholics were anxious not to lend fuel to the idea that devotional excess sapped the virility of the nation. At the same time, there was a validation of women's role in both devotional and social activity. One of the

[39] 'Ancient and Modern Processions: since with sectarian progress religious processions are proscribed or greatly restricted, much more frequently do we see processions of a longer and more dangerous kind': *L'Eco d'Italia*, 44, no. 6 (1892), p. 1.

[40] Ibid., nos 97, p. 3, 98, p. 3; *Pro Porta Pila: Numero unico dell' Eco d'Italia* (22 Dec. 1892), passim.

[41] See D. Cambiaso, 'L'anno ecclesiastico e le feste dei santi in Genova nel loro svolgimento storico', *Atti della Società Ligure di Storia Patria*, 48 (1917), pp. 28–130. See also the regular Diario religioso of *La settimana religiosa*; 'Ai divoti di S. Giuseppe', ibid., a.1, no. 9 (26 Feb. 1871), pp. 76–9.

Catholic journals in Genoa produced a supplement for women called *La donna e la famiglia: scritti di istruzione, educazione e ricreazione per le donne*. It laid great stress on the moral role of women in the household, and on their responsibility to maintain Marian devotion. But it also publicized meetings of women's associations in Germany and America, and produced a spirited denial of the prejudice that not just Italian men but Italian women (whether because of the climate or their spirit of devotion) were given up to languid abandon and the proverbial *dolce far niente*. It emphasised that a wide range of occupations – both salaried and voluntary – were undertaken by aristocratic, middle-class, artisan, and labouring women, who combined labour outside the home with rushing back to care for their children. Such a level and variety of activity went unrecognized by the state, which disadvantaged women in the Civil Code, and seemed to be unknown to foreign observers, who needed to be made aware of the heroic ability of Italian Catholic women to carry out effectively so many useful roles.[42]

Although the balance of intellectual traditions, both within and outside Catholicism, was particular to each region of Italy, Genoa was not unique in having a rich religious debate in which the need to reinforce devotional practices and to demonstrate their centrality to an appreciation of civil life was related to wider philosophical questions about the role of the Church in modern society. This explicit integration of what have come subsequently to seem discrete areas of concern was expressed especially through Catholic journalism, and through the extensive publication of occasional pamphlets. Just as in Britain, the vast expansion in periodical literature helped in the reinforcement of intellectual connections.

One of the most prominent figures in Catholic journalism in Italy was the Genoese Gaetano Alimonda, whose eloquence led to his being described as the 'Lacordaire d'Italia', a 'novello Bossuet'. From 1864 to 1877 he held a series of Sunday conferences in the cathedral of San Lorenzo in Genoa, which were published under the title *I problemi del secolo XIX*. One of the four main 'problems' which he addressed was that of the economy. He set out by attacking the notion of examining the economy as an autonomous sphere of human activity; criticized the impact of a self-help ethos which urged men never to be content; and stressed the complexity of labour as chastizement, expiation, and

[42] *La donna e la famiglia: scritti di istruzione, educazione e ricreazione per le donne*, 4 (Genoa, 1865), pp. 211–15.

mastery of the earth. He noted the injunctions of economists to method, and underlined the fundamental method of a Christian life. From this he acknowledged the merits of the division of labour, claiming classical authority for it, and pointing out that this doctrine, consistently sustained, would allow the priest his role as much as the gasworker. Employing a similar rhetorical approach to that of Ruskin, he took what seemed to be familiar and accepted concepts, and gave them fresh meanings in a fundamentally new and different epistemological framework. He provocatively used Marx to imply the failure of modern economics to think through its metaphysics: to take note of the crucial distinction between the categories of quality and quantity in the interpretation of labour.[43]

In picking up this distinction in Marx, Alimonda showed his affinity with a much wider movement in nineteenth-century Catholicism: the revived emphasis on philosophy to underpin Catholic engagement with modern thought, and specifically the renewed authority given to Thomas Aquinas and through him to Aristotle. Aristotle had distinguished between the worth of activities in terms of the *telos* or end being pursued. This distinction could be analytically crucial in confronting the generally prevalent utilitarian theory, by which actions were judged solely by their effectiveness in producing the single end of utility.[44] It thus offered a radical challenge to what was still a conventional economic treatment of work in terms of the production of value in exchange. Within Italy, key figures in this neo-Thomist revival were Padre Liberatore, promoter of *La civiltà cattolica* and later to be the principal drafter of *Rerum novarum*; Salvatore Talamo, who wrote about the Aristotelianism of the Scholastics and used it as a tool with which to analyse the development of modern materialism;[45] and Guiseppe Toniolo, for whom Aristotle and Aquinas were fundamental to his project to make ethics intrinsic rather than extrinsic to economic law.[46] Talamo and Toniolo collaborated in the establishment of the *Rivista internazionale di studi sociali* in 1893, which built on the

[43] G. Alimonda, *I problemi del secolo XIX. Conferenze del Cardinale Alimonda recitate nella metropolitana di Genova*, 4, *Problemi economici* (Genoa, 1876), p. 232, and conferences 5 and 6, passim.

[44] Cf. 'Le due economie', *La civiltà cattolica*, ser.3, a.7, 3 (1856), pp. 257–72, 465–85.

[45] See S. Talamo, *Svolgimento del materialismo contemporaneo* (Naples, 1874); idem, *L'Aristotelismo della scolastica nella storia della filosofia*, 3rd edn (Siena, 1881).

[46] F. Vito, 'G. Toniolo e la cultura economica dei cattolici italiani', in G. Rossini, ed., *Aspetti della cultura cattolica nell'età di Leone XIII* (Rome, 1961), pp. 10–19; R. Aubert, 'Aspects divers du Néo-Thomisme sous le pontificat de Léon XIII', in ibid., pp. 135–209.

work which Liberatore and his associates, as well as Cantù, had done in the previous generation. In its first number, *La civiltà cattolica* proclaimed confidently that Protestant rationalism was unable to produce social unity because its moral ideas were not grounded in metaphysics.[47] Or, as Toniolo was to put it, there was a concealed metaphysics, which subordinated values to facts.[48] Liberatore went on to sing the praises of Aquinas as both a Catholic and an Italian philosopher, whose thinking could help to expose the utopian fallacies of foreign critics.[49] Rather like *Rerum novarum*, Leo XIII's encyclicals of 1878 and 1879, *Inscrutabili Dei* and *Aeternis patris*, which established neo-Thomism as the official theology of Catholicism, were phrased in such a way as to give scope for both liberal and conservative interpretations. In some ways their intellectual contribution, or rather their recognition of an intellectual contribution, was far more fundamental to the development of Catholic thinking on work than that of *Rerum novarum*.

In an 1873 address on the ethical element in economic laws, Toniolo praised the Italian tradition of studying public economy which by definition considered economic life as an aspect of civilization, and which could lead to a greater sense of proportion and harmony than the British tradition as it had developed after Adam Smith seemed to him to possess.[50] This may have come to seem over-sanguine, but the eighteenth-century Italian tradition did leave its legacy, partly because political economy remained closely linked to jurisprudence and in many cases to the study of canon law. However, subsequent developments in Italian academic and political life were to have the effect of obscuring this holistic cultural tradition, even down to the present day. During his brief incumbency of the Chair of Political Economy at Turin in 1849, Emilio Broglio felt it necessary to attack the inclusive-

[47] 'Una replica intorno all'antagonismo fra il cielo e la terra', *La civiltà cattolica*, ser.1, a.1, 2 (1850), pp. 260–1.

[48] G. Toniolo, 'Dell'elemento etico quale fattore intrinsico delle leggi economiche', *Trattato di economia sociale e scritti economici II* in *Opera omnia di Giuseppe Toniolo*, ser. 2, 2 (Vatican City, 1949), pp. 266–92. See also P. Pecorari, *Toniolo. Un Economista per la Democrazia* (Rome, 1991), p. 44; A. Acerbi, 'Giuseppe Toniolo, tra filosofia neoscolastica e scienza economica', in *Contributi alla concoscenza del pensiero di Giuseppe Toniolo* (Pisa, 1981), pp. 59–85.

[49] F. Traniello, 'Cultura ecclesiastica e cultura cattolica', in *Chiesa e religiosità in Italia dopo l'Unità (1861–1878)* (Milan, 1973), p. 22. Liberatore published a collection of articles from *La civiltà cattolica*, as *Principî di economia politica* (Rome, 1889). An English version (tr. E. H. Dering) appeared as *Principles of Political Economy* (London and New York, 1891).

[50] Toniolo, 'Dell'elemento etico', p. 291.

ness of the Aristotelian approach in order to try to establish what he felt to be the necessary autonomy of the discipline of economics.[51] This was to be asserted conclusively by his successor in the Chair, Francesco Ferrara, who was identified by subsequent historiography as bringing 'system' to the study of economics. It was system run by the crudest invisible hand. To Ferrara it was self-evident that whilst Christianity might speak to the heart, men were more receptive to an appeal to their interests; and that application of cool economic reasoning would automatically result in moral benefits for all.[52] Although some eclecticism remained, by the end of the nineteenth century, utilitarian and positivist approaches to political economy predominated in Italian university circles, synchronizing with the ideology of the liberal state. There was little interest there in the questions about economics and religion raised by either Weber or Sombart when they were first published. The subsequent association of Catholic corporatism with fascism, and the more recent reaction against post-war Catholic political power, have contributed to a striking lacuna in Italian perspectives on the nineteenth century, where what is looked for is evidence of secular rationalism rather than creative Catholicism.

In Britain, the home of 'puritan economics', notwithstanding religious critiques and other challenges to classical economics, the neo-classical reformulation of political economy from the 1880s continued to treat labour only in the context of the production of exchange value in the market. In the article on 'The English School of Political Economy' in Palgrave's influential *Dictionary of Political Economy* (1891–4), the influence of Carlyle and Ruskin was held to be important, although economists kept 'in mind the distinction of economic theory from a mere record of facts or a mere utterance of philanthropic aspiration'.[53] Elsewhere in the *Dictionary*, the then newly established *Economic Review*, organ of the Oxford-based Christian

[51] L. Pallini, 'Tra politica e scienza: le vicende della cattedra di economia politica all'Università di Torino 1800–58', in M. M. Angello et al., eds, *Le Cattedre di economia politica in Italia. La diffusione di una disciplina 'sospetta' (1750–1950)*, 3rd edn (Milan, 1992), pp. 170–2.

[52] F. Ferrara, 'Caratteri essenziali dell'economia politica', in R. Bocciarelli and P. L. Ciocca, eds, *Scrittori italiani di economia* (Rome, 1994), p. 7. On Ferrara's dogmatism see also R. Romani, *L'economia politica del Risorgimento italiano* (Turin, 1994), p. 188. See also Achille Loria's article on the Italian School of Economists in R. H. I. Palgrave, *A Dictionary of Political Economy*, 3 vols (London and New York, 1891–4), 2: 466–7, in which he emphasises the 'objective and positive' enquiry which succeeded to Ferrara's extreme dogmatism.

[53] Palgrave, *Dictionary*, 1: 735.

Social Union, which set out to examine the relationship between ethics and economics, was described as not really being strictly economic in its preoccupations.[54] In the article on Aristotle it was pointed out that his economic views depended on the ethical principle that conduct (*praxis*) and not the production of commodities (*poiesis*) was the end of man. The subsequent comment was that this perhaps prevented him from understanding even the economic structure of the society in which he lived. It certainly made his methodological approach seem, to readers of the *Dictionary of Political Economy*, entirely irrelevant to the understanding of late-nineteenth-century economics.[55] Arguably the overwhelming influence of Hume on the British philosophical tradition in this context made it difficult for a more fundamental challenge to the analytical conventions of economics to succeed; although the revival of Christian moral philosophy in the last quarter of the century did help to give intellectual reinforcement to an organic approach to economic problems pursued within the churches. The impact of Aristotle and Aquinas was meanwhile felt in a Catholic context at Stonyhurst. Charles Devas, also a disciple of Ruskin, used the distinctions between *praxis* and *poiesis* to develop a compelling argument for the scientific status of an ethical economics.[56]

To say, however, that the ideals of Christian political economy did not succeed in transforming the methodology of economics is less pertinent than to point to the fact that the pursuit of these ideals was an aspect of increasing Christian confidence over the second half of the nineteenth century. In both Protestant and Catholic contexts a devotional revival, an attention to the detail of the daily, weekly, monthly interrelationship of worship with the reality of work, was the practical counterpart to the raising of related and fundamental philosophical questions. Ruskin pointed to the fact that devotion to the Madonna was that part of the Catholic faith 'least comprehensible by the average realistic and materialistic temper of the Reformation'. He then built on this observation to argue that veneration of the Virgin Mary had been one of the noblest aspects of Catholicism:

54 Ibid., 1: 736.

55 Ibid., 1: 55.

56 C. S. Devas, *Political Economy*, 3rd edn (London, New York, Bombay, and Calcutta, 1910), pp. 636–7; cf. idem, 'The restoration of economics to ethics', *International Journal of Ethics*, 7 (1896–7), pp. 191–201.

> I am certain that to the habit of reverent belief in, and contemplation of, the character ascribed to the heavenly hierarchies, we must ascribe the highest results yet achieved in human nature, and that it is neither Madonna-worship nor saint-worship, but the evangelical self-worship and hell-worship . . . which have in reality degraded the languid powers of Christianity to their present state of shame and reproach.[57]

Ruskin wilfully neglected the extensive and effective evangelical self-criticism which had been produced in the second half of the nineteenth century, and which had precisely been one element in the revival of the languid powers of Christianity. But he was right to point to the continued Protestant misunderstanding of Catholicism, and hence failure to engage with constructive aspects of Catholic tradition. The dangers of the unthinking assimilation of Anglo-Saxon Protestant values to the working of individualist economic laws remained, as was to be seen when America welcomed with open arms Talcott Parsons's translation and interpretation of Weber. In terms of economic thought it has perhaps been easier in some respects for Catholic contributions to retain a more effective counter-cultural dimension. But only now, as a few influential voices within the economics profession have begun to be raised in support of a more humane economic ethic, and have begun to confront analytically issues of quality of life, does a fresh look at the richness and vitality of nineteenth-century debates seem of more than passing historical interest.

Wadham College, Oxford

[57] Cook and Wedderburn, *Works of Ruskin*, 28: 82 (May 1874).

'A FRIENDLY AND FAMILIAR *BOOK FOR THE BUSY*': WILLIAM ARTHUR'S *THE SUCCESSFUL MERCHANT: SKETCHES OF THE LIFE OF MR SAMUEL BUDGETT*[1]

by MARTIN WELLINGS

SIR Henry Lunn (1859–1939), former Wesleyan minister and missionary turned journalist, ecumenical pioneer, and successful entrepreneur, wrote several volumes of autobiography in the first third of the twentieth century. Reflecting some fifty years later on the strengths and weaknesses of the Methodism of his youth in *Chapters from My Life* (1918), he wrote:

> Our pulpits in the '70s . . . had largely lost touch with the Catholic idea of poverty as one of the great virtues. Some years earlier a much-revered President of the Wesleyan Conference had written two widely different books. One was a powerful assertion of the need for the Baptism of the Holy Spirit in Christian work. The other was a glorification of a rich Methodist tradesman. Both books had a large circulation.[2]

The 'much-revered President' was William Arthur (1819–1901), President of the Conference in 1866, and his 'two widely different books' were *The Tongue of Fire* (1856) and *The Successful Merchant: Sketches of the Life of Mr Samuel Budgett, late of Kingswood Hill* (1852). *The Tongue of Fire*, hailed as a spiritual classic in the nineteenth century and much reprinted then and thereafter, examined the role and importance of the Holy Spirit in Christian life and work.[3] *The Successful Merchant*, written four years earlier and equally successful in publishing terms, was more controversial in subject-matter and message. As will be seen, it attracted mixed reviews, and some contemporaries shared Henry Lunn's disquiet at the portrayal of the central character. Arthur himself dedicated the book 'to the young men of commerce', and claimed that

[1] The research for this paper has been furthered by the staff and facilities of the Wesley and Methodist Studies Centre at Oxford Brookes University, and by the library of the Wesley Historical Society based at the W.M.S.C.

[2] Henry S. Lunn, *Chapters from My Life* (London, 1918), p. 21.

[3] *Methodist Times* (London), 14 March 1901, p. 186; *Methodist Recorder* (London), 14 March 1901, p. 3.

his purpose was to meet the need for a Christian 'Commercial Biography', thereby encouraging informed reflection on the relationship between faith and work.[4] This paper seeks to place *The Successful Merchant*, described by its author as 'a friendly, familiar *book for the busy*',[5] in context in the genre of Methodist biographical literature, in the social and ecclesiastical setting of mid-nineteenth-century Wesleyanism, and in the debate on work and wealth which has been a strand in Methodist identity, history, and historiography since the days of the Wesleys.[6] First, however, some attention must be given to the book itself, its author, and its hero.

William Arthur was born in Kells, County Antrim, in February 1819. After a very brief career in the corn business, Arthur was accepted as a candidate for the Wesleyan Methodist ministry in 1837, and sent to train in England. While at the Wesleyan Theological Institution at Hoxton he volunteered for missionary service, and left for India in April 1839. He spent less than two years in the subcontinent, however, being forced by deteriorating health to return home in 1841. Arthur continued to work under the auspices of the Wesleyan Methodist Missionary Society (W.M.M.S.), first as an advocate for missions, then in France from 1846–9, and finally as a member of the secretariat. Apart from three years as President of Methodist College, Belfast (1868–71), he remained in London until the early 1890s, first as a secretary of the W.M.M.S. (1849–68), then as Honorary Secretary (1871–88), and finally in retirement. The closing years of his life were spent in Cannes, where he died in March 1901, sixty years after his return from India.[7]

The *Methodist Recorder* devoted four pages of its edition of 14 March

[4] *Methodist Times*, 14 March 1901, p. 184; George John Stevenson, *Methodist Worthies*, 6 vols (London, 1884–6), 3, p. 388; William Arthur, *The Successful Merchant* (London, 1852) [hereafter *SM*], title page and p. v.

[5] Ibid., p. vii.

[6] See, for instance, David J. Jeremy, 'Introduction: debates about interactions between religion, business and wealth in modern Britain' and W. R. Ward, 'Methodism and wealth, 1740–1860', in David J. Jeremy, ed., *Religion, Business and Wealth in Modern Britain* (London, 1998), pp. 1–28, 63–9; John Walsh, 'John Wesley and the community of goods', in Keith Robbins, ed., *Protestant Evangelicalism: Britain, Ireland, Germany and America, c. 1750–c. 1950*, *SCH.S*, 7 (Oxford, 1990), pp. 25–50; Michael R. Watts, *The Dissenters*, 2 vols (Oxford, 1978–95), 2: 327–46.

[7] Stevenson, *Methodist Worthies*, 3, pp. 382–96; *Methodist Recorder*, 14 March 1901, pp. 11–14; *Methodist Times*, 14 March 1901, pp. 184, 186; *DNB Supplement, January 1901-December 1911*, 3 vols (London, 1912), 1: 64; Norman W. Taggart, *William Arthur. First Among Methodists* (London, 1993).

1901 to Arthur's life and career, including detailed reminiscences by J. H. Rigg, a friend since 1845.[8] A recurrent feature of that career until his withdrawal to Cannes in the early 1890s was the oscillation of bouts of poor health with strenuous activity as preacher, lecturer, author, and ecclesiastical statesman.

It was during one such period of involuntary leisure provoked by ill-health in the summer and autumn of 1851 that William Arthur found time to write *The Successful Merchant*.[9] The hero of the title, Samuel Budgett, was a self-made man who rose from comparatively humble origins to own and control the leading wholesale provision business in the west of England. Budgett was born in Somerset in 1794, the son of a small tradesman. He quickly demonstrated an aptitude for commerce, and by the age of twenty-two was established in partnership with his elder half-brother as a shopkeeper in Kingswood, near Bristol. Samuel was the driving force in turning the business from retail to wholesale trading, expanding the Kingswood premises and then relocating the centre of operations to Bristol. When he died in April 1851 the *Bristol Times and Bath Advocate* reported that 'By his energy, ability, and great activity, he raised from small beginnings what is, we believe, the largest business in the west of England, and which turns nearer millions than thousands in the course of the year, giving employment . . . to hundreds.' Even allowing for some exaggeration in the reported turnover of the business, the title of Arthur's memoir was clearly well chosen.[10]

The Budgetts were not only successful entrepreneurs, but also committed and generous Wesleyan Methodists. Samuel was a Local Preacher and Sunday School teacher, as well as a lavish benefactor of Kingswood Methodism, as was his brother Henry Hill Budgett (1778–1849). Samuel's eldest son, James Smith Budgett, married the youngest daughter of Thomas Farmer of Gunnersbury House, lay treasurer of the W.M.M.S., and both he and his brothers William and Samuel junior continued the family tradition of generosity to Methodist causes.[11] Furthermore, Henry Budgett's second wife, Sarah, who died

[8] *Methodist Recorder*, 14 March 1901, pp. 11–14.

[9] *SM*, p. v.

[10] *DNB*, 3, p. 226; *Bristol Times and Bath Advocate* (Bristol), 3 May 1851, p. 5; 10 May 1851 (2nd edn), p. 5; *Watchman* (London), 7 May 1851, p. 149; *Wesleyan Methodist Magazine* (London), June 1851, pp. 606–7.

[11] Ibid., May 1855, pp. 471–2; John Telford, *The Life of James Harrison Rigg, DD, 1821–1909* (London, 1909), pp. 105, 109–10; *Methodist Recorder*, 10 July 1874, p. 369 (family donations to The Leys School, Cambridge).

in 1839, and Samuel's second son, Edwin, who died of cholera ten years later, were the subjects of pious memoirs.[12]

Connexionally as well as commercially, therefore, Samuel Budgett was a promising topic for the ready pen of William Arthur, facing 'the prospect of a long involuntary leisure' and seeking 'designs for improving it by literary occupation'.[13] Arthur was already acquainted with the family, perhaps through the Farmers, and was in Bristol at the time of Samuel Budgett's death, and he suggested that he should undertake the writing of a memoir. The result, *The Successful Merchant*, published in January 1852, achieved enormous sales, so that 'the name of the author became as familiar to the general public as it had previously been to his own denomination.'[14] Within a year *The Successful Merchant* had run through three editions, and by 1877 it had reached its forty-third edition in Great Britain, having sold 84,000 copies. American sales, beyond the control of Arthur and his publishers, reputedly exceeded British ones, and there were versions in Welsh, Dutch, French, and German. The American children's writer, Helen Cross Knight, reworked the story into an edifying tale for the young, entitled *No Gains without Pains. A True Life Story for Boys* (1867), which itself ran into multiple editions; while *The Successful Merchant* also formed the basis for H. Noel's tract, *The Merchant of Kingswood* (1882).[15]

The book was hugely influential in a variety of ways. The Revd Edward Boaden wrote to the *Methodist Times* in March 1901 that 'for a few years after its publication, whether it was commended or adversely criticised, one would hardly attend a public meeting of any kind without hearing some quotation from that book or some reference to it.'[16] Setting aside reward and reputation, and picking up the theme of his stated aim in writing the book and dedicating it to the 'young men of commerce', Arthur claimed in the 1877 preface that 'Not a few have said that the reading of it had marked a turning-point in their character, and therefore in their career.'[17]

The scope and structure of Arthur's memoir may be reviewed

[12] John Gaskin, *A Memoir of the Late Mrs Sarah Budgett, of Kingswood-Hill, Bristol* (London, 1840); Anon., *Recollections of Mr Edwin Budgett, Late of Kingswood-Hill, near Bristol, by a Ministerial Friend* (London, 1850).

[13] *SM*, p. v.

[14] Stevenson, *Methodist Worthies*, p. 388.

[15] See the preface to the 43rd edn of *SM*, reprinted in the Author's Uniform Edition of 1885, pp. x–xiii [hereafter *SM(AUE)*].

[16] *Methodist Times*, 28 March 1901, p. 222.

[17] Prefaces to the 1877 and 1885 edns: *SM(AUE)*, pp. xi, xv.

briefly. *The Successful Merchant* offered a study of Samuel Budgett's life, career, and character combining thematic and chronological approaches. Arthur began with Samuel's funeral, creating an impression of Kingswood, of the community's response to Samuel's death, and of the sheer scale of the business enterprise which he had established. Succeeding chapters sketched Samuel's early life, his 'toils and troubles' and his 'rise and progress', identifying the qualities undergirding his success: intuition, thorough organization, ability to concentrate on the business in hand, diligence, punctuality, and sound judgement of commerce and character. Attention then turned to his management of employees and to his activities as a local benefactor, zealous Wesleyan, and head of a large family and household. After a chapter on 'the Inner Life', the book concluded with a lengthy narrative of Samuel's last illness and death, drawn from an account by a young friend, later identified as Miss Charlotte Shumm of Bath.[18] Use was made throughout of family letters (with names carefully deleted) and of recollections submitted by clergymen and ministers, particularly the Wesleyan Benjamin Carvosso and the Anglican John Gaskin, Samuel's nephew by marriage and the biographer of his sister-in-law. Arthur also incorporated published sources, conversations with employees, and extracts from Samuel's reminiscences, noting sadly that a journal of his early years had been 'burnt up by his own hand'.[19]

The result was a lengthy biography of almost 400 pages – if indeed a '*book for the busy*', then for the busy with some leisure for reading – blending narrative, dialogue, testimony, quotation, and theological reflection. Arthur was inclined to interrupt the narrative with lengthy didactic, ethical, or literary digressions, so that, for example, the second chapter began with a ten-page essay on the rise and progress of commerce throughout the world, while incidents in Samuel's life led into general comments on such topics as the apprenticeship system and the superficiality of popular culture.[20] An otherwise sympathetic reviewer in the *Baptist Magazine* commented that there was 'too great a display of "fine writing"' and 'too much preaching'; the *Christian Observer*, less sympathetically, concluded its review, 'If it had been half as long, it would have been twice as good.'[21]

18 Ibid., p. 450.

19 *SM*, p. 341.

20 Ibid., pp. 19–28, 107–16, 128–32.

21 *Baptist Magazine* (London), 44 (Jan. 1853), p. 27; *Christian Observer* (London), 192 (Dec. 1853), p. 865.

In writing a spiritual biography William Arthur was claiming his place in a well-established and popular strand of Christian literature, although as will be seen, *The Successful Merchant* modified the tradition in several significant ways. As a genre, spiritual biography was firmly rooted not least in the broad heritage of evangelical Protestantism, where exemplary lives played a major part in shaping experience, forming spirituality, reinforcing faith, and guiding Christian practice. Arguably nowhere was this heritage more vigorously expressed than in Wesleyan Methodism, whose strong literary sub-culture may be traced to John Wesley's recording and publication of his own spiritual experience, and to his dissemination of the spiritual biographies of others through his Christian Library and *Arminian Magazine*. Several volumes of the Christian Library, published between 1749 and 1755, were wholly devoted to religious biographies, and Wesley repeatedly urged the Methodists to read particularly the lives of Haliburton, de Renty, Lopez, and Brainerd. When the *Arminian Magazine* began in 1778 biographies and autobiographies were included as standard items.[22]

This pattern, set by Wesley, continued into the nineteenth century. The first article in the monthly *Magazine* (*Methodist Magazine* from 1798 and *Wesleyan Methodist Magazine* from 1822) was inevitably a memoir, sometimes serialized over several issues; briefer accounts of the lives and deaths of society members appeared regularly; and the receiving of obituaries of the travelling preachers was an important part of the business of the annual Conference. More substantial memoirs appeared in book form. At the time of the publication of *The Successful Merchant*, John Mason, the Connexional Book Steward, was advertising a twelve-volume Library of Christian Biography, edited by Thomas Jackson; Jackson's two-volume *Lives of Early Methodist Preachers*; and biographies of David Stoner, William Carvosso, Rowland Peck, Lady Maxwell, Hannah Ball, Mary Cooper, and Elizabeth Mortimer. In an evangelical constituency where novel-reading might still be regarded with some suspicion, biographies could offer pious readers excitement and adventure without spiritual risk.[23]

[22] Margaret P. Jones, 'From "the state of my soul" to "exalted piety": women's voices in the *Arminian/Methodist Magazine*, 1778–1821', *SCH*, 34 (1998), pp. 273–86.

[23] Watts, *Dissenters*, 1: 168–79; Isabel Rivers, '"Strangers and pilgrims": sources and patterns of Methodist narratives', in J. C. Hilson, M. M. B. Jones, and J. R. Watson, eds, *Augustan Worlds: Essays in Honour of A. R. Humphreys* (Leicester, 1978), pp. 189–201; Henry

In his brief preface to the original edition of *The Successful Merchant* Arthur contrasted the popular reputations of biographers and historians, declaring that 'Biographers, like portrait painters, are a suspected race: it is generally taken for granted that they paint men as they ought to be; while to the historian you must look for the delineation of men as they are.' He went on to claim that 'in the picture you are asked to look upon, an effort has been made to insert, with a firm hand, every real scar.'[24] Despite Henry Lunn's complaint that Arthur 'glorified' Samuel Budgett, *The Successful Merchant* was certainly not pure panegyric. Undoubtedly the general tone of the book was very positive, both in the author's own comments on his hero and in the judgements quoted from other sources, but there was another side to the story. Arthur reported Samuel's self-deprecation and nervousness, and described his spiritual struggles, especially, but not exclusively, in early life. This might be seen as standard fare in a narrative of this type, a common staging-post on the journey of faith, but it might not be expected that the biographer of a 'successful merchant' would also include a detailed description of his hero's faltering start in business, including his dismissal from his apprenticeship by his own brother for 'want of ability'.

Arthur was prepared, moreover, to examine and to criticize aspects of Samuel's business practice. His enthusiasm for striking an advantageous bargain was singled out for particular criticism: 'The danger of Mr Budgett did not lie in an excessive love of money, but it did lie in an excessive love of a good bargain.' This 'natural passion for successful trade' was '*the* defect of his character', illustrated by the young Samuel's insistence on taking a pair of stays as a pledge of payment for a donkey, and then insisting on retaining the pledge when the donkey subsequently died. One of Arthur's moral essays followed on from this account of Samuel's love of 'keen trading', leading to reflection on commercial maxims commonly invoked to justify the practice and on the Christian duty to be both commercially competent and 'just and brotherly'. The other area of business practice singled out for criticism was that of 'leading articles': selling some goods at a loss in order to entice customers to buy other products. While accepting the sincerity of the Budgetts in all their dealings, Arthur regarded this practice in

D. Rack, *Early Methodist Experience: Some Prototypical Accounts* (Oxford, 1997); Doreen Rosman, *Evangelicals and Culture* (London, 1984), pp. 184–93. Mason's catalogue was bound in the endpapers of *SM.*

[24] *SM*, pp. vi–vii.

general as against the public interest and 'decidedly to be condemned'.[25]

It may be seen that William Arthur set himself against what he perceived to be the general expectations of biography in frankly criticizing his main character. He developed and subverted the genre of religious biography more fundamentally, however, by taking for his subject a businessman and by making the context of work and commerce central rather than peripheral to the narrative. It has been persuasively argued by Jane Garnett that *The Successful Merchant* was one of a number of books published in the mid-nineteenth century which signalled a shift in the evangelical perspective on the world of work. It is suggested that earlier generations of evangelical authors presented exemplary lives without reference to employment, or portrayed business largely as a snare or a distraction from the spiritual. *The Successful Merchant*, and books like it, represented an attempt by evangelicals to develop a positive casuistry for Christians engaged in commerce, as part of a wider project to relate Christian teaching to social and economic theory and practice.[26]

Although it has not been possible to test this theory in detail by examining the full range of early and mid-nineteenth century biographies, a few examples from the period do support William Arthur's claim that 'Commercial Biography' was a neglected field of religious literature. In the brief memoirs published in the *Wesleyan Methodist Magazine,* the focus of attention tended to be conversion and activity within the life of the Methodist society, culminating in an edifying death, and in many cases the subject's business life was rapidly dismissed or passed over altogether. When, for example, Arthur's tutor at Hoxton, John Hannah, wrote a memoir of the prominent Leeds Methodist William Gilyard Scarth for the *Magazine*, Scarth's business as a master dyer received no mention whatsoever.[27] Fuller biographies took the same approach. Edwin Budgett (1829–49)

[25] *SM*, pp. 61–2, 341, 117, 53, 81, 46–7, 142–3.

[26] Jane Garnett, 'Evangelicalism and business in mid-Victorian Britain', in John Wolffe, ed., *Evangelical Faith and Public Zeal. Evangelicals and Society in Britain 1780–1980* (London, 1995), pp. 59–76; E. J. Garnett, 'Aspects of the relationship between Protestant ethics and economic activity in mid-Victorian England' (Oxford University, D.Phil. thesis, 1986), esp. pp. 149–202.

[27] *Wesleyan Methodist Magazine*, June 1855, pp. 481–9; Margaret Batty, *Stages in the Development and Control of Wesleyan Lay Leadership 1791–1878* (Peterborough, [1988]), p. 120; W. R. Ward, ed., *The Early Correspondence of Jabez Bunting 1820–29* (London, 1972), pp. 162–3 and n.1.

was involved in the family business before his early death during a cholera epidemic; but conversion, Christian work, religious conversation, and spiritual progress took up the bulk of the memoir written by 'a Ministerial Friend'.[28] Arthur's fellow Wesleyan Gervase Smith's *The Chequered Scene: or, Memorials of Mr Samuel Oliver*, published in 1853, included a brief chapter on 'Business', but paid more attention to Oliver's retirement through ill-health and resignation to financial ruin than it did to his business ethics.[29] Admittedly Oliver's career was considerably more exotic than Samuel Budgett's, including military service in Africa and India before conversion at the age of forty-five, but nonetheless *The Successful Merchant* was marked out by its emphasis on commerce, and by its positive engagement with the challenges and dilemmas of business life, from apprenticeship and adulteration to excess profits and employee welfare. This was recognized by the reviewers in a range of evangelical periodicals. The *Baptist Magazine* remarked that 'Religious biography has been, for the most part, confined to ministers of the gospel, or such prominent laymen as never can be models for the many.'[30] The *Eclectic Review* congratulated Arthur on breaking 'comparatively new ground' in taking such a subject.[31] The *Watchman and Wesleyan Advertiser*, perhaps predictably, was enthusiastic in its praise: 'We are acquainted with nothing similar or second to it.'[32] The *Christian Observer* commented with disdain that 'there is nothing of the impression made by a Christian of the highest class. Furthermore the mercantile tone of the book is of the lower and narrower kind, and the style is in many parts (if we may coin or use the word) "shoppy" to the last degree',[33] so inadvertently confirming the point that Arthur was subverting the accepted genre of religious biography in order to reach the burgeoning class of small tradesmen, warehousemen, and clerks with the story of an appropriate role-model. Although *The Successful Merchant* conformed to the pattern of traditional memoirs to the extent of observing that Samuel gradually withdrew from business in later life and devoted more time to Bible

[28] *Recollections of Mr Edwin Budgett*, pp. 54–5, 59.

[29] Gervase Smith, *The Chequered Scene: or, Memorials of Mr Samuel Oliver, for some Years an Officer in the Twenty-First Regiment of Light Dragoons in Africa and India: with References to Protestant Missions on those Continents* (London, 1853), pp. 116–29, 184–5.

[30] *Baptist Magazine*, 44 (1853), p. 27.

[31] *Eclectic Review* (London), n.s. 3 (May 1852), p. 631.

[32] *Watchman*, 7 Jan. 1852, p. 6.

[33] *Christian Observer*, 192 (1853), p. 865.

study and spiritual reflection,[34] he remained nevertheless first and foremost a merchant, and this was central to the narrative, rather than an interlude, an afterthought, or an embarrassment.

William Arthur was not alone in his concern for 'the young men of commerce'. He collaborated with eleven other Wesleyan ministers in delivering a series of Wednesday evening lectures in the City of London in the spring of 1852 to audiences of businessmen and City workers. The series, published as *Religion, in its Relation to Commerce and the Ordinary Avocations of Life*, covered such topics as 'Industry prompted by conscience and not by covetousness', 'Christian frugality and care, distinguished from selfishness', 'The rule of Christian equity applied to commercial transactions', 'Danger and safety in commercial difficulties and reverses', and 'The claims of commerce and those of life, health and religion'. Arthur's lecture on 'The dangers and right use of commercial prosperity' did not refer explicitly to Samuel Budgett, but the figure of the 'successful merchant' could be detected in the examples of good practice scattered through the text.[35] This concern was not a Wesleyan monopoly. Evangelicals of various traditions in this period were engaged in the quest to link personal morality and business ethics, using the pulpit, the press, and a range of denominational and undenominational agencies to do so. In seeking to understand what prompted this pan-evangelical endeavour, Arthur's memoir may be located more firmly in its contemporary setting.

The concerns exemplified by *The Successful Merchant* may be explored in relation to three overlapping contexts in the mid-nineteenth century. The broadest and most general of the three was the context of the world of commerce, with its practical and ethical challenges. Economically the period was one of both opportunity and instability. Legislative changes, beginning with the repeal of the usury laws in 1832 and the passing of the Municipal Corporations Act in 1835, increased scope for commercial enterprise, while regulatory measures failed to keep pace with an increasingly complex business world. Expansion, opportunity, and aspiration therefore marched hand in hand with fraud, speculation, and recurrent crises. Christians were caught up in this situation as winners and losers, as employers and as members of the aspiring white-collar sector, as victims or sometimes as

[34] *SM*, p. 355. Compare the conventional account of his illness and death in ch.10.

[35] *Watchman*, 7 April 1852, p. 110; 2 June 1852, p. 174; W. H. R[ule], ed., *Religion, in its Relation to Commerce, and the Ordinary Avocations of Life* (London, 1852).

perpetrators of commercial malpractice, and as pastors offering moral guidance in competition with the flourishing literature of secular self-help. Evangelicals of different hues were moved by pastoral and apologetic motives to participate in contemporary debates and to address the needs of the business world from a Christian perspective, recognizing that 'in this busy country there is no small danger of separating trade from Christianity'.[36]

The second context was that of the social composition of English Christianity, and in particular given William Arthur's background, that of Wesleyan Methodism. Despite the difficulties of evidence and methodology,[37] Michael Watts's work on nineteenth-century Dissent has drawn two interesting conclusions in this regard. First, taking England and Wales as a whole, Nonconformity, including Wesleyan Methodism, continued to appeal primarily to the working classes in the first half of the nineteenth century. Second, however, in the larger urban centres there was a trend towards increasing respectability from the 1840s onwards. Unusually, surviving evidence from Leeds allows a comparison to be made across the period from 1810 to 1870, and it indicates that local Wesleyanism saw a steady rise in the proportion of businessmen, retailers, and white-collar workers from the 1840s to the 1860s, and a corresponding decline in the proportion of unskilled workers.[38] It might be argued, then, that books like *The Successful Merchant* appealed to an expanding section of the Wesleyan and broader Nonconformist urban constituency, representing lower-middle-class and 'respectable' working-class aspirations, and addressing their ethical dilemmas in the changing world of work. Anecdotal evidence of the impact of the book on individuals, buttressed by the solid statistics of its sales, shows that Arthur succeeded in reaching a wide readership; the groups identified by the Leeds evidence, 'men from the counting-house or the shop',[39] would be plausible purchasers and readers of the memoir.

The third context for *The Successful Merchant* was that formed by the

[36] Garnett, 'Evangelicalism and business', pp. 59–76; *Eclectic Review* (1853), p. 631.

[37] See, for example, R. B. Walker, 'The growth of Wesleyan Methodism in Victorian England and Wales', *JEH*, 24 (1973), pp. 267–84; Clive D. Field, 'The social structure of English Methodism: eighteenth-twentieth centuries', *British Journal of Sociology*, 28 (1977), pp. 201–2; idem, 'The social composition of English Methodism to 1830: a membership analysis', *Bulletin of the John Rylands Library*, 76 (1994), pp. 153–69; Watts, *Dissenters*, 2: 303–27.

[38] Ibid., pp. 593–601.

[39] *SM*, p. vii.

economic ethic of Wesleyan Methodism, shaped by the movement's ideological legacy and modified by the realities of connexional politics in the difficult years after 1845. The Methodist attitude to wealth and the contribution of Methodism (and evangelicalism in general) to Britain's industrial and commercial development have fuelled intense historiographical debate, at least since the publication of the Weber thesis in 1905.[40] As John Walsh has shown, John Wesley's teaching and example set out a radical lifestyle for the people called Methodists, summed up in Wesley's sermon on 'The use of money' in three injunctions: 'Gain all you can', 'Save all you can', and 'Give all you can.'[41] Echoed by Arthur in *The Successful Merchant*, Wesley's triple rule remained official Methodist teaching as part of the Connexion's doctrinal standard throughout the nineteenth century.[42] The pattern of hard work, frugality, and sacrificial giving, however, was not always maintained even in the early days of Methodism, much to Wesley's despair. Despite their founder's warnings, Methodists became affluent, and this ambivalence continued after his death. Adam Clarke, preaching at Spitalfields in the 1790s, so emphasised the duties of men of business that

> an eminent merchant who had heard the sermon overtook him on the way home, and observed, 'Mr Clarke, if what you have said today in the pulpit be necessary between man and man, I fear few commercial men will be saved.' 'I cannot help that, sir,' replied he: 'I may not bring down the requirements of infinite justice to suit the selfish chicanery of any set of men whatever.'[43]

Nonetheless, Methodists continued to prosper, and in the years after Waterloo the connexional leadership worked hard to cement an alliance between the Conference and a respectable laity, consciously repudiating radicals and revivalists in the process.[44] The triumph and

[40] Jeremy, 'Introduction', pp. 13–28; Watts, *Dissenters*, 2: 327–46.

[41] Walsh, 'Wesley and the community of goods', pp. 35–6, 44–50; Albert C. Outler, ed., *The Works of John Wesley, vol. 2: Sermons II, 34–70* (Nashville, TN, 1985), pp. 263–80.

[42] *SM*, pp. 138–9. Wesley's published sermons were part of the doctrinal standard of Wesleyan Methodism under the 1784 Deed of Declaration, until modified by the Deed of Union in 1932.

[43] J. W. Etheridge, *The Life of the Revd Adam Clarke, LL.D.*, 2nd edn (London, 1858), p. 167.

[44] David Hempton, *The Religion of the People: Methodism and Popular Religion c.1750–1900* (London, 1996), pp. 91–108; idem, *Methodism and Politics in British Society 1750–1850* (London, 1984), pp. 85–115.

cost of respectability were demonstrated in 1827, when connexional machinery was used on distinctly dubious grounds to over-rule the leaders and local preachers of the Leeds East circuit, who had objected to the installation of an organ in the new Brunswick chapel. The organ was seen as a concession to the tastes and preferences of wealthy seatholders and trustees, and it became a symbol of social, political, and ecclesiological conflict extending far beyond Leeds. The organ controversy resulted in a Pyrrhic victory for the Conference, but the cost in terms of local resentment and secession foreshadowed the bitter conflicts of the 1840s.[45] It should not be forgotten that Arthur wrote *The Successful Merchant* against the background of a great upheaval in Wesleyan Methodism, as opposition to Jabez Bunting and his allies came to a head in the Fly-Sheet controversy of 1849–52; nor that part of the rhetoric of the reformers was that authentic Methodism had been robbed of its spiritual power by an alliance of clericalist bureaucrats and wealthy laymen.[46] When it is remembered that one of the cocktail of charges levelled at what James Everett called 'the Clique, that ruled the Conference, that ruled the People' was that it was in the pocket of 'some hundred rich men',[47] and that not only was Arthur a colleague of Bunting on the staff of the Mission House and a defender of Conference policy, but also that James Budgett's father-in-law Thomas Farmer was a prominent and wealthy Buntingite, it is not surprising that Arthur's memoir and Samuel Budgett's character received less than complimentary reviews in the *Wesleyan Times*, the reformers' newspaper.[48]

Notwithstanding the vitriol of the *Wesleyan Times* and the establishment disdain of the *Christian Observer*, *The Successful Merchant* was generally well received by press and public alike. For William Arthur it brought a considerably enhanced reputation in the evangelical world, as well as the financial rewards of successful authorship. More significantly, it indicated the determination of evangelical Christians to engage positively with the world of work and commerce, taking seriously the ethical challenges of the day and the pastoral needs of

45 Batty, *Wesleyan Lay Leadership*, pp. 117–50.

46 Hempton, *Methodism and Politics*, p. 198; Benjamin Gregory, *Side-Lights on the Conflicts of Methodism 1827–1852* (London, 1898), chs 7–11.

47 Batty, *Wesleyan Lay Leadership*, p. 244.

48 Taggart, *William Arthur*, p. 76. Farmer was co-treasurer of the 1852 testimonial fund for Bunting and Robert Newton: Telford, *James Harrison Rigg*, p. 98; Thomas Jackson, *The Life of the Revd Robert Newton, DD* (London, 1855), pp. 324–39.

urban congregations, whether composed of successful merchants, ambitious clerks, or victims of collapsing credit. In terms of Wesleyan Methodism, Arthur's memoir set the seal on thirty years of collaboration between a lay elite and the connexional hierarchy, acknowledged the commercial base of Wesleyan prosperity, and opened up a new style of exemplary literature. Its influence may be assessed by comparing a contemporary judgement on the memoir with a telling sequel. On 14 February 1852 Benjamin Gregory wrote privately to his brother: 'Have you read *The Successful Merchant*? 'Tis in my opinion as to both composition and tendency a great lowering of Arthur. It ought to have been entitled "The art of getting a camel through the eye of a needle".'[49] Within twenty years of this scathing comment, and revealing imitation to be truly the sincerest form of flattery, Gregory had published his own commercial biography, *The Thorough Business Man: A Memoir of Mr Walter Powell* (1871).[50] By this time the place of the successful entrepreneur was well established both in the polity and the literature of Wesleyan Methodism.

[49] Benjamin Gregory, *Autobiographical Recollections* (London, 1903), p. 400.
[50] Ibid., p. 434, comments on Gregory's lack of business experience!

USEFUL INDUSTRY AND MUSCULAR CHRISTIANITY: GEORGE AUGUSTUS SELWYN AND HIS EARLY YEARS AS BISHOP OF NEW ZEALAND

by ALLAN K. DAVIDSON

CHARLES Kingsley in 1855 gave the following dedication to his novel, *Westward Ho!*:

> To the Rajah Sir James Brooke, K.C.B., and George Augustus Selwyn, D.D., Bishop of New Zealand this book is dedicated, by one who (unknown to them) has no other method of expressing his admiration and reverence for their characters.
>
> That type of English virtue, at once manful and godly, practical and enthusiastic, prudent and self-sacrificing, which he has tried to depict in these pages, they have exhibited in a form even purer and more heroic than that in which he has drest it.[1]

Brooke, the adventurer, soldier, and colonial administrator, and Selwyn, the missionary colonial bishop, appealed to Kingsley as exemplars of what he called 'Christian manliness'. One of Kingsley's reviewers, T. C. Sandars, described Kingsley as 'spreading the knowledge and fostering the love of a muscular Christianity'.[2] The defining characteristics of this 'muscular Christianity', a term with which Kingsley was uneasy, were 'an association between physical strength, religious certainty, and an ability to shape and control the world around oneself'.[3]

Additional elements defining Selwyn's Christian manliness were his immense energy and his concern that time be used so that not a moment was wasted. These elements found expression both in his own life and action and in his description and implementation of what he called 'useful industry' at the college he founded in New Zealand.

[1] Charles Kingsley, Dedication to *Westward Ho!*, Feb. 1855.

[2] T. C. Sandars' review of Kingsley's *Two Years Ago* (1857), cited in Donald E. Hall, 'Muscular Christianity: reading and writing the male social body', in idem, ed., *Muscular Christianity. Embodying the Victorian Age* (Cambridge, 1994), p. 7.

[3] Ibid.

Ironically, in the light of Kingsley's vigorous reaction against both Tractarians and Evangelicals, Selwyn was thought by some to be too closely identified with the Oxford Movement, while others, such as John Keble, were concerned about his involvement with the Evangelical Church Missionary Society (CMS).[4] In choosing Selwyn for his *Westward Ho!* dedication, Kingsley was promoting his own brand of Christian anthropology and apologetic. Kingsley's heroes were both his own invention and the creation of his age. There was little room for subtle nuances alongside Kingsley's hagiographical representations of Christian manliness. This paper, in examining Selwyn's understanding of work and time, provides critical insights into his embodiment of muscular Christianity.

* * *

Norman Vance, in describing Christian manliness, refers to the way in which it was characterized by 'self-assertion and determination rather than humbler, more passive qualities of patience and heroic martyrdom'. Those who best displayed Kingsley's ideals 'were Christian soldiers on active service for the benefit of the whole nation'.[5] Manliness was expressed in the individual's boldness, honesty, plainness and defiance of authority, stoicism, and violent energy. Dennis Allen, reflecting on muscular Christianity in Thomas Hughes's *Tom Brown's Schooldays*, concluded that the 'essence of work' was 'not in the pursuit of Mammon', but through the labours of 'each individual to make things "a little better"'.[6]

Selwyn exemplified many of these qualities. Kingsley's attraction to him was no doubt reinforced by the publicity given to Selwyn during his visit to England in 1854–5 when he returned from New Zealand to consult with legal and ecclesiastical authorities regarding Church constitutional matters. Selwyn was already well known for his self-sacrifice, physical exploits, his walking long distances in New Zealand, and his voyages to Melanesia in small vessels under his own command. As the first bishop appointed under the Colonial Bishoprics Fund, Selwyn was a pioneer in creating church structures in a colonial

[4] Allan K. Davidson, *Selwyn's Legacy. The College of St John the Evangelist, Te Waimate and Auckland, 1843–1992, A History* (Auckland, 1993), pp. 10–11, 16, 68–9.

[5] Norman Vance, *The Sinews of the Spirit. The Ideal of Christian Manliness in Victorian Literature and Religious Thought* (Cambridge, 1985), p. 24.

[6] Dennis W. Allen, 'Young England: muscular Christianity and the politics of the body in "Tom Brown's Schooldays"', in Hall, ed., *Muscular Christianity*, p. 126.

environment. He was also deeply involved in supporting and working with the CMS missionaries who had been labouring among Maori in New Zealand since 1814.

Underlying Selwyn's character was a very strong work ethic which shaped his episcopate and his relations with those who worked with him. His attitude to work was infused with a strong sense of devotion to duty and reinforced his vocation which his first biographer characterized as his 'deacon episcopate'.[7] Service was a key component of Selwyn's ministry. How far this originated from his understanding of his vocation and how far it was pathological, or a combination of both, is open to debate. Certainly the evidence from his early years points towards a 'a strong self-willed child' who combined resolution with unselfishness, which according to his sister, 'made him energetic and ready to assist in any emergency which might arise in the nursery'.[8] While coming from a professional family (his father was a noted constitutional lawyer) Selwyn showed an 'indifference to comfort' which 'enabled him in later years to endure so much hardness on board ship, in camp and on Melanesian coral-reefs'.[9]

As a student at Eton he became involved in rowing, choosing always to take the 'bad oar'.[10] In 1829, while at St John's College, Cambridge, Selwyn rowed in the inaugural Oxford–Cambridge boat-race and was a member of the losing crew. He was an advocate of exercise, walking on one occasion from Windsor to London 'in thirteen hours without stopping'. A strong swimmer, Selwyn promoted daily bathing, becoming 'the President of a Society which was called "The Psychrolutic Club"' which required its members to bathe 'five days in every week for a whole year'. Together with William Evans, a drawing master at Eton, he established a '"swimming system," by which no boy was allowed to boat [at Eton] until he has "passed" in swimming'.[11] These interests in rowing, walking, and swimming, were part of the cult of athleticism which Kingsley and others sanctified as expressions of manliness.

Reflecting on his time as a student at Cambridge when he was giving advice to his younger son, John, Selwyn confessed that a lack of

[7] H. W. Tucker, *Memoir of the Life and Episcopate of George Augustus Selwyn*, 2 vols, (London, 1879), 2: 382.

[8] Ibid., 1: 6.

[9] Ibid., 1: 7.

[10] Ibid., 1: 11.

[11] Ibid., 1: 18.

resolution meant that 'I lost much time there.' Drawing on the apostle Paul's allusion to the athletic example, which Vance credits with inaugurating the tradition 'of moral manliness',[12] Selwyn encouraged his son with an understanding of the 'Christian life' which

> in all its varieties is nothing but pressing towards a mark: and *that* mark must be a distant one; not a boat-race to-day, or a drill to-morrow, or a party the next day, but a fixed and steady sight of a distant prize, to be won only by long and steady perseverance in well doing.[13]

Selwyn's academic career at Cambridge was marked by his second placing in the Classical tripos in 1831 and his election as a fellow of St John's. He became an assistant master at Eton, as well as a private tutor, and following his ordination served as curate in Boveney and then in the adjoining parish of Windsor. It is said that he 'soon made a very deep mark upon the neighbourhood by his indomitable energy, and by the true spirit of Christian self-oblivion which he displayed in all that he undertook.'[14] Reflecting on his role, Selwyn remarked to a friend, 'I believe that, as clergymen, we ought . . . to be willing to be tied like furze-bushes to a donkey's tail, if we can thereby do any good by stimulating what is lazy and quickening what is slow.'[15]

Underlying Selwyn's appointment as Bishop of New Zealand in 1841 was a strong sense of duty and family honour. His brother William, who was involved in the Church Society of New Zealand, which was attempting to establish the Church of England in the colony, was offered the bishopric. Writing to William Gladstone, a contemporary at Eton, Selwyn declared, 'I know of no limit to the duty of obedience either of a Priest to the Church, or a wife to her husband, and therefore I can say nothing but go at all sacrifices.'[16] William, however, turned it down because of opposition from his wife and father-in-law. George Selwyn was upset by his brother's refusal and let it be known that he would take up the position if it was offered to him in order to recover the family honour. When the Bishop of London and secretary of the Colonial Bishoprics Fund made a formal offer,

[12] Vance, *Sinews of the Spirit*, p. 26.

[13] Tucker, *Selwyn*, 1: 15.

[14] G. H. Curteis, *Bishop Selwyn of New Zealand and Lichfield* (London, 1889), p. 11.

[15] Tucker, *Selwyn*, 1: 24.

[16] BL, MS Add 44,299, fols 77–8: G. A. Selwyn to W. E. Gladstone, Eton College, Windsor, 20 May 1841.

Selwyn replied that 'Whatever part in the work of the ministry of the Church of England as represented by her Archbishops and Bishops may call upon me to undertake, I trust I shall be willing to accept it with obedience and humility.'[17] Sarah, his wife, whom he had married in 1839, reflected in her old age how her husband 'was quite ready to take his education and his wife and all besides into any sphere to which he might be called by lawful authority.' Although Sarah told George that she 'did not like it', she hoped she would 'never hinder him from doing what he thought was right. He said he could only look on this as a call to go, and so it was settled.'[18] This subordination of the wife to the husband's vocation was typical of the period. While Sarah was a person in her own right, she was relegated to the role of helpmate, mother, and bishop's wife.

Selwyn brought to his work as Bishop of New Zealand great energy. He was cast in what was an unusual situation at that time, being both a missionary and colonial bishop. He brought together support from the Evangelical CMS who paid half his stipend, the High Church Society for the Propagation of the Gospel which gave him both finance and personnel, the New Zealand Company which was promoting emigration, and the Colonial Office which paid the second half of his stipend. The tensions between missionary interests to Maori, the indigenous people, and ministry to the growing settler community were to define many of the struggles of Selwyn's episcopacy in New Zealand. Selwyn's churchmanship was also somewhat ambiguous and the cause of some disagreements. He was traditional High Church but influenced by the Oxford Movement and the renewed vigour which it brought to episcopal authority and the centrality and autonomy it gave to the Church. His close friend and the organizer of a great deal of his financial support, Edward Coleridge, took him to Oxford before he left for New Zealand to meet with the 'Oxford Apostles', J. H. Newman and John Keble. Selwyn, however, tried to remain aloof from party disputes, seeking to work with people from across the theological spectrum.

Coleridge, in describing Selwyn's farewell sermon at Windsor, refers to the difficulty he had in restraining 'my own mind from something of Idolatry for the man; his appearance so simple, open, devout, yet for

[17] Tucker, *Selwyn*, 1: 65.

[18] Auckland, Museum Library (hereafter AML): 'Reminiscences by Mrs S. H. Selwyn 1809–1867', typescript (Auckland, 1961), p. 13.

his station so fresh and young; his manner so quiet and unassuming yet so serious, earnest and influential.' Referring to what Selwyn said, Coleridge drew attention to his 'self forgetfulness', his 'intensity of devotion to his cause', his 'undervaluing of his sacrifices', and his 'magnifying of his privileges and blessings'.[19] We see in Coleridge's hero worship an anticipation of the attraction that Kingsley and others found towards Selwyn.

Before he even arrived in New Zealand Selwyn imposed his disciplined approach on those who accompanied him. The *Tomatin* sailed from Bristol on Boxing Day 1841 and within ten days 'a regular system of Instruction was commenced, and, with the exception of a few days, maintained throughout the whole voyage.'[20] Writing to his mother, Selwyn recorded:

> Our day is spent thus:
> 8 o'clock Prayers
> 10 New Zealand lesson [Maori language]
> 11 Greek lesson
> 1 Hebrew lesson
> 2 Mathematics
> We have taken different departments for the study of the New Zealand language . . .
> I am studying practical navigation under our Captain (a most intelligent man) in order that I may be my own *Master* in my visitation voyages.[21]

Sarah Selwyn reported, 'We have a most orderly industrious party, the 1st quality, owing to their being most of them, well conditioned nice people; the last, is in consequence of George's examples and rules', with 'George being chief Professor'. As they neared the equator there was 'a general hue and cry for a Midsummer vacation on acc[oun]t of the heat', but Selwyn, ever the taskmaster, was described as 'hard-hearted and will only promise 3 days under the line'.[22]

[19] Auckland, St John's College (hereafter SJC), Misc Arch 17/1: Edward Coleridge, 'Account of the Dinner and Meeting at Eton and Windsor on the 30th and 31st Oct 1841'.

[20] AML, Selwyn Papers, MS 273, vol. 5, typescript, pp. 4–6: [T. Whytehead,] 'Journal kept by one of the passengers on board the *Tomatin* with extracts from Bishop Selwyn's letters, Dec. 26 1841 to 11 Nov. 1842'.

[21] AML, MS 273, vol. 1, typescript, p. 6: G. A. Selwyn to his mother, *Tomatin*, 18 Jan. 1842, Lat. 6 N., Long. 21 W.

[22] SJC, Selwyn Papers, Misc Arch 9/10, vol. 2, p. 2: Sarah Selwyn to her aunt, *Tomatin*, 18 Jan. 1842.

Selwyn led by example. William Bambridge, a lay assistant, described how Selwyn 'with shirt sleeves turned up and shewing as much dexterity as any of them' sheared a sheep on board the *Tomatin.* He commented, 'I suppose he lived a systematic life and has made a point of following out the old maxim "Whatever is worth doing, is worth doing well". His Lordship won't allow the plan of skimming the surface instead of sifting a matter to the foundation to know the why & the wherefore.'[23] There was almost a sense in which Selwyn acted as the 'superman' who was able to match others in strength and intelligence in order to assert his leadership.

After their arrival in New Zealand, Bambridge noted that 'His Lordship sets us an example with respect to working wh[ich] I think few can follow.'[24] During his first visitation throughout his new diocese which 'extended over more than six months', Selwyn traversed '2,277 miles . . . 762 on foot, 86 on horseback, 249 in canoes or boats, and 1,180 by ship.'[25] On his return from another visitation Bambridge noted, that 'The principal feature in the Bishop's travelling is that he never seems to be tired. . . . The natives who accompany the Bishop say that they are very weary, but the *Pihopa* [Bishop] is never weary.'[26]

Physical work played an important part in Selwyn's plans for developing the church in New Zealand. The College of St John the Evangelist, which he established at Waimate in 1843 and shifted to Auckland in 1844, was the 'key and pivot' in his schemes. A multi-level institution, it was designed to train ordinands, educate boys in a grammar school, prepare Maori teachers, and give schooling to Maori boys. Among the other activities Selwyn incorporated into his College were a hospital, building and printing departments, farming, gardening, and tree planting. It was an ambitious plan, and Selwyn gained a large amount of financial support which was used to buy 1,300 acres of land in Auckland and to erect buildings. Everyone in the College was expected to take part in 'Useful Industry', which along with 'True Religion' and 'Sound Learning', made up the trinity in the College's motto, *Religio, Doctrina, Diligentia.*

Selwyn's philosophy was a mixture of pragmatism in the colonial

23 Wellington, Alexander Turnbull Library (hereafter ATL), Microfilm MS501: William Bambridge, Journal, 3 Jan. 1842.

24 Ibid., 20 April 1843.

25 Tucker, *Selwyn*, 1: 132.

26 ATL: Bambridge, Journal, 31 Aug. 1843.

context where he lacked money to employ artisans and an idealism which harked back to medieval monasticism and the work of monks, with him claiming that 'he was wont to act, "on the best precedents of antiquity".'[27] Biblical sanction was given to his scheme by drawing up 'St Paul's Rule and Practice' which listed six verses which reinforced 'work with your own hands', 'if any would not work, neither should he eat', 'labouring night and day ... we would not be chargeable unto any of you', 'labouring ye ought to support the weak'.[28] In outlining his 'General Principles', Selwyn indicated that all students and scholars 'shall employ a definite portion of their time in some useful occupation in aid of the purposes of the Institution.'[29] Selwyn argued that 'Even if industry were not in itself honourable, the purpose of the institution would be enough to hallow every useful art, and manual labour, by which its resources might be augmented.' Industry and self-denial were '*the only real endowment of St John's*'[30] and for Selwyn '*it is the motive which sanctifies the work*'. He urged members of the College 'to carry into the most minute detail of their customary occupations the one living principle of Faith, without which no work of man can be good or acceptable in the sight of God.'[31] In giving a theological and biblical justification for the priority he placed on work, there was a danger that Selwyn could hide behind these idealistic and high sounding principles and place a burden on his staff and students which exceeded their capacities.

Reflecting his own ethnocentrism, Selwyn was critical of Maori 'indolence' and was afraid that English boys 'would sink to the same level'. His institution was intended

> To raise the character of both races, by humbling them; to hinder, so far as positive institutions may avail, the growth of that shabby, mean, and worthless race of upstart gentlemen, who are ashamed to dig but not to beg, whose need never excites them to industry, and whose pride never teaches them self-respect.[32]

St John's, for Selwyn, was intended to be a 'place of holy rest, and yet of

[27] Tucker, *Selwyn*, 1: 134.
[28] Ibid., pp. 134–5; I Thess. 4.11; II Thess. 3.8; I Thess. 2.9; Acts 20.34.
[29] Tucker, *Selwyn*, 1: 135.
[30] Ibid., 1: 136.
[31] Ibid., 1: 138.
[32] [G. A. Selwyn,] *A Journal of the Bishop's Visitation Tour Through His Diocese*, Church in the Colonies, 20 (London, 1849), p. 23.

charitable energy'.[33] Most of those who lived at the College, however, found little rest, and the energy expected of them was not always given charitably.

In part the difficulty was that Selwyn in acting as the 'superman' set such high standards for himself and also expected others to meet them. One of his students recalled how 'Someone was remonstrating' with Selwyn 'as to the amount of work he was doing', to which 'he replied that he would rather wear away than rust away.'[34] William Cotton, Selwyn's domestic chaplain, noted that Selwyn acted as 'an architect planning St. John's College',[35] building supervisor,[36] and builder. Selwyn was unhappy with the progress made on the temporary buildings and 'To shame all our idlers, he took ye whole party onto the hill to cut *toitoi*, a sort of rushy grass which is used for roofing.'[37] Selwyn, however, confessed to Edward Coleridge that 'there is something in the multitude of petty details with which I am conversant, which overloads the mind for the time, and destroys its elasticity.' For Selwyn there was the frustration that 'all the details of every kind of work come back upon the principal agent: I seem to know the length and breadth of every stone and plank.'[38]

Selwyn felt very responsible for ensuring the success of his undertaking. On one occasion when wheat needed to be harvested and no outside labour was available, Selwyn cancelled all teaching. Following a short service in the Chapel at five o'clock and breakfast, Selwyn, the masters, and all the students took to the fields, bringing the harvest in within a week. Selwyn rewarded everyone with a Harvest Home.[39] In leading by example, Selwyn expected others to work as hard as he did. When the College was short of firewood, he took the schooner and some students to a place where wood had been cut, and 'having denuded himself of his episcopal breeches and gaiters, and donned a pair of trousers, commenced operations', loading twenty tons of wood.[40]

33 G. A. Selwyn, *An Idea of a Colonial College. A Sermon Preached in the Chapel of St. John the Divine, Bishop's Auckland* (Eton, 1848), p. 8.

34 SJC, MS 10/5/10, p. 9: Edward Hammond, 'Personal Reminiscences of Bishop Selwyn'.

35 AML, Microfilm 35: William Cotton, Journal, 4 Sept. 1844.

36 AML, Microfilm 36: ibid., 12 Feb. 1845.

37 Ibid., 4 March 1845.

38 AML, MS 273, vol. 1, p. 183: G. A. Selwyn to [E. Coleridge], St John's College, 30 Nov. 1847.

39 SJC: Hammond, 'Reminiscences', pp. 19–21.

40 Ibid., p. 24.

Critical questions were raised by both observers of and participants in Selwyn's College. John Greenwood, a student at the College, wrote in 1852 that 'One of the reasons for my thinking of leaving this place, is the constant work, work, work, from morning to night, without break or stop. I cannot say what it may do to others, but it is making me morose, unfeeling, cynical and discontented.'[41] T. H. Smith, both a student and tutor, complained that they did not have time to look at their books. The mornings were 'devoted to out-door work and the afternoon to "scholastic glory" (as you call it)'.[42] He vented his disgust that 'the boys are taken away so much for other work that you can hardly make any impression upon them during school hours which will last till you have another opportunity of following it up.'[43] Taking over the position as 'House Steward' with responsibility for meals and cleaning, Smith sarcastically wrote that Selwyn 'would have us turn out washerwomen if he could rather than pay one'.[44] William Williams, a CMS missionary, who sent two of his sons to the College, reflected a common concern about it, that 'There is much outside shew, but little reality.'[45] Jane Williams in 1847 noted that 'A great point is made of out-door work, which is all very good in N[ew] Zealand, provided school hours are well employed, but they were not.'[46] The Williamses withdrew their son Leonard, a future bishop of Waiapu, from the College and sent him to England for further education.

Selwyn had put in place a comprehensive educational, ecclesiastical, and industrial institution. It was, however, impossible to sustain the College in the form he had outlined. He blamed the way in which it was failing on the lack of capable assistants, but this was only a partial explanation. The CMS missionaries, who were suspicious of Selwyn's Tractarian connections and what they saw as basic flaws in the arrangements at St John's, lost confidence in Selwyn and his College and did not continue to send their own children or Maori students. Robert Maunsell, a CMS missionary, declared that 'The Bishop's College is a most extraordinary failure', and charged Selwyn with being 'more able as a theorist than a practical man' whose 'narrow 14th

[41] ATL, MS Microfilm 194: John Greenwood, Diary 1850–5, 17 July 1852.

[42] AML, MS 283, p. 167: Thomas Henry Smith, Letters to his brother, 22 June 1847.

[43] Ibid., 25 Nov. 1847, p. 233.

[44] Ibid., 6 Jan. 1848, p. 256.

[45] Frances Porter, ed., *The Turanga Journals 1840–1850. Letters and Journals of William and Jane Williams, Missionaries to Poverty Bay* (Wellington, 1974), p. 395.

[46] Ibid., p. 425.

century notions' got in the way of 'the good which he has already done'.[47] A homosexual scandal at the College was the occasion rather than the cause for closing it in 1853.[48] J. F. Lloyd, who had joined the College staff in 1849, noted that 'This blow was a very severe one to the poor Bishop who had spent a vast amount of labour & energy & intellect as well as money in planning & carrying out the College.'[49]

Reflecting on Selwyn's qualities, Lloyd wrote that:

> he is certainly one of the most remarkable men of the age, a man of great & most varied powers of mind, extraordinary self denial, & most profound & enlarged views of religion, I never knew any man that has laboured as he has done, he allows himself no recreation, but works incessantly, & his work is no light work, but real hard laborious work, few men w[oul]d hold out for one year under his work, but he has an iron constitution & frame. – He is no tractarian, as some people report, in fact tractarianism cannot exist in the atmosphere of a Colony like this.[50]

There was, however, a tendency, seen in Kingsley's *Westward Ho!* dedication, to idealize and romanticize Selwyn's attributes. There was little acknowledgement in the published record that the hero also had feet of clay. John Greenwood, sailing with Selwyn, noted that he was

> very fond of quoting a Man of War's orders & regularity against us; but he does things Man of War fashion when it suits His own purpose . . . His ruling passion appears to be the love of power, to gratify which he will interfere & meddle in the most frivolous as well as the most important things.[51]

Selwyn was, in modern language, a 'workaholic' who was consumed by his vocation and had difficulty in delegating work to people he did not trust. He also had a short fuse when it came to his temper. Leonard Williams noted that 'sometimes he gets very *riri* [angry] and blows nearly everyone sky high.'[52] Greenwood, after being what he thought

[47] Helen Garrett, *Te Manihera. The Life and Times of the Pioneer Missionary Robert Maunsell* (Auckland, 1991), p. 166.

[48] Davidson, *Selwyn's Legacy*, pp. 67–9, 78–81.

[49] ATL, MS J. F. Lloyd Papers 1786, Folder 1: J. F. Lloyd to Ellen [F. Lloyd], Auckland, 28 Dec. 1853.

[50] Ibid.

[51] ATL, Greenwood, Diary, 12 Feb. 1850.

[52] AML, MS 335, A/3, f.220: William Leonard Williams to Jane Williams, St John's College, 13 Feb. 1847.

was 'unjustly reprimanded' by Selwyn, was told by Lloyd 'that the Bishop was not angry with me, but that he so often seemed angry when he was not.' This could indicate both the stress and frustration under which Selwyn often worked. Greenwood noted that after being on the receiving end of the bishop's 'severe & angry displeasure & scolding . . . the next time one meets the B[isho]p after one of these passages, He is as smiling and open as if nothing had happened.'[53] Selwyn, however, had many redeeming qualities, and among them were the many hours he spent nursing the sick and his ministry to the dying.

Selwyn viewed time as 'a precious commodity'. He went to extreme lengths in setting 'a time limit for meals – ten minutes for dinner, grace included!' until a doctor 'informed him he was not only making his men eat like pigs, but he was ruining their digestions. The rule was relaxed.'[54] Whenever there was a rare lapse and Selwyn overslept, he was, as Cotton noted on one occasion, 'always rather cross during the rest of the day . . . He looks as if he had got out of bed on the wrong side and has been in rather a nice sort of humour for finding fault with trifles.'[55] Despite the punishing regime under which he lived, Selwyn was physically strong and generally kept good health. On one infrequent occasion when he had a cold and toothache he had taken the day 'to lie by'. Sarah, ever the long-suffering wife, noted that 'a day's rest seems to be sometimes so imperatively called for tho' it is never taken unless he is driven to it.'[56] Lady Mary Martin, the Selwyns' good friend, was aware more than anyone of the costs of his work, noting that after the war in the north in 1845 'he was very worn'.[57] Hammond recalled visiting Selwyn several times at the end of the day and found him 'lying on the sofa thoroughly exhausted – the strong man bowed low – scarcely able to articulate a word. But he was always his own robust self again the next morning at chapel.'[58]

One of Selwyn's few forms of relaxation was also intimately connected with his work. Vicesimus Lush referred to him 'as our own "sailor bishop"'.[59] Selwyn was very much at home on the sea.

[53] ATL, Greenwood, Diary, 12 Feb. 1850.

[54] Sybil M. Woods, *Samuel Williams of Te Aute* (Christchurch, 1981), p. 69.

[55] AML, MS 85, typescript: Cotton, Journal, 21 Aug. 1845.

[56] AML, MS 273, vol. 2, p. 551: Sarah Selwyn to Mrs Coleridge, Te Waimate, 3 July 1844.

[57] Ibid., p. 687: Mary Ann Martin to Edward Coleridge, Taurarua, 11 Aug. 1845.

[58] SJC: Hammond, 'Reminiscences', p. 9.

[59] Alison Drummond, *The Auckland Journals of Vicesimus Lush 1850–63* (Christchurch, 1971), p. 89.

Hammond recalled seeing him in a strong wind and 'a nasty sea . . . rigged out in a full set of oilskins', looking 'every inch the sea captain'.[60] Referring to his need of a new boat Selwyn informed Coleridge, 'I have no house of my own' and that 'After all, the cost of my carriage, which I can steer myself, will not exceed that of an English Bishop's new Coach which he must have a Coachman to drive and a footman to open the door.'[61]

As well as sailing around the coast of New Zealand, Selwyn embarked on an ambitious missionary undertaking in Melanesia. Given the demands of pioneering episcopal ministry in New Zealand among Maori and migrants and the huge geographical area he was responsible for, some saw this new venture as foolhardly. Between 1847 and 1860 'Selwyn spent approximately thirty-one months, or twenty-two per cent of his time on ten voyages to the islands north of New Zealand.'[62] There was a heroic and romantic dimension to these voyages, with Selwyn sailing in the early years in his small twenty-one ton schooner, the *Undine*, in uncharted waters among often hostile people. Robert Maunsell, reflecting the CMS opposition towards what became known as the Melanesian Mission, referred to it as Selwyn's 'quixotic mission'.[63] Settlers were alarmed at Selwyn spending so much time outside 'his diocese proper',[64] where he was accused of '"yachting" among the Solomon and other groups'.[65] In his defence Selwyn indicated that during his voyages in 1852 'my charge, journals, study of languages, navigation, and the chief part of my correspondence have been accomplished'.[66]

In undertaking the Melanesian Mission Selwyn developed a unique missionary methodology based on bringing Melanesians to Auckland for teaching and then returning them to their islands where it was hoped they would become evangelists among their own people. While his strategy was innovative its success was limited, and required considerable modification and eventually replacement before the

60 SJC: Hammond, 'Reminiscences', p. 39.

61 SJC, Australian Joint Copying Project (hereafter AJCP), Microfilm 1095: G. A. Selwyn to E. Coleridge, St John's College, 27 Jan. 1847.

62 Hugh Laracy, 'Selwyn in Pacific perspective', in Warren Limbrick, ed., *Bishop Selwyn in New Zealand 1841–68* (Palmerston North, 1983), p. 121.

63 SJC, CMS Correspondence, AJCP Microfilm 228, Reel 56: Robert Maunsell, Annual letter, Kohanga, Waikato River, 19 Jan. 1857.

64 Tucker, *Selwyn*, 1: 281.

65 Ibid., 1: 375.

66 Ibid., 2: 13.

Melanesian Mission began to become the Church in Melanesia.[67] That Selwyn attempted the Mission at all is remarkable testimony to his energy and missionary vision and the merger of what Sohmer has identified as 'action and self-denial in mission'.[68]

* * *

This paper has concentrated on Selwyn's understanding of work and the way in which he embodied that before 1855 and as a result became an ideal for Kingsley of 'Christian manliness' and for his age an exemplar of 'muscular Christianity'. After his return from England in 1855 Selwyn was preoccupied with developing a constitution for the Church in New Zealand which was formulated in 1857; subdividing his diocese and sharing in synodical government with other bishops, clergy, and laity; handing over the work of the Melanesian Mission to John Coleridge Patteson who was consecrated as a missionary bishop in 1861; and providing ministry during the trying years of the New Zealand wars from 1860 to 1867. He returned to England for the first Lambeth Conference and took a leading part in its deliberations. He was offered the see of Lichfield which he only accepted after the intervention of Queen Victoria. His sense of duty was reflected in his comment that 'As a solider of the Church I shall probably feel bound to do whatever my commander-in-chief bids me.'[69] Selwyn, after settling affairs in New Zealand, returned to Lichfield in 1869, actively undertaking an energetic episcopal ministry until his death in 1878.

Selwyn was a bishop for thirty-seven years who worked tirelessly for what he believed in. The legacy of his work, as one of his biographers indicated, remains paradoxical.[70] Constantine Dillon, no friend of Selwyn, pointed to this in describing the failure at St John's College, but also noting that people nevertheless recognized him as 'a 13th Apostle and call him the blessed Bishop'.[71] 'Useful Industry' emerged in the various forms that St John's College took over the years, but it never again played the central defining role that Selwyn

[67] David Hilliard, *God's Gentlemen. A History of the Melanesian Mission 1849–1942* (St Lucia, 1978).

[68] Sarah H. Sohmer, 'Christianity without civilization: Anglican sources for an alternative nineteenth-century mission methodology', *Journal of Religious History*, 18 (1994), p. 193.

[69] Tucker, *Selwyn*, 2: 239.

[70] J. H. Evans, *Churchman Militant. George Augustus Selwyn Bishop of New Zealand and Lichfield* (Wellington, 1964), pp. 252–3.

[71] C. A. Sharp, ed., *The Dillon Letters. The Letters of the Hon. Constantine Dillon 1842–1853* (Wellington, 1954), p. 89.

had given it.[72] What Selwyn had been unable to accomplish no one else attempted. The Christian manliness which he exemplified was achieved at great personal cost to himself and Sarah. Selwyn poignantly wrote after the death of their daughter Margaret, who lived for five months, 'I had only know her for twelve days, and those full of business, so that I can scarcely call her features to mind.'[73] Yet for Selwyn, the personal qualities that this essay has highlighted, such as his devotion to duty and his demanding work ethic, undergirded by his athleticism and physical energy, were used to express his sense of vocation. Work was not an end in itself.

Time was something which Selwyn felt that he, and all who worked with him, should be accountable for using well. As a result he put enormous pressures on himself and those around him which led some to feel that he expected too much of people. Selwyn gained a reputation for being a strict disciplinarian, seen, for example, in his question and answer to his theological students at Lichfield: 'Is it *rest* that you require? . . . Rest is like a top when it is "asleep". It is then at full and steady work; and it is only when it begins to lose its speed that it begins to fall.'[74] Yet while the time-pressure Selwyn put on himself and others was largely self-inflicted, it was driven by his high sense of duty, the enormous tasks before him, and the self-sacrifice he was willing to make in attempting to accomplish the work which he thought necessary for building up the Church in New Zealand and Melanesia. While Selwyn was admired by some as an example of muscular Christianity, the very things which contributed to this, such as his self-sacrifice and preoccupation with time and work, caused a negative reaction in others who worked closely with him.

Underlying Selwyn's activism there was a theological understanding of work and time which he expressed in his charge to his clergy in 1847: 'The loftiness of His [God's] work is the proof both of His sufficiency, and of our unfitness for His ministry.' Selwyn concluded with the words of the seventeenth-century Archbishop of Glasgow, Robert Leighton, 'So the more a man rightly extols this his calling, the more he humbles himself under the weight of it.'[75] Tucker in his

[72] Davidson, *Selwyn's Legacy*, pp. 109, 129, 135, 153, 160, 220.

[73] Evans, *Selwyn*, pp. 191–2.

[74] 'Bishop Selwyn', *New Zealand Methodist*, 20 July 1889, p. 1.

[75] [G. A. Selwyn], *A Charge Delivered to the Clergy of the Diocese of New Zealand, at the Diocesan Synod, in the Chapel of St John's College, on Thursday, September 23, 1847* (London, 1849), pp. 104–5.

evaluation of Selwyn noted that 'He was hard and exacting' and that 'he never praised men for doing their duty'. This is what he expected of people because it was so much a part of himself. Tucker, without saying as much, links the thoughts of Selwyn and Leighton in stating that

> If at any time he [Selwyn] exacted from others more than they could perform, his very strictness was but the result of his humility; he never realized the fact that he could do more, physically and intellectually, than other men; so lowly was his opinion of himself, that he thought all men could do as he did, and was content with no smaller measure of service.[76]

Whether this accurately captures Selwyn is debatable. What is not in debate is Selwyn's strong and compelling sense of duty which took him to the other side of the world where, through his work, he left his distinctive imprint, with all its paradoxes, on the church which he led as Bishop of New Zealand.

St John's College, Auckland, New Zealand

[76] Tucker, *Selwyn*, 2: 380.

WORK, LEISURE, AND REVIVAL: THE INTEGRATION OF THE 1859 REVIVAL INTO THE WORKING AND SOCIAL LIVES OF THE TOWNSFOLK, FERMFOLK, AND FISHERFOLK OF ABERDEENSHIRE

by K. S. JEFFREY

OFTEN the timing and manner of revivals have been significantly influenced by the working and leisure patterns of the contexts within which they have occurred. Seventeenth- and eighteenth-century Scottish awakenings appeared most regularly within agrarian towns and villages during their summer communion seasons. Often they took place around the times of planting and harvest, with the result that the period between May and October was often considered the 'holy season'.[1] The appearance of these movements was appreciably affected by the annual agricultural cycles of work and rest. At the start of the nineteenth century the ability of these popular communion festivals to engender religious enthusiasm began to decline when, under the influence of an increasingly enlightened culture, they became more respectable and organized. In addition, new measures emerged which sought to attract the urban masses and they gradually undermined the old models of revivalism.[2] Many of these 'modern' techniques were designed to compete against other social attractions for the attention and time of the city dweller.[3] The 1859 revival hence presents an opportunity to examine how religious movements had changed and become related to the use of time by the middle of the nineteenth century.

A noticeable feature of the 1859 religious movement, as it affected the north-east of Scotland, was the manner in which it appeared in a variety of separate social contexts. The revival began in Aberdeen in September 1858. The initial fervour climaxed in December and receded in March, but was re-ignited in August 1859 and continued

[1] L. E. Schmidt, *Holy Fairs: Scottish Communions and American Revivals in the Early Modern Period* (Princeton, NJ, 1989), pp. 3–29, 156.

[2] R. Carwardine, *Transatlantic Revivalism: Popular Evangelicalism in Britain and America, 1790–1865* (Westport, CT, 1978), pp. 71–80.

[3] K. T. Long, *The Revival of 1857–8: Interpreting an American Religious Awakening* (Oxford, 1998), p. 28.

throughout the autumn. During the subsequent year the same pattern was repeated, with religious enthusiasm rising in the summer and subsiding in late October. Meanwhile, the agricultural farms and villages of the region began to experience the revival in the spring of 1859. The movement proceeded more steadily for several years amongst the fermfolk, although there were particular periods of spiritual fervour between July and October during 1859, 1860, and 1861. Finally, the awakening was a dramatic, intense, and short-lived event in the lives of the Moray Firth fisherfolk. It broke out around the beginning of February 1860 and had disappeared almost completely by the end of April. The timing, length, and manner of the revival were influenced, to a considerable extent, by the working and leisure patterns of the three distinctive situations in which it appeared.

* * *

The first context which needs to be considered is the city of Aberdeen itself. By the middle of the nineteenth century the city's economy was based largely on the production of textiles. The New Statistical Account of 1843 estimated that up to 12,300 people, who constituted 46 per cent of the city's workforce, were employed in the processing of flax, cotton, and wool.[4] Nevertheless, Aberdeen's economic base was fairly diverse. An extensive programme of civic improvements created a building boom around the middle of the century that produced a large number of jobs for quarrymen, masons, and labourers. In addition, there were six ship-building yards at Footdee, a small fishing community near the harbour, which employed hundreds of wrights and carpenters. Moreover there were rope, comb, and paper mills, not to mention a thriving machine engineering industry. The traditional artisan society continued to make up a large section of the labour force, with 4,000 hand-loom weavers, 800 shoemakers, 600 carpenters, 500 tailors, 500 blacksmiths, and 200 cabinet-makers and upholsterers.[5] There was also a substantial middle class. By 1861 there were 80 doctors, 170 male teachers and professors, 200 female teachers, and 500 commercial clerks working in Aberdeen.[6] Furthermore, 3,500 female domestic servants were employed in the city.[7]

[4] A. A. MacLaren, *Religion and Social Class* (London, 1974), p. 2.

[5] R. Duncan, *Textiles and Toil: The Factory System and the Industrial Working Class in Early Nineteenth Century Aberdeen* (Aberdeen, 1984), p. 3.

[6] J. Valentine, *Aberdeen as it Was and Is* (Aberdeen, 1871), p. 26.

[7] Duncan, *Textiles and Toil*, p. 4.

This heterogeneous population did not share a standard, universal working lifestyle. Factory workers, the majority of whom were young unmarried women, laboured for approximately ten hours each day following the 1844 Factory Act.[8] Those involved in the building trade worked for sixty hours each week in the summer and forty-seven hours during the winter.[9] During the same period advocates worked from 10.00 a.m. to 4.00 p.m., walked home for their evening meal, and resumed their labours from 6.00 until 8.00 p.m.[10] Thus most city people followed a rigid daily work routine which occupied approximately ten hours for six days of each week. The rise of Aberdeen's factory-based economy had been accompanied by new work disciplines. They undoubtedly affected the people's appreciation of the value of time with the result that, from the 1840s, the townsfolk began to draw a sharp demarcation between their working hours and 'free time'.[11]

Many of the leisure activities pursued in mid-nineteenth-century Aberdeen were class based. The city continued to have a larger proportion of licences to the population than any other town in Scotland and the public house remained central to the social life of the working classes.[12] However, they also enjoyed outdoor games such as quoiting, which resembled bowls. Meanwhile the middle classes indulged themselves in separate pursuits such as horse-racing and cricket.[13] The first Aberdeenshire Cricket Club, formally constituted in 1857 by the lawyer James Forbes Lumsden, was 'composed chiefly of law clerks and university students'.[14] Finally the theatre, whose season ran from September to March, was the most popular pastime for those wealthy enough to afford it.[15] Thus each community within the city occupied its spare time with various social activities according to its taste and means. Nevertheless, the changes in work patterns that accompanied the economic developments around the middle of the nineteenth century affected the recreational activities of many people.

[8] E. J. Evans, *The Forging of the Modern State: Early Industrial Britain 1783–1870* (London, 1983), pp. 228–32.

[9] W. H. Fraser, *The Coming of the Mass Market 1850–1914* (London, 1981), p. 18.

[10] L. MacKinnen, *Recollections of an Old Lawyer* (Aberdeen, 1935), p. 111.

[11] E. P. Thompson, 'Time, work-discipline and industrial capitalism', *P&P*, 38 (Dec. 1967), p. 90.

[12] A. S. Cook, *Pen Sketches* (Aberdeen, 1901), p. 232.

[13] W. Skene, *East Neuk Chronicles* (Aberdeen, 1905), p. 16.

[14] W. Carnie, *Reporting Reminiscences* (Aberdeen, 1902), p. 35.

[15] Skene, *East Neuk*, pp. 16–22.

The rise of disciplined hours of work, particularly in the factories, created regular time for leisure. As a result new opportunities of exercise and entertainment began to emerge as museums, art galleries, and public libraries opened in the city.[16] Also the popular temperance movement was established in 1839. It encouraged the pursuit of new social activities, the most popular of which was the soiree, a Saturday evening gathering that included recitations and singing.[17] In addition, between 1840 and 1865 there were seventeen philanthropic and religious societies established in Aberdeen which sought to occupy the new free time which many of the townsfolk had begun to possess.[18] The growth of the city and the rise of the factory-based economy had created a new recreational market.[19] Accordingly, during the years immediately preceding the revival, a new range of leisure activities was beginning to compete for the free time which the people of Aberdeen had begun to enjoy.

Within this busy city the revival ebbed and flowed between September 1858 and April 1861. There were at least four periods of intense religious activity which illustrate how the city movement was affected by the working and leisure patterns of the urban context. The first 'season of grace' began in the summer of 1859 during the course of a number of evening open-air meetings. In April the members of the Aberdeen Free Presbytery 'had resolved to go out to the lanes and streets to preach the gospel as widely as they could'.[20] As a consequence it was reported that 'open-air preaching has never been so common in this city as it has been for a fortnight past [29 July 1859] . . . hundreds have listened to the offer of salvation who had never done so before.'[21] George Campbell, the Free North Church minister, remarked how 'it was quite uncommon to have less than a thousand people who could be gathered in the thoroughfares' to listen to the revivalist.[22] Summer evening open-air evangelistic meetings became an important hallmark of the revival. Their success can be largely attributed to the fact that they offered, to many townsfolk, an alternative, cheap form of popular entertainment during the long, warm nights of the summer months.

[16] Fraser, *Coming of the Mass Market*, pp. 208, 214.

[17] *Northern Temperance Record*, March 1841.

[18] *Aberdeen Almanac 1860* (Aberdeen, 1860), p. 241.

[19] B. Harrison, 'Religion and recreation in nineteenth century England', *P&P*, 38 (Dec. 1967), p. 111.

[20] *Aberdeen Free Press*, 13 April 1860, p. 6.

[21] Ibid., 29 July 1859, p. 6.

[22] Ibid., 13 Jan. 1860, p. 6.

The Music Hall rallies, held during the autumn of 1859, marked the second important period in the city revival. One local minister recalled how in the 'autumn [of 1859] Aberdeen became again deeply moved . . . [when] the whole community seemed to feel the influence at work . . . a feeling of solemnity seemed to pervade the life of the city'.[23] The catalyst and principal focus of this heightened state of religious excitement was a series of twelve Sunday evening revival meetings that were held in the newly-opened Music Hall. The first, addressed by Reginald Radcliffe, attracted 9,000 people, only a third of whom were able to gain admittance.[24] These occasions constituted possibly the most successful period of the revival. Undoubtedly, the day and timing of these gatherings accounted for their popularity in the city. They were held during the only period of the week when everyone was on holiday. Thus the working and leisure habits of the townsfolk had a significant effect upon the timing and manner of this city movement.

Finally, there were two periods of fervent revival activity, during the autumn of 1858 and the summer of 1860, when there were short, intensive evangelistic campaigns that were organized to coincide with local holidays. One local observer noticed how at the height of the Cattle Show in October 1858 'when thousands of strangers from the adjoining counties were in town, and when thousands of sight seeing town's people were moving about, it was reckoned a seasonable opportunity to circulate religious tracts and papers amongst the crowds on the Links.'[25] Indeed, the revival leaders organized 'a goodly number of extraordinary services [which] were thus held during the week, all with a view to the revival of God's work and the salvation of souls.'[26] Similarly a two-day revival rally was held at the Links in Aberdeen in August 1860, where it was anticipated that 'many people will naturally congregate, it being the evening of the Cattle Show.'[27] In addition, special services were organized for the working people on the Saturday afternoon, when 'most of them have the half holiday' and consequently they were 'present in great

[23] T. T. Matthews, ed., *Reminiscences of the Revival of Fifty Nine and the Sixties* (Aberdeen, 1910), pp. 54, 113.

[24] *Banffshire Journal*, 18 Oct. 1859, p. 5.

[25] Anon., *Times of Refreshing: Being Notices of the Religious Awakenings which have Taken Place in the UK, with Special Reference to the Revival in Aberdeen* (Aberdeen, 1859), p. 12.

[26] Ibid.

[27] *Stonehaven Journal*, 28 July 1860, p. 3.

numbers'.[28] Special revival services were meticulously planned to suit the holidays and leisure patterns of those who lived in the city. The leaders of the Aberdeen movement were anxious to target the free time of the townsfolk.

Perhaps the defining features of the Aberdeen revival were the two daily prayer meetings, which clearly illustrate how the social patterns of the city affected the manifestation of this religious movement. These gatherings were modelled on the famous businessmen's prayer assemblies of the American revival of 1857–8. They had been designed to encourage working men to take a break for prayer during their lunch hour and were highly organized. The directions stipulated that the opening hymn, Bible reading, and prayer were not to occupy more than twelve minutes, and that at 12.55 the leader should announce the closing hymn, with 'any one having the floor yielding immediately'.[29] The Aberdeen leaders of the revival organized two similar prayer meetings which attracted an attendance of more than 1,000 people each day.[30] The first of these, held between 2.00 and 3.00 p.m., 'gathered together [people] from the drawing room, lowly hearth side, shop and office'.[31] The second meeting, conducted between 8.00 and 9.00 p.m., was arranged specifically 'for the convenience of the working people'.[32] The times of these gatherings and the particular audiences they targeted suggests that the work and leisure patterns of the city commanded a vital influence over the nature of this religious movement. The Aberdeen revival was carefully planned to fit around the disciplined working routines of the townsfolk, and to target their free time.

* * *

In contrast to the events in Aberdeen, the progress of the revival in rural areas followed a very different pattern. Two types of people laboured in rural Aberdeenshire in the middle of the nineteenth century. Firstly there were independent farmers who owned small holdings. They constituted the largest section of Aberdeenshire's agrarian population in 1859. Each day they followed a natural,

[28] *Peterhead Sentinel*, 24 Aug. 1860, p. 3.

[29] Long, *Revival of 1857–8*, p. 83.

[30] *Stonehaven Journal*, 24 Feb. 1859, p. 3.

[31] Omicron, *Five letters on the Religious Movement in Aberdeen: with an Appendix on the Nature, Probability and Necessity of a Religious Revival* (Aberdeen, 1859), p. 4.

[32] *Aberdeen Journal*, 2 Feb. 1859, p. 3.

unregimented rhythm that included milking the cow, tending the sheep, and toiling in the fields. They did not adhere to a rigid work pattern.[33] The second class of agricultural labourer, however, conformed to a more disciplined daily routine. These men and women were employed in teams on larger farms that were owned by wealthy, 'improving' farmers who had developed a greater sense of time-thrift.[34] In the second half of the nineteenth century horsemen were expected to work from 4.45 a.m. to 8.00 p.m., with two hours off for meals, while cattlemen were required to labour from 5.30 a.m. until 8.00 p.m. each evening.[35] As a result these men and women separated their work and leisure time more exactly.[36] Moreover, during the summer extra help was required to cut and dry the peat.[37] The busy, tireless industry of the farming community often continued until the end of September, which the *Farmer's and Grazier's Calendar* 'considered the harvest month'. During this period it encouraged farmers to 'engage plenty of assisting hands for this important season'.[38] Nevertheless, there were two basic patterns of farm work during this period. The lives of the small-holding farmers followed an undisciplined, rhythmic routine, while the agricultural employee had more definite patterns of labour.

Their way of life meant that a serious distinction between 'work' and 'rest' did not arise amongst the self-employed farmers. Rather, the two activities merged in an indistinguishable manner as families laboured together in their fields and yards. Thus a large proportion of the fermfolk did not consider time as a vacuum that was filled either with work or play, for they considered both as inextricably bound together.[39] It appears from anecdotal testimony, however, that farm employees had a more distinct appreciation of their free time, which many of them spent visiting one another. Regularly, many of them would spend the evening drinking or indulging in fornication. For example, the Horseman's Wood was a local fraternity that attracted a large number of young ploughmen. This organization was frequently reported to occupy the free time of many farm workers with endless

33 Thompson, 'Time, work-discipline', p. 60.

34 Ibid., pp. 61, 77.

35 I. Carter, *Farmlife in North East Scotland* (Edinburgh, 1979), p. 112.

36 Thompson, 'Time, work-discipline', pp. 61, 77.

37 M. Gray, 'North east agriculture and the labour force, 1790–1875', in A. A. MacLaren, ed., *Social Class in Scotland: Past and Present* (Edinburgh, 1976), p. 88.

38 *Aberdeen Almanac 1860*, p. 12.

39 Thompson, 'Time, work-discipline', p. 61.

evenings of drinking.[40] Nevertheless, most farming people did not enjoy exact periods of rest, and thus many of them did not value leisure time spent in recreational activities.

It is significant then, that the 1859 revival followed an annual cycle within the farming communities over the course of three years. Each year there was a regular rhythm of spiritual fervour followed by decline. The period of intense religious activity began each year towards the end of spring and lasted until the beginning of October. During these months there were scores of open-air rallies, many of which were held on Sunday evenings in fields close to the local churches.[41] Also, there were countless midweek services conducted in village and town squares. At New Pitsligo, for example, a series of meetings was led by two Free Church ministers, whose words, it was reported, were 'listened to reverently by large numbers, many of whom, on week nights, are to be seen anxiously listening in their working clothes'.[42] What is notable is that the revival flourished in these communities during their busiest period of the year. It appears the religious fervour may have been imported by the influx of additional labourers who swelled the agricultural communities during these months. However, there were two other principal factors that serve to explain why this movement affected these people at this particular time.

Firstly, the leaders of the religious movement targeted the principal holidays in the agricultural calendar. The biannual feeing markets, at which labourers were hired on six-month contracts, were great farming public festivals which attracted enormous crowds of people.[43] Regularly, they were frowned upon on account of 'the very serious moral mischiefs and dangers' that accompanied them.[44] Nevertheless, the revivalists grasped these occasions and used them for their own purposes. Donaldson Rose, the Free Church minister of Kinnethmont, described his experience at the Huntly feeing market in 1859 as 'one of the most remarkable days in my life – perhaps one of the most remarkable days I will ever see in this world'.[45] He

[40] Carter, *Farmlife*, p. 154.

[41] *Aberdeen Free Press*, 12 Oct. 1860, p. 6.

[42] *Banffshire Journal*, 21 June 1859, p. 6.

[43] W. Alexander (ed. I. Carter), *Rural Life in Victorian Aberdeenshire* (Edinburgh, 1992), p. 50.

[44] *Aberdeen Free Press*, 20 May 1859, p. 4.

[45] *A Report of a Conference on the State of Religion and Public Meeting, held in the Free Church, Huntly, January 5, 1860* (Aberdeen, 1860), p. 21.

reported how he saw 'old men, and young lads, and intelligent tradesmen – all assembled together, and the room crowded over and over again by the anxious, many of whom had been arrested in the market . . . those solemn meetings and solemn dealings will never be forgotten.'[46] Other rural ministers reported similar experiences as the religious movement thrived during these occasions. The successful targeting of these events demonstrates why the revival affected these communities during the summer, and how its appearance was influenced by these agricultural holidays.

More importantly, the cyclical nature of the agricultural revival can be explained by the traditional, rural communion season. These holy events acted as the catalyst to this movement and were the means by which it was sustained. They were a week-long series of religious services that were held, usually twice a year during spring and summer, and which culminated in the celebration of the sacrament of the Lord's Supper on a Sunday. Often these periods became particularly sacred moments in the lives of these communities. In 1859 they were charged with particular spiritual anticipation and excitement. Robert Reid, the Free Church minister at Banchory, recounted how the revival had begun in his parish 'the week after the Spring Communion, on the first Sabbath of May, which not a few had felt to be a very solemn season to their souls'.[47] Alexander Reid, the Free Church minister at Portsoy, described how the revival had begun to affect his congregation following a summer communion season.[48] In addition David Henry, the Free Church minister at New Marnoch, recalled 'in noticing any special means adopted, we may mention that, previous to the Communion last summer, a course of meetings was held for conference and prayer. . . . The effect, by the blessing of God, was an awakened attention to divine things.'[49] These great religious festivals became hugely popular events in Aberdeenshire between 1859 and 1862 as the summer months became again a 'holy season' and a 'time for the harvest of souls'.[50] The communion seasons, which were knitted into the annual rhythms of planting and harvest, had the most profound

[46] Ibid., p. 21.
[47] Ibid., p. 7.
[48] Ibid., p. 11.
[49] Ibid., p. 32.
[50] Schmidt, *Holy Fairs*, pp. 29, 215.

influence on the timing and manner of the 1859 revival in rural Aberdeenshire.

* * *

The final group affected (somewhat belatedly) by the '1859 revival' was those engaged in the fishing industry, inhabitants of the Moray Firth villages. Two distinct fishing industries operated here around the middle of the nineteenth century. The first involved men working in small boats in teams of four and lasted from September to May. This inshore fishing for haddock and cod suited the smaller villages which lacked harbours, because only lighter boats, which could be hauled over the beaches, were used. As a result fishermen rarely sailed more than an hour's journey from their village and returned home each night.[51] The herring industry constituted the second commercial enterprise of the same fishermen. It required twenty-five-foot boats that were manned by six men. Consequently, such fishing was carried out from the larger towns that had harbours which allowed these boats to land. Thus, most of the fisherfolk, including wives and children, deserted their village homes, from June to August, and spent the summer living in the adjacent ports of Peterhead and Fraserburgh.[52] Life was arduous for the wives and children who lived in these villages. Each day, between September and May, the women prepared the baits on up to 500 hooks. In addition, they dried the fish and then walked long distances selling them to the neighbouring agricultural communities.[53] During the summer they cured the herring and prepared them for the markets. Essentially, however, the daily tasks of the fishing people were irregular because they followed the rhythms of the tides of the sea. Consequently the fisherfolk disregarded 'clock time' and followed a more flexible pattern of work.[54]

Nevertheless, during the busy period of the herring season, between June and September, the fishermen had little time to devote to social activities. John McGibbon, a local writer in the last quarter of the nineteenth century, observed how 'fishermen have to be content with very few holidays during the [herring] fishing season . . . even funerals

[51] J. S. Smith and D. Stevenson, eds, *Fermfolk and Fisherfolk: Rural Life in Northern Scotland in the Eighteenth and Nineteenth Centuries* (Aberdeen, 1989), p. 38.

[52] M. Gray, *The Fishing Industries of Scotland, 1790–1914: A Study in Regional Adaption* (Oxford, 1978), p. 48.

[53] Ibid., p. 24.

[54] Thompson, 'Time, work-discipline', p. 59.

are so arranged as to take up as little time as possible, and are usually over in time to allow the men to sail to the fishing grounds, and shoot their nets, that night.'[55] However, it appears the fisherfolk had more time to relax during the shorter days of winter when they were at home and when the demands of work were less onerous. In the winter it was anticipated that 'there will be no regular work for weeks. The boats and gear will be overhauled, and nets spread out to air and dry in the fields. . . . It will be a month of weddings. The lights will go out late, in some cases not till morning . . . they do not get up early in these days of semi-holiday.'[56] The leisure patterns of the fishing villages were closely related to the annual cycle of their working routines. There was little time to relax at the height of the herring season in the summer, while during the winter the village fishermen could afford to spend more time relaxing at home.

The timing and the brief, unplanned nature of the Moray Firth revival demonstrates clearly how it was influenced by the work and rest habits of the fishing people. It began in Portknockie on 28 January 1860 and subsequently affected every fishing village and town between Burghead and Gardenstown within the following few weeks. The revival brought life in these villages to a complete standstill. Work was temporarily suspended as people spent whole days at religious meetings.[57] At Banff it was reported how 'religion has become the talk of the town, the theme of remarks in the place of business as well as in the place of prayer . . . the current of men's thoughts seems to be turned altogether in the direction of religion.'[58] At Portessie it was recorded that 'many have scarcely taken food for some days', such was the excitement generated by this movement.[59] Moreover, the revival appeared in an unpremeditated manner. Services were not planned and targeted for particular times. On the contrary, they took place whenever and wherever the people gathered together. The peculiar nature of this movement was only possible within a community where people could afford to suspend their labours indefinitely and devote their entire attention towards religious concerns. Yet it had waned by the end of April 1860. The demise of the movement was precipitated by the demands of the busy herring season when the people had to

55 J. McGibbon, *The Fisherfolk of Buchan* (Edinburgh, n.d.), p. 141.
56 J. Leatham, *Fisherfolk of the North-East* (Turiff, 1930), p. 7.
57 *Aberdeen Free Press*, 24 Feb. 1860, p. 6.
58 Ibid., 20 April 1860, p. 7.
59 Ibid., 24 Feb. 1860, p. 6.

emigrate from their close-knit villages into the larger, heterogeneous fishing towns. Wholehearted attention towards religious matters was forced to recede in order to allow the annual rhythms of life to proceed. Nevertheless, it is clear that the fervency and brevity of the fisherfolk's revival was directly affected by the nature of their winter work habits.

Perhaps the principal feature of the fisherfolk's religious movement was the evening revival service which usually began around 7.00 p.m. and continued throughout the night. John Stark, the biographer of the United Presbyterian minister John Murker, who led the revival in Banff, wrote, 'on the night between Saturday the 10th and Sabbath the 11th March, the meeting lasted from seven in the evening till about six of the following morning.'[60] Moreover, John McGibbon described how James Turner, a celebrated Methodist evangelist, conducted gatherings in his cooperage. He recalled how 'the meeting would begin as soon as the coopers left off their barrel making for the day, and would last long into the night, and often the coopers would have to wait in the early mornings until the prayer meeting broke up and the fishermen went off to their homes.'[61] In addition, John Forrester, a United Presbyterian minister, complained of the 'utter impossibility [that] exists of getting the people to retire. In many instances, the benediction has been pronounced again and again, and the people peremptorily told to withdraw, but, in spite of all this, they would sit still, . . . anxious to have their burdened souls lightened.'[62] The spontaneous, undisciplined nature of these all-night meetings, upon which the fishing revival flourished, prospered among these people because they occurred during a holiday period when the fisherfolk could afford to suspend work and devote all their time and energy to religious matters. Such protracted meetings, the chief characteristic of the fishing revival, were undoubtedly fashioned by the work and rest patterns of these communities.

* * *

It is clear that the timing and manner of the 1859 revival was significantly determined by the separate labour and leisure patterns of the these three different communities in Aberdeenshire. Firstly, the

[60] J. Stark, *John Murker* (Banff, 1887), p. 165.
[61] McGibbon, *Fisherfolk*, p. 76.
[62] *Banffshire Journal*, 27 March 1860, p. 5.

organizers of the city revival planned its evangelistic meetings very carefully. They paid careful attention to the social lives of those they hoped to reach, organizing services around factory hours in an attempt to compete against the other social attractions of the city. The rural revival was a semi-planned religious movement. The targeting of the feeing markets by its leaders reveals how they sought to take advantage of the local holidays when people were free to attend to religious matters. Yet the spiritual potency of the traditional communion season, within which the strength of the rural revival lay, demonstrates how the older religious habits of the fermfolk had the most important influence upon the timing of the movement. By contrast, the Moray Firth revival was a wholly spontaneous, unplanned religious awakening. During the winter the fisherfolk could afford to give undivided attention to religious matters. Consequently, the revival did not need to be planned or accommodated around disciplined working hours, nor did it have to compete against rival leisure activities. Accordingly, each manifestation of this religious movement was substantially affected by the work and rest patterns of the people amongst whom it was experienced.

THE SABBATH QUESTION IN VICTORIAN SCOTLAND IN CONTEXT

by †DOUGLAS M. MURRAY

THE question of the observance of the Sabbath as a day of rest arose most notably in Scotland during the Victorian period over the running of Sunday passenger trains. In the 1840s Sabbatarians were successful in stopping a passenger service between Edinburgh and Glasgow, but failed to prevent the introduction of a similar service in 1865.[1] The controversy which was aroused over this issue in the 1860s has been called the 'Sabbath War' and it centred round Norman MacLeod, the celebrated minister of the Barony Church in Glasgow and one of Queen Victoria's favourite preachers.

The Glasgow presbytery of the Church of Scotland had issued a pastoral letter in November 1865 against the running of Sunday trains and ordered it to be read out from all pulpits. MacLeod read the letter but then told his congregation why he disagreed with it.[2] At the subsequent meeting of the presbytery, MacLeod attacked what he considered to be a Pharisaical attitude to the keeping of the Lord's Day. He distinguished between the Sabbath as referred to in the fourth of the Ten Commandments, and the Lord's Day as found in the New Testament.[3] The fourth commandment, he said, no longer had authority in the Church of Christ.[4] He thought that the Decalogue, in the sense of a binding rule, had been 'abrogated by being nailed to Christ's cross, with the whole Mosaic economy, and buried in the grave with Jesus'.[5] The Sabbath 'ceased to exist as a law to Christians, on the morning when Christ rose from the dead'.[6] MacLeod, however, still wished Sunday to be observed in a distinctive way as a holy day, a day of rest and worship for Christians.[7]

[1] C. J. A. Robertson, 'Early Scottish railways and the observance of the sabbath', *ScHR*, 57 (1978), pp. 143–67; R. Douglas Brackenridge, 'The "Sabbath War" of 1865–66: the shaking of the foundations', *Records of the Scottish Church History Society*, 16 (1966–8), pp. 23–34.

[2] Donald MacLeod, *Memoir of Norman MacLeod, D.D.*, 2 vols (London, 1876), 2: 189–90.

[3] Norman MacLeod, *The Lord's Day: Substance of a Speech Delivered at a Meeting of the Presbytery of Glasgow, on Thursday, 16th November, 1865* (Glasgow, 1865), p. 9.

[4] Ibid., p. 18.

[5] Ibid., pp. 19–20.

[6] Ibid., p. 36.

[7] Ibid., pp. 38–9.

MacLeod's positive view of the keeping of the Lord's Day was lost sight of in the ensuing controversy carried on in pamphlets and in the press. Some of his fellow ministers passed him in the street, while one even hissed at him.[8] One observer thought that, since MacLeod had questioned the validity of the Ten Commandments, the easiest answer to Norman was to go into his house and steal his silver spoons.[9] This remark was a neat way of referring to the issue and at the same time drawing attention to the minister's love of the good things of life. MacLeod was only admonished by the presbytery, and celebrated suitably with champagne afterwards. Although he feared that his attitude might be challenged at the subsequent meeting of the General Assembly, no one raised the issue. In the Free Church, too, the more liberal Sabbatarian views of Walter C. Smith, minister of the Tron Church in Glasgow, simply resulted in his admonition by the Assembly in 1867, much to the dismay of more conservative opinion.[10] In addition, both ministers went on to be elected as moderators of the General Assemblies of their respective churches, MacLeod in 1869 and Smith in 1893.

In seeking to understand the nature of this controversy, it is important to see the Sabbath question in context. In the first place the Scottish debate took place in relation to the parallel discussion south of the border. In Scotland, as in England, the concern over the issue of Sabbath observance had arisen as a result of the Evangelical revival. Before this period Evangelicals were not necessarily strict in their observance of the Sabbath. For example Sir Henry Moncrieff, the aristocratic cleric and leader of the Evangelical party in the Kirk, entertained his friends after family prayers on a Sunday evening to 'roasted hens, a goblet of wine, and wholesome talk'.[11] It was the Evangelical revival of the early nineteenth century which turned the Sabbath into 'the stern thing it later became'.[12] A new stridency and a more uncompromising tone entered the debate.[13] Many Evangelicals left the Church of Scotland at the Disruption in 1843, under the

[8] MacLeod, *Memoir of Norman MacLeod*, 2: 190.

[9] Andrew L. Drummond and James Bulloch, *The Church in Victorian Scotland 1843–1874* (Edinburgh, 1975), p. 309.

[10] J. R. Fleming, *A History of the Church in Scotland 1843–1874* (Edinburgh, 1927), pp. 218–20; *Proceedings of the Free Church General Assembly, 1864–68* (Edinburgh, 1868), pp. 349–51.

[11] Henry Grey Graham, *The Social Life of Scotland in the Eighteenth Century*, 4th edn (London, 1937), p. 365.

[12] T. C. Smout, *A Century of the Scottish People 1830–1950* (London, 1986), p. 196.

[13] John Wigley, *The Rise and Fall of the Victorian Sunday* (Manchester, 1980), p. 30.

leadership of Thomas Chalmers, to form the Free Church. It is significant that the first Assembly of that Church held a debate on the question of Sunday trains.[14] One of the most active campaigners on this issue at the national level was Sir Andrew Agnew, who became the member of Parliament for Wigtonshire in 1830, and was an elder of the Free Church.[15]

Those who wished to take a more liberal view were also influenced by the debate in England. In the published version of his speech to the presbytery of Glasgow, Norman MacLeod acknowledged his indebtedness to the Bampton Lectures of 1860 by John Augustus Hessey, headmaster of Merchant Taylors' School, entitled *Sunday, its Origins, History, and Present Obligations*.[16] It has been said that this book 'did more than any previous publication in English to shake the Sabbatarian theory, while the moderation of the author and his earnest plea for the Christian Sunday as a divine institution, made a real impression on the unbiased religious mind'.[17] Hessey spoke of the confusion of thought which resulted in the Lord's Day being regarded as identical with, instead of at the most analogous to, the Sabbath of the fourth commandment.[18] He pointed out that a legalistic interpretation of Sabbath observance in the Church developed during the medieval period, was rejected by the Reformers, but became more prominent as a result of the influence of Puritanism in the seventeenth century. Hessey made several references to the situation in Scotland, pointing out that Knox, like Calvin, had repudiated a strict Sabbatarian position, although he was supposed, incorrectly, to have introduced this view into Scotland.[19] It is interesting to note that MacLeod's opponents in the presbytery debate recognized that the Reformers gave an 'uncertain sound' on this subject, and they thought that the Roman Catholic Church had taken a more biblical view.[20] Hessey favoured the keeping of Sunday as a day of rest, but said that 'sobriety is not sadness, still less is it abstinence and mortification'.[21]

[14] Drummond and Bulloch, *Church in Victorian Scotland*, p. 22.

[15] Wigley, *Rise and Fall of the Victorian Sunday*, pp. 35–42.

[16] Macleod, *The Lord's Day*, p. 6; John Augustus Hessey, *Sunday, its Origins, History, and Present Obligations*, 3rd edn (London, 1866).

[17] Fleming, *History of the Church in Scotland*, p. 213.

[18] Hessey, *Sunday*, p. 3.

[19] Ibid., p. 15.

[20] *The Sabbath. Report of the Proceedings of the Established Church Presbytery of Glasgow, November 16, 1865* (Glasgow, 1865), pp. 26, 75.

[21] Hessey, *Sunday*, p. 231.

He opposed the legalizing of Sunday trading for profit, but allowed that trains should run, provided the employees were assured of adequate periods of rest. He also thought that parks and other open spaces should be made freely available to the public.[22] He considered, however, that the whole area was one in which it was difficult to be consistent. What was important was that Sunday be seen as the Lord's Day and not as the Sabbath.

The second context in which the Sabbath question should be seen is as part of the general movement of change in the Victorian Kirk. A more liberal view of the Sabbath was held by those who had become dissatisfied with the theology of the Westminster Confession of Faith. Those Evangelicals who held a traditional view, on the other hand, could point to the Confession as supporting their position. The Confession was the subordinate standard of the Kirk in matters of doctrine and was enshrined as such in Acts of Parliament.[23] It had also been adopted enthusiastically by the Free Church. According to the Confession, the Sabbath of the Old Testament had been changed into the Lord's Day as the Christian Sabbath.[24] It spoke of it as a day of holy rest, not only from work, but also from 'worldly employments and recreations'. The whole time should be taken up in the public and private exercise of worship and in duties of necessity and mercy. Robert Jamieson, minister of St Paul's Church and the chief spokesman of the presbytery of Glasgow's position, pointed out that those who challenged the traditional view had to recognize that they were also challenging the standpoint of the Church's doctrinal standard.[25]

MacLeod realized the significance of the stance which he had taken. He said at the time:

> The smaller question is fast merging into the higher one, of whether we are to gain a larger measure of ministerial liberty in interpreting those points in our Confession which do not touch the essentials of the Christian faith. If the Assembly passes without my being libelled, I shall have gained for the Established Church, and at the risk of my ecclesiastical life, freedom in alliance with law, and for this I shall thank God. But should they drive me out,

[22] Hessey, *Sunday*, pp. 237–9.

[23] Douglas M. Murray, 'Theological identity in a pluralist age: the future of the Church's Confessional Standards', *Theology in Scotland*, Occasional Paper 2 (1977), pp. 42–3.

[24] *Westminster Confession of Faith* (Edinburgh, 1880), XXI, pp. 76–7.

[25] *The Sabbath*, pp. 10, 82.

> that day will see national evangelical liberty driven out for many a day from the dear old Church.[26]

It should be noted that MacLeod was deeply influenced by the theology of his cousin, John McLeod Campbell, who was deposed from the ministry of the Church of Scotland in 1831 for departing from the teaching of the Westminster Confession.[27]

Campbell taught a doctrine of universal atonement and stressed the importance of the relation between the incarnation and the atonement. As a result of the publicity surrounding his case, and the influence of his later book, *The Nature of the Atonement*,[28] Campbell 'set going a ferment of dissatisfaction with the stereotyped theology associated with the inflexibilities of old style Calvinism'.[29] Norman MacLeod was supported by others who wished to change the Kirk's relationship to its Confession of Faith. Principal John Tulloch of St Mary's College, St Andrews, expressed general agreement with MacLeod's position in an address which he gave on the place of the Westminster Confession.[30] Tulloch pointed out the historical circumstances in which the Confession had been written. It was, he said, 'the manifesto of a great religious party' and, as with all such doctrinal statements, was not to be taken as an absolute expression of Christian truth.[31]

The connection between the Sabbath controversy and the confessional issue was identified by James MacGregor, minister of the Free High Church in Paisley. He was the author of *The Sabbath Question: Historical, Scriptural and Practical* (Edinburgh, 1866), the most substantial work to be written against MacLeod's arguments from the traditional point of view. He saw the attack on the Sabbath as the first manoeuvre in a campaign against the Church's basic principles.[32] MacGregor pointed out that the Westminster Confession declared 'the morality and permanent obligation of the whole Ten Commandments of the Decalogue', as clearly as it declared 'the Trinity of persons in the

26 MacLeod, *Memoir of Norman MacLeod*, 2: 191.

27 Peter L. M. Hillis, 'Towards a new social theology: the contribution of Norman MacLeod', *Records of the Scottish Church History Society*, 24 (1990–2), p. 266.

28 John McLeod Campbell, *The Nature of the Atonement*, with a new introduction by James B. Torrance (Edinburgh, 1996).

29 John McIntyre, *Prophet of Penitence: Our Contemporary Ancestor* (Edinburgh, 1972), p. 4.

30 Margaret Oliphant, *A Memoir of the Life of John Tulloch, D.D., LL.D.*, 2nd edn (Edinburgh and London, 1888), p. 220.

31 Ibid., p. 222.

32 James MacGregor, *The Sabbath Question: Historical, Scriptural and Practical* (Edinburgh, 1866), p. 18.

Godhead, or the Incarnation of God's Word, or the Atonement by His death'.[33] He viewed the antiSabbatarians as part of a general movement to undermine the Christian faith which was epitomized by the writings of Strauss and Rénan on the Continent, and by the publication of *Essays and Reviews* in England. MacGregor was right to draw attention to the influence of biblical criticism in the controversy since scholars had drawn a clear distinction between the Jewish Sabbath and the Lord's Day. Scotland's most controversial biblical scholar, William Robertson Smith of the Aberdeen Free Church College, changed his view of the Sabbath as he developed his critical work on the Bible. As a student he had criticized his father, who was a minister of the Free Church, for sending him letters which arrived on the Sabbath, and he agonized over whether or not to take a walk on a Sunday afternoon.[34] But he came to agree with the view of Hessey that the Lord's Day and the Sabbath were two separate institutions, and in later years he wrote letters and enjoyed a quiet afternoon stroll on Sundays.[35]

For MacLeod the Sabbath question was also closely connected to the mission of the Church in society. In his speech before the presbytery he had spoken of the way in which the Church should put forward its positive view of Sunday as the Lord's Day. Rather than insisting that the law should support a strict Sabbatarianism, the Church should seek to convince people about the truth of Christ's teaching. Thus for MacLeod evangelism was the issue rather than legislation.[36] It would be far better if people wished to observe the Lord's Day voluntarily, and as a result of coming to faith in Christ. MacLeod thought that the Church of Scotland had failed the poorer sections of the population in the task of home mission. New churches had been built in Glasgow, for example, but only two of them were in the east end of the city where the need was greatest.[37] If this challenge was not met then, said MacLeod to his brethren, 'all we talk about will pass, as it ought to do, as mere talk, as an easy orthodox way of advocating the Sabbath as a doctrine, but not the difficult way of getting it kept as a holy duty and blessed privilege.'[38]

[33] MacGregor, *Sabbath Question*, p. 39.

[34] John Sutherland Black and George Chrystal, *The Life of William Robertson Smith* (London, 1912), p. 86.

[35] R. Douglas Brackenridge, 'Sunday Observance in Scotland, 1689–1900' (University of Glasgow, Ph.D. thesis, 1962), p. 201.

[36] MacLeod, *The Lord's Day*, pp. 42–3.

[37] Ibid., p. 44.

[38] Ibid.

MacLeod could speak on this subject with authority because some years before he had begun evening services in the Barony Church for working people.[39] As a result of this venture a separate congregation, the Barony Mission Church, was founded in 1855.

The Sabbath issue was also linked, in MacLeod's view, to the movement for liturgical renewal in the Kirk. If more people were to be persuaded to spend the day in worship rather than in other pursuits, the Church would have to examine its liturgical practices and seek to make its services more attractive.[40] MacLeod's attitude to the Sabbath was not new, since a similar position had been taken previously at the General Assembly by those who were also involved in the revival of worship. In 1847 Robert Lee, minister of Greyfriars in Edinburgh, had spoken in similar terms to those later used by MacLeod. He referred to the Pharisaical attitude of those who wished to prevent passenger trains running on a Sunday.[41] Lee was the pioneer of change in the worship of the Kirk, and his lead was followed by the Church Service Society which was founded in 1865, the year in which the 'Sabbath War' began.[42] MacLeod had spoken out at the Assembly in favour of Lee's innovations and was one of the original members of the Society.[43] In 1863 William Milligan and Robert Story, two prominent members of the Society,[44] had spoken in favour of the opening of the Botanic Gardens in Edinburgh on Sundays.[45] Story, who later became principal of the University of Glasgow, spoke on this issue at a Church Congress held at Aberdeen. He answered the objection that the opening of public parks and galleries on Sundays would mean additional work for others. He said that 'it would not entail a quarter of the amount exacted every Sunday from the great army of beadles, door-keepers, and organists, whose labour is considered essential to the proper assembling of ourselves together.'[46] He also thought that there were many people who would

[39] Hillis, 'Towards a new social theology', pp. 281–2.

[40] MacLeod, *The Lord's Day*, p. 47.

[41] Robert Herbert Story, *Life and Remains of Robert Lee, D.D.*, 2 vols (London, 1870), 1: 128–30.

[42] Douglas M. Murray, 'Disruption to Union', in Duncan B. Forrester and Douglas M. Murray, eds, *Studies in the History of Worship in Scotland*, 2nd edn (Edinburgh, 1996), pp. 91–4.

[43] MacLeod, *Memoir of Norman MacLeod*, 2: 1813.

[44] Murray, 'Disruption to Union', pp. 95–6.

[45] *Memoir of Robert Herbert Story D.D., LL.D., by his Daughters* (Glasgow, 1909), p. 77.

[46] Ibid., p. 339.

be willing to perform this service on Sundays, including those who were unemployed for the rest of the week.

William Milligan, professor of biblical criticism at Aberdeen, was the author of a book entitled *The Decalogue and the Lord's Day*, published in 1866.[47] Milligan argued for both continuity and discontinuity between the old and new covenants. Christ had fulfilled the law and hence the absolute requirement of the fourth commandment had to go. Even those who argued for a strict observance had to reinterpret the Decalogue, since it was the first, and not the seventh, day which they now wished to observe. Yet the Lord's Day should still be kept, he said, only without the scruples by which 'freedom and joyfulness are limited or destroyed'.[48] A more spiritual rather than a less spiritual Sunday observance was called for, one which was free from legalism. Milligan would later become the first president of the Scottish Church Society, the expression of the Scoto-Catholic movement in the Kirk. The Society favoured a credal, rather than a confessional doctrinal statement, and was in favour of a weekly celebration of the Lord's Supper.[49] James Cooper, who had studied under Milligan at Aberdeen, and was the secretary of the Society, thought that Scotland would oscillate between an 'ultraJudaic Puritanism' and an 'irreligious license' about Sunday until the Church returned to the true celebration of the resurrection of Jesus, which was made in the celebration of the Lord's Supper on the Lord's Day.[50]

The renewal in public worship, along with the movement away from the doctrines of the Westminster Confession, the increasing impact of biblical criticism, and a new concern for evangelism, played an important role in the acceptance of a more liberal view of Sabbath observance. As MacLeod said to the presbytery of Glasgow, the Sabbath question went deeper than they might choose to think.[51] It was but one area in which the Church in Scotland experienced radical change during the Victorian period.[52] In addition those who advocated a more

[47] William Milligan, *The Decalogue and the Lord's Day, with a Chapter on Confessions of Faith* (Edinburgh, 1866).

[48] Ibid., p. 45.

[49] Murray, 'Disruption to Union', pp. 95–6.

[50] James Cooper, *The Lord's Day: its Divine Sanction; and how to Sanctify It* (Aberdeen, 1898), p. 14.

[51] MacLeod, *The Lord's Day*, p. 47.

[52] A. C. Cheyne, *The Transforming of the Kirk: Victorian Scotland's Religious Revolution* (Edinburgh, 1983), p. 162.

liberal view of the Sabbath were also at the forefront of reform in other aspects of the life of the Kirk.

It would be a mistake, however, to think that Sabbath observance was uniform during the nineteenth century. The popular picture of Victorian Scotland as a church-going, Bible-reading nation, whose Calvinist citizens abstained from alcohol and observed the Sabbath in a strict fashion, was true of only a minority of the population. Scotland in the mid-nineteenth century was in general terms a land of two nations, the middle classes who reaped the rewards of the new industrial prosperity, and the working classes who shared little of the growing national wealth.[53] The second group was the larger and the Presbyterian Churches, as MacLeod had pointed out, could not claim to have had much impact on this section of the population.[54] A stricter observance of the Sabbath was carried out in the main by the religious middle classes in the towns and cities and, as the century progressed, by those in the highlands who were influenced by the Evangelical revival and supported the Free Church.[55] Thus the third context in which the issue should be seen is the change from a predominantly agricultural to an industrial community and the variety of Sabbath observance which resulted from that change.

It was not the case, for example, that no passenger trains ran on a Sunday before the mid-1860s. One German traveller, Theodore Fontane, found this to be true during a visit to Scotland in 1858. He described the problems of the Sabbath in this way:

> A Sunday in Scotland is for the traveller like a thunderstorm at a picnic. You get wet, you can't go on, and all your good humour vanishes. We had seen all the sights of Stirling and were horrified at the thought that for the next twenty-four hours we should have nothing but an old copy of *The Times* and a silent table d'hote.[56]

But he was not, after all, stranded in Stirling. He was able to catch an early morning train to Perth. The train had started its journey in

53 Donald C. Smith, *Passive Obedience and Prophetic Protest, Social Criticism in the Scottish Church 1830–1945* (New York, 1987), p. 190.

54 Drummond and Bulloch, *Church in Victorian Scotland*, p. 2.

55 Brackenridge, 'Sunday Observance', p. 251. Cf. Smout, *Century of the Scottish People*, p. 183.

56 Theodore Fontane, *Across the Tweed: Notes on Travel in Scotland, 1858* (London, 1965), p. 115. I am grateful to Dr Alastair J. Durie of the University of Glasgow for this reference.

London the evening before and was able to continue on its way in Scotland on the Sabbath. Fontane explained the situation in this way:

> This business of an early train which thus desecrates the Sunday is very like that of champagne on the table of a Turk – it passes under another name. This Sunday train is really a Saturday evening train. The whole thing works as follows. The Great Northern Railway, which traverses England and Scotland from head to foot, runs a daily express which leaves London in the evening; now if a traveller boards it in London on a Saturday evening with the intention of going to Perth and Aberdeen *via* Edinburgh, this is entirely in accordance with prevailing law and custom; even the church-mindedness of a Scot can hardly object to it. After all, it isn't the traveller's fault that the express doesn't go faster than it actually does, and consequently the Saturday has to borrow a bit of Sunday. It is only the act of making use of this train after it has actually touched Scottish soil that is frowned upon, as it is natural enough that it should be; but there is no limit to the license accorded to foreigners.[57]

And it was not only some passenger trains which ran on the Sabbath; goods trains had been running for some years, and the mail was carried by train and was collected and delivered on Sundays.[58] In addition, ships entered and left Scottish ports, and ferries operated.[59] Sunday pleasure boats became popular because, following the passing of the Forbes MacKenzie Act in 1853, which closed public houses on a Sunday, it was still possible to purchase alcohol if one was a *bona fide* traveller.[60] Trips 'doon the water' on the Clyde remained common until an Act was passed in 1882 outlawing the sale of drink on boats on Sundays as well.[61] In Glaswegian patois to this day, to be 'steaming' is to be intoxicated![62]

Why was the introduction of a regular passenger train service such an important issue for Sabbatarians when there were many other breaches of the Sabbath? One reason was that the railways were run by

57 Fontane, *Across the Tweed*, p. 115.

58 Brackenridge, 'Sunday Observance', pp. 166–9, 189, 196.

59 Ibid., pp. 163–4.

60 Alastair J. Durie, 'The development of Scottish coastal resorts in the central lowlands, *c.* 1770–1880: from Gulf Stream to Golf Stream', *The Local Historian*, 24 (1994), p. 211.

61 Smout, *Century of the Scottish People*, p. 157.

62 Durie, 'Development of Scottish coastal resorts', p. 211.

public companies in which Sabbatarians could exercise pressure, by seeking to influence the shareholders, and by purchasing shares themselves.[63] The steamboats were owned by private companies and were less open to such pressure. It may be, too, that as one pamphlet claimed, the Churches depended for financial support on the donations of the shipowners.[64] Not all forms of Sunday travel were opposed in any case. It was admitted that some traffic was permissible, such as the journey of necessity or mercy. The most celebrated incident which highlighted this type of journey involved the Duchess of Sutherland in 1849. She was refused a seat on the Sunday mail train in order to visit her dying father, but he had died by the time she arrived on the Monday.[65]

For James MacGregor it was the public nature of the running of passenger trains on a Sunday which was the most objectionable factor. The operation of Sunday trains was a case of 'ordinary, systematic, open, and flagrant secular traffic' on the Lord's Day. He put his concern in this way:

> There may be Sabbath desecration which is not traffic; for example in the case of needless Sabbath walking; or Sabbath riding in one's carriage. There may be Sabbath traffic which is not ordinary or systematic, but only incidental and extraordinary; for example, when a car or a train is hired for an emergency of real or alleged necessity or mercy. And there may be ordinary systematic Sabbath traffic which is not open and flagrant but is carried on privately, removed from the public view. But the Sabbath railway business is . . . a traffic which, from its very nature, is always and necessarily open and flagrant, in full view of nation and Church.[66]

There was an important distinction, in his view, between private and public transport. No general rule could be applied to the question of taking a cab or using a private carriage on a Sunday. In relation to these matters he did not think that the apostolic principle applied very clearly or strongly. But it did apply most certainly in the case of buses, steamers, and trains which carried 'an ordinary systematic traffic on the Lord's Day'.[67] In making this distinction MacGregor laid himself open

[63] Robertson, 'Early Scottish railways', pp. 149–50.
[64] Ibid., p. 146.
[65] Ibid.
[66] MacGregor, *Sabbath Question*, p. 300.
[67] Ibid., pp. 352–3.

to the charge, which had been made by Robert Lee, of denying the public the right to choose for themselves whether or not they travelled on a Sunday.[68] Those who did not possess private means of transport were being denied the use of the only form of transport available to them.[69]

Work on a Sunday which was considered necessary was not opposed, such as that of a physician, or of a clergyman. Clearly many people employed domestic servants for whom the Sabbath was like any other day, except that they would be expected to attend church in addition to carrying out their normal duties. Factories, such as those involving iron and chemical processes, could not easily close down for one day. In 1875 the Free Church synod of Glasgow and Ayr reported that of the 150 iron works in Scotland, 125 remained in continuous operation.[70] Later in the century the leaders of the Free Church were embarrassed by Keir Hardie's attack on one of their most prominent members, Lord Overtoun. Hardie lambasted him for the poor working conditions in his chrome factory in Glasgow, including 'the hypocrisy of a self-proclaimed Sabbatarian making Sunday a day of labour'.[71] Before the end of the nineteenth century the Churches no longer opposed all commercial work on the Sabbath but tried to keep it within reasonable limits. There would inevitably be a difference of opinion, however, on what constituted those acceptable bounds. The antiSabbatarian lobby, like Hardie, were quick to point out the inconsistencies of those who upheld a strict observance. Sir Andrew Agnew was himself said to have used his own carriage on a Sunday to get to Parliament in time for a debate on one of his own Bills in favour of a strict Sabbath observance.[72] The keeping of the Sabbath, even for a strict Sabbatarian, could never be a question of black and white.

University of Glasgow

68 Story, *Robert Lee*, pp. 129–30.
69 Robertson, 'Early Scottish railways', pp. 147–8.
70 Brackenridge, 'Sunday Observance', p. 204.
71 Callum G. Brown, *Religion and Society in Scotland since 1707* (Edinburgh, 1997), p. 127.
72 Robertson, 'Early Scottish railways', p. 148.

INDUSTRIAL DAY-DREAMS: S. E. KEEBLE AND THE PLACE OF WORK AND LABOUR IN LATE VICTORIAN AND EDWARDIAN METHODISM

by TIM MACQUIBAN

DISCUSSION of the use of time in industrial Britain hardened in the nineteenth century into debates about the morality of work and its rewards, about the ethics of labour and the exploitation of the labourer, issues neglected in a Methodism dominated by the prevailing social thought of evangelicalism which persisted throughout most of the century. While much valuable work has been done recently on a re-assessment of the place of Wesleyan Methodist businessmen's influence in politics, commerce, and industry in the heyday of Victorian and Edwardian Britain,[1] not so much has been done on the attitudes to poverty and wealth, work, and wages from within the Church establishment, or investigation of how ministers were shaping or reflecting social and political attitudes. This paper seeks to identify the particular contribution of one pivotal figure, Samuel Keeble (1853–1947) whose work deserves a more detailed biography than the Wesley Historical Society lecture published in 1977.[2] His mentor, Hugh Price Hughes, a Wesleyan revivalist but less clearly a Christian socialist, created the environment in which the Wesleyan Methodist Union of Social Service (WMUSS) emerged, through which Keeble was able to channel much of his energies in the promotion of social issues, including those concerning work and labour.[3] It is their contribution that this essay seeks to highlight.

Those who emphasised the social service element of Methodism and its attitude to work of course looked to their founder, John Wesley, as the inspiration for such activity. Methodists gathering at the first Conference of the WMUSS in 1909 claimed their place in the apostolic succession 'of those Oxford men who visited the sick and

[1] Notably in David Jeremy, *Religion, Business and Wealth in Modern Britain* (London, 1998).

[2] Michael S. Edwards, *S. E. Keeble: the Rejected Prophet* (Broxton, 1977).

[3] Christopher Oldstone-Moore, *Hugh Price Hughes: Founder of a New Methodism, Conscience of a New Nonconformity* (Cardiff, 1999).

those in prison, and who preached the gospel to the poor'.[4] They were reclaiming a radical concern for social reconstruction by rediscovering Wesley who had said that 'Christianity is essentially a social religion', in defence of the poor and in attack on those who exploited them and misused wealth.[5] The later involvement of some Methodists (albeit more non-Wesleyans) in the Trade Union movement and in Chartist and radical politics was cited by them as the response of authentic 'Wesleyan' Methodism to the concerns of the urban poor and growing working class/proletariat, in the fusion of evangelical proclamation and social action, challenging the fatalism of Calvinism. The divide of religious and social ethics highlighted by Tawney in his analysis of the *Rise of Capitalism* came under close scrutiny from churchmen of the late nineteenth century onwards.[6] Nigel Scotland sees such Methodist involvement as endowing the 'labouring classes with a heightened social awareness and a strong sense of justice, manifested in the strength of themes of brotherhood, the priesthood of all believers and social justice, in an affirmation of spiritual and social equality.'[7]

* * *

From those with Wesley's radical social conscience, and under the influence of F. D. Maurice and the Christian Socialists, emerged the charismatic figure of Hugh Price Hughes who, in 1884, proclaimed: 'The great need of our time is for Christian Socialism.' Arthur Porritt called him 'The Day of Judgement in breeches' as a measure of his notoriety.[8] In 1889 he founded a new and radical work in the West London Mission, the exemplar of much subsequent Methodist social action, focusing often on the provision of work and gainful employment in wholesome activities off the streets. He thus reclaimed the cities of England as targets of a more aggressive Christian evangelism, through the creation of central halls as part of the so-called Forward Movement. A characteristic statement which epitomizes his whole approach is found in the collection of his sermons, *Social Christianity*, published in that same year, 1889: 'Christ came to save the Nation as

[4] *Social Science and Service: Report of the Oxford Conference of the WMUSS* (London, 1909).

[5] Quoted in J. Ernest Rattenbury, 'John Wesley and social service', in Samuel Keeble, ed., *The Citizen of Tomorrow* (London, 1906), p. 54.

[6] David Jeremy, *Capitalists and Christians* (Oxford, 1990), p. 57.

[7] Nigel Scotland, 'Methodism and the English Labour Movement 1800–1906', *Anvil*, 14 (1996–7), pp. 36–48.

[8] Jeremy, *Capitalists and Christians*, p. 59.

well as the Individual . . . it is an essential feature of his mission to reconstruct society on the basis of Justice and Love.'[9]

But this did not lead Hughes to espouse the political aspects of the emerging socialist movement in Britain. Through the creation of mission centres and social work agencies, with a freedom to innovate rarely allowed by the Wesleyan Methodist Conference in terms of independence and the suspension of itinerancy, the Church was challenged to divert its resources and to change radically in its approach to the cities.[10] His slogan was 'regenerate, regenerate, regenerate', both spiritually and materially, in a crusade of social and moral purity which did not hesitate to use every organ of government, local and national, in support of the so-called 'Nonconformist Conscience'. This was a natural response to the publication of Andrew Mearns's book *The Bitter Cry of Outcast London* (1883) which awakened the nation's conscience. J. E. Rattenbury later assessed Hughes as 'primarily a Methodist evangelist with the old message of salvation for sinful men', whose Forward Movement 'shook Methodism out of her self-complacency and bade her look out on the heathen masses'. Rattenbury saw it as the last great attack made on pagan England, a rebuke to the earlier torpidity of a 'red and green baize pews . . . and mahogany pulpit' type of religion which had often ignored the plight of the poor.[11] This was a 'whole gospel of personal salvation and social service' in equal measure. The gospel of personal redemption and social reconstruction were to belong together.

Hughes's *Essential Christianity* (1894) pays tribute to the success of Booth's Salvation Army and criticizes the 'delusion of Socialism' which seeks to meet bodily needs alone, thinking that the social environment was all important. Government, whether central or local, was to be in the service of the people, otherwise it was not Christian. He quotes Benjamin Franklin in support of his case, in reminding his readers and listeners that 'whoever introduces into public affairs the principles of Primitive Christianity will change the face of the world.' Christianity, he asserts, is the only creed which will heal the social woes of

[9] H. P. Hughes, *Social Christianity* (London, 1890), p. viii.

[10] Henry D. Rack, 'Wesleyan Methodism 1849–1902', in R. E. Davies, A. R. George and G. Rupp, eds, *A History of the Methodist Church in Great Britain*, 4 vols (London, 1965–88), 3: 132–6.

[11] J. E. Rattenbury, 'Methodist Evangelism', in J. Scott Lidgett, ed., *Methodism in the Modern World* (London, 1929), pp. 169–92.

humanity. To be a Christian is not to subscribe to the ethical idea of this creed, but to do the will of God and show the love of Christ in social service. He pointed to the 'supreme curse of modern history' which was 'the fatal divorce between Personal Christianity and Social Christianity'. The integration of the Church into society was to infuse the ethical teaching of Christ into all aspects of life. It was 'applicable to business, pleasure, politics as well as to prayer meetings and sacraments'.[12] Much of his message was propagated through the columns of the newspaper he founded to challenge the more conservative views of the Methodist establishment found in the *Methodist Recorder*. His *Methodist Times*, the voice of the emerging 'Social Christianity' emphasis in the Church, was widely read by American Methodists as well as British Methodists.

* * *

While Hughes represented a social but conservative egalitarianism within Wesleyan Methodism, eager to bridge the gap between Church and working classes,[13] Samuel Keeble, a younger minister, epitomized a more radical stream of Social Christianity which eventually broke with Hughes, leading on to a more overt association with socialism and communism in the twentieth century. It was on Keeble that 'a strip of Hughes' mantle fell' in the attempt to argue powerfully for the 'direct application of the ethical standards of Christianity as tests, and Christian principles as guides, to these [social and economic] problems'.[14] Edwards's biographical sketch is subtitled 'The rejected prophet', an indictment of Methodism's reluctance to espouse his more radical programme. Yet his socialism was not doctrinaire. He was neither a Fabian nor a member of the Independent Labour Party formed in the 1890s. Whilst Keeble was influenced by Ruskin and Marx, introducing the work of the latter to many Methodists for the first time in the 1880s, Thompson attributes to him the credit for paving the way for the 'new social gospel' in England.[15] Keeble read *Das Kapital* with enthusiasm, agreeing with many aspects of Marx's

[12] H. P. Hughes, *Essential Christianity* (London, 1894), p. 174; see also D. P. Hughes, *The Life of Hugh Price Hughes* (London, 1905), ch. 14, 'Citizenship in London', pp. 329–82.

[13] For the background to this, see K. S. Inglis, *Churches and the Working Classes in Victorian England* (London, 1963).

[14] Samuel Keeble, *Industrial Day-Dreams* (London, 1896) [hereafter *IDD*], pp. vii–viii.

[15] David M. Thompson, 'The emergence of the Nonconformist Social Gospel', in K. Robbins, ed., *Protestant Evangelicalism: Britain, Ireland, Germany and America c. 1750–1960*, *SCH.S*, 7 (Oxford, 1990), pp. 255–80.

social and economic analysis, but thought it marred by 'materialistic philosophy, Hegelian jargon and economic errors'.[16] He wrote later that 'a purified Socialism is simply an industrially applied Christianity', with a naïve earnestness which did not endear him to many Methodists.[17] Although he maintained the primacy of Social Christianity which 'professes subordination to no debatable theory; it simply claims to be an effort to apply Christianity to problems which Socialism has neither created nor cured', many saw in his writing and preaching the socialist agenda. He drew on a ministry in industrial cities in the North of England (Leeds, Chester, Sheffield, and Manchester) where he encountered opposition for perceivably preaching politics in the pulpit and talking more about housing than about heaven. In Chester, he described the Methodists as 'hard to enthuse, lukewarm, discontented and reactionary; they have no care for Social Christianity'.[18]

Initially, Hughes took him up and engaged him to write a column called 'Labour Lore' in the *Methodist Times,* which he edited from 1889 to 1895. Hughes's growing impatience with the stridency of Keeble's views led him to prevent publication of an article in the *Times* on Marx in 1891, with a disclaimer that 'Our labour correspondent sometimes expresses strong opinions with which we do not agree.' This was perhaps a reference to Keeble's attack on employers as 'human vampires', and his support for striking workers in docks and factories and on the railways. He was a member of a delegation which called on the Prime Minister to campaign for the introduction of an eight-hour day. By 1900, Hughes's autocratic editorial control led Keeble to part company with the *Methodist Times.* He published a rival newspaper, the *Methodist Weekly*, which lasted for three years, an organ for challenging the imperialist anti-Boer, pro-war stance of Hughes and others in the Wesleyan Methodist establishment. Yet Hughes helped Keeble to publish his first major book, *Industrial Day-Dreams* (1896), when the Methodist Bookroom turned it down. Only 208 copies were sold and 267 had to be bought back, a measure of the lukewarm response it met. A series of studies in industrial ethics and economics, it is a landmark in the development of Nonconformist social radicalism, influencing many Christians like Philip Snowden who subsequently made a

16 Edwards, *Keeble*, p. 13.
17 *IDD*, p. 13.
18 Edwards, *Keeble*, p. 15.

significant contribution to the emerging Labour Party.[19] The book is a stalwart defence of the social gospel against Christian individualism on the one side and socialist collectivism on the other, taking on both in equal measure.

> Against Christian Individualism, which demands the 'simple Gospel' Christian Socialism maintains that the Christian Gospel is two-fold – individual and social. The Social Gospel is as sacred and as indispensable as the individual Gospel – the two are complementary, and the neglect of either always brings its penalties. . . . That Gospel, contends Christian Socialism, is far from being 'simple' . . . it is profound and manifold – and is bent upon saving not only the individual but also society, upon setting up in the earth the Kingdom of Heaven.[20]

Socialism, which uses physical force, which undermines the family, which cramps the place of religion, is condemned, while that which affirms peace and justice, brotherhood and equality, is truly Christian. By the time the book was published in a second edition only nine years later, it was generally acceptable and more widely read, for reasons which will become apparent as we see the developments of the first decade of the new century unfold.

* * *

From the inspiration of Hughes's Forward Movement, and in the confident spirit of the progress of the Liberal Party in politics, came the WMUSS. One stream of influence was the so-called 'nonconformist conscience' and enthusiasm for moral and social reform which permeated Wesleyanism in the 1890s. A Wesleyan Methodist Sociological Society had been proposed in 1899 but had few supporters. Keeble, with the support of S. F. Collier of the Manchester Mission (the *Methodist Weekly* had been published in the city), persuaded the annual conference meeting at Bristol in 1905 to authorize the creation of the Union, modelled on the Anglican Christian Social Union but with more official status, to 'try to awaken the social conscience of the Church'. This was an important date in the history of a Church which traditionally had kept at arms' length issues of social policy in the

[19] J. M. Turner quotes Morgan Phillips' remark that the Labour Party owed more to 'Methodism than to Marx' in his article 'Methodism 1900–1932', in Davies, George, and Rupp, *A History*, 3: 349–61.

[20] *IDD*, pp. 62–3.

enforcement of the unwritten but powerful 'no-politics' rule. It represented the 'rising tide of social sympathy in the Wesleyan Methodist Church' and buried the legacy of Buntingite hostility to radical politics and social reform for the time being. The Union was established 'to study social science, pursue social service and discuss social problems . . . with the view to educate public opinion and secure improvement in the conditions of life'.[21] Samuel Keeble was its first President. The influential Scott Lidgett, Warden of the Bermondsey Settlement in London, a sympathetic supporter of social reform and labour affairs and active in local city politics in the Progressive Party, elected as an Alderman on the London County Council, was its Vice-President.[22] J. Ernest Rattenbury, then serving at the Nottingham Mission, and subsequently for eighteen years at the West London Mission, was a further Vice-President. W. F. Lofthouse, who taught at Handsworth Theological College in Birmingham, and would emerge as a very significant theologian and apologist for the importance of social ethics and the social agenda, was its Secretary.[23]

Despite its small membership, in its early years the Union produced some impressive studies, which stimulated interest in social service. But its lack of commitment to any political party or creed led to disagreement over objectives. Lidgett wanted (in line with Hughes) social reform without socialism while Keeble took progressively a more radical stance and ended up in isolation. The formation of the Sigma Club in 1908, comprising sixty-five Methodist ministers with a more socialist focus, was in frustration at the failure of the Church to move more quickly, but it provoked the creation of anti-Socialist societies within Methodism and Nonconformity to counter its limited influence.[24] Nevertheless, *The Citizen of Tomorrow: A Handbook on Social Questions* (1906), published at the beginning of the term of office of the Liberal Government on its landslide victory, was well received, selling over 10,000 copies and playing a major educational role in sensitizing the Methodist people and persuading them of the value of social reform and progress. It was followed in 1907 by *The ABC Annotated Bibliography on Social Questions*, and in 1909 *The Social*

[21] *Social Science and Service*, p. v.

[22] E. S. Waterhouse, 'The public servant', in R. E. Davies, ed., *John Scott Lidgett: a Symposium* (London, 1957), p. 162.

[23] Edwards, *Keeble*, p. 28.

[24] David Bebbington, *Evangelicalism in Modern Britain: a History from the 1730s to the 1980s* (London, 1989), p. 215.

Teaching of the Bible, all edited by Keeble. In 1909 a significant conference was held in Oxford by the Union, marking, it claimed, 'the entry of the Wesleyan Methodist Church into the arena of constructive social reform'. As well as a keynote address from Scott Lidgett on 'The Church and Social problems', it included contributions from Percy Alden M.P. on 'Unemployment: its causes and remedies', and one from Keeble himself on 'The Moralization of Economic Relations'. Arguing for the Christianization of social and political life by the churches from their ethical superiority, he addresses himself to employers and workers alike, urging an 'economic chivalry' which would render them less selfish and more conscientious in response to 'our Lord's Golden Rule', that is the 'law of reciprocity, equality, fairness and justice', a socialism of the Sermon on the Mount to be taught through the home, the Sunday School, and the church. This vague and idealistic communitarian spirit which experimental religion can provide is necessary so that 'ethics and economics are for ever joined together by God . . . let no man put them asunder.'[25]

* * *

In his *Industrial Day-Dreams* Keeble, like Hughes before him, is anxious to avoid the criticism that he preaches Christian Socialism. In his opening essay he writes, 'Social Christianity . . . professes subordination to no debateable theology; it simply claims to be an effort to apply Christianity to problems which Socialism has neither created nor cured.'[26] He spends half the book on a critical examination of the theories of German, French, and English Socialism before examining particular aspects of contemporary debate. He attacks Christian individualism which draws on a spirituality which he judges is unethical and antisocial and other-worldly, 'travestying the good gospel of God'.[27] In contrast to capitalists and socialists alike, he declares the 'true value of labour' as production and the rights of the workers for just wages to be paramount.[28] He criticizes the law of supply and demand which 'brings in its wake oppression, injustice, misery and destitution', proposing in its place the 'law of service, not

[25] *Social Science and Service*, pp. 188–201.

[26] *IDD*, p. 7.

[27] Quoted in C. W. Cheatham, 'Social Christianity. A study of English nonconformist social attitudes, 1880–1914' (Vanderbilt University, Ph.D. thesis, 1982), p. 195.

[28] *IDD*, chapter on 'The Labour Theory of Value', pp. 106–17.

selfishness' in a mutuality of interest.[29] His solution is to allow social reforms which would modify and improve both supply and demand in regulating production and distribution, implying more than a passing nod of approval at the collectivist solutions of socialists. In a sermon delivered on Labour Sunday in the John Street Wesleyan Chapel, Chester, before the Fabian Socialists in 1893, he urged all Christians to examine the economic and social causes of poverty and remember the benefits of pre-competition pre-industrial Britain where community was more important than competition. He urged employers to view their workers not as 'producing-power' but as 'brothers in industry'.[30] Central to the question of fairness was the 'living wage'.[31] Attacking traditional evangelical quietism in matters of wage bargaining, he drew on a range of material, biblical and socio-economic (quoting the recent work of Thorold Rogers), to justify his call for a fixed minimum wage. His dream was for a large number of Christians 'bent upon applying the principles of the Sermon on the Mount most rigorously to their own financial and industrial affairs, without mercy to their own selfishness and class prejudice'. Only thus could a new industrial era be ushered in.[32] In an essay on 'The claims of manual labour', Keeble idealizes such work as God-given. In such 'the manual toiler is brought into fellowship with Nature, as he pits his thews and sinews against it'. He concludes with Emerson that 'labour is God's education' fitting human beings for society. The chief duty of man is 'to earn his bread by the labour of his hands' so 'nothing but a revived sense of the dignity of labour . . . will save us from straying far from the assigned path of social and spiritual well-being.'[33]

In his *Christianity and our Wages System*, one of the *Social Tracts* produced by the WMUSS in 1907, Keeble contrasts the profits of businessmen since 1891 with the declining wages of the workers. He cites the example of railway companies to demonstrate the unequal distribution of wealth. Was it a coincidence that the most prominent Methodist businessman of the day, Sir Robert Perks, was a major shareholder of one of these?[34] What should his fellow Christians do about this without recourse to violent or revolutionary changes? He

[29] Ibid., p. 137.
[30] Ibid., p. 160.
[31] Ibid., pp. 165–84.
[32] Ibid., p. 192.
[33] Ibid., p. 200.
[34] See Jeremy, *Religion, Business and Wealth*, ch. 4.

proposes that attention be given to three areas. First, he urges all Christians to adhere to the principle of justice and apply ethical Christianity to their sharing of prosperity. They should be model employers and exemplary workers. Secondly, he defends the involvement of Christians in Trade Unionism and the Co-operative Movement as the natural way of ending the 'dualism of capital and labour' by securing more equitable means of production and distribution. Thirdly, in a wave of enthusiasm for the election of fifty-four Labour members to the 1906 Parliament, he applauds the political and moral actions which may be taken in response to this preponderance of Christian influence, calling in particular for the establishment of a network of Labour Exchanges and the implementation of a minimum wage. He calls for the Church to expel any 'exploiter of labour . . . with all his ill-gotten gains'.[35]

In his *The Idea of the Material Life and other Social Addresses* (1908) Keeble does not draw back from a fierce attack on 'brute corporations, individual Calibans who "fear not God nor regard men"' and 'unmerciful businessmen who need to be imbued with Christian conceptions of humanity and the inherent dignity of work'.[36] The latter is central to that which makes the human being made in the image of the divine. To work is divine; to be idle is to practise immorality.[37] In an industrial society, Keeble argues, there must be limits to competition. Christian principles must inform the ethics of business and the humanization of economics. Otherwise competition will result in social unrest and discontent.

In his essay 'The Penalty of Wilful Idleness', there is a strong analysis of the text from II Thessalonians 3.10 ('If any man will not work . . .'). Idleness which is wilful is sinful. The Christian Church cannot condone its members who refuse to work: 'The only way for a Christian to be prosperous . . . is to work for God, Christ and humanity . . . it is the non-worker in the Church who starves . . . and also sins.'

He pricks the Christian conscience to respond to the fifty thousand underfed, underpaid, and unemployed people in London, victims of the sweating system. He rejects the criticism that the unemployed are all 'drinkers, idlers, loafers, inefficients, and ne'er-do-wells'. He rounds on the idle poor and the idle rich alike, who should both be punished;

35 *Social Tracts*, no. III, pp. 12–20.

36 Samuel Keeble, *The Idea of the Material Life* (London, 1908), p. 13.

37 Ibid., pp. 35–6.

they should be offered the healthy alternative of work with no false charity or taxed out of existence.[38]

* * *

The period 1905 to 1914 was the heyday of interest in and the influence of Social Christianity within Methodism. Disillusionment with the Liberal Government's ability to deliver aspects of its agenda and the outbreak of war in 1914, as well as the innate conservatism of many Wesleyan Methodists and the hostility of its increasingly middle-class constituency, interrupted the progress of such ideas and influences.

The rationale of the WMUSS was that it took further the emphasis which the Forward Movement had placed on the duty of public service, in fighting for social reconstruction.[39] The long-term effect of the Union was felt more by those who served in political life than in the life of the Methodist Churches. From a prevailing ethos of seeking after a form of limited collectivism to replace the worst aspects of the laissez-faire politics of earlier Liberalism, the political mood of Wesleyanism became divided. This mirrored also the crisis in the Liberal Party on which it had pinned so many hopes, and the failure to follow up the social welfare policies of Lloyd George, the architect of the radical programme. The Liberals declined, to the benefit of the nascent Labour Party whose policies, including the nationalization of the means of production, they feared to trust.[40] A number of Methodists joined the new party and abandoned a Liberal Party which lost its radical cutting edge.

The First World War blunted the impact of the social gospel in Britain by calling into question the Labour leanings and more pacifist stance of its more radical figures like Keeble in what David Bebbington has called 'the Great Reversal'.[41] While the Social Creed in the United States was adopted and expanded by most of the Methodist Churches there, the Wesleyan Methodists at home hijacked the movement by creating a Department of Temperance and Social Welfare in 1918, diverting most of its energies into the areas of moral rather than social welfare. The demon drink and the gambler's curse

38 Ibid., ch. IX, pp. 201–19.
39 See Rattenbury, 'Wesley and social service', pp. 51–68.
40 See Turner, 'Methodism', p. 358.
41 Bebbington, *Evangelicalism*, pp. 214–15.

were more worthy of attention than the devils of poverty and unemployment, war and waste. The WMUSS withered on the vine of temperance in 1926.

While social gospellers in both American and British Methodism were sensitized to the conditions of workers and cities, they lacked the concise goals and objectives to widen their local concerns. Their social diagnosis and plans for ameliorative action through the central halls and missions established in most cities were more successful than the wider application of a programme for social reform, which could be more generally effective. Like Washington Gladden's comment on the American counterpart, it contained primarily a 'mystical propheticism with practical emphasis'.[42] Keeble's prophetic isolation was marked after the publication of his last great book in 1921, *Christian Responsibility for the Social Order*, foreshadowing much that William Temple was to publicize more prominently in the Life and Work movement in the next two decades. Increasingly Keeble became involved with the organizations he was to put his stamp upon, particularly the Conference on Christian Politics, Economics and Citizenship (COPEC), meeting in 1924, and the League of Nations. He moved steadily leftwards, with great but unfounded hopes for the collectivist solution.

This short paper cannot do justice to the importance of the two great figures of Social Christianity in British Methodism, Hughes and Keeble. It is nevertheless clear that in the period 1887 to 1910 they made a considerable contribution in their differing ways to the cause of Social Christianity in British Wesleyan Methodism, which in turn contributed to the significant development of the social gospel in Britain and the re-evaluation of the place of work in religious life in society and the relationship of the Methodist Churches to the labour movement. 'From Welfare to Work' was a theme pre-empted in much of the discussion within Methodism, exposing the fault-lines between the individualistic and collectivist approaches reflected in the preaching and practice of religious groups in the twentieth century, culminating in the *Unemployment and the Future of Work* report of 1997.[43]

Westminster Institute of Education, Oxford Brookes University

[42] Washington Gladden, *Recollections* (New York, 1909), p. 19.

[43] Report published by Council of Churches for Britain and Ireland. See unpublished paper by Tim Macquiban, 'Welfare to work: Protestant and Catholic responses in thought and action'.

MARIANNE FARNINGHAM: WORK, LEISURE, AND THE USE OF TIME

by LINDA WILSON

IN 1907, aged seventy and nearing the end of her long life as a journalist and writer, Marianne Farningham published her autobiography. She gave it the forthright title *A Working Woman's Life*, thus indicating that in her old age she constructed her identity as that of both 'woman' and 'worker', closely bound up with her gender as well as with the type of life she had lived. Looking back from the perspective of the early twentieth century, although with a view of life largely shaped in the 1840s and 1850s, she recounted, amongst other things, the joys of her work, the perils of overwork, and the pleasures of relaxation. Her writing accordingly included several passages addressing matters relating to the use and abuse of time.

She was actually born not Marianne Farningham but Mary-Ann Hearn, in 1834 in a small village in Kent. Later she took its name, Farningham, as her nom-de-plume. Her formative years were shaped not only by family and village, but also by the traditional rural Baptist church at nearby Eynsford to which her family belonged. She remained within that denomination all her life, although her sympathies grew wider. Most of her adulthood was spent in Northampton, initially as a teacher before she became a full-time journalist. She was a member of College Street Baptist chapel, where she ran a girls' class for many years. By the time she wrote her autobiography in the early 1900s, her understanding of work, leisure, and the use of time had mellowed a little since she first put pen to paper on the subject in the late 1850s and early 1860s, and she was less anxious about every moment being wisely used, but her basic opinions remained the same. In 1861 she had declared 'we live for work, for service, for some good end, and not for self-gratification merely',[1] and her autobiography with its emphasis on her work is a testimony to that belief. But she also believed in the need for play: 'we do well to take all the happiness we can find in the world,' she wrote of the need for relaxation, 'seeing that our Father in heaven has sent it on purpose

[1] Marianne Farningham, *Life Sketches*, 1st ser. (London, 1861), p. 66.

for us.'[2] Marianne's views on the subject of work and leisure were strong and straightforward and would have struck a chord with her readers. She is of interest to us today for several reasons. Uncovering the history of women such as Marianne Farningham is part of the important process of rediscovering women's history within nineteenth-century Nonconformity, one that until recent years has been neglected by gender and ecclesiastical historians alike. She is also of significance because her writings shed light on popular evangelicalism during a period of over fifty years, including attitudes to the use of time.

Marianne produced regular poetry, prose, and fiction for the weekly *Christian World*, which at its peak around 1880 had a circulation of 130,000.[3] Her first piece for the paper was published in its inaugural number in 1857, and she continued to write for it until just before her death, becoming salaried in 1867. She covered a wide variety of topics through poetry, prose pieces, and serialized fiction, and also contributed to (and from 1885 edited) the 'Sunday School Magazine'. Many of her short pieces were later published as collections in book form, with titles such as *Girlhood*, *Boyhood*, and *Homely Talks about Homely Things*. Marianne thus had a wide readership, and, if often sentimental, was an accessible as well as a prolific writer. Her name would have appeared in print in many dissenting households at least once a week for over fifty years, and would have been familiar in evangelical circles.

This is demonstrated, for instance, when she was introduced to the Baptist preacher Charles Spurgeon, in the summer of 1867. She had recently been appointed as a full-time contributor, after ten years of writing part-time. They were near contemporaries in age. Many years later, Marianne remembered the occasion:

> Between the afternoon and evening services Mr Whittemore introduced me to Mr Spurgeon.
> 'So you are the great Marianne Farningham,' he said.
> And I replied 'So you are the great Charles Spurgeon.'
> After this, and the tea we had together, we were friends for the rest of the years.[4]

[2] Marianne Farningham, *Girlhood* (London, 1869), p. 39.
[3] James Munson, *The Nonconformists* (London, 1991), p. 73.
[4] Marianne Farningham, *A Working Woman's Life* (London, 1907), p. 148.

Such a comment by Spurgeon, even in jest, was an indication of just how well known she was. Another indication of her fame comes from a much later stage in her life, when Lloyd George, sharing a public platform with her in the little Welsh town of Barmouth only a few years before her death, admitted that her weekly writings had been one of the influences that had shaped his character.[5] Her popularity was demonstrated, too, by the way people crowded in to hear her when, several years running, she undertook lecture tours.[6] In addition, for many years, hardly a week went by without her receiving 'letters of appreciation and thanks from strangers'.[7] Her wide readership, and the response of some of those who read her, indicates that as well as reflecting the culture she lived in and wrote for, Marianne also helped to shape its attitudes.

She especially hoped to influence her younger readers. As someone whose main church activity was leading a thriving class for teenage and young adult girls, she had a particular concern with that age group, and it appears that she had at least some degree of success. One correspondent wrote, on the occasion of the jubilee of *The Christian World*, to thank her for her book, *Girlhood*: 'My aunts gave it to me when I was sixteen, and it was my monitor in many ways . . . your book strengthened my principles and helped me to view life and its responsibilities in a different light; in fact I cannot express all it did for me.'[8] This was just the kind of result which encouraged Marianne. In her writing she was concerned with many aspects of young people's lives, but one of those was work, leisure, and time, an area of some anxiety in the years when she was first writing.

Commenting about this aspect of early nineteenth-century evangelicalism, Doreen Rosman has argued that even those who believed in the value of leisure had 'unease about their use of time'. This, she observed, was particularly evident amongst dissenters.[9] In the 1850s and 1860s, when Marianne Farningham was in the early years of her journalistic career, it could be argued that this unease had grown, and was verging on obsession. This was the period during which, as David Bebbington has noted, 'the cult of duty, self-discipline and high

[5] *The Christian World*, 25 March 1909: account of sermon at Barmouth following Marianne Farningham's death.

[6] Farningham, *Life*, p. 156.

[7] Ibid., p. 266.

[8] Ibid., pp. 266–7.

[9] Doreen Rosman, *Evangelicals and Culture* (London, 1984), p. 121.

seriousness was at its peak'.[10] In this climate an anxiety existed amongst evangelicals which led them to be insistent about the importance of using every moment wisely, to work hard, and to be cautious about the way their increasing leisure was spent. Some of Marianne's early pieces demonstrate this sense of worry. In *Life Sketches*, for instance, a collection of short articles published in 1861, she suggested that it was good to be constantly busy, because time must not be wasted. 'When tempted to be inert and slothful', she argued, 'let us remember that there is much to do; time is very short, and we have "not a minute to spare".'[11] Evangelicals were conscious that one day each individual would have to give an account to God for his or her life. Part of this account, in an age of railway timetables and increased clock consciousness, would be for the use of their time.[12] Marianne was fearful that her readers might be wasting some of their precious minutes. A rather trite poem dating from 1860 encapsulates this fear:

> Only a day – a little day! –
> Full half its hours were wasted.
> We trifled in its morning prime,
> Forgetting how it hasted . . .
>
> Only a day – we might have helped
> To stem the raging waters;
> We might have blessed and comforted
> Earth's wretched sons and daughters.[13]

Half a day spent relaxing with friends was thus portrayed as an unsuitable use of time, and the implication was that to enjoy leisure was sinful if there was work, especially philanthropy or mission, waiting to be done.

Such a sentiment did not appear in quite the same form in her later writings. The near obsession with the use of time disappeared. What remained was a belief in a disciplined and careful use of time. Whereas in 1860 she had written urgently about the need not to waste time, and in 1861 with enthusiasm about the fast pace of life, only a few years

[10] David W. Bebbington, *Evangelicalism in Modern Britain* (London, 1989), p. 105.

[11] Farningham, *Sketches*, pp. 39–40, 66.

[12] Ibid., p. 17.

[13] Marianne Farningham, *Lays and Lyrics of the Blessed Life*, 4th edn (London, 1860), pp. 63–4.

later she had a more balanced approach. In *Home Life*, published in 1869, she suggested that 'we live too fast, we work too hard, there is too great a strain both on body and mind.'[14] Relaxation was not only permitted, but vital, to alleviate this strain, whether through reading aloud in the family circle, or taking a walk in the country. It did not even need a clear purpose. She did not 'believe that time absolutely given up to fun and nothing else is wasted. On the contrary, so it be free from sin, it is well spent.'[15] Approval of the need for leisure was thus given. As Marianne's early attitudes to the use of time mellowed so that she was more comfortable with leisure, she was reflecting the experience of the evangelical community – and indeed, middle-class culture as a whole – as it came to terms with the extra time available for relaxation and worked out how best to fill it.[16] The subtle changes in her writing mirrored the developments in evangelical attitudes over these years.

One must not over-emphasise the change, however. All through her life she taught that leisure time was a gift from God, which should be enjoyed for its own sake, as well as for the beneficial effect it could have on work. 'To those who live to purpose, who devote the far greater part of their time to *duty*, there come many pleasures', she wrote in a very early piece;[17] and in her autobiography she wrote at length about some of those pleasures, especially travel and the enjoyment of nature.

Leisure always remained, in her view, something that came after the necessary work had been done. In one early contribution, entitled 'Drudgery', she discussed ordinary everyday tasks, asserting that leisure is only genuinely enjoyable if people have worked first.[18] She stressed a similar point in her biography of Grace Darling, published in 1875 under the pseudonym of 'Eva Hope'. Grace was portrayed as a good and cheerful worker, but Marianne suggested that 'it was a happy time for her when the work of the day was done, and she was able to sit down by the fireside, and read from her favourite books.'[19] Work was

[14] Marianne Farningham, *Home Life* (London, 1869), p. 38.

[15] Ibid., p. 41.

[16] See Peter Bailey, *Leisure and Class in Victorian England* (London, 1978), ch. 3, on the middle classes and the new leisure in the mid-Victorian period.

[17] Farningham, *Sketches*, p. 22.

[18] Ibid., p. 67; a similar sentiment is expressed in *Home Life*, p. 88.

[19] Eva Hope, *Grace Darling* (London, 1875), p. 56. In addition to her journalistic work, Farningham wrote several biographies and edited at least three collections of poetry, all under a second pseudonym of Eva Hope which, as she commented later (Farningham,

thus the purpose of life, leisure the earned relaxation bodies and minds needed in order to work more effectively.

This belief in the primacy of work was evident in both her early pieces and her later writings. In *Girlhood* (1869) she stressed 'the great truth that there is dignity in labour';[20] and in her autobiography declared that although her life had 'been very full of interests, yet in a very real sense my work has been my life.' It was made most fulfilling by the knowledge that people appreciated her work. Knowing that she was able 'to write that which was acceptable and useful to people' was a strong motivation to continue.[21] Part of the pleasure of the writing, therefore, came from a sense of purpose and usefulness, and thus she found it difficult when in old age she had to work less. One friend suggested that in the last year before she died 'the hardest part of all she had to bear was the enforced surrender of so much of the work she loved'.[22] Her work had become intimately bound up with her sense of self.

How did Marianne define work? Referring to herself she primarily meant paid work, although she did regard teaching her weekly girls' class as 'this most delightful work'.[23] When addressing her readers, however, she often made no distinction between unpaid and paid work, consistently using a wider understanding of the subject, especially with regard to women. It was not a question of being rich or poor, she insisted, but to do with having a purpose in life, and believing that 'there is dignity in labour'.[24] Work was portrayed by her as a blessing, not a curse: 'We should be miserable without it, and perhaps it contributes more to our happiness than anything else', she insisted.[25] She stressed that work could be a pleasure as much as a duty, and she certainly regarded her own work in that light, declaring in her autobiography that 'after fifty years of work, I love it almost as much as ever'.[26] Work

Life, p. 131), was 'about the weakest [name] we could have found.' The account of Grace Darling is almost certainly fictional: see Richard Armstrong, *Grace Darling: Maid and Myth* (London, 1965), p. 62. Whilst, as Armstrong argued, this work is 'bad beyond belief' as a biography (p. 10), it provides a useful reflection of the beliefs and attitudes of the author.

20 Farningham, *Girlhood*, p. 34.

21 Farningham, *Life*, p. 141.

22 Supplement to *The Christian World*, 18 March 1909, personal tribute by Jennie Street.

23 Farningham, *Life*, p. 262.

24 Farningham, *Girlhood*, pp. 30–5.

25 Farningham, *Sketches*, p. 66.

26 Farningham, *Life*, p. 273.

was the main purpose of her existence, a perception she probably shared with many of her contemporaries.

She urged her positive view of work on her readers. For instance, in an item in *Girlhood* entitled 'Work', Marianne insists to her youthful audience that 'Very probably it is the greatest good that could happen to you', and contrasts it with the bored and useless life of a lady of leisure.[27] The key here is the contrast between usefulness and uselessness, rather than between paid or unpaid work, or between the private or public spheres. 'There is not one of you but may be of use in God's world',[28] she wrote in *Girlhood*. This same attitude is reflected in her book on Grace Darling, where she suggested that

> She seems to have been actuated every day by the one desire, to do her duty. She wished to serve God, obey her parents, and do any good work that might be in her power. And who does not see how much better she was than a useless fine lady, who could do nothing but pass her life in idleness?[29]

Thus Marianne believed that work should be the means of fulfilment and purpose, and by her own account this was also her experience. The way to be happy, she believed, was to be useful.[30]

Working could also bring financial independence, an advantage relished by Marianne. In a collection published in 1861, she commented that it was sad that many young women thought of work as vulgar, and believed that it was a disgrace to earn.[31] By contrast, she believed that there was no need for single women to be dependent on other men in the family.[32] This demonstrates that she was conscious of being a *woman* worker, as she was later very aware of her position as the only woman on Northampton School Board for its first six years. Her own identity appears to have largely been located within the world of paid work.

Her love of work was also demonstrated in her explanation of an illness, a serious breakdown early in 1889 due to overwork and anxiety.

27 Farningham, *Girlhood*, pp. 30–1.

28 Ibid., p. 17.

29 Hope, *Darling*, p. 294.

30 Marianne Farningham, *Little Tales for Little Readers* (London, 1869), p. 102.

31 Farningham, *Sketches*, p. 135. For further discussion of her view of women and work see L. Wilson, '"Afraid to be singular"; Marianne Farningham and the role of women', in S. Morgan, ed., *Strategies of Subversion: Women, Religion and the Dynamics of Feminism: Britain 1750–1900* (forthcoming).

32 Farningham, *Life*, p. 234.

Family problems contributed to the collapse, but she had thirty years of constant work behind her. Although she had travelled, she always wrote articles as she went, and so rarely, if ever, had a complete break. She explained in her autobiography:

> A few weeks ago I looked through some old volumes of our journals, at the British Museum, and was really amazed at the output of my pen. It made me a little tired even to recall those years of work. The wonder was that the breakdown had not come at some previous time during the thirty years. But I had not realized how hard I was working, because the work to me was so intensely interesting, and I loved it so much.[33]

This comment indicates the extent to which, as she herself admitted, her work was her life.[34] There is another element here, however. During this period many Nonconformist ministers had breakdowns, to the extent that the experience almost came to be regarded as proof of a life dedicated to serving God. They then often used the opportunity to go on extended tours of the continent, which is exactly what Marianne herself did. Thus, in highlighting this part of her life, she was constructing her identity not only as a female worker, but as the equivalent of a minister. She put herself very clearly in the male world of work.

For Marianne, work was given by God, and he was essential for the process of effective work: without Christ, she believed, people would be poor workers.[35] She described the writing process as being 'really helped to write', presumably by God.[36] Work, therefore, should be undertaken in order to serve both others and God, and those are the criteria by which success should be judged. Near the end of her life, she wrote that she knew she had not been able to do 'any great thing which would impress the world, and cause me to be kept in remembrance, but have hoped that I should be able to do a great many little things which might tell on individuals. My desire has been to "serve my generation, and fall asleep".'[37] She failed to distinguish here between small acts of kindness and her work of journalism, by which she reached many thousands, but she was stressing that view of work as the

[33] Farningham, *Life*, p. 215.
[34] Ibid., p. 141.
[35] Farningham, *Girlhood*, p. 36.
[36] Farningham, *Life*, p. 141.
[37] Ibid., p. 275. The biblical quotation is from Acts 13.36.

primary purpose of life which she had first written about nearly fifty years earlier.

Leisure also remained important in her thinking, even though she overworked, failing to take her own advice. Recreation, she suggested, was necessary, but she was concerned about the kind of pleasures her readers enjoyed. They had to be suitable and not sinful, however that was defined. She suggested to the young readers of *Girlhood* that a useful rule for leisure activities was to 'never engage in anything upon which you cannot ask God's blessing'.[38] One of the best activities was undoubtedly an enjoyment of nature. 'Do you ever sit under the shade of a tree on a hill', she wrote, 'and look over a beautiful landscape until your heart has grown full, and the tears have come unbidden to your eyes?'[39] On a similar note, in her autobiography, she recalled her childhood garden, musing that she 'must have spent hours . . . leaning against that wall and looking out into the world of summer'.[40] She gave the impression that she could have stayed leaning there for ever, looking at the fields beyond her garden. Whether that was her experience as a child, or a reflection of her attitude in old age, cannot now be unravelled, but what is clear is that by the time she came to write those words she could quite happily envisage time spent just daydreaming, or looking at the scenery, in a very relaxed frame of mind. Such an appreciation of nature could also be usefully coupled with another important element, exercise. During her years of full-time writing, her preferred pattern of work included a morning walk, and she also suggested this to others.[41] In 1869 she advised her young female readers to have regular cold baths and frequent exercise in fresh air, suggesting at least one walk a day, preferably in the morning, although not before breakfast.[42] The following year she gave similar advice to boys, adding that to sit in front of a fire with a book in winter could lead to mental illness.[43] A walk thus combined two virtues: the need for exercise and fresh air, and the enjoyment of nature.

Holidays, of course, gave scope for all these pleasures and more, and they were on the increase for the lower middle class during this period. In *Girlhood* she insists that holidays are a good thing, and suggests

[38] Farningham, *Girlhood*, p. 43.
[39] Ibid., pp. 40–1.
[40] Farningham, *Life*, p. 22.
[41] Ibid., p. 139.
[42] Farningham, *Girlhood*, pp. 67–9.
[43] Marianne Farningham, *Boyhood* (London, 1870), p. 40.

frequent ones, either by the sea or in the country.[44] She took plenty herself, though she usually wrote when travelling, using what she saw as material for short prose pieces. On several occasions she also took some of her girls' class away together. Several of them had never seen the sea: 'holidays were not so easy and common then as now' and they were thrilled at the sight.[45] Her own holidays ranged from short trips within England to a Cook's tour of the Holy Land, paid for by a friend.[46] But if these holidays were often more busy than relaxing, her cottage in Barmouth, which she rented from the mid 1880s, did provide a place for retreat, rest, and the enjoyment of nature. She was so thrilled with having 'a cot of my very own' where she could retreat when strength and health were at a low ebb, that she declared that she could not 'imagine why the plan is not more often tried'.[47] Whether through holidays or just regular walks, Marianne believed in the recuperative power of nature and exercise.

She approved of indoor leisure activities too, but still with the proviso that they had to be of the kind which God would also approve. In an early piece she emphasised the pleasures of listening to a lecture, or attending a concert. The latter she saw as a foretaste of heaven.[48] She was thus a woman of her time, enjoying the new forms of relaxation which were developing with the increase of leisure. Much pleasure, she believed, could also be gained from an evening at home. She was a subscriber to the sentimental Victorian view of the home, and stressed its virtues at every opportunity. Within its walls, she believed, brothers could be restrained from sin, girls could find useful occupations for at least some of their time, fathers could be refreshed after a busy day, and children could be encouraged to talk, play, and study. Mothers, it seems, were meant to facilitate this situation. Home could and should provide a place of love and encouragement.[49]

It is not surprising, therefore, that the home-based activity of reading had a prominent place in her thinking and practice. Marianne believed that 'there may be as much good in a thoroughly good novel

[44] Farningham, *Girlhood*, p. 42.

[45] Farningham, *Life*, p. 122.

[46] Ibid., pp. 179–87.

[47] Ibid., pp. 230–4.

[48] Farningham, *Sketches*, p. 23.

[49] Farningham, *Home Life*, pp. 7–31, 57–60. For home and Nonconformist women, see L. Wilson, '"She succeeds with cloudless brow" . . . How active was the spirituality of Nonconformist women in the home during the period 1825–75?', *SCH*, 34 (1998), pp. 347–59.

as in a sermon',[50] and considered that a house was not 'properly furnished' without a supply of 'really good books'.[51] She was clearly more open-minded than the previous generation in her home church of Eynsford Particular Baptist. She recalled that her mother 'did not like my always having a book in my hand or pocket, and would have been better pleased if I had been equally fond of the brush or the needle';[52] and that as a child she was 'taught that it was wicked to read novels', though by whom she does not make clear. When her pastor, Jonathan Whittemore, gave her a copy of Shakespeare as a gift, one lady in the congregation 'begged me to let her burn it'.[53] Marianne, however, kept the book and continued her voracious reading.

Yet, although reading was always a great pleasure to her, her advice to others indicates that she remained extremely cautious about what constituted 'really good books'. Some novels and periodicals, she suggested, were 'full of hidden stings and secret mischief',[54] others were 'silly and quite useless',[55] or even 'vile'.[56] Her advice to girls was that if there were passages in a book which could not be read aloud to the men in the family without blushes the book should be discarded.[57] Accordingly, the definition of a good book (the only sort worth reading) was restricted to one which had a moral purpose, a view which reflected the theory if not the practice of many of her contemporaries.

Marianne also believed in restricting time spent reading. To both young men and women she insisted that it was important not to read when there was still work to be done. 'Books can be so bewitching that everything else is neglected for them', she wrote in *Girlhood*, an indication of her own fondness for them.[58] The remedy, she suggested, was to set aside part of the day for reading, and to be careful about keeping to it.[59] She also advised young people that they should 'read only good books in a proper way, and at a suitable time',[60] and there is

[50] Farningham, *Girlhood*, p. 47.
[51] Farningham, *Home Life*, p. 52.
[52] Farningham, *Life*, pp. 22–3.
[53] Ibid., p. 71.
[54] Farningham, *Home Life*, p. 54.
[55] Farningham, *Girlhood*, p. 46.
[56] Farningham, *Boyhood*, p. 54.
[57] Farningham, *Girlhood*, p. 46.
[58] Ibid., p. 44.
[59] Ibid., p. 45.
[60] Farningham, *Boyhood*, pp. 54–6.

every indication that she kept her own advice. Thus an anxiety about the use of time, and about leisure in particular, had been reduced by 1869 through developing means to control the potential dangers of free time. This was a perspective which Marianne continued to maintain, although by the time she wrote her autobiography it was less of a pressing issue.

Another facet of rest amongst evangelicals in this period was of course the Sabbath, and here too Marianne's slowly changing views mirror those of the wider Nonconformist community. In her early writings, she was very particular about the use of Sunday. She saw it as a day given over to recuperation, and to thinking and reading about God. Whilst in the 'busy, bustling week, we have only had snatches of the promises – hasty glances into the loving face of the Redeemer', on Sunday there is 'time to sit and enjoy the good things spread before us to our hearts' grateful content'.[61] Her belief clearly was that Sunday was a much-needed opportunity for refreshment. At this stage, however, she was quite rigid in her interpretation of Sabbath. She criticized people who allowed the postman to call on Sunday and ate hot dinners cooked by someone else, calling this by implication a 'desecration of the Sabbath'.[62] It did not continue to be a frequent theme, however. She spent her Sundays at College Street Chapel, and took her girls' class on a Sunday afternoon, but wrote very little in later years, or in her autobiography, about the Sabbath as an issue. It appears that, on the whole, she kept out of any debate on the subject.

One of the lectures which Marianne Farningham gave was called 'The Rush and the Hush of Life', which she delivered over two hundred times to a total of several thousand people,[63] an indication that the subject of the use of time, and the need for space to relax and develop spirituality, was very much a topical one in the last quarter of the century. She consistently saw work as not only the main purpose of life, but the main source of a person's fulfilment. She was aware too of her own position as a working woman, and was more than a little proud of her own achievements. Perhaps unrealistically, she imagined that this could be the same for a factory hand or servant girl as it was in her own situation, where she loved working so much that she did not notice she was overworking until she had a breakdown.

[61] Farningham, *Sketches*, pp. 9–11.

[62] Ibid., p. 128.

[63] Farningham, *Life*, p. 165.

As well as the primacy of work, she wrote about the importance of leisure. She was a strong advocate of the recuperative power of nature, and the importance of exercise. In her talk of usefulness, in the way she discussed small matters and gave them dignity, and in her plain and straightforward, if often sentimental, style, her writing was accessible to those she most cared about. Her personal faith and her simple expression of it was at the heart of her appeal to so many readers.[64] In her writing she was not an innovator or a great thinker, although her views did develop along with those of the wider evangelical community. Reading her work thus gives an insight into popular evangelicalism in the second half of the nineteenth century. Her readers were men and women who, whether or not they found their identity in work as Marianne did, worked conscientiously, were self-conscious about their use of time, and were becoming more relaxed about enjoying the expanding variety of leisure available to them. Above all, however, they, like her, understood the whole of their lives in the light of their faith.

Open Theological College, Cheltenham

[64] It is interesting that she regarded it as self-evident that 'my writings have appealed most of all to the working-classes': Farningham, *Life*, p. 269.

'A PECULIARLY ENGLISH INSTITUTION':[1] WORK, REST, AND PLAY IN THE LABOUR CHURCH

by KRISTA COWMAN

THE Labour Church held its first service in Charlton Hall, Manchester, in October 1891. The well-attended event was led by Revd Harold Rylett, a Unitarian minister from Hyde, and John Trevor, a former Unitarian and the driving force behind the idea. Counting the experiment a success, Trevor organized a follow-up meeting the next Sunday, at which the congregation overflowed from the hall into the surrounding streets. A new religious movement had begun.[2] In the decade that followed, over fifty Labour Churches formed, mainly in Northern England, around the textile districts of the West Riding of Yorkshire and East Lancashire.[3] Their impetus lay both in the development and spread of what has been called a socialist culture in Britain in the final decades of the nineteenth century, and in the increased awareness of class attendant on this. Much of the enthusiasm for socialism was indivisible from the lifestyle and culture which surrounded it. This was a movement dedicated as much to what Chris Waters has described as 'the politics of everyday life . . . [and] of popular culture' as to rigid economistic doctrine.[4] This tendency has been described as 'ethical socialism', although a more common expression at the time was 'the religion of socialism'.[5]

The enthusiasts who preached of the religion of socialism sought

[1] John Trevor, *The Labour Church in England: an Unspoken Address to the Foreign Members of the International Socialist Congress, London, July 1896* (London, 1896).

[2] For detail of these early services see Stanley Pierson, 'John Trevor and the Labour Church movement in England, 1891–1900', *ChH*, 29 (1960), pp. 463–78.

[3] John Belchem, *Popular Radicalism in Nineteenth Century Britain* (Basingstoke, 1996), p. 161.

[4] Chris Waters, *British Socialists and the Politics of Popular Culture* (Manchester, 1990), pp. 13–14.

[5] On the division between ethical and economistic socialism, see, for instance, Eleanor Gordon, *Women and the Labour Movement in Scotland* (Oxford, 1991), esp. p. 261. Early uses of the phrase 'religion of socialism' include William Morris, Preface to the *Manifesto of the Socialist League*, (London, 1895), cited by R. A. B., 'Studies in the religion of socialism', *The Labour Prophet* (April, 1897), pp. 51–2; Katherine St John Conway and John Bruce Glasier, *The Religion of Socialism* (Manchester, 1894); R. Blatchford, *The New Religion* (London, 1892); Stephen Yeo, 'A new life: the religion of socialism in Britain, 1883–1896', *History Workshop Journal*, 4 (1977), pp. 5–56.

more than the replacement of one system of production and distribution with another. Their aim was the total transformation of all levels and aspects of society. This would involve the creation of a 'New Life' in which not just work, but also leisure and the way in which free time was spent would be transformed. Precious hours away from work were to be occupied with a variety of activities aimed both at self-improvement and at developing a sense of comradeship amongst socialists. Brass bands, drama groups, choirs, sewing circles, and rambling associations were as important as the many educational classes which socialist societies ran for their membership.[6] Although the socialist content of many of these leisure pursuits may be difficult to quantify, their main purpose was to further a sense of comradeship in members and thus strengthen the socialist movement through ensuring that its followers spent as much of their free time together as was possible.

John Trevor's decision to found a separate Labour Church struck a chord amongst those more attracted to cultural manifestations of socialism. Many of these came from religious backgrounds, but found that their espousal of socialism made them uncomfortable in existing churches. There were, in the later nineteenth century, strong links between not just the established church but also nonconformists and the dominant, anti-socialist political parties.[7] Yet for many socialists, religious affiliations were not lightly broken. As Hugh McLeod has remarked, the Labour Church filled a vacuum in the lives of socialists who found that they had lost their faith, but not their need for spirituality or the associated rituals of religion and its 'Sunday home'.[8]

Trevor himself claimed that he quit his former Unitarian ministry after a 'conversation with a working man who had formerly been a member of his congregation' but was now uncomfortable with its middle-class atmosphere.[9] More serious than this particular discomfort of individuals, however, was the feeling amongst many Christians that the organized church had gone too far from its roots. Socialists, S. G. Hobson explained to Cardiff sympathizers, had been 'practically forced

[6] For a broad overview, see Waters, *British Socialists.*

[7] Hugh McLeod, *Religion and Society in England 1850–1914* (Basingstoke, 1996), p. 208. For a discussion of the breadth of denominations actively criticized by the Labour Church, see K. S. Inglis, 'The Labour Church movement', *International Review of Social History*, 3 (1958), pp. 445–60.

[8] McLeod, *Religion and Society*, pp. 208–9.

[9] Henry Pelling, *The Origins of the Labour Party*, 2nd edn (Oxford, 1965), p. 133.

into the formation of a new church because the old established churches are altogether far too committed to an endorsement of the worst aspect of latter-day industrialism'. Similarly, Philip Wicksteed, Trevor's Unitarian mentor, felt that the established churches' efforts to 'ignore class distinctions' had led them to 'receive the capitalist, the landlord, or the rich professional man', at the expense of the class-conscious socialist worker.[10] A Labour Church, whose first principle was 'that the labour movement is a religious movement', was a logical attempt to counter such problems. Not only would this Church work as the conscience of the wider movement, 'preserving the higher socialist mission against the materialism . . . of political action' as Stanley Pierson has expressed it, it would also attempt to counter 'the opposition of the orthodox churches to socialism' through its members' determination to live a lifestyle which personified the establishment of heaven on earth.[11]

There are many different interpretations of the nature of Labour Church theology, and the extent to which it was adhered to by those attending the movement's services. In recent decades it has been portrayed as everything from a vague association of 'mere political clubs' to an attempt 'to harness religious aspirations' which 'could not be met in a purely political body'.[12] By the turn of the century, it is clear that there was a split within the Labour Church movement between those who wished to remain a Church, and those who saw the role of the organization as purely propagandist, yet exactly how far particular congregations – many of which were numbered in the thousands rather than the hundreds in their heyday – followed each faction is hard to disentangle.[13] Part of the difficulty in interpreting the Labour Church lies in its incredibly short life, which can largely be explained by the chronological limits of British socialist culture previously mentioned. Few Labour Churches survived for a long

[10] S. G. Hobson, *The Possibilities of the Labour Church: an Address to the Cardiff Labour Church* (Cardiff, 1893), p. 4; Philip H. Wicksteed, *What does the Labour Church stand for?* (London, 1892).

[11] S. Pierson, *British Socialists: The Journey from Fantasy to Politics* (Cambridge, MA, 1979), p. 29. See also Eleanor Keeling, 'The New Faith', *Labour Prophet* (April, 1894), pp. 37–8.

[12] Stephen Mayor, *The Churches and the Labour Movement* (London, 1967), p. 67; Owen Chadwick, *The Victorian Church, part 2, 1860–1901*, 2nd edn (London, 1972), p. 276; Pelling, *Origins of the Labour Party*, p. 132.

[13] For details of the split between John Trevor and Fred Brocklehurst, portrayed as the main advocate of a propagandist role for the Labour Church, see John Saville and Richard Storey's biographical sketch of Trevor in J. M. Bellamy and J. Saville, eds, *Dictionary of Labour Biography*, 6 (London, 1982), pp. 249–53.

enough period to allow adequate assessment of the strengths and weaknesses of each side in retaining congregations.[14] There is broad agreement, however, that in the crucial decade of the 1890s Labour Churches were a vital means of spreading a particular synthesis of religion and socialism, best described by Hugh McLeod as 'the religion adopted by the kind of working man who preferred the ILP [Independent Labour Party] to the SDF [Social Democratic Federation]'.[15] Central to this was what Trevor described as their 'incontinent . . . desire to have God's kingdom set up on earth'.[16] This belief led Labour Church followers to repudiate the more placatory aspects of later Victorian religion which promised equality in the hereafter as either a compensation or a reward for hardships endured on earth. It also led them to deal with complex issues, especially for those who attempted to retain a religious dimension in their political work. Some of the most difficult debates were those occasioned by the attitude of the Labour Church to both work and leisure, and it is on these that the remainder of this paper will concentrate.

Adherents of the Labour Church trod an intricate line around the question of work. On the face of it, the position of an avowedly pro-socialist organization on the issue would appear to be straightforward. The Church had been formed in part as a response to perceptions of class in existing churches, especially when these appeared to forgive the sins of the master more readily than those of the servant. Predictably, the Labour Church repudiated ideas of divine drudgery, concentrating on the claim to 'a fair share of life for those who do a fair share of labour'.[17] There was no belief, however, in an equality of the work across all levels of society. Implicit within the Labour Church was a view that the work done by working men (and occasionally women) was morally superior to that done by employers. Many of the hymns in *The Labour Church Hymn Book*, developed explicitly to 'emphasize the religion . . . of actual everyday life', reinforced this idea.[18] Idleness was

[14] Few Labour Churches survived beyond the end of the Boer War, the main exceptions being Birmingham, Leek, and Norwich. See the 'Readers' Comments' between Henry Pelling and K. S. Inglis, *International Review of Social History*, 4 (1959), pp. 111–13.

[15] Hugh McLeod, *Class and Religion in the Late Victorian City* (London, 1974), p. 62.

[16] *Labour Prophet* (April, 1892), p. 28.

[17] Philip Wicksteed, 'Is the Labour Church a class church?', *Labour Prophet* (Jan. 1892), p. 1.

[18] John Trevor, 'Preface', *The Labour Church Hymn Book* (London, 1895), p. 1. For a useful discussion of the *Labour Church Hymn Book* and its relationship to similar contemporary collections, see Waters, *British Socialists*, pp. 114–16.

to be avoided, and work sought out, as in Sydney Dyer's *Work, for the night is coming* (hymn number 77):

> Work, for the night is coming
> Work through the sunny noon
> Fill Brightest hours with Labour
> Rest comes sure and soon.

'He livest longest who can tell of true things only done each day', intoned Hymn 59, whilst others spoke of 'work for everyone in every hour of every day' or warned 'do not then stand idly waiting.' And if there were any doubt at all as to what constituted work, or a worker, in the eyes of the Labour Church, then the hymn book's version of the National Anthem would remove it, with its stirring opening 'God save the working man, peasant or artisan.'[19]

Although this standpoint was doubtless popular amongst Labour Church congregations, many of whom were drawn from the doggedly Marxist Social Democratic Federation, it left the organization wide open to accusations that it was an irreligious class church, aimed more at promoting disharmony than at any higher function.[20] The Revd Joseph Dawson, a Wesleyan minister, published a vicious attack on the Labour Church which warned:

> should the movement spread we shall probably have, as a result from it, and a set-off against it, the establishment of a Capitalist Church; and thus, instead of two forces, – Capital and Labour – simply making war in the industrial realm, we shall have them marshalled against each other under the banner of religion, and crossing swords on the Sabbath as well as on the week day.[21]

A similar attack was made by the Revd Dr Charles Leach. This London clergyman had attended a meeting at Bradford where he was horrified to hear Keir Hardie proclaim that within the established churches, 'Christianity is dead . . . and only awaits a decent burial.' Leach wrote an article in the *Bradford Observer* venting his concerns about the

[19] T. W. Chignell, 'Happy are they'; H. Bonar, 'He liveth long who liveth well'; Mrs M. E. Pickering, 'Helping along'; Mrs Gates, 'If you cannot on the ocean'; Anon., 'God Save the Working Man': *Labour Church Hymn Book*, nos 80, 59, 53, 45, 12.

[20] See, for example, the account of the funeral of George Evans of the SDF and Labour Church, *Labour Prophet* (May 1893), p. 36.

[21] *Labour Prophet* (Oct. 1892), p. 80.

teachings of the Labour Church. 'He that sets class against class, he that sets a man against his master, the poor against the rich, is as much the enemy of the one as he is of the other.'[22]

There were attempts from within the Labour Church to repudiate these accusations. The Revd J. Harker, who styled himself minister of the Labour Church at Bolton, published in pamphlet form a sermon in reply to the Revd Dawson explaining that, sadly, the capitalist church was already in existence:

> It is formed in every West End and wealthy suburb of our large towns, and most of our town churches are Capitalist churches. It is the tendency everywhere to build Capitalist churches, and to make more of the Capitalist than any other man. . . . It is the Capitalist Church that necessitates a Labour Church![23]

Keir Hardie, whose fiery words had been singled out for particular attack in the *Bradford Observer* article, stood by his original speech and responded in similar vein. The Labour Church existed, he claimed, because existing churches had turned their back on Labour: 'The Church has turned its back upon Christ. . . . [It] worships respectability, and puts its ban on poverty. It takes the slum owner and the sweater to its bosom and hands their victims over to everlasting perdition.'[24] These responses, however, were not typical. There were amongst Labour Church congregations many socialists who may have felt uncomfortable with the politics of other churches, but would have been quite comfortable with their predominantly middle-class base.[25] Hence a coherent position on what constituted 'work' became increasingly elusive within the literature of the Labour Church. The failure of existing churches to be inclusive to all, whilst excluding those who stood against the values of the Labour movement, had partially provoked the Labour Church into existence. The issue, however, appeared as difficult for socialists as capitalists to resolve satisfactorily.

Less contentious was the opposite side of the coin, the question of how the Labour Church ought to conceptualize and promote leisure. This too was important to the organization from its inception. The

22 *Labour Prophet* (Nov. 1892), p. 84.

23 Ibid. (Oct. 1892), p. 80. Harker, a Congregationalist minister, had moved himself, his Congregational Church, and its congregation, into a Labour Church with help from local socialists. See Pierson, 'John Trevor and the Labour Church movement', p. 467.

24 *Labour Prophet* (Nov. 1892), p. 84.

25 Pierson, *British Socialists*, pp. 37–8.

Church's fifth principle stated 'that the development of Personal Character and the improvement of Social Conditions are both essential to man's emancipation from moral and social bondage'.[26] Discussions of leisure allowed the broader labour movement to point to some of its successes. They also allowed the Labour Church to point to what was distinctive about its message within this broader movement. Other socialist groups could rejoice in the fact that 'the eight hour day [was] within measurable distance, and the Saturday half-day an accomplished fact', but only the Labour Church could consider how best working men and women could use this extra time to enrich their lives on a deeper level.[27]

As already suggested, Trevor and his supporters strongly believed that the individual members of the Church represented the physical embodiment of God, and that a large part of their work was in establishing heaven on earth rather than in the afterlife. As part of his quest for the 'Kingdom on Earth', Trevor initiated in the *Labour Prophet* (the journal of the Labour Church movement) a fierce debate about whether Labour Clubs (the majority of which in this instance were associated with Labour Churches or populated by Labour Church members) ought to serve alcoholic drink. This question, with its particular inference for those who believed that their bodies represented more than mere humanity, was exactly the kind of issue on which 'New Life' adherents would be expected to take a view. The results, given the extent of support for teetotalism amongst prominent socialist leaders, were quite mixed, but say something interesting about the faith that some Labour Church members held in their ability to provide a space for leisure quite different from anything within secular society. A majority of writers felt that prohibition ought to be the norm. Some argued from a position of teetotalism themselves, such as Thomas Chew who feared that he and other abstainers would be 'practically prohibit[ed]' from attending if drink were served.[28] Others also worried that the presence of drink would put off particular members, either younger supporters of both sexes, or 'sensitive and moral women'.[29] Class and pragmatism were further reasons for abstinence. One writer warned that 'the seduction of the wine cup

[26] The five principles of the Labour Church can be found in each edition of *The Labour Prophet*. They are also repeated in Pelling, *Origins of the Labour Party*, pp. 135–6.

[27] Tom Mann, 'The workman's wife', *Labour Prophet* (Feb. 1892), pp. 9–10.

[28] *Labour Prophet* (March 1893), p. 22.

[29] Ibid. (April 1893), p. 31.

of the rich has its counterpart in the ale glass of the workers . . . [and that] the advance guard . . . cannot afford . . . to emulate the fashions of the classes'; whilst Robert Blatchford, no abstainer himself, believed that socialist leisure was still important work, and that no one 'will wish to have a drink and gossip in any kind of workroom or study'.[30] Supporters were equally concerned about the potential for prohibition to narrow the movement, but felt that this would also happen if moderate drinkers were banished, with one correspondent from Rusholme warning that a successful movement required 'the combined and brotherly efforts of drinkers and abstainers'.[31] Most interesting with regard to the feelings of Labour Church supporters about leisure were the letters which supported drink within Labour Clubs as an antidote to the misuse of alcohol in less controlled arenas. W. H. Drew, the vice-president of Bradford Trades Council, explained that, in his town, fellow socialists agreed that they ought to provide for the wants of the moderate drinker 'in a purer moral atmosphere than usually obtains in the public house'. No one would be forced to buy drink, which was not always the case in commercial centres.[32] Bradford socialists at least were confident that they were providing a higher form of leisure than purely secular groups.

The Labour Church believed that this higher form of leisure was crucial in allowing the individual members to achieve their full potential for life. The richer life that they promised was underpinned with particular cultural forms, with space for 'writers, scientific men, musicians, actors' and others to 'feed their sense of beauty . . . reminding them of the meaning of life'.[33] Essential to this was a view that leisure provided opportunities for all to engage in 'the exercise of creative power' which underpinned much of the discourse on this theme within the Labour Church. Leisure was of vital importance, for it was where the seeds of the 'New Life' were to be sown and nurtured. Eleanor Keeling, secretary of the 'pioneer' group which was dedicated to working up areas for new Labour Churches, was quite clear that they offered something distinctive in this area. Something could be gained from time spent at the Labour Church which the wider socialist movement was ignoring. She explained:

[30] *Labour Prophet* (March 1893), p. 22; ibid. (May 1893), p. 35.
[31] Ibid. (March 1893), pp. 22–3.
[32] Ibid. (May 1893), pp. 34–5.
[33] Wicksteed, 'Is the Labour Church a class church?', p. 1.

> Ordinary meetings where the economics of Socialism are preached and discussed, are not calculated to raise and purify [the] thoughts. One is apt to become sordid and materialistic . . . forgetting that it is not much use nourishing and developing a body, be it never so healthy and beautiful, unless it be inhabited by an equally healthy soul.[34]

Keeping the soul nourished was the aim of much of the cultural activity of the Labour Church, which separated it somewhat from the broader attempts at associational culture practised by other socialist groups such as the *Clarion* movement.

Souls, however, were difficult to isolate, and their nourishment not as straightforward as Keeling may have hoped. Many socialist meetings failed dismally to separate their working-class audiences from the miserable surroundings of their daily lives. Robert Blatchford complained after attending a particularly depressing labour function in Lancashire (not attached to a Labour Church) that 'the fact is that those people had never been taught to be happy', and that until this state of affairs was altered the movement was 'doomed to march miles behind a Labour band which plays "the Marseillaise" in several keys, and none of them the right one'. The food was dreadful, he complained, the sandwiches thick and poorly presented, the cake 'beneath criticism'. Further, he worried that many would simply feel that these things were 'good enough for a lot of working folks, but . . . it was not good enough, just because they were working folks, only the best the world could give them would be good enough for them'.[35]

In seeking to uplift attenders, the format of the Labour Church was more useful than that of many political meetings. Although the organization tried to avoid regular ministers and set rituals, its use of music was consistent, and appeared to be welcomed.[36] Trevor himself recommended three hymns in each service.[37] Alf Mattison, secretary of one of the largest Labour Churches at Leeds, believed that music was in part the reason for the success in that locality, as 'the singing of our labour hymns . . . [has been] very inspiring and it is something in which all can join'; whilst the secretary of Bolton Labour

[34] *Labour Prophet* (May 1894), p. 63.

[35] Robert Blatchford, 'A plea for pleasure', ibid. (July 1894), pp. 84–5.

[36] Joseph Clayton, *The Rise and Decline of Socialism in Great Britain, 1884–1924* (London, 1926), pp. 95–6.

[37] *Labour Prophet* (June 1895), p. 89.

Church felt that 'the heartiness and vigour with which Labour hymns are sung is in pleasing contrast to the conventional style of most churches and chapels.'[38]

As well as aspiring to provide enjoyable ways of passing free time, the Labour Church also attempted to encourage its members to look to it rather than other institutions for some of the more profound areas of their life beyond work. Its attempts at rites of passage, discussed in detail by K. S. Inglis, again show the Labour Church as a cultural rather than a political phenomenon.[39] Christening 'troubled' R. Morley, the secretary at Halifax, who was grateful that his Church had 'managed to steer clear of such service' for unspecified reasons.[40] The Labour Church in Leeds was less anxious about this function and proudly reported its first christening in 1897, in which it was hoped that the child 'when it grew so as to be able to take its place in the Battle of Life . . . would be found in the ranks of the "despised," fighting for Love, Truth and Justice'.[41] Leeds was also the only Labour Church to be registered for marriages; but no record of any such service remains. Burials were more common, with Halifax again reporting that members had 'talked over the advisability of compiling something ready for the death of any members. We have some now who apparently will not be long with us.'[42] Unfortunately, there is no record of who these unfortunate members were, nor of their reaction to this news. Details of similar services elsewhere do exist, however, in which the simplicity and relevance of the Labour Church speakers appear to be the most distinctive factor.[43]

Along with many other aspects of the rich political culture which inspired and nurtured it, the Labour Church did not survive the nineteenth century.[44] Individual socialist leaders like Hardie and Philip Snowden persisted in using Christian rhetoric, but were no longer able to locate this within a particular organization. Former supporters

[38] *Labour Prophet* (Sept. 1894), p. 128; ibid. (Aug. 1893), p. 80. See also Inglis, 'The Labour Church movement', and the account of Philip Wicksteed reprinted from the *Manchester Guardian* in the *Labour Prophet* (Jan. 1892), p. 10.

[39] Inglis, 'The Labour Church movement', pp. 451–2.

[40] *Labour Prophet* (Sept. 1894), p. 128.

[41] Ibid. (Dec. 1897), p. 140, cited by Inglis, 'The Labour Church movement', p. 452.

[42] *Labour Prophet* (Sept. 1894), p. 128.

[43] See, e.g., John Trevor's account of the service he held for John Smith of Salford, *Labour Prophet* (May 1893), p. 39.

[44] There were a few exceptions, noted above, but representing more what Inglis refers to as a 'broad front political body' than an attempt at a religious group. See Pelling and Inglis, 'Readers' Comments'.

finally decided for themselves the incompatibility of being both a Church and a propagandist body by committing themselves decisively to different groups which were either one or the other.[45] Henry Pelling rightly observes that, due to the close if unofficial links between the Labour Churches and the ILP, it was unlikely that the downturn in the fortunes of the latter should escape the former. K. S. Inglis agrees, but adds that the particular synthesis of religion and propaganda was fated to failure.[46] Both of these explanations satisfy, but must not be taken as a denial of the success of the movement in its prime. Its best epitaph comes from Henry Myers Hyndman, a speaker, but never a particular supporter, who recalled one of the Bradford meetings: 'packed . . . some 1500 people. . . . The great towns of Yorkshire are getting far beyond mere "Labourism". . . . [P]eople get wildly enthusiastic.' This enthusiasm for a politics which addressed itself to leisure as well as work was notably absent in parliamentary politics in the next decade.

Leeds Metropolitan University.

[45] For example, Enid Stacy, who had written regularly for *The Labour Prophet*. She married a minister and combined the two difficult roles of parish wife and socialist propagandist, but rarely attempted to do both simultaneously. See her letters in Salford, Working Class Movement Library, Angela Tuckett papers.

[46] Inglis, 'The Labour Church movement'; Pelling and Inglis, 'Readers' Comments'.

THE POPE, LABOUR, AND THE TANGO: WORK, REST, AND PLAY IN THE THOUGHT AND ACTION OF BENEDICT XV (1914–22)

by JOHN F. POLLARD

EVER since Leo XIII promulgated his encyclical *Rerum novarum*, 'On the Conditions of the Working Classes', in 1891, successive popes have added to the corpus of Catholic teaching on social/labour questions. Pius X, for example, published an encyclical specifically addressing the vexed question of 'interconfessional' Christian trade unions in Germany, and Pius XI published no fewer than three encyclicals on social questions in the space of twelve months – *Quadragesimo anno* of May 1931, *Nova impendet* of October 1931, and *Caritate Christi compulsi* of May 1932.[1] Recent popes, John XXIII, Paul VI, and John Paul II, have been equally prolific in their commentaries on the labour question.

The notable exceptions were Pius XII (1939–58) and Benedict XV (1914–22). The fact that Benedict did not make a major public pronouncement specifically on the labour question is at first sight a little puzzling when one considers that during the course of his albeit short pontificate significant developments took place in the history of labour in Italy. In the immediate post-war period, both the Marxian Socialist working-class movement and the smaller Catholic labour movement, each with affiliated peasant leagues, co-operatives, credit unions, and mutual benefit societies, reached a high point of development. Moreover, his reign also saw the Bolshevik Revolution in Russia, and related insurrections and agitation in various parts of Europe, including Italy. Relations between capital and labour were, therefore, burning issues of the hour for Catholics, as well as all socially and politically conscious people in Europe at that time.

This paper will trace the development of Benedict XV's ideas on social issues, and in particular those on labour (work), rest, and play, with an especial emphasis, as far as the latter is concerned, on the 'abuses' thereof. It will then examine how he applied his ideas, both as

[1] For the texts of all these encyclicals see C. Carlen, IHM, ed., *The Papal Encyclicals*, 6 vols (Raleigh, NC, 1990), 3–4.

Archbishop of Bologna from 1907 until 1914, and as Pope between 1914 and 1922. Since Benedict is the least known of twentieth-century popes, it would be helpful to begin with a brief biographical sketch.[2]

* * *

Benedict XV was born Giacomo Della Chiesa, of a noble Genoese family, in 1854. After completing his legal studies at the University of Genoa in 1875, he went to Rome to train for the priesthood. Here he was 'talent-spotted' by Mgr Rampolla Del Tindaro, at that time Under Secretary, but later Vatican Secretary of State, and sent for further study to the Academy of Noble Ecclesiastics, the training ground of future Vatican diplomats and curial bureaucrats. After a short spell in the Madrid nunciature, he returned to Rome and eventually rose to be Under Secretary of State in 1901. The turning point in his career came with the death of Leo XIII three years later. In the subsequent conclave the election of Rampolla was blocked by an Austrian veto. Had Rampolla been elected, Della Chiesa might well have become his Secretary of State. Instead the election of Cardinal Giuseppe Sarto, Patriarch of Venice, as Pius X, and the replacement of Rampolla by Raphael Merry Del Val as Secretary of State, caused serious problems for Della Chiesa. He found himself increasingly at odds with Pius and Merry Del Val over their policies on 'modernism' and relations with France such that, in 1907, he was removed from the Vatican, being made Archbishop of Bologna. Though deprived of the cardinal's hat which usually went with that archbishopric until May 1914, he was, nevertheless, eminently papabile when Pius X died three months later. Della Chiesa's election as Benedict XV on 3 September still came as a surprise to many, but it can be attributed to the fact that of all the serious candidates he had by far the best mix of curial, diplomatic, and pastoral experience required of a pope who (as it turned out) would have to guide the Church through the horrors and dangers of the First World War.

* * *

Given his background and upbringing, it is hardly surprising that his views on the 'social question' were fairly conventional ones for an Italian priest ordained in the last quarter of the nineteenth century.

2 The most recent biography of Benedict XV is J. F. Pollard, *The Unknown Pope: Benedict XV (1914–1922) and the Pursuit of Peace* (London, 1999).

metropolitan see, he almost certainly wrote it. In the letter the bishops declared themselves to be above and beyond 'the struggles between the various classes by nature of [our] ministry', but they omitted the usual, almost obligatory, condemnation of Socialism and stressed the legitimacy of the right of class organization, a courageous stand in view of the attitude of the Vatican at this time.[19]

But the actual experience of labour conflict and its effects was not the only influence on the development of Della Chiesa's thinking on the labour question during his time as Archbishop. Other influences were at work. Della Chiesa was not reputed to be an intellectual, and there is no clear evidence of his reading habits. It is not even known, for example, whether he read the works of Professor Giuseppe Toniolo of the University of Pisa, who was Italy's leading Catholic social theorist at this time. Toniolo advocated the idea of corporations, mixed associations of workers and employees, an essentially neo-Thomist re-evocation of the guilds of a mythical, medieval golden age of European Catholicism.[20] Certainly, there is no identifiable trace of corporativism in Della Chiesa's teaching. On the other hand, judging by his decision as pope to call in Mgr Pottier, the Belgian Christian Democratic pioneer, to pronounce on the Catholic integrity of the economic and social policies of the *Partito Popolare Italiano*, founded in 1919, it would appear that he was familiar with and sympathetic to that man's thought.[21] Pottier was a strong advocate of autonomous, Christian unions, and even of the participation of Catholics in unions that were not even Catholic-based.[22]

There is also strong circumstantial evidence of Italian Christian Democratic influences on Della Chiesa at this time. By the beginning of the twentieth century, the Italian Christian Democrats, led by two priests, Romolo Murri and Luigi Sturzo, and by the Milanese Catholic lawyer, Filippo Meda, had become the dominant influence in the *Opera dei Congressi*, the umbrella organization for the various associations and activities of the Italian Catholic movement. Some of the most radical and dynamic of these activities were created or at least sponsored by them, like the *Capellani del Lavoro* experiment in the

19 L. Bedeschi, *Il modernismo e Romolo Murri in Emilia-Romagna* (Parma, 1967), p. 158.

20 Misner, *Social Catholicism*, p. 286.

21 Vatican City, Affari Ecclesiastici Straordinari [Archives of the Council of the Public Affairs of the Church, hereafter Vatican, AAEESS], 953–4, Italia 1918–1921 file, 348, 'Mons. Pottier sulla questions del movimento democratico ed il ruolo della Chiesa'.

22 Misner, *Social Catholicism*, pp. 259–60.

industrial hinterland of Milan which was very similar to the French worker-priest movement, but one which preceded it by thirty years.[23] The Christian Democrats were also very active in the organization of Catholic labour unions, especially in the countryside of northern and eastern Italy, and were consequently involved in a rash of strikes in the 1890s and early 1900s.[24] But it was the political ambitions of the Christian Democrats that were eventually to fall foul of the papacy and bring about their downfall. At the turn of the century, the Christian Democrats were chafing against the ban on Catholics participating in Italian politics, the *Non expedit*, which had been imposed by Pius IX in the 1860s as a protest against the Italian invasion of the Papal States. Many wished to enter parliamentary politics in order to achieve legislative implementation of their labour and social reform programme. It is known that even before his elevation to the see of Bologna, Della Chiesa had had cordial relations with Sturzo, encouraging him in his pioneering work organizing peasant leagues and municipal reform in his native Sicily.[25] He was equally encouraging to his fellow-Genovese, Giambattista Valente, who was active in the formation of Catholic labour unions among industrial and transport workers in northern and central Italy.[26] He was also close to another Christian Democratic leader, Angelo Mauri, who went on to became a key figure in the *Partito Popolare*.[27] These, and his other Christian Democratic contacts, suggest that by the end of his time as Archbishop, Della Chiesa had been fully exposed to Christian Democratic ideas, especially in relation to the labour union question, but which, in his typically prudent fashion, he kept largely to himself. In other words, he was a closet 'Christian Democrat'.

Della Chiesa had good reason to be cautious at this time. Whereas the aristocratic Leo XIII had been patient with the Christian Democrats, limiting himself to strictures about their political ambitions in his encyclical *Graves de communi re* of 1901, his plebian successor Pius X was rather less tolerant. It did not help that so many of their leading lights were suspected of 'modernism'. In 1905 Pius X dissolved the

[23] L. Bedeschi, *I capellani del lavoro: aspetti religiosi e culturali della societa lombarda negli anni della crisi* (Milan, 1977).

[24] Ibid., p. 211.

[25] G. Mellinato, 'Benedetto XV e il PPI', *La civiltà cattolica*, 144 (1993), 3, pp. 277–8.

[26] L. Bedeschi, *I pionieri della Democrazia Cristian: modernismo cattolico, 1896–1906* (Milan, 1966), p. 347.

[27] Ibid., p. 135.

Opera, which had become by now deeply divided between supporters and opponents of Christian Democracy. As Catholic activists sought to meet the Socialist challenge by extending their own network of labour unions and peasant leagues, they were hampered by the reverberations of this conflict at a local level, and by the bishops' concern to enforce Rome's demands to isolate and neutralize the Christian Democrats.[28] In Bologna, one of the centres of Christian Democracy, Della Chiesa seems to have had success in resisting some of these pressures.[29]

Catholic trade union organizers came under particular pressure in the latter part of Pius X's reign. There were demands that Catholic unions should be mixed, that they should include employers as well as workers, and there was the question of the morality of strike action. It was implicitly permitted as a weapon of last resort by *Rerum novarum* but regarded with disapproval by the ecclesiastical authorities. It is significant in this regard that when the Bishop of Bergamo, Radini-Tedeschi, gave his moral and material support to a strike of textile workers at Ranica in his diocese in 1909, he did so without the approval of the Vatican.[30] In these circumstances, it is hardly surprising that the growth of Catholic trade unionism in Italy was difficult and slow: in 1910, according to government statistics, the membership of Socialist trade unions stood at over 650,000, whereas that of the Catholic unions at only 104,000, and two-thirds of those were female workers.[31] But in 1914, Pius X came close to banning Christian trade unions altogether. Padre Monetti wrote a series of articles and published them in the Jesuit journal *La civiltà cattolica* between February and May of that year. In them he inveighed against the 'excesses' of existing Catholic trade union organizations and challenged their moral legitimacy, intending to prepare the way for their eventual condemnation.[32] In all probability, only the death of Pius X in August 1914 prevented a condemnation of Catholic trade unionism tout court.[33]

* * *

28 Pollard, 'Religion and the Italian working class', p. 171.

29 Bedeschi, *Il modernismo*, pp. 77–8.

30 I. Lizzola and E. Manzoni, 'Proletariato Bergamasco e organizzazioni cattoliche: lo sciopero di Ranica (1909)', *Studi e ricerche di storia contemporanea*, 15 (1981), pp. 15–18.

31 D. D. Horowitz, *Storia del movimento sindacale in Italia* (Bologna, 1966), pp. 186–7.

32 *La civiltà cattolica*, 65 (1914), 1, pp. 385–400, 'Sindacalismo cristiano?'; 2, pp. 385–99, 'Sindacalismo cristiano?', pp. 546–59, 'Sindacalismo cristiano?'.

33 Misner, *Social Catholicism*, pp. 286–7.

Against this background, the changes in papal policy on the labour question which followed the election of Cardinal Della Chiesa in September 1914 can only be described as revolutionary. His elevation to the papal throne, in fact, brought about a break with a number of his predecessor's key policies. Though Benedict reaffirmed Pius X's strictures on 'modernism' in his first encyclical, *Ad beatissimi*, of November 1914,[34] he stopped the anti-modernist witch-hunt, banishing its chief 'witch-finder', Umberto Benigni, from the Vatican. He and his Secretary of State, Cardinal Pietro Gasparri, reversed the policy of intransigence towards anti-clerical France which had been maintained by Pius X and Merry Del Val, and adopted a more active diplomatic policy aimed at breaking out of the isolation into which Pius and his Secretary of State had effectively shut the Vatican. Following the example of Leo XIII and Rampolla, they sought to establish equidistance between France and the other Entente powers, on the one hand, and Germany and Austria-Hungary on the other.

Benedict's policy on the labour question was an equally decisive reversal of the policy of the previous reign. His pronouncements on labour and social questions marked a return to the principles of *Rerum novarum*. In *Ad beatissimi* he attacked 'class hatred' and Socialism, but like Leo XIII he was even-handed.[35] Throughout his pontificate, Benedict repeatedly affirmed the dignity and rights of workers, and the obligation of Catholics to contribute actively towards the moral and material progress of the labouring classes, and he reiterated these themes in his very last consistory of December 1921.[36]

The first clear signal of the new policy came in 1915 when Benedict replaced a group of leading figures at the head of the Italian Catholic movement. The safe, conservative Count Medolago Albani made way for the more progressive Count Zucchini as president of the *Unione Economico-Sociale*, the branch of the movement responsible for supervising the trade unions.[37] In addition, Angelo Mauri was made the secretary-general of the *Unione*.[38] At the same time, Luigi Sturzo was appointed president of the *Unione Popolare*, the cultural, educational,

[34] Carlen, *Papal Encyclicals*, 4: 146.

[35] Ibid., pp. 144–5.

[36] See AFDC, file on 'Visite', 34, 'Discorso ai rappresentanti del Sindacat Catholique des ouvriers des Chemins de Fer Nederlandais', May 1921, and *La civiltà cattolica*, 72 (1921), 4, p. 387.

[37] G. B. Valente, *Aspetti e momenti dell'azione sociale dei cattolici italiani (1892–1926)* (Rome, 1968), p. 140.

[38] Bedeschi, *Pionieri*, p. 347.

and recreational arm of the Catholic movement and the precursor of the future Catholic Action organization.[39] The Christian Democrats had returned in force to the leadership of the movement after a break of nearly twelve years.

More dramatic developments were to come. In 1919 Benedict gave his permission to Giambattista Valente to found an 'aconfessional' and autonomous confederation of all the Catholic trade unions – the *Confederazione Italiana del Lavoro* (CIL). The confederation was 'aconfessional' in that it could theoretically recruit non-Catholic workers, and it was 'autonomous' in that it was separate from and independent of the Catholic movement and the Church hierarchy. This new status enabled it to be officially recognized by the Italian state. Within a few years, membership of the unions under its authority increased tenfold, reaching a peak of over 1,100,000 in 1920.[40] Likewise, Benedict liberated the political potential of Italian Christian Democracy by allowing the formation of the *Partito Popolare Italiano* and by ordering that the *Non expedit* should be finally permitted to lapse. Like the CIL, the *Partito Popolare* was meant to be both aconfessional and autonomous. Benedict expressed the hope that the party would 'facilitate in every way the penetration and realization of Christian social doctrine'.[41] He even gave guarded approval of its policy of giving votes to women;[42] a far cry indeed from the policies of Pius X.

* * *

But even for Benedict there were limits to the autonomy of Catholic trade unionism, and in his view these limits were passed during the 'Red Two Years'. This was a period of working-class militancy, strikes, riots, and occupations of the land and factories, which convulsed Italy between the end of the war and the autumn of 1920. Against a background of Bolshevik-style uprisings and short-lived governments in various parts of eastern and central Europe, these events produced a very real fear on the part of the political establishment and the middle classes that revolution was imminent in Italy also. Benedict's concern was about Catholic trade-union and other activists imitating the militant tactics of their Marxist counterparts in the Socialist-

39 G. De Rosa, *Luigi Sturzo* (Turin, 1977), p. 186.

40 Valente, *Aspetti e momenti*, p. 140.

41 F. Traniello and G. Campanini, eds, *Dizionario storico del movimento cattolico in Italia, 1860–1980*, 3 vols in 5 (Turin, 1981–4), 2/i: 33.

42 Mellinato, 'Benedetto XV e il PPI', p. 75.

dominated trade union confederation, the CGL. (The Communist Party did not emerge in Italy until 1921.) The *estremista* faction of the Catholic trade union movement, headed by Cremonese peasant leader Guido Miglioli, with supporters in other parts of northern Italy like Bergamo and Verona, were doing just that in 1920. Their militant tactics in struggles with the landowners over tenancy agreements and sharecroppers' contracts, and their support for co-operation with the Socialists, led them to be dubbed the 'white Bolsheviks'.[43] In March 1920, Benedict wrote a public letter to Mgr Marelli, the Bishop of Bergamo, warning against the adoption of Socialist methods of class struggle by the diocese's Catholic trade union organization, the *Ufficio del Lavoro*, and advising the Bishop not to hesitate, if he felt it necessary, to remove the organization's officers, which Mgr Marelli duly did.[44]

If Benedict issued no encyclical on social/economic questions, then his letter to Bishop Marelli constitutes an unofficial substitute, containing as it does a fairly comprehensive restatement of established Church teaching on the ethics of industrial relations and the conduct of Catholic trade unionism. Like Leo XIII before him, he utterly rejected the theory and practice of class struggle, and with them Socialism. On the other hand, he reaffirmed the legitimate right of workers to organize themselves in unions to bring about an improvement in their material situation in a peaceful fashion.[45]

In 1920 Benedict told his friend Carlo Monti, who acted as his link with the Italian government, that he intended to publish an encyclical condemning Communism.[46] It is certainly not surprising that he considered doing so in 1920 because in the summer of that year working-class militancy culminated in the occupation of the factories of northern Italy, which was interpreted by many as the prelude to revolution. It was against this background, and the broader one of reports coming into the Vatican of the persecution of the Church by the Soviet regime in Russia and the short-lived Soviet governments in Bavaria and Hungary, that Benedict issued a *motu proprio* in which he condemned Communism, or as he described it, 'the utopian dreams of

[43] J. M. Foot, '"White Bolsheviks"? The Catholic Left and the Socialists in Italy, 1919–1920', *HistJ*, 40 (1997), pp. 415–33.

[44] *La civiltà cattolica*, 71 (1920), 2, p. 104.

[45] Ibid., p. 101.

[46] A. Scottà, ed., *La concilizaione ufficiosa: diario del barone Carlo Monti lincaricato d'affari del governo italiano presso la Santa Sede (1914–1922)*, 2 vols (Vatican City, 1997), 2: 491.

a universal Republic' and 'absolute equality of men'.[47] It is significant that the document was addressed not just to the Italian bishops, but to those of the whole world. No trace of an encyclical has been found in Benedict's private papers or the Vatican Archives, but the *motu proprio*, a papal statement of admittedly lesser significance than an encyclical, served as a more than adequate substitute until Pius XI's encyclical, *Divini redemptoris*, of 1937.

* * *

Another major concern of Della Chiesa and his fellow bishops in the pre-War period was with the ways in which the new patterns of work consequent on industrialization affected the labouring classes. Female labour evinced particular anxiety because of both the potential damage to family life, and also because of the vulnerability of young girls to immoral influences in the working environment.[48] The new work patterns in both industry and agriculture also violated the sanctity of Sunday as a day of rest and worship. The records of provincial councils and diocesan synods, as well as those of episcopal visitations in a number of areas of northern and central Italy in the early 1900s, are full of complaints about the fact that many workers were unable to fulfil their obligation to attend Mass.[49] In response to this situation, there developed an Italian equivalent of the Lord's Day Observance Society, *La Pia Opera per la sanctificazione delle feste*.[50] The battle to safeguard the *riposo festivo* became a major task of Catholic Action, which Benedict created as Pope following the reorganization of the Italian Catholic movement in the wake of the foundation of the *Partito Popolare* and CIL. Along with a battle for 'public morality' – a campaign against cabarets, dance halls, and immodest dress – it remained a major objective of Catholic Action throughout the reign of Benedict's successor, Pius XI.[51]

In Benedict XV's thinking about rest and recreation, especially in

[47] A. Scottà, *I vescovi veneti e la Santa Sede nella guerra 1915–1918*, 3 vols (Rome, 1991), 3: 452.

[48] See A. Kelikian, 'Convitti operai cattolici e forza lavoro femminile', in A. Gigli Marchetti, ed., *Donna Lombarda* (Milan, 1992), pp. 180–6.

[49] See, for example, F. Agostini, ed., *Le visite pastorali di Giuseppe Calligari nella diocesi di Padova(1884–88/1893–1905)* (Rome, 1981), pp. 132–4.

[50] U. Lovato and A. Castellani, 'Il beato Leonardo Murialdo e il movimento operaio cristiano', in *Italia Sacra: Spiritualità ed azione del laicato cattolico* (Padua, 1969), p. 608.

[51] J. F. Pollard, *The Vatican and Italian Fascism, 1929–1932: a Study in Conflict* (Cambridge, 1985), p. 112.

relation to the labouring classes, the Tango takes on something of a symbolic function. He was extremely scandalized by the vogue for the Tango which swept Italy, and Europe, in the pre-First World War period, and actually denounced it as 'the height of public immorality'.[52] (Curiously, jokes are still told about Benedict and the Tango in Italy today.) Like his fellow bishops, when Archbishop of Bologna he saw leisure time/recreation as a potentially major occasion of sin for the labouring classes, so denunciations of the Tango, and more generally of dance halls and most public entertainments, were frequent in his diocesan bulletin.[53] Not surprisingly, therefore, he also regarded the Carnival as an apotheosis of evil. Clergy were forbidden to be near places where the 'carnivalesque follies' took place, and the duty of attendance at expositions of the Blessed Sacrament and services of reparation to the Sacred Heart for the 'obscene, immoral and blasphemous' behaviour of the revellers were enjoined upon the laity.[54] Throughout the reigns of both Pius X and Benedict XV, the ecclesiastical hierarchy also remained extremely ambivalent towards a new form of recreation, the cinema, forbidding the clergy (though not the laity) from frequenting it; despite the fact that religious films were being produced by a specifically Catholic company, *Unitas*, and were being shown in parish halls.[55]

But recreation/leisure was not just a question of 'public morality', it was also a key battleground in the incessant war which developed with the Marxian-inspired working-class movement. As it developed, that movement very consciously sought to build a comprehensive counter-culture to that of the Church, using *circoli operai* (workers' clubs), social centres, theatrical and musical associations, creches, and cheap restaurants to serve the worker and his family in competition with the Catholic parish and its initiatives. In its definitive form, this culture was characterized by all manner of secular events and heroes to compete with the public demonstrations of Catholic piety and loyalty, particularly the celebration of saints' days.[56] According to the nineteenth-century Anarchist leader Mikhail Bakunin, who spent a

[52] As quoted in *La civiltà cattolica*, 71 (1920), 3, pp. 290–1.

[53] *Il corriere della sera*, 23 Jan. 1922, p. 2.

[54] *Bollettino diocesano di Bologna*, 4/v (Feb. 1914), p. 116, 'avvertimenti ai Sacerdoti per Carnevale'; AFDC, Documenti, dispense ecc. del Msgr Giacomo Della Chiesa durante sua permanenza nell'Arcivescovado di Bologna, 'Fervorino per funzione di riparazione al Sacro cuore di Gesul' (no date).

[55] Traniello and Campanini, *Dizionario storico*, 1/i: 304.

[56] Pollard, 'Religion and the formation of the Italian working class', p. 167.

long period in Italy, Italian peasants were superstitious and 'they loved the Church because it interrupted the monotony and misery of country life with its theatrical and musical ceremonies.'[57] The Church quickly found that as the processes of industrialization and agricultural modernization in Italy proceeded apace its capacity to command the attention of the labouring classes, especially in industrial towns and agro-villages, could no longer rest on the colour of traditional ceremonies. Della Chiesa in Bologna realized that more was needed than existing parish facilities could provide.[58] And as Howard Bell has demonstrated from his detailed study of the struggle between Catholics and Socialists in Sesto San Giovanni, an industrial satellite of Milan which later earned for itself the title of 'the Stalingrad of Italy', the development of Catholic recreational and sporting facilities were more often than not a response to a perceived threat from the working-class movement.[59]

After 1920, Benedict gave responsibility for recreational and sporting activities among Catholics, both youth and adults, to the Catholic Action movement.[60] Its networks of parochial youth clubs, sporting clubs, recreational halls, and eventually small cinemas, were to survive the 'demolitions' of Fascism in the late 1920s, and further threats in the 1930s, to become a key element in the strong Catholic 'subculture' of the post-Second World War period.[61]

* * *

Giacomo Della Chiesa was essentially conservative and conventional in his upbringing and outlook, and this is most clearly demonstrated by his instinctive feelings about work, rest, and play. Yet the radical streak already discernible in his comments on *Rerum novarum* in 1897 was to become very manifest after he became pope, most clearly after the end of the War. In the letter written on his behalf by the Cardinal Secretary of State to Mgr Pottier on 18 December 1918 he posed three questions:

57 As quoted ibid., p. 165.

58 Traniello and Campanini, *Dizionario storico*, 1/i: 176–7.

59 D. Howard Bell, *Sesto San Giovanni: Workers, Culture and Politics in an Italian Town 1880–1922* (New Brunswick, NJ, 1986), p. 60.

60 It is significant that Benedict's reign witnessed the formation of the Catholic boy scout movement in Italy, affiliated to Catholic Action and the Italian Catholic Sports Association: see Traniello and Campanini, *Dizionario storico*, 1/ii, pp. 373–4.

61 Pollard, *Vatican and Italian Fascism*, pp. 107–8.

> Is it opportune for the Church to involve itself in the ideas which are currently dominant? . . . What liberties pertaining to the people could the Church take under its patronage without detriment to essential Christian principles? . . . What definite steps may the Church take in order to develop a line of action in the direction indicated?[62]

Clearly these questions were prompted by the radically transformed state of Europe at the end of the First World War, in particular the prevalence of Wilsonian principles of national self-determination and democracy in the vanquished states and the impact of the Bolshevik Revolution, which had unleashed a ferment of agitation and expectation among the working classes, what Pottier described as 'la quattrième état'.[63] The choice of Pottier, a long-standing proponent of Christian Democracy on the socioeconomic and political planes, is indicative of Benedict's willingness to be bold in responding to the pressing questions of the hour at war's end. In fact, as far as Italy was concerned, he had already made his response, by permitting the establishment of both the *Partito Popolare* and the Catholic trade union confederation, by the time he received Pottier's reply written on 15 February 1920.[64]

This response to the signs of the times was undoubtedly revolutionary by comparison with the policies of both Benedict's predecessor Pius X and his successor Pius XI. Maybe it was even premature. Certainly Pius XI, and probably the bulk of the Italian bishops and clergy, was more than happy to stand by as both the *Partito Popolare* and the CIL disappeared in the 'demolitions' of Fascism in the late 1920s. For Pius XI, Fascism was the answer to the threat of revolution, not experiments in lay Catholic autonomy in the political or trade union field. But if Benedict was a man before his time, then the experience of both Catholic trade unionism and political Catholicism in post-Second World War Italy (even allowing for the ignominious collapse of the Christian Democratic Party in a welter of corruption scandals in the 1990s) ultimately vindicated his boldness.

Anglia Polytechnic University

[62] Vatican, AAEESS, 953–4, Italia, 1918–1921, 'Mons. Pottier sulla question del movimento democratico e la Chiesa': letter from Pottier to Gasparri, 15 Feb. 1920.

[63] Ibid.

[64] Ibid.

FROM SHOOTING TO SHOPPING: RANDALL DAVIDSON'S ATTITUDES TO WORK, REST, AND RECREATION

by STUART MEWS
(*Presidential Paper*)

IF Jose Harris was right when she asserted that 'there was no such thing as a homogeneous Victorian work ethic' and that a history of work, especially between 1870 and 1914, can only be written on the basis of the reported observations of, and reflections on, the work of individual farms, factories, homes, offices, and workshops,[1] she would find few better sources than the astonishing variety of personal experiences and insights of Randall Davidson (1846–1930), England's longest-serving Archbishop of Canterbury.[2] Davidson's early career touched a range of contacts from middle-class urban Edinburgh, to the Lowland small country estate, English public school, and Oxford college; as well as the doctor-dominated private sickroom, smart shooting parties on grouse moors, the staid Lambeth Palace bureaucracy, the tradition-infested Court at Windsor, the arcane Board of the British Museum, and the privileged confines of the House of Lords and West End clubs with their opportunities for strategic socializing and quiet persuasion. At the same time there was a coming to terms with the new consumer society as manifested in the new shopocracy of retail stores like Debenhams. These different worlds imposed their own power-structures, work expectations, and demands on both providers and purchasers. They produced their own stresses and strains which called for mitigation. The huge range of what constituted work was part of the concerns of the socially-alert clergyman in late Victorian Britain, none more so than Randall Davidson, who can be profitably considered as an exponent of, participant in, and observer of the place of work and use of time in his society.

Though Queen Victoria once wondered if her latest ecclesiastical

[1] Jose Harris, *Private Lives, Public Spirit. A Social History of Britain 1870–1914* (Oxford, 1993), p. 125.

[2] G. K. A. Bell, *Randall Davidson*, 2 vols (Oxford, 1935); Stuart Mews, 'Randall Davidson', *New DNB* (Oxford, forthcoming).

favourite was ambitious,[3] Davidson, then Dean of Windsor, would never have thought in such terms. Rather, he would have talked the language of service. George W. E. Russell, grandson of a Duke of Bedford, Liberal politician, and ardent High Churchman, went to Harrow only five years after Davidson. 'I can remember quite clearly', he recalled, 'that, even in my Harrow days the idea of Life as Service was always present to my mind: and it was constantly enforced by the preaching of such men as Butler, Westcott, and Farrar.'[4] In Russell's case, the influences of school reinforced the teaching of an evangelical home, and propelled him into a life of public service via social work, the new London County Council, and hence into the House of Commons and on to the Liberal Front Bench.

Life as service was the creed of the new professionals of late Victorian Britain. Harold Perkin has written convincingly of the development of the professional ideal alongside the older aristocratic and entrepreneurial codes. The professional ideal was essentially to be found in the ethos of the reformed civil service – 'your obedient servant'.[5] In Davidson's case the ideal of service implanted at Harrow had initially to co-exist, as we shall see, with more brutal rural pursuits in the holidays.

Davidson was inclined to be anxious. Sir Edward Grey once asked of him, 'Who was that bishop with such a puzzled face?'[6] Philip Bell has written of Davidson's 'massive calm';[7] but Owen Chadwick may be nearer the truth when he writes of Davidson looking 'for the shadows of tigers behind all the bushes in the jungle'.[8] Asquith, with the superiority and self-assurance of Balliol man, told Arthur Benson that in any other profession Davidson would not be 'a *first-rate* man – but a very good one'.[9] It was Asquith who once tried to calm Lloyd George in a tense Commons debate in 1915 by whispering, 'They call the Archbishop of Canterbury "God's own Butler".'[10] Davidson was God's own butler in the sense that he was always well prepared, desired to

[3] Queen Victoria to Sir Henry Ponsonby, 24 Dec. 1889: Bell, *Davidson*, 1, p. 185.

[4] George W. E. Russell, *Fifteen Chapters of Autobiography* (London, 1915), p. 339. H. M. Butler became Master of Trinity College, Cambridge; B. F. Westcott became Bishop of Durham; F. W. Farrer became Dean of Canterbury.

[5] Harold Perkin, *The Rise of Professional Society* (London, 1990), p. 2.

[6] David L. Edwards, *Leaders of the Church of England 1928–44* (Oxford, 1971), p. 237.

[7] P. M. H. Bell, *Disestablishment in Ireland and Wales* (London, 1969), p. 298.

[8] Owen Chadwick, *Hensley Henson. A Study in the Friction of Church and State* (Oxford, 1983), p. 139.

[9] David Newsome, *On the Edge of Paradise. A.C. Benson: the Diarist* (London, 1980), p. 123.

[10] *Lloyd George: Diary by Frances Stevenson*, ed. A. J. P. Taylor (London, 1971), p. 40.

please, and did his best to ensure that the life of the household ran smoothly and efficiently. But that did not make him a doormat, and there were times when his best service was offered through reasoned and principled but always courteous criticism.

For a real butler's assessment of Davidson, there is the memorandum prepared by Mrs Davidson's companion Mary Mills, for George Bell's use in writing the outstanding official biography. She recalled the butler at a big country house where the Davidsons often stayed saying, 'I like the Archbishop, he is the nicest gentleman that ever comes here. Why, in all the years he has been coming here, I have never heard him say, "one damn".'[11] Mary Mills went on to write that he was always 'anxious and ready to help'. Whoever sought his advice would receive his whole attention. When members of the household complained at busy periods about the time being given to individuals seeking his help, the Archbishop would say, 'What am I here for? Is it not to help; and remember that for so and so, it is his life – emphasising the words "his life".'[12]

Davidson's formative years were spent in a world of game and guns. Born in Edinburgh in 1846, the son of a timber merchant, personally devout, who took his son for a Presbyterian baptism, the family moved during Randall's early childhood to a new house set in 240 acres at Muirhouse on the shore of the Firth of Forth. It meant, he recalled, being 'indoctrinated in all sorts of country things'.[13] There were plenty of rabbits, birds, fish, and a pony. Davidson always considered himself fortunate in reaching his settled convictions 'in surroundings which taught me instinctively to grasp the lay view, and sometimes the sporting view on all sorts of questions'.[14] This cryptic comment appears to have been quoted by George Bell from an autobiographical memorandum, which is no longer to be found amongst the Davidson Papers at Lambeth.[15]

The significance of Davidson's 'sporting view' as a preparation for the life of a priest and (later) bishop needs closer consideration. His

[11] London, Lambeth Palace Library [hereafter LPL], Bell Papers, vol. 222, fol. 17: Mary Mills Memorandum, 1932.

[12] Ibid., fol. 18.

[13] Bell, *Davidson*, 1: 10.

[14] Ibid., 1, p. 33.

[15] I owe this information, as well as invaluable help with the Davidson Papers, to Melanie Barber, whose own 'Randall Davidson: a partial retrospective', is in Steven Taylor, ed., *From Cranmer to Davidson. A Church of England Miscellany*, Church of England Record Society, 7 (Woodbridge, 1999), pp. 387–438.

enjoyment of country pursuits was to have dire consequences, which affected the rest of his life, and probably influenced his use of his time and the significance he gave to work, rest, and play. On two occasions he almost lost his life. At fourteen he was nearly drowned, and at eighteen accidentally shot. Shooting rabbits seemed innocuous for someone as experienced as Davidson, but it was a young friend who accidentally pulled a trigger, and lodged around 160 shot near the top of Davidson's thigh. The doctor who attended was so certain that death was inevitable that he did not consider amputating the leg, the normal procedure in such cases. Against all the odds Davidson recovered; though the effects of the accident remained for the rest of his life. Sir Thomas Barlow, his doctor, noted that Davidson was always liable to attacks of lumbago, partly induced by damage to the muscles of his hips. A 'formidable hernia' on the right side was a life-long inconvenience. Davidson had to wear a truss, but the rupture often came down while he was preaching. If he could get by himself, noted Barlow, 'he was fairly dodgy and could get it back'. Diet was important. Davidson liked tripe, and it was good for him.[16]

After the shooting accident, there followed many months in bed at home, then crutches, and five months later a return to Harrow in a semi-invalid state. His subsequent career at Trinity College, Oxford, was disappointing, ending with an undistinguished third-class degree, after a collapse during schools.[17]

Davidson had always wanted to be ordained. He had been confirmed into the Church of England whilst at Harrow by his father's old friend A. C. Tait, then Bishop of London, later to be Archbishop of Canterbury, and later still to become Davidson's father-in-law. After Oxford the restoration of his health was paramount. That meant plenty of fresh air and exercise. Guns and game were the answer. For the next four years it is tempting to say that Davidson lived the life of a young gentleman of leisure, but that would be to simplify his actions and attitudes. James Obelkevich has argued that the gentry were set apart in Victorian society by their rejection of the gospel of work;[18] but Davidson was as self-driven as any Victorian entrepreneur. The methodical, relentless, even ascetic way in which he sought to

[16] London, Wellcome Library, 108/82: 'Memorandum on Archbishop Davidson's Illnesses', Typescript by Sir Thomas Barlow.

[17] Bell, *Davidson*, 1: 18–25.

[18] James Obelkevich, *Religion and Rural Society. South Lindsey 1825–1875* (Oxford, 1976), p. 40.

regain his health by the patient mastery of the art of the shoot must surely have won the admiration of even Max Weber. This was not the carefree playtime of a young gentleman but the calculated use of time in a disciplined way for the attainment of specific goals. Now the time had come to put away childish things, and it was not rabbits but grouse and pheasants which were his quarries, and the means to his ends. From 1869 to 1873 Davidson kept a meticulous record of the daily bag in his Sportsman's Note-book.[19] A Fenland farmer recalled that in the 1840s the bag was not itemized but weighed: 'it was a good sport for a party to kill a peck'.[20] By the time Davidson began to shoot, precision was expected, both of aim and in the recording of results. He began the entries soon after his twenty-first birthday, which might suggest that either the new notebook or a new gun was a birthday present. Davidson went out shooting, usually with friends, on 17, 19, 20, 21, 23, and 24 August 1869. On the first day he and a friend bagged forty-one grouse, a snipe and a hare. In those first six days 138 hits were scored, mostly of grouse. In August and September Davidson recorded over 300 kills. He continued shooting with great regularity for the next four years.[21] Sometimes he went out on his own, usually with a few friends. Living in shooting country, it not surprisingly never seems to have occurred to him that the slaughter of birds might raise moral questions. In 1870 few people cared. There had always been bishops like Blomfield of the huge pre-1834 diocese of Chester who disliked their clergy riding to hounds, mainly on the grounds that it was an unseemly waste of a clergyman's time;[22] but G. W. E. Russell insisted that in the evangelical circles of his youth shooting was seen as different from hunting and 'no one condemned shooting'.[23]

Shooting became part of the modernization of the countryside. As Richard Holt points out, the rich began to prefer shooting to hunting in the late nineteenth century. 'If the golden age of fox-hunting was the first half of the nineteenth century, the shooting of large numbers of carefully preserved game-birds such as grouse, pheasant and partridge with ever more accurate and powerful firearms was the

[19] LPL, Davidson Papers, vol. 734: Sportsman's note-books 1868–73.

[20] *The Reminiscences of Albert Pell*, ed. Thomas Mackay (London, 1908), p. 100.

[21] LPL, Davidson Papers, vol. 734.

[22] C. J. Blomfield, *Primary Charge to the Clergy of the Diocese of Chester* (London, 1825), pp. 29–30. On the clergy and hunting see J. T. Williams, 'Bearers of moral and spiritual values: the social roles of clergymen and women in British society, c.1790–c.1880, as mirrored in attitudes to them as foxhunters' (Oxford University, D.Phil. thesis, 1987).

[23] G. W. E. Russell, *The Household of Faith* (London, 1906), p. 234.

passion of late Victorian and Edwardian England' – and also, we might add, of Scotland. Holt suggests that shooting 'was essentially private whereas hunting was part of the public life', and that access came only through 'intimate networks of friendship and influence'.[24]

In November 1872 Davidson visited Egypt with the most significant of his old Oxford chums, Crauford Tait, son of the Archbishop of Canterbury. They both enjoyed shooting. Crauford reported back home, 'We went to the first station on the Cairo Railway for some snipe-shooting, but only succeeded in bagging five snipe, which we plucked, cooked, and ate for lunch.'[25] Davidson was much more satisfied, 'We had a great deal of shooting, especially pigeons, but also water-fowl.'[26]

With so much practice, Davidson soon became a first-class shot, and in his own words 'was consequently invited to all kinds of rather select shooting parties'.[27] On 29 September 1873 he went out shooting with one of Scotland's wealthiest landowners, the Earl of Aberdeen (about 58,000 acres). On Christmas Eve it was the Earl of Haddington, owner of a mere 34,000 acres, and his three brothers, with Sir John May. Davidson was always good at hob-nobbing. The following year he put his name down for the Athenaeum.[28] Meanwhile he was also able to arrange two shoots with the decisive contact of his life, Crauford Tait. On 13 September 1873 Crauford and Randall with two other guns bagged twenty-five partridges and four hares. They went out again on 12 October. During this period, Randall was meant to be preparing for ordination, which he had begun as one of Vaughan's 'doves', private pupils of the Master of the Temple, C. J. Vaughan, a former head-master of Harrow.

The gun was given up when ordination loomed. His last shots were fired on 27 December 1873. Two months later he was ordained, on 1 March 1874, by Archbishop Tait, the transition from country sportsman to dapper deacon being symbolized by the Archbishop's insistence that he should remove his heavy, sporty moustache.[29] Henceforth he was known amongst his fellow curates as 'the Dean'.[30]

[24] Richard Holt, *Sport and the British: a modern History* (Oxford, 1994), p. 54.
[25] William Benham, *Catherine and Crauford Tait. A Memoir* (London, 1881), p. 308.
[26] Bell, *Davidson*, 1: 34.
[27] Ibid., 1: 30.
[28] Ibid., 1: 159.
[29] Ibid., 1: 38.
[30] Ibid., 1: 36.

He never pulled a trigger again. There was, however, always riding and fishing, and foreign travel. A visit to Palestine in March 1876, paid for by a wealthy fellow-curate, gave the opportunity for 'long, hard rides every morning and sundown'.[31] Fishing was a life-long pursuit. Having begun as a boy, he was still fishing in his seventies. In 1922 his wife Eadie described how 'R caught 2 salmon . . . R stuck to it like a man, even when he backed and sat down in a burn.'[32] On another occasion, 'last night the moon rose out of a cloud. . . . At this moment – whrr – went the reel and a fish was on and R. played him and brought him in – such a beautiful thing.' Eadie, herself now 66, was as elated as the Archbishop. 'I feel rather like the women at the Gladiatorial shows! Seeing anything so beautiful fight for its life and be gradually brought in!'[33]

During his three-year curacy at Dartford, which began in 1874, Davidson maintained his close friendship with Crauford Tait, and would be often invited back to dine at Lambeth Palace. Crauford was now his father's chaplain and was keen for Randall to be his successor. Despite some initial hesitation from the Archbishop – perhaps he still worried about the moustache – Davidson was appointed in 1877, and was soon in his element at the centre of church affairs. After counting and recording the bag, visitation returns held no terrors, and the interpersonal skills acquired in coping with beaters and swells came in useful when drafting the Archbishop's replies to indignant correspondents. Another moment of high symbolic significance in the transition from sportsman to ecclesiastical bureaucrat occurred when Archbishop Tait insisted on checking visitation returns as they rode together on horseback along the Embankment on a windy day.[34]

So completely did Davidson immerse himself in the Archbishop's way of thinking that he came to be increasingly trusted to speak on behalf of his master. This in turn gave increasing influence over the management of events and situations, sometimes leading some participants to suspect that he might have exceeded his authority. Bramwell Booth, sent by his father, the redoubtable General of the Salvation Army, to attempt the difficult task of negotiating a working agreement with the Church of England in 1882, blamed Davidson for their failure, ostensibly over the General's authority. The truth was that

31 Ibid., 1: 36.

32 M. C. S. M[ills], *Edith Davidson of Lambeth* (London, 1938), p. 209.

33 Ibid., p. 211.

34 LPL, Claude Jenkins Papers, 562: MS Journal of R. T. Davidson, 1877–8.

Davidson was not as pessimistic of Anglican prospects as some of the bishops as they contemplated the threats of disestablishment and secularism, and was more aware of the reluctance of the parochial clergy to share spiritual authority in their localities with Major Barbara, especially when the Army was being engulfed by tales of scandal and impropriety.[35]

Davidson was now moving with assurance in the highest circles of Church and State. Tait's death had led to a meeting with Queen Victoria, who was to prove to be another powerful patron – providing his health was equal to the duties demanded of him. By 1883 the Archbishop's bundle of letters was brought to his chaplain in bed, even on Sunday.[36] In May of that year they included the momentous news that the Queen had asked for him to be the next Dean of Windsor. Westcott, now back in Cambridge, wrote, 'There is no place, I think in which you could have had a nobler opportunity of doing good service.'[37]

The move to Windsor brought new contacts for which old country skills could prove useful. Riding in the Great Park with Captain Bigge became the basis for an 'intimate friendship' which lasted over fifty years with the man who, as Lord Stamfordham, was to become Private Secretary to King Edward VII.[38] As Archbishop of Canterbury Davidson would have had good reason to be thankful for this crucial friendship forged through riding in the park.

Queen Victoria was quick to appreciate her new Dean's many gifts, and within a year had appointed him a Trustee of the British Museum in succession to Prince Leopold. This was to thrust him into the centre of the late-Victorian debate about work, rest, and recreation. Should the British Museum be open on Sunday? The new Archbishop, Edward Benson, thought not, agreeing with his predecessor. Letters sent to both Archbishops from the Lord's Day Observance Society had been answered by Davidson, on their behalf. It came as a great blow to the Society when Dean Davidson appeared to break ranks. He explained to the Society's secretary that 'I am one of those who believe that it is a mistake, both on religious and other grounds, to keep the doors of the

35 For a detailed discussion of Davidson's role see Stuart Mews, 'The General and the Bishops. Alternative responses to de-Christianization', in T. R. Gourvish and Alan O'Day, eds, *Later Victorian Britain* (Houndmills, 1988), pp. 221–4.

36 Bell, *Davidson*, 1: 63.

37 Ibid., 1: 68.

38 Ibid., 1: 80.

Museum closed when so many other doors leading to evil and not to good stand open.'[39] The Dean moved towards this goal in a way which was to become typical. Knowing that his episcopal superior, the Archbishop, was also a Trustee, he was pleased that the topic was already in the secretary's report so that he 'did not have to initiate the matter'.[40] After a long debate, it was Davidson who moved the resolution on which the Trustees voted. In his typically crab-like way of proceeding, he proposed that the Treasury should be asked to provide a sum, not exceeding £500, to enable the Natural History Museum at Kensington to be opened on an experimental basis on Sunday afternoons. Archbishop Benson voted against, but the majority, including the Prince of Wales, Lord Rosebery, and Sir John Lubbock, carried the day.[41] This produced consternation amongst the Sabbatarians, but at once established Davidson as a man of independent views who might take an advanced line on social questions, though without going so far that he might lose Court and Cabinet approval. The British Museum Trust brought Davidson into contact with Sir John Lubbock (later Lord Avebury), banker, scientist, M.P. for London University, and a man with a mission to humanize the workplace, reduce the hours of toil, and promote intellectual curiosity amongst the people.[42]

In 1891, at the age of 42, Davidson was appointed Bishop of Rochester – then a huge diocese which included all of London south of the Thames. Eleven days after his consecration, in which he shared a service with Mandell Creighton, he began to feel unwell, and began vomiting blood. The Queen's physician, Sir James Read, referred him to Sir Thomas Barlow, who diagnosed a serious stomach ulcer and ordered him to go immediately to bed, and be a complete invalid for three months.[43] George Bell commented, 'nevertheless with his extraordinary capacity for getting things done',[44] Davidson kept the diocese running from his bedroom, and did masses of reading of demanding books like Charles Booth's recently published *Life and*

[39] Ibid., 1: 111. For the significance of Davidson for the Sunday question see John Wigley, *The Rise and Fall of the Victorian Sunday* (Manchester, 1980), pp. 113, 145–6, 160–1, 191.

[40] Bell, *Davidson*, 1: 110.

[41] LPL, Davidson Papers, 84, fol. 36: R. T. Davidson to Henry Davidson, 19 Jan. 1885.

[42] Horace G. Hutchinson, *Life of Sir John Lubbock*, 2 vols (London, 1914).

[43] LPL, Davidson Papers, 577: Journal, 4 May 1891, fols 33–4.

[44] Bell, *Davidson*, 1: 205; LPL, Davidson Papers, 577, fol. 65.

Labours of the People of London, as well as giving serious attention to his own devotional life.[45]

After his death, Mary Mills wrote that Davidson 'was always determined to make "the best use of the time"'. 'Now', he would say, as illnesses of varying levels of magnitude struck him down, 'we must make the best of these days; don't let us just waste or fritter [them] away. Let us have some clear plan.'[46] It was Mary Mills's impression that many important interviews took place during times of illness – in fact he had to be ill indeed for his zest for work to be overcome.[47] The Wesleyan leader Scott Lidgett clearly regarded discussions with Davidson in his bedroom as a rare mark of ecumenical favour.[48]

Davidson maintained his interest in the day of rest. In 1892 he agreed to present a petition to Convocation on behalf of the Sunday Society for the opening of museums, public libraries, and art galleries on Sunday afternoons. The clergy newspaper the *Guardian* described his speech as one of great courage. The files at Lambeth show just how thoroughly it was prepared. He presented facts and figures from different parts of England which effectively undermined those frequently heard assertions that no one wanted to visit a museum, a library, or a gallery on a Sunday.[49] He drove home his point by quoting a clerk, living in dingy lodgings with a fellow clerk: 'I want to know', he had asked, 'how you clergy think that a man like me ought to spend a wet Sunday?'[50] Following the Convocation debate a committee chaired by Davidson was set up to bring back proposals for action. These accepted the strength of the case for access to libraries, museums, and galleries by people whose only day of leisure was Sunday. This was too radical for the bench of bishops, and a decision was delayed for a year. When it came to the vote, in July 1894, Davidson unusually found himself supported by only one other bishop. Against him were not just the more elderly and conservative bishops such as Ellicott, Bickerstaffe, and Durnford, but to his amazement he failed to bring round the ex-headmasters, Frederick Temple and George Ridding. Even the outwardly worldly-wise Mandell Creighton

[45] LPL, Davidson Papers, 577, fols 49–50.
[46] LPL, Bell Papers, vol. 222, fol. 14.
[47] Ibid., fols 15–16.
[48] J. Scott Lidgett, *My Guided Life* (London, 1936), p. 253.
[49] LPL, Davidson Papers, 492.
[50] Bell, *Davidson*, 1: 221.

deserted him. 'They all spoke as men belonging to another generation than ours', Davidson later commented sadly.[51]

Translation to Winchester in 1895 seemed to transform Davidson's health. He continued to take an interest in issues of rest and recreation, warning his diocesan conference of the effects of Sunday cycling on church attendance.[52]

During his time at Winchester, Davidson became interested in the campaign waged by Sir John Lubbock and others to reduce the hours worked by shop assistants and improve their conditions. In the drapery trade it was quite common for girls in their late teens to work from 8.30 a.m. to 9.30 p. m. for five days a week, and until midnight on Saturday. Often they lived in and were given inadequate food. Twenty minutes were usually allowed for a lunchtime break, and fifteen minutes for tea. Over a period of more than twenty years Lubbock formed pressure groups, conducted a vigorous press campaign, and introduced Bills in the Commons to provide statutory bank holidays, reduce the hours of trading, and even make it compulsory for shops to provide seats for lady shop assistants.

When Lubbock introduced his Shops Early Closing Bill in 1895 it was resented by many shopkeepers as high-handed interference by the state into the right of an employer to drive a bargain with his staff.[53] Petitions in support of Lubbock's Bill were signed by the Archbishop of Canterbury, the Bishop of London, Cardinal Manning, and five hundred other bishops, priests, and Nonconformist ministers.[54] Yet though passing through the Committee stage, the Bill ran out of Parliamentary time and lapsed.[55]

A new approach was then launched by those who wanted to keep the state out. Sir John Blundell Maple, a Conservative M.P. and owner of a furniture store, claimed that more success had been achieved by voluntary measures.[56] This idea appealed to many concerned middle-class churchgoers. Considerable efforts were made by the voluntarists to swing public and especially religious opinion behind them. The Voluntary Early Closing Association listed as its President the

[51] Ibid., I: 222.

[52] P. C. Hammond, *The Parson in the Victorian Parish* (London, 1977), p. 104; Anthony Russell, *The Clerical Profession* (London, 1985), p. 250.

[53] W. B. Whitacker, *Victorian and Edwardian Shopworkers* (Newton Abbot, 1973), p. 122.

[54] Ibid., p. 120.

[55] Ibid., p. 123.

[56] Ibid., p. 124.

Archbishop of York, and its Vice-Presidents included the Bishops of London (Creighton), Ripon (Boyd Carpenter), and Davidson of Winchester. The main Nonconformist heavyweight to lend support was the Baptist F. B. Meyer.[57]

Special sermons were preached on behalf of Voluntary Early Closing by Dr Monroe Gibson at St John's Wood Presbyterian chapel, on 12 March 1899,[58] and on 7 May by Wilson Carlile, the founder of the Church Army. Carlile's sermon was a classic: shops could close earlier if people would do their shopping early. That made sense, but the ardent evangelist could not leave it there. 'Your chance of purchasing is almost over', he told the congregation,

> Do you see that man just inside the shop? He is turning the handle of the cog-wheel connected with the shutters, and they are coming down, down, down. When they have reached the bottom and the shop is closed, it will be too late to do our shopping. We should have shopped early. 'Those who seek me early shall find me'. Jesus Christ, the son of the proprietor, whom you crucified on the cross, is standing behind the counter waiting to serve you. Come and buy, without money, and without price. Come and shop early, soon the shutters of time will go down and your opportunity will be lost forever.[59]

Voluntary Early Closing attracted not only those churchgoers who were unhappy about the dangers of state interference, but also those who wished to be free to pay low wages. When a supporter of Lubbock's legislative approach informed Davidson that men like Maple were mean employers, he resigned from the Association, though few would have known because he chose to do it privately.[60]

That was in June 1899, but the treatment of shop assistants would not go away, and a month later another Bill sponsored by Lubbock reached the House of Lords.[61] This was a Bill to require employers to provide seats for female shop assistants in retail shops. Perhaps it was

[57] W. Y. Fullerton, *F. B. Meyer: a Biography* (London, n.d.), p. 111.

[58] *Special Sermon on 'Early Closing' by Rev. J. Monroe Gibson, Preached by desire of the Voluntary Early Closing Association* (London, 1899).

[59] *Rev. Wilson Carlile on Early Shopping*, Issued by the Voluntary Early Closing Association (London, 1899).

[60] LPL, Davidson Papers, 64, fols 306–37: Shop Early Closing Bill 1896–1900.

[61] M. Irwin, 'The Shop Seats Bill movement', *Fortnightly Review*, 66 (1899), pp. 123–31.

because he knew from personal experience the value of rest that Davidson took the debate so seriously. The very idea of seats behind the counter was ridiculed by many, and became the subject of the inevitable cartoon in *Punch*.[62] Preliminary correspondence in the *Times* was largely derisive, and Lady Frances Balfour denounced what she called 'the grandmothers' armchair bill'.[63]

Opposition to the measure was led for the West End stores by Frank Debenham, himself an exemplary employer, who objected to the principle of state interference. Lubbock encouraged the creation of a League to Secure Seats for Young Women in Shops. Patrons were the Duke of Westminster, the Bishop of London (Mandell Creighton), and the Dean of Westminster (George Bradley). A notable collection of the great and the good lent their names in support. They included peeresses (the Duchess of Westminster, and the Countesses of Aberdeen, Carlisle, and Warwick), bishops' wives (Louise Creighton and Lavinia Talbot), and wives of the radical intelligentsia (Mrs J. W. Benn, Mrs Bertrand Russell). The token Nonconformists were Mrs Hugh Price Hughes and Mrs Mark Guy Pearse. Catch any of them, with the possible exception of the two Wesleyans (Mrs Hughes and Mrs Pearse), on the wrong side of the counter!

The League's calling card[64] summed up its appeal in verse:

> Weary of strain of body and brain,
> With aching feet and swollen vein;
> A shop girl climbed to her bed at night
> Scarce praying for the morning light.

The Bishop of Winchester was not one simply to give an opinion. When he knew that the matter was to be debated in the Lords, he wanted facts. He bought trade papers like the *Drapers Record*, and a relevant number of the *Lancet*. He sent trusted friends to discover information. He went himself round shops and stores, like Marshall and Snelgrove.[65] The *Pall Mall Gazette* reported that Davidson horrified the Lords with his account of his pilgrimage through certain drapery establishments in London. Some girls had laughed at what they

62 The cartoon is reproduced in Lee Holcombe, *Victorian Ladies and Work: Middle Class Working Women in England and Wales 1850–1914* (Newton Abbot, 1973), p. 128.

63 *Times*, 8 July 1899.

64 LPL, Davidson Papers, 517, fol. 121.

65 Ibid., fol. 199.

called 'an episcopal visitation'.[66] According to that report, Davidson's words 'fell with something like a shock upon the nerves of his peers: "I went behind the counter in each shop".'[67] Talk of the leprosy of trade!

The Prime Minister himself, the Marquess of Salisbury, intervened in the debate with the intention of having the Bill thrown out. He poured scorn on Davidson's contribution. Who knew best about shop girls, the Lord Bishop of Winchester or Mr Pollock, the general secretary of the Scottish Shopkeepers' Assistants' Union, who was much less enthusiastic for change?[68] The peers came down on the side of the Bishop, and rejected the great Lord Salisbury by the convincing vote of 73 to 28. The Bill received the Royal Assent, and for all I know shops are still required to provide seats for lady shop assistants.

Frank Debenham, magnanimous in defeat, thanked the Bishop for his interest. 'The result of the debate . . . was largely attributable to your own speech, and its influence on public opinion is bound to be great.'[69] Whether the public conscience was touched cannot be easily assessed. A young couple of Scottish Socialist activists seem to have been impressed, and wrote to Davidson for help in another measure to improve working conditions. They were a Mr and Mrs Ramsay Macdonald.[70]

This incident occurred one hundred years ago in what I believe is a revealing vignette, but receives little more than a page in Bell's great biography. However, Bell did make two significant observations. Firstly, that it was unusual in the late nineteenth century for bishops to take any part in the Lords in business which was not ecclesiastical. Secondly, that this was the first time that Davidson had taken such a significant part in changing the laws governing 'general social welfare'.[71] It also reveals Davidson's willingness to campaign for the easily forgotten army of working women. Most of his early life had been spent in exclusively male company: Harrow, Oxford, the shoot,

[66] *Pall Mall Gazette*, 12 July 1899.

[67] Bell, *Davidson*, 1: 322; *The Drapers' Record*, 15, 22 July 1899. The official record of the speech, in *Parliamentary Debates (authorised edition)*, 4th ser., 74 (6–21 July 1899), col. 445, has a different form of words: 'I have gone behind counters and held investigations while sales were going on.'

[68] Ibid., col. 450. Pollock was 'not quite clear that it would be practicable to insist on seats being provided', and had fears about the knock-on effects of their introduction.

[69] LPL, Davidson Papers, vol. 517, fols 196–7: F. Debenham to R. T. Davidson, 14 July 1899.

[70] Bell, *Davidson*, 1, p. 322.

[71] Ibid., 1, p. 321.

Grillions (his London club), clergy gatherings. In these circles women and their problems were either invisible or the objects of mirth. After the first defeat of the Shop Seats Bill in the Commons in 1898, Lord Wemyss wrote to Salisbury expressing the hope that Parliament 'having taken shop girls seats in hand has thus touched bottom in social legislation'.[72] Wemyss, like Davidson, had been born in Edinburgh and began his education as he did, at Edinburgh Academy, followed also by public school in England and Oxford. They were both crack shots. But there the similarity ends. Wemyss became a Conservative M.P. before inheriting an estate and peerage. Davidson's understanding of life was influenced by his accident and the need to recover, the teaching of Butler and Westcott at Harrow, the insight afforded by his shared hosting with Eadie of the hundred-strong Ladies' Bible Class they started together at Windsor, and the contact with Lubbock through the British Museum Trustees.

The purpose of this paper has been to shed light on one prominent late Victorian bishop's attitudes to work, rest, recreation, and the use of time. Those attitudes were shaped by his own personal experiences and ideological formation. In Davidson's case shooting, which began as a country pursuit, a form of recreation, was transformed into a work discipline by his need to recover his own health. Sunday was regarded by most Victorian clergy as a means of enforcing godly discipline, but for Davidson it was also an opportunity to enrich the drab lives of poor people. The campaigns to humanize the work-place were recognitions of the consequences of the huge developments of trade and commerce. They were especially responses to the poor pay, long hours, and bad conditions of work for women. In the late Victorian world of rapid social change the concerns of Randall Davidson offer rare insights into some of the many worlds of work.

University of Gloucestershire

[72] Hatfield House, Salisbury MS: Wemyss to Salisbury, 5 May 1899.